Financial Inclusion Regulatory Practices in SADC

Against a background of calls to prioritise the improvement of financial inclusion in Africa, this book provides an analysis of current financial inclusion measures in Southern Africa. Evaluating the existing strengths and weaknesses of financial inclusion in Africa, it identifies opportunities to improve inclusive financial services and aid poverty reduction in the region. With a focus on South Africa, Namibia, Botswana, and Zimbabwe as case studies for assessing current financial inclusion in the context of particular challenges faced by unbanked and underbanked customers, who are easy targets for cybercriminals due to low levels of digital literacy, it looks into the regulation and promotion of financial inclusion in Southern Africa. The book explores financial inclusion in the context of digital transformation in the 21st century, examining the regulation and promotion of financial inclusion in the context of digital transformation, as well as the challenges related to financial inclusion. Suggesting improvements to aspects of company law, securities and financial markets in the Southern African Development Community region, the book offers a comprehensive study on the regulation and promotion of financial inclusion in the Southern African Development Community region. It will be essential reading for students and academics researching financial inclusion, international economic law and development.

Howard Chitimira is Research Professor and Professor of Securities and Financial Markets Law at the Faculty of Law, North-West University, South Africa

Tapiwa Victor Warikandwa is Senior Lecturer in Private and Commercial Law at the University of Namibia

Financial Inclusion Regulatory Practices in SADC

Addressing Prospects and Challenges in the 21st Century

Edited by Howard Chitimira and Tapiwa Victor Warikandwa

Routledge
Taylor & Francis Group
LONDON AND NEW YORK

First published 2023
by Routledge
4 Park Square, Milton Park, Abingdon, Oxon OX14 4RN

and by Routledge
605 Third Avenue, New York, NY 10158

Routledge is an imprint of the Taylor & Francis Group, an informa business

British Library Cataloguing-in-Publication Data
A catalogue record for this book is available from the British Library

ISBN: 978-1-032-43915-0 (hbk)
ISBN: 978-1-032-43916-7 (pbk)
ISBN: 978-1-003-36940-0 (ebk)

DOI: 10.4324/9781003369400

Typeset in Times New Roman
by Deanta Global Publishing Services, Chennai, India

This book project is dedicated to everyone who has actively worked to promote financial inclusion in the world, including individuals, policymakers, governments, financial service providers and other key stakeholders. Financial inclusion is the provision of usable and affordable financial goods and services, such as payments, transactions, savings, credit and insurance, to both individuals and enterprises in a sustainable and ethical manner. Their efforts are noteworthy at a time when, regrettably, Africa has lagged behind other continents in the use of financial inclusion as a political instrument to create inclusive growth. In Africa, fewer than one in every four adults has access to a bank account with a reputable financial service provider. However, more people will be able to invest in their families and themselves if financial inclusion is prioritised and supported in Southern Africa and the rest of Africa due to increased household savings, investment capital, the expansion of the entrepreneur class and better access to financial services. The end of poverty will coincide with the realisation of sustainable development goals. For policymakers in Southern Africa who are yet to actively embrace financial inclusion, as well as the rest of Africa, we urge them, in the context of this book project, to prioritise financial inclusion as a means of achieving sustainable development.

Contents

Contributors

Marvin R. Awarab School of Law, University of Namibia

Yvette Basson Department of Mercantile and Labour Law, University of the Western Cape, South Africa

Howard Chitimira Faculty of Law, North-West University, South Africa

Tendai D. Svotwa Department of Graduate Studies, Botho University, Gaborone, Botswana

Friedrich Hamadziripi Postdoctoral Fellow, Faculty of Law, North-West University, South Africa

Vimbai Jana Doctoral Candidate, Faculty of Law, North-West University, South Africa

Neels Kilian Faculty of Law, North-West University, South Africa

Louis de Koker La Trobe Law School, La Trobe University, Australia; Department of Mercantile and Labour Law, University of the Western Cape, South Africa

Tinashe Kondo Department of Mercantile and Labour Law, University of the Western Cape, South Africa

Eugene L. Libebe School of Law, Faculty of Commerce, Management and Law, University of Namibia

Phemelo T. Magau School of Law, University of KwaZulu-Natal, South Africa

Charles Makanyeza Namibia Business School, University of Namibia

Nednah Maraga Department of Law and Paralegal Studies, Ba Isago University, Botswana

Olipha Mpofu Department of Accounting and Finance, Ba Isago University, Botswana

Gertruida van Niekerk Faculty of Management and Law, University of Limpopo, South Africa

Ashley B. Nyaude Department of Mercantile Law, Faculty of Law, University of Pretoria, South Africa

Jean Jacques du Plessis Deakin Law School, Deakin University, Australia

Elize Shakalela School of Law, Faculty of Commerce, Management and Law, University of Namibia

Lineekela Usebiu School of Law, Faculty of Commerce, Management and Law, University of Namibia

Tapiwa V. Warikandwa School of Law, Faculty of Commerce, Management and Law, University of Namibia

Eukeria Wealth School of Accounting, Faculty of Commerce, Management and Law, University of Namibia

About the editors

Professor Howard Chitimira (co-editor of the book) is a full Professor of Law and Research Professor at the Faculty of Law, North-West University, South Africa. He is also an advocate of the High Court of South Africa and a National Research Foundation (NRF) rated legal scholar. Prof Chitimira holds the degrees Bachelor of Laws (LLB) (Cum Laude) from the University of Fort Hare (UFH); Master of Laws (LLM) from UFH and Doctor of Laws (LLD) from the Nelson Mandela Metropolitan University (NMMU). For his doctorate, he specialised in securities and financial markets law. To date, he has published three books and over 50 journal articles in this field. Prof Chitimira is a reviewer and editorial board member of several law journals in South Africa and elsewhere, as well as an external examiner for LLB, LLM and LLD degrees at several universities. He serves on editorial boards of journals and is a member of several academic and related associations. For instance, Prof Chitimira is an Assistant Editor of the *Potchefstroom Electronic Law Journal* and an Editorial Board Member of the *Journal of Corporate & Commercial Law & Practice*. He has acted as a Guest Editor for the *Interdisciplinary Journal of Economics and Business Law* and the *Namibia Law Journal*. He was appointed by the Academy of Science of South Africa (ASSAF) on behalf of the Department of Higher Education and Training (DHET) to serve on an ad hoc ASSAF Consensus Panel to peer review new applications and re-applications of journals for DHET accreditation on 11 October 2019. To date, he has delivered numerous keynote speeches on securities and financial markets law in South Africa and elsewhere. Prof Chitimira was invited to comment on the Financial Action Task Force's Recommendation 1 on Risk-Based Measures to Proliferation Financing in August 2020. He successfully launched the annual Corporate and Financial Markets Law Conference in 2019.

Dr Tapiwa V. Warikandwa (co-editor of the book) holds a Doctor of Laws in International Trade Law. He is a Senior Lecturer and Head of Department in the Faculty of Law at the University of Namibia. He specialises in international trade law, labour law, indigenisation laws, mining law and constitutional law among other disciplines. Prior to coming to Namibia, Dr Warikandwa worked as a legal officer and later legal advisor in the Ministry of Public Service Labour and Social Welfare in Zimbabwe. Key among his duties was legal drafting. Dr Warikandwa worked with the law reviser of the Ministry of Justice in Zimbabwe in reviewing laws administered by the Ministry of Public Service Labour and Social Welfare. Dr Warikandwa also completed ordinary and advanced training in labour law making at the International Labour Organization's International Training Centre in Turin, Italy. On numerous occasions, Dr Warikandwa was actively involved in the activities of the Cabinet Committee on Legislation on behalf of the Ministry of Public Service Labour and Social Welfare. Dr Warikandwa has since written books on labour law and women's rights in South Africa and Namibia among others, as well as publishing articles in accredited peer-reviewed journals such as *Law, Development and Democracy*, *Speculum Juris*, *Journal for Black Studies*, *Potchefstroom Electronic Law Journal*, *Comparative International Law Journal for Southern Africa*, *The African Journal of International and Comparative Law* and *Juridical Tribune*, among others. He was also a Post-doctoral Fellow and has also worked as a Senior Lecturer at the University of Fort Hare in South Africa. Dr Warikandwa studied for his Bachelor of Laws, Master's degree and Doctoral degree at the University of Fort Hare in South Africa. He currently is the Chief Editor of the *Namibian Law Journal*.

Preface

This book project was thought necessary by the editors to study the developments towards achieving financial inclusion in the Southern Africa Development Community (SADC) region and provide advice on the subject to the rest of Africa and other regional blocs throughout the world. The book's concept is based on the understanding that, on average, financial inclusion in the SADC region is low and substantially differs between countries. The nations in the region also varied significantly in terms of the quality of financial inclusion and access levels. The fundamental basis of the book project is the understanding that financial inclusion is a crucial enabler of the United Nations' Sustainable Progress Goals (SDGs), which include, among other things, ensuring economic development and eliminating poverty. The main argument of the book project is that more laws and regulations should be passed in order to increase the area's financial inclusion.

The SADC Council of Ministers endorsed the SADC Strategy on Financial Inclusion and Small and Medium Enterprises Access to Finance in September 2016, which will expedite financial inclusion programs in all SADC member states. The book discusses issues pertaining to financial inclusion and the advancements made in the area in that direction. The idea that formerly mistreated and excluded poor clients are demonstrated to develop towards financial inclusion is implicit in this technique. This book will also look at the numerous issues surrounding financial inclusion in the SADC region. Financial inclusion is the provision of usable and affordable financial goods and services, such as payments, transactions, savings, credit and insurance, to both individuals and enterprises in a sustainable and ethical manner. Since financial inclusion is linked to both economic growth and the eradication of poverty, it has drawn attention. In order to overcome the challenges in reaching the SDGs, one of the key objectives of this book project is to align financial inclusion as a policy and regulatory tool.

This book project uses data on personal, business and government payments to link observed financial inclusion metrics to potential implications for macroeconomic factors like economic growth, employment, wages and poverty. The relationship between financial inclusion and the macroeconomic sphere is becoming more prominent. Financial education-related topics will also be discussed to assist marginalised individuals in making the shift from solely using cash for transactions to formal financial services that can be accessed via a mobile phone or other digital technologies. Other economic blocs around the world may find the discussions in the book instructive. The SADC will see sustainable development as a result of these developments.

To ensure inclusivity, equal access to opportunities and regional economic growth and development, the authors of this book – all authorities in fields related to law and economics – will argue that individuals and businesses need access to a variety of financial institutions and products in a stable competitive market. Once all economic sectors and the entire people have access to and are proficient consumers of pertinent financial services to satisfy their needs, the SADC region will experience sustainable growth and development. We will also achieve the SDGs. The adoption of ways to advance financial inclusion in SADC (and beyond) and lower the cost of cross-border payments, utilising among other mechanisms, digital financial inclusion, is thus emphasised in the book. Thus, this book discusses the strategy for SADC's financial inclusion. The authors examine stakeholder involvement, policy and regulatory alignment and strategy development in a few SADC member nations. The writers try to address the challenges, requirements and conditions unique to the chosen jurisdictions. The authors also suggest that SADC member states coordinate their legislative and policy initiatives in order to address local issues and advance regional financial integration.

Financial inclusion, it will be claimed, enables people and organisations within SADC to engage in economic activity and, as a result, trade. The requirement of financial inclusion for business growth as well as its significance in transitioning the informal to the formal business sector will be underlined. Small businesses, which are more likely to lack access to finance, such as in the digital era, will be the growth engines for intra-African commerce (particularly in the context of the recently launched Africa Continental Free Trade Area Agreement). The argument made in the book is that in order for such a goal to be accomplished, people and businesses must be financially involved. Financial inclusion is, therefore, necessary to ensure economic transformation and advancement in the SADC region. One of the major subject topics that will be explored in the book is digital financial inclusion. Some contributors in the book will talk about how the SADC region has to adopt digital financial inclusion concepts if financial inclusion is to be completely realised. Therefore, each chapter of this book has undergone a double-blind peer review by reviewers who cannot be identified to determine its academic rigour and fitness for publishing.

Acknowledgements

Without the suggestions, help and support of several people, this book project could not have been finished. In this regard, we would like to extend our profound gratitude to those listed below:

- All blessings and good things originate from the All-Powerful God. He deserves all honour, gratitude and adulation. Everything in heaven and on earth is yours, therefore the greatness, power, glory, majesty and splendour are all yours, Lord.
- Our parents, who taught us about the omnipotent God as children.
- We are grateful for the support that each of our families, friends and colleagues gave us while we were working on this project.
- We value the knowledgeable support provided by the assigned Routledge editors, who competently assisted us throughout the publication process.
- We appreciate the authors' efforts in contributing to the success of this project by writing the book's chapters.
- We also want to express our gratitude to everyone who helped with this initiative and whose excellent work made it a success.

1 An introduction to financial inclusion as an enabler of 21st-century Sustainable Development Goals

Howard Chitimira and Tapiwa V. Warikandwa

1.1 Introduction

Financial inclusion is one of the 17 Sustainable Development Objectives (SDGs) that the United Nations (UN) has set for the year 2030, and it is given high emphasis in eight of those goals.[1] SDG 1, which focuses on eradicating poverty, is among them. In order to eradicate hunger, achieve food security and advance sustainable agriculture, SDGs 2 and 3 call for prioritising health and well-being, SDG 5's goal is achieving gender equality and empowering women economically and SDG 8 promotes job creation and economic growth. SDG 9 supports infrastructure, business and innovation, and SDG 10 aims to reduce inequality.[2] SDG 17 enhances the means of implementation, which emphasises savings mobilisation for investment and consumption that can stimulate growth and also acknowledges the implied importance of greater financial inclusion.[3]

Financial inclusion is not specifically included in any of the UN's 17 SDGs, but it may be inferred that it is a key enabler of those goals.[4] The objectives of ensuring that everyone has access to savings accounts, loans, insurance and other financial services are not specifically mentioned, despite the fact that objectives like inclusive growth and greater equality are straightforward to discern.[5] We do not believe that individuals who created the feasible SDGs had financial inclusion-related issues specifically left out. Instead, we will show how the SDGs could progress concerns linked to financial inclusion in this chapter. The conceptual framework on SDGs and financial inclusion presented in this chapter, among other things, will serve as a guide for the opinions presented by the numerous contributors to this book.

Financial inclusion can aid in the achievement of more general development objectives as well as overall economic growth. According to a 2016 McKinsey Global Institute report, digital finance alone could help billions of people by fostering inclusive growth and increasing the gross domestic product (GDP) of emerging nations by US$3.7 trillion over the next ten years.[6] According to the findings of a long-term impact study on Kenya's M-PESA mobile money service, mobile money has successfully improved the financial well-being of low-income women and members of households headed by women. It has also assisted an estimated 200,000 households, or the equivalent of 2% of the country's population, in escaping poverty.[7] In addition, there

DOI: 10.4324/9781003369400-1

is mounting proof that financial inclusion encourages domestic savings, increases tax revenue and enhances financial and economic stability.

Banks, cooperatives, microfinance institutions, money transfer companies and mobile network providers can all enter new financial markets thanks to the UN Capital Development Fund's (UNCDF) last-mile financing methods.[8] The UNCDF works to ensure that the right financial products – savings, credit, insurance, payments and remittances – are available to people, especially the unbanked and underbanked, as well as micro-, small- and medium-sized businesses, at a fair price and in a sustainable way.[9] The UNCDF places a special emphasis on women since there is mounting evidence that women who have access to savings achieve better economic outcomes, including higher productivity, incomes and investments in their companies.[10] Savings help stabilise incomes during economic shocks, giving women more financial liberty and decrease the risk that they may sell assets to pay for medical emergencies. Financial inclusion should be prioritised by the Southern African Development Community (SADC) and the rest of Africa. The population's economic potential to combat poverty and advance income distribution is fostered by extending financial inclusion. This study aims to investigate the relationship between financial inclusion and the SADC region's progress in reaching the SDGs in terms of eradicating poverty. The intellectual and contextual basis for this book project is introduced in this chapter. Additionally, it offers a summary of the chapters that will be covered in the book.

1.2 Background information on financial inclusion

The World Bank defines financial inclusion as the accessibility of individuals and organisations to beneficial and fairly priced financial goods and services that meet their needs for payments, transactions, savings, credit and insurance that are offered in a sustainable and responsible manner.[11] Financial inclusion includes both the feature of high-quality product and service delivery as well as the accessibility and use of financial services by individuals and businesses. It is necessary for both an individual's and the economy's overall responsible financial progress and well-being. According to the World Bank, in order to achieve the global goal of universal financial access (UFA), a comprehensive approach that addresses both the supply and demand sides should have been adopted by 2020.[12]

1.2.1 Key indicators of financial inclusion

The first and most crucial step towards increased financial inclusion is having access to a transaction account that allows people to exchange and store money. Therefore, ensuring that everyone has transaction accounts is the most crucial component of financial inclusion.[13] The ability to manage short-term financial requirements, long-term planning and even preparing for unforeseen future events are all made possible by having financial access. However, simply holding an account is not enough to achieve the objective of financial inclusion. Therefore, the second aspect of financial inclusion, using these financial services, must get equal attention.[14]

According to the Global Findex database, 515 million persons globally opened accounts with financial institutions or mobile money providers between 2014 and 2017. Approximately 69% of adults currently have an account, up from 51% in 2011 and 62% in 2014. About 65% of those over the age of 25 are women; 52% of payments are made or received by adults. Approximately 87% of small and medium-sized enterprises (SMEs) have accounts with a formal financial institution. Globally, 30% of people have received government handouts or wages that have been directly deposited into their accounts.[15] The aforementioned statistics demonstrate that economies all over the world are getting closer to the goal of financial inclusion by adhering to the G20 High-Level Principles for Digital Financial Inclusion, UFA by 2020, the SDGs, national financial inclusion strategies, financial consumer protection and literacy and many other initiatives already taken in this direction.

1.2.2 Financial inclusion and the SDGs

The SDGs were established by the UN General Assembly in September 2015 for the year 2030; 193 members of the General Assembly, comprising both developed and developing states, have endorsed the agenda for these objectives, which were formed following years of discussion and debate. The SDGs are a collection of 17 goals.[16] Financial inclusion helps with sustainable development goals being achieved. It offers a wide range of benefits, including increasing the use of digital platforms, lower transaction costs, increased female entrepreneurship, higher earning potential and lower transaction costs. Even while financial inclusion does not specifically aim to achieve the SDGs, expanding access to financial services has opened the door for the achievement of a number of SDGs.[17] Some of the 17 SDGs have been recognised by the World Bank as being made possible by financial inclusion. Increasing financial inclusion may aid in achieving several SDGs. For instance, if people have better access to financial services, particularly in distant places, they can have better access to money and other related financial services in SADC countries or any other country.[18] As a result, people can leave poverty, enabling the realisation of SDG 1, which sets a focus on eliminating severe poverty. Thanks to better and extended access to avenues for raising income, access to insurance and improved credit facilities, those employed in primary sectors such as agriculture and fisheries can manage their finances during the planting or fishing season and produce larger harvests.[19] SDG 2 relates to reducing hunger and fostering food security, and this not only increases food production in the nation but also creates food security in the economy. Farmers' financial inclusion may lead to higher planting season investments. As envisioned in SDG 2, higher yields and advancements towards enhanced food security are the outcomes. After their earnings were placed into a new bank account, Malawian farmers increased their spending on equipment by 13% and the value of their agricultural produce by 21%.[20]

Due to the marginalised coastal and inland populations' limited access to financial institutions in countries like Namibia, small-scale fishery households and their enterprises are likely to have few options for financing and managing cash flows for personal necessities or company developments.[21] The access vacuum is filled by informal lenders, who may also be the primary fish customers or boat owners. In rural and underserved coastal fishing areas, financial inclusion can increase a household's financial resilience.[22] Therefore, it is essential to remove the current barriers preventing SSF households in the SADC region from becoming financially included. These barriers include a lack of formal identification, insufficient financial skill and literacy, a lack of assets for collateral and physical distance from a financial institution. The provision of a range of financial services other than credit, the collection of financial data, financial literacy, de-risking financial institutions and client understanding are some of the solutions to these issues that must be made available to enable fishing households to maintain control over their earnings and savings.[23] Financial inclusion can help reduce the numerous vulnerabilities of low-income inland and coastal fishing households and rural communities and increase economic resilience, particularly among the SSF sector in countries like Namibia.[24]

SDG 3 relating to obtaining good health and well-being is more likely to be achieved when individuals are able to escape poverty, are guaranteed food security and have access to numerous insurance options.[25] Regarding SDG 3, financial inclusion can support health. Therefore, clinic appointments for children can be paid for by parents using a savings account. The price of out-of-pocket medical treatment is one of the key things that keep people in poverty.[26] For instance, according to a Kenyan study, increasing people's access to safe places to deposit money led to a 66% rise in health spending.[27] Jordan has remarked that insurance can help women manage health-related shocks and pay for medical expenses that might otherwise interfere with their economic activities and result in them losing income.[28]

The barrier of financial limitations that prevents people from pursuing higher education has been lifted by the expansion of funding choices. Parents who invest in their children's education help to accomplish SDG 4, which is focused on fostering high-quality education.[29] Female company owners are now more motivated than ever to tackle projects that were previously out of their reach as a result of financial inclusion. In order to advance gender equality (SDG 5), women's empowerment must increase.[30] When there is financial exclusivity, the link between smaller aspirations and larger socio-economic goals is weakened. These five SDGs provide a strong framework for achieving additional, more general socio-economic goals, such as SDG 8's ambition of "Promoting shared economic growth" and SDG 9's purpose of "Promoting innovation and sustainable industrialization."[31]

Financial inclusion warrants continued attention, which will be done in this book, given the relationship between financial inclusion and overall economic growth. Achieving the SDGs will likely be a more challenging objective for SADC and the rest of Africa without financial inclusion.[32] More people need to be enrolled in the banking system or have access to financial services because of the link between financial inclusion and development. In this book, academics with a broad range of experience in the field will highlight the potential role that financial inclusion may play in reaching a number of SDGs, among other concerns. Most of the SDGs' goals, including ending poverty, creating jobs, advancing gender equality and promoting good health, are strongly tied to financial inclusion, as this chapter has already mentioned. Financial inclusion is a critical strategy for ensuring economic growth and development in SADC since those who can utilise financial services have more protection and privacy over their money. Savings accounts, for instance, make it easier for people to save, which promotes increasing income and saving. This was seen in Nepal, where providing women with a basic bank account increased their assets by 16%.[33] A government programme in India to open banks in rural regions helped to cut rural poverty by as much as 17%.[34]

Increasing account ownership would advance the gender equality objective of SDG 5. Consider the fact that the bulk of the 1.1 billion individuals who are economically excluded are poor women.[35] Compared with a comparable group of women in Kenya who did not obtain savings accounts, the daily expenditure of female market vendors increased by 37%.[36] Additionally, digital technology can support financial inclusion and help achieve significant SDGs.[37] People can borrow money from distant family and friends in times of need thanks to digital financial payment options like a mobile phone linked to a bank account, which reduces the likelihood of falling into poverty.[38] A study of the programme found that users of Kenya's M-Pesa mobile phone-based money platform are more likely to receive remittances when faced with a financial shock, such as a job loss.[39]

There is growing proof that digitising payments for health, education and other social safety nets not only dramatically helps individuals but also improves efficiency for governments and assistance organisations by reducing transaction costs and leakage. By eliminating intermediaries who steal money, automating government transfers in India decreased the need for bribes by 47% and improved beneficiary payouts.[40] In addition, despite more accessibility, there are still disparities in how different communities use digital financial services. Above 70% of adults in both Europeand Central Asia use at least one type of digital payment, compared with 9% of people in the Middle East.[41] Financial services are becoming more widely available thanks to mobile devices, especially for people who reside in rural locations that are underserved by traditional banks; 12% of phone-based payments made by adults in Sub-Saharan Africa (SSA) are made via mobile money accounts, with Kenya having the highest number at 55%.[42]

The main argument of this book is that given the link between financial inclusion and development, governments should keep pressing for more access to and use of financial services. Prioritising financial services does not deprive other SDG objectives of funding. The information gathered so far actually provides a strong argument that financial inclusion helps to create the circumstances necessary to achieve a number of the SDGs. The UN has set out to use global resources in collaboration with significant financing partners like international, multilateral institutions, regional development banks, member countries and the private sector to mobilise the approximately US$3 trillion in financing needed to achieve the SDGs of the 2030 Agenda.[43] Even though some people may view extreme climate risks as long term, the current effects of extreme weather events, the water crisis, loss of biodiversity and the ensuing unintended consequences, such as illegal migration brought on by global inequalities, are symptoms of a crystallisation of the climate crisis.

By 2030, efforts to battle climate change could have saved at least US$26 trillion, and the world could have created at least 380 million new jobs and at least US$12 trillion in market opportunities as a result of reaching the SDGs.[44] In order to help poor economies transition to sustainability without waiting for new loans or debt write-offs, big finance has revived proposals for a financial green revolution supported by worldwide multilaterals acting as first-loss absorbers or insurers. A key component of achieving the funding of the SDGs is the payment systems that will serve as the framework for transaction settlement. When compared with portfolio loan and equity flows, diaspora remittances, which contributed 9% of GDP in 2015, are more regular and in many cases equal to or even exceed official development assistance.[45] As part of the SDGs, the UN has set the objective that the average cost of remittances made through official channels will drop from 6.5% in 2020 (the lowest in history) to 3% by 2030.[46] Therefore, in order to encourage larger cash flow, increased activity, and economic redistribution, it is imperative that these remittances reach the micro-beneficiaries in more efficient, affordable and secure methods. Financial accessibility is still needed for sustainable development.

Global efforts to enhance financial inclusion could assist the world's poorest citizens, notably women, who control a rising number of micro-, small-, and medium-sized enterprises, yet make up a relatively smaller portion of the world's wealth. Payment systems are typically severely regulated globally due to the systemic hazards they pose. As a result, entry barriers are significantly higher and global cooperation is needed to synchronise goals and make genuine progress. Paper money has replaced barter, commodity money and coins as the primary form of money used as a means of exchange for the previous 10,000 years.[47] Automated teller machines (ATMs) were the only useful advancement made by banks in the previous 20 years, according to Paul Volcker in 2009.[48] Despite having a significant impact on the payments system, ATMs, credit cards and even chequebooks, smartphones have led to the widespread usage of mobile money and e-wallets.[49]

Cryptography and distributed ledger technology are continuing to drive a boom in the use of bitcoin and stablecoins.[50] Some countries have even looked into the possibility of utilising cryptocurrency as a secondary national currency. The introduction of dematerialised payments would have a huge impact on the global payments system. The "blood arteries" that support the financial viability of infrastructure projects are the financial architecture of the SDGs. Digital collection techniques, for instance, enhance tax collection and the payment of public goods. The micro-population would also receive additional benefits from the SDG finance thanks to aid, financial transfers and remittances.[51] Consideration in the past has been given by other scholars to the approach adopted in the spectrum or a maturity model[52] for environmental, social and corporate governance (ESG) and impact commitment outlines the advancements occurring across payment systems in connection with the SDGs.[53] The traditional bank investor serves as the model's starting point. This investor makes investments while looking for the best risk-return frontier in an effort to maximise shareholder value.[54] The typical investor would engage in regulatory arbitrage and harm the environment in the absence of legislation (such as carbon taxes), as they are not particularly concerned with internalising the external or social costs of conducting business. Its importance is further strengthened in the context of "blend finance", a key instrument for funding the SDGs that focuses on early-stage venture capital or private equity initiatives with a mix of social and financial benefits.

Huge sums of money would need to be invested, current systems would need to be revolutionised and impact investment projects with ESG prospects would need to be taken into account in order to implement sustainable projects on a large scale and keep global temperatures to 1.5°C over pre-industrial levels.[55] This function is played by fintech companies, which are still working to digitise money and the impact model that results from techfin companies adopting a strategy of monetising data. The type of investments needed in the payments industry to spark SDG benefits for citizens will surely be impact investments.[56] To meet the objectives of financial inclusion, cost reduction and enhanced affordability of remittances, central banks would need to embrace a hybrid digital currency architecture that provides backups for intermediaries. The infrastructure for interoperability with financial systems around the world would be made possible and a crowding-out of financial intermediaries would be avoided.

A reasonable return would need to be paid in order to attract private capital using a combination of seigniorage and charity. For instance, the Rockefeller Foundation, the Bill and Melinda Gates Foundation and the Mastercard Foundation would provide catalytic money to finance financial inclusion targets in a sustainable way, preventing costs from being passed on to final consumers.[57] Public financial and political risk protection from multilaterals like The World Bank Multilateral Investment Guarantee Agency would support these first-loss ventures.[58] Private funding might be used to expand these projects while still providing owners with a decent profit. In order to address the issues with financial inclusion that are unique to developing countries, involve small business owners and entrepreneurs in the economic tax system and boost long-term tax collections – several initiatives have the potential to be implemented. These initiatives will increase financial inclusion, promote investment in fragile economies and resolve the contradictions and denials of greenwashing at some corporations in established capital markets.

SDG 17, "Partnership for the Goals", will be essential in the race for greener, digital, cleantech assets, an end to poverty, the eradication of hunger, good health for all, clean energy, clean water, zero hunger and other SDG targets as all stakeholders will cooperate rather than compete towards a common goal. The Covid-19 pandemic has accelerated the digital revolution, causing a global wave of central banks to adopt digital money in order to maintain the central supply of currency.[59] Customers and the payments system may benefit more from these retail central bank digital currencies. A hybrid architecture supported by financial intermediaries would be preferable to a direct form because it would limit anonymity through early identification and eventual expiration, minimise privacy concerns, encourage private sector engagement and boost system confidence.[60]

The UN's SDGs of eradicating poverty, improving health and education and reducing inequality may all be directly impacted by access to finance.[61] To ascertain whether a person's socio-economic status and demographic characteristics, such as income and education, have an effect on their ability to receive credit, some participants in this book will meticulously assess the growing amount of empirical data. In several chapters, it will also be claimed that obtaining funding is made simpler for households and business owners by having a higher level of education and/or financial literacy. Traditional financial institutions are less likely to extend credit to persons with lower incomes and less wealth. In impoverished countries, women are more likely to be rejected, refused access to official loans and charged higher costs. People with disabilities, people of colour, immigrants and people who identify as racial or ethnic minorities are more likely to be excluded from the official credit markets. We find that the aforementioned credit-challenged social groupings commonly use pricey pawnbrokers or payday lenders. These findings show a startling similarity between developed and poor countries. Finally, we provide recommendations for future research on achieving SDGs through financial inclusion and access to credit by highlighting a number of shortcomings in the existing literature and empirical data.

This book is divided into 15 chapters. In Chapter 1, authors Howard Chitimira and Tapiwa V. Warikandwa make the case that financial inclusion is essential to achieving the UN SDGs, which will be a key factor in reducing poverty and promoting shared prosperity around the world. To this end, Chitimira and Warikandwa stress the need for governments and investors to recognise the importance of financial inclusion in achieving the SDGs because economic growth is a key long-term driver of company sales and profitability, which in turn supports asset prices. The fact that some of the 17 goals are made possible by financial inclusion emphasises how crucial it is. The chapters of the book, all of which were written by authorities on the topic of financial inclusion, will also be summarised in this chapter.

Louis de Koker, in Chapter 2, reflects on the history of South Africa's Exemption 17 and the challenges under a risk-based approach. He argues for a partial return to a rule-based approach, at least in relation to a tiered customer due diligence framework. De Koker notes that South Africa was the first nation to permit easier methods of client identification in support of its financial inclusion initiatives. Exemption 17, the initial solution that was offered, was well-intentioned but not workable. The development and acceptance of tier-based customer due diligence measures in Pakistan, Mexico, Nigeria and other nations were influenced by later evidence-based enhancements that were significantly more successful. After adopting a risk-based strategy, South Africa revoked the laws on rule simplification and required banks and other financial service providers to implement appropriate identity verification requirements.

In Chapter 3, Neels Kilian explains the differences between South Africa and the United Kingdom in regard to financial inclusion in insurance law. The chapter does not discuss legislation relevant to insurance law principles, since both jurisdictions require an application form for insurance to be completed, and after the information on the application form has been accepted, the policy contract (often referred to as the policy wording) will be sent to the policyholder. This chapter highlights the importance of the questions asked on the insurance application form. Such questions are commonly referred to as underwriting questions. Both jurisdictions ask similar underwriting questions, however, they have a dissimilar approach to vague or unspecific questions.

In Chapter 4, Jean Jacques du Plessis explores some of the unique aspects of South African company law and its approach to corporate governance. Du Plessis illustrates that by adopting the all-inclusive stakeholder approach, South Africa has been ahead of many other jurisdictions. The focus in the United States has shifted to a more stakeholder-orientated approach since about 2017. Du Plessis concludes that no fundamental change in South African company law or corporate governance models is required. Du Plessis then recommends that in future the focus needs to be on ensuring that South African corporations adopt the approach in South African legislation and the King Reports and that all stakeholders work together to ensure a long-term and sustainable future for South African corporations.

In Chapter 5, Eukeria Wealth, Tendai D. Svotwa and Charles Makanyeza seek to unravel the status of the financial education system in Namibia in a bid to identify the related constraints and proffer possible solutions. They argue that with the current global financial crisis, the need for financial education for the common man and society at large cannot be overemphasised. They conclude by arguing that financial education programmes cannot be a one-size-fits-all and there is a need for tailored curriculum and targeted content that address Namibia's unique needs.

In Chapter 6, Howard Chitimira and Friedrich Hamadziripi point out that most studies on financial inclusion in South Africa have been restricted to "cash" forms of micro-credit and unconsciously neglected the role of asset-based funding in promoting financial inclusion. They further argue that, in South Africa, the provision of trade finance has been largely left to the private sector. Banks and other private institutions remain key players in the financial inclusion of SMEs in South Africa through the provision of micro-credit. The authors conclude that trade finance could be an alternative means of micro-credit to promote the financial inclusion of the poor and SME owners in South Africa.

In Chapter 7, Olipah Mpofu and Nednah Maraga argue that mobile money (MM) has become a powerful means of achieving financial inclusion (FI) and sustainable development, especially in Africa. MM transactions, which have been regarded as a tool for FI through serving the underserved and unbanked population, are equally at the forefront of Covid-19 prevention. The call for adherence to Covid-19 protocols such as social distancing and mobility restrictions have become a substantive motivating factor in the adoption of MM services. The past two decades have seen the rapid growth of MM in developing economies. At the same time, FI has topped most of the developmental agendas. MM has proved to be an enabler of FI in many economies, however, some have failed to fully utilise the sector. Mpofu and Maraga thus explore the challenges of implementing MM services and barriers to the adoption of MM in Botswana. They envisage that this study would proffer to policymakers on how to enhance MM to improve FI, prevent the spread of Covid-19 and ultimately achieve sustainable development.

In Chapter 8, Tendai D. Svotwa, Charles Makanyeza and Eukeria Wealth argue that despite the major roles played by women in entrepreneurship and leadership, several challenges have been observed in the quest to financially include women in the formal financial system. They point to the existence of a myriad of challenges in the SADC region that militate against the inclusion of women in the formal financial services sector. These include the reluctance by banks to advance credit to rural communities and the poor and the demand for collateral/security by financial institutions when they advance loans to women. In this chapter, Svotwa, Makanyeza and Wealth reveal that Namibia and South Africa have higher rates of financial inclusion compared with Botswana and Zimbabwe.

In Chapter 9, Gertruida van Niekerk makes the case that access to digital financial services (including smartphones, websites, computers and ATMs) can be a solution to enable people to use their bank accounts regularly. She further points out that challenges to using digital financial services that poor and low-income earners in rural South Africa experience include insufficient information and communications infrastructure, no access to smartphones and/or cell phone data, the digital capability of individuals and the lack of digitised informal trading. Van Niekerk then recommends that broadband network and data coverage be raised into underserved areas and that point of sale (POS) technology at spaza shops and informal vendors be extended so that customers can pay digitally. She concludes by observing that digital transformation can assist poor and low-income earners in rural South Africa who have bank accounts to overcome challenges so that they can use their bank accounts regularly.

Tinashe Kondo and Yvette Basson, in Chapter 10, observe that economically excluded persons are unlikely to utilise banking services as they are not participating effectively in the economy, and thus lack financial resources. In this vein, they discuss the curious case of the Gauteng Township Economic Draft Bill. The Bill seeks to regulate the management of the township economy. In its first draft, the Bill sought to limit the participation of foreign nationals without permanent residency status from participating in certain sectors of the township economy. A reason for this was the interpretation of s 22 of the Constitution of the Republic of South Africa, 1996, as only guaranteeing the right to freely choose a trade, occupation profession to citizens, and, by extension, to permanent residents. This had potential implications for a number of socio-economic rights for certain classes of foreign nationals. Thus, Kondo and Basson explore how such an economic exclusion of refugees may potentially jeopardise the project of meaningful financial inclusion.

In Chapter 11, Howard Chitimira and Phemelo T. Magau point out that in an effort to provide financial assistance to unemployed people during the lockdown, the government introduced the Covid-19 Social Relief Distress (SRD) grant. The SRD grant, also known as the special R350 Covid-19 grant, has been welcomed by many as one of the relief measures the government put in place and extended its provision several times to try to sustain the people most affected by the pandemic. However, as Chitimira and Magau observe, the administration of this grant has not been without challenges, thus thwarting the objective of this grant and resulting in some poor and unemployed persons not accessing the grant on time or at all. Accordingly, Chitimira and Magau examine the process of administering the SRD grant in the context of the financial inclusion of poor and unemployed persons in South Africa. They discuss the role of selected key role-players involved in the provision and administration of the SRD grant. Such role-players include the South African Social Security Agency (SASSA), the South African Post Office (SAPO) and the Department of Social Development (DSD). The role played by these institutions is discussed to investigate whether they have adopted and put adequate measures in place to promote financial inclusion of the poor and unemployed persons in the provision and administration of the SRD grant. Moreover, Chitimira and Magau outline the advantages and disadvantages of the SRD grant in South Africa.

In Chapter 12, Eukeria Wealth, Tendai D. Svotwa and Charles Makanyeza point out that more than 60% of Africa's youth are unemployed, and a significant portion often transition into adulthood without access to financial services. Wealth, Svotwa and Makanyeza attribute this development to the fact that the youth are perceived as a high-risk and low-value sector. These challenges act as barriers to financial freedom and economic emancipation of young people, exposing them to financial fragility compared with adults. Wealth, Svotwa and Makanyeza thus explore the relationship between financial inclusion and youth empowerment in order to inform policymakers on possible interventions.

In Chapter 13, authors Friedrich Hamadziripi and Vimbai Jana contend that the low uptake of formal financial services by poor and marginalised people in Zimbabwe is fuelled by supply induced barriers such as profit motives by financial institutions that result in financial services becoming expensive to access. They further note that poor and marginalised people also struggle to comply with the minimum account opening or loan requirements needed by financial institutions in the formal financial sector. Furthermore, regulatory barriers such as rigid banking laws have also contributed to the low uptake of formal financial services in Zimbabwe. The purpose of this chapter, according to Hamdziripi and Jana, is to analyse the policies and statutory regulations relating to the promotion of financial inclusion in Zimbabwe. Most importantly, the 2016–2020 national financial inclusion strategy (NFIS) was launched by the Reserve Bank of Zimbabwe (RBZ) in March 2016. They also considered it worthy to analyse the progress made and the challenges faced by the government of Zimbabwe towards achieving financial inclusion.

In Chapter 14, Tapiwa V. Warikandwa, Eugene Libebe, Elize Shakalela, Lineekela Usebiu and Marvin R. Awarab make the case that farmers and marginalised as well as poor persons in Namibia have consistently tried to adjust to weather fluctuations by modifying irrigation and crop choices, but only recovered minimal lost revenues. Farmers and marginalised as well as poor persons may be unable to adjust successfully to the negative effects of climate change due to significant financial hurdles. The authors point out that farmers, for example, may not have the funds or credit to invest in more hardy seeds or irrigation technologies. Furthermore, the authors note that farmers may lack access to cheap insurance policies that might help offset losses caused by extreme weather. As the effects of climate change become more severe, it is vital to assist the poor in adapting to these problems and empowering them to lessen their environmental impact. Warikandwa, Libebe, Shakalela, Usebiu and Awarab thus explore new ways that financial services and products may address the threats that climate change poses to the poor and marginalised persons in Namibia.

In the final chapter, Chapter 15, Ashley B. Nyaude observes that deposit insurance policies and procedures as expressed in the International Association of Deposit Insurers Core Principles for Effective Deposit Insurance Systems and individual deposit insurer mandates affect financial inclusion, primarily through policies and practices governing membership, coverage, funding and public awareness. The author further observes that Zimbabwe is characterised by incredible human and economic hardships, including bank failures, low-capacity utilisation, nation-wide lockdowns attributable to the devastating effects of Covid-19, the Covid-19 pandemic and inflationary pressures. Therefore, in the chapter, Nyaude examines the measures taken by the Deposit Protection Corporation of Zimbabwe to protect bank depositors and promote financial inclusion to pronounce on whether it adequately achieves this goal.

1.3 Conclusion

Financial inclusion has been emphasised in certain policy documents as a means of eradicating poverty in developing nations. It provides the ability of poor families to lessen financial shocks, make human capital investments in health and education and/or engage in modest asset accumulation in order to take advantage of appealing investment opportunities in their economies. However, it has been shown that most SSA countries' banking systems are either unable or unwilling to serve the poorest segments of the population. As a result, SSA still has a lot of work to do to encourage growth and end poverty. Therefore, this chapter has detailed the numerous scenarios in which researchers will examine the various ways that financial inclusion may help achieve the UN's SDGs of ending poverty, protecting the environment and ensuring that everyone enjoys prosperity by 2030. The debates also bring to light a few pressing problems. One crucial conclusion is that the poorest SADC citizens may not receive the knowledge and skills they require to find ways out of poverty from financial inclusion alone. Financial inclusion must aim to boost people's sense of control over their circumstances and their faith in that ability in order to aid the masses of the SADC and people in other regions of the world to escape poverty.

Notes

1 United Nations (n.d) https://sdgs.un.org/2030agenda, accessed 10 July 2022.
2 United Nations (n.d) https://sdgs.un.org/2030agenda, accessed 10 July 2022.
3 United Nations Capital Development Fund (n.d.) https://www.uncdf.org/financial-inclusion-and-the-sdgs, accessed 11 July 2022.
4 Klapper et al. (2016), 1, para. 2.
5 Klapper, L (2016).
6 McKinsey Global Institute (2016), 2.
7 Kuzmina (2018).
8 United Nations Capital Development Fund (n.d.) https://www.uncdf.org/lmftf/what-is-the-last-mile-finance-trust-fund, accessed 11 July 2022.
9 UNCDF (2020).
10 UNCDF (n.d.) https://www.uncdf.org/f4f/womens-empowerment, accessed 8 July 2022.
11 The World Bank (2022).
12 The World Bank (2020).
13 Maas (2018).
14 Global Partnership for Financial Inclusion (n.d) https://databank.worldbank.org/data/download/g20fidata/G20_Financial_Inclusion_Indicators.pdf, accessed 6 July 2022.
15 The World Bank (2021).
16 UN Department of Economic and Social Affairs: Sustainable Development. https://sustainabledevelopment.un.org/sdgs, accessed 7 July 2022.
17 United Nations Conference on Trade and Development (2015). See also C Emebinah 'Enhancing financial inclusion toward the SDGs' 2021, available at https://impactentrepreneur.com/enhancing-financial-inclusion-toward-the-sdgs/, accessed on 4 July 2022.
18 Hope (2018).
19 Oxford Business Group (2017).
20 Klapper (2016).
21 Food and Agriculture Organisation of the UN (2020).
22 Prathap (2011), 79–105.
23 Pomeroy et al. (2020). See also Stopler and Walter (2017) 581.
24 Matongela (2014), p171.
25 The World Bank (2013).
26 The World Bank (2014).
27 The World Bank (2019).
28 Avitsian (2020).
29 United Nations International Children's Emergency Fund (2018).
30 Robino et al. (2020).
31 Ahmed (2019), 1–17.
32 Lipper and Benton (2020).
33 Salman and Nowacka (2020), 3.
34 Government of India (2020).
35 Klapper (2016).
36 Klapper (2016).
37 Tay et al. (2022), 1–10.
38 Klapper (2016). See also Ozili (2018), 329–340.
39 Donovan (2012), 2647–2669.
40 Adam and Fazekas (2021), 2–14.
41 Khera et al. (2021), 6.
42 Ahmad (2020), 753–792.
43 Economic Commission for Latin America and the Caribbean [ECLAC] (2018).
44 United Nations Development Programme (2019).

45 Barne and Pirlea (2019).
46 UN (2022).
47 Peneder (2022), 175–203.
48 The Wall Street Journal (2009).
49 Lei et al. (2022), 1071–1087.
50 Arner et al. (2020), 2–28.
51 Akanle et al. (2022).
52 Saskia et al. (2016), 312–323.
53 Mohabbati-Kalejahi et al. (2022), 1222.
54 Saskia et al. (2016), 312.
55 Tiefenbacher (n.d.).
56 ECLAC (2018).
57 Sklair and Gilbert (2022), 51–77.
58 Matsukawa and Habeck (2007), 1–88.
59 Wang et al. (2022).
60 Soderberg (2022).
61 Vorisek and Yu (2020), 1–29.

Bibliography

I Adam & M Fazekas 'Are emerging technologies helping win the fight against corruption? A review of the state of evidence' (2021) 57 *Information Economics and Policy* 2.

A H Ahmad 'Mobile money, financial inclusion and development: A review with reference to African experience' (2020) 34 *Journal of Economic Surveys* 753.

S M Ahmed, J Jassim, A Basharat & W Malik 'Microfinance poised to play a vital role in achieving developmental objectives of the government' (2019) 38 *MicroNote* 1.

O Akanle, D Kayode & I Abolade 'Sustainable development goals (SDGs) and remittances in Africa' (2022) 8 *Cogent Social Sciences* 2037811.

D Arner, R Auer & J Frost *Stablecoins: Risks, Potential and Regulation* (Bank for International Settlements working papers no. 905, 2020) 2.

T Avitsian 'The healthcare system in Jordan' 2020, available at https://borgenproject.org/the-healthcare-system-in-jordan/, accessed on 6 July 2022.

D Barne & F Pirlea 'Money sent home by workers now largest source of external financing in low- and middle-income countries (excluding China)' 2019, available at https://blogs.worldbank.org/opendata/money-sent-home-workers-now-largest-source-external-financing-low-and-middle-income, accessed on 6 July 2022.

K P Donovan 'Mobile money, more freedom? The impact of M-PESA's network power on development as freedom' (2012) 6 *International Journal of Communication* 2647.

ECLAC 'Data, algorithms and policies: Redefining the digital world' 2018, available at https://repositorio.cepal.org/bitstream/handle/11362/43515/4/S1800052_en.pdf, accessed on 8 July 2022.

Economic Commission for Latin America and the Caribbean (ECLAC) 'The 2030 agenda and the sustainable development goals: An opportunity for Latin America and the Caribbean' 2018, available at https://repositorio.cepal.org/bitstream/handle/11362/40156/25/S1801140_en.pdf, accessed on 10 July 2022.

C Emebinah 'Enhancing financial inclusion toward the SDGs' 2021, available at https://impactentrepreneur.com/enhancing-financial-inclusion-toward-the-sdgs/, accessed on 4 July 2022.

Food and Agriculture Organisation of the UN 'Voluntary guidelines for securing sustainable small-scale fisheries in the context of food security and poverty eradication'

2020, available at https://www.fao.org/voluntary-guidelines-small-scale-fisheries/news-and-events/detail/en/c/1333232/, accessed on 10 July 2022.

Global Partnership for Financial Inclusion 'G20 financial inclusion indicators', available at https://databank.worldbank.org/data/download/g20fidata/G20_Financial_Inclusion_Indicators.pdf, accessed on 6 July 2022.

Government of India 'Poverty alleviation in rural India - Strategy and programmes' 2020, available at https://niti.gov.in/planningcommission.gov.in/docs/plans/planrel/fiveyr/10th/volume2/v2_ch3_2.pdf, accessed on 7 July 2022.

A Hope 'Women, trade and financial inclusion, Tralac 30 August 2018' 2018, available at https://www.tralac.org/blog/article/13422-women-trade-and-financial-inclusion-in-sadc.html, accessed on 7 July 2022.

P Khera, S Ng, S Ogawa & R Sahay *Measuring Digital Financial Inclusion in Emerging Market and Developing Economies: A New Index* (IMF working paper on monetary and capital markets department, March 2021, WP/21/90, 2021).

L Klapper 'See also Ozili, PK (2018) Impact of digital finance on financial inclusion and stability' (2016a) 18 *Borsa Istanbul Review* 329.

L Klapper 'Financial inclusion has a big role to play in reaching the SDGs' 2016b, available at https://blogs.worldbank.org/developmenttalk/financial-inclusion-has-big-role-play-reaching-sdgs, accessed on 10 July 2022.

L Klapper, M El-Zoghbi& J Hess 'Achieving the sustainable development goals: The role of financial inclusion' (2016) *United Nations Secretary General's Special Advocate for Inclusive Finance for Development* 1, para. 2.

A Kuzmina 'Kenya case study part II: M-PESA vs the market' 2018, available at https://medium.com/what-the-money/kenya-case-study-part-ii-m-pesa-vs-the-market-107ef4559497, accessed on 11 July 2022.

H Lei, J Lan & K Sleiman 'An empirical study on investigating mobile payment effect on automated teller machine use' (2022) 10 *Open Journal of Business and Management* 1071 at 1087.

L Lipper & T G Benton *Mega-Trends in the Southern African Region. SADC Futures: Developing Foresight Capacity for Climate Resilient Agricultural Development Knowledge Series*. CCAFS Report (2020).

T Maas 'The importance of financial inclusion in socio-economic development' 2018, available at https://hollandfintech.com/2018/07/the-importance-of-financial-inclusion-in-socio-economical-development/, accessed on 7 July 2022.

A M Matongela 'Understanding the state of financial inclusion in Namibia' (2014) 5 *Research Journal of Finance and Accounting* 171.

T Matsukawa & O Habeck *Review of Risk Mitigation Instruments for Infrastructure Financing and Recent Trends and Developments, Trends and Policy Options No. 4* (2007) 1.

McKinsey Global Institute *Digital Finance for All: Powering Inclusive Growth in Emerging Economies* (2016) 2.

N Mohabbati-Kalejahi, S Alavi & M A Zahed 'Sustainable development goals (SDGs) as a framework for corporate social responsibility (CSR)' (2022) 14 *Sustainability* 1222.

Oxford Business Group 'The report: The Philippines 2017' 2017, available at https://oxfordbusinessgroup.com/philippines-2017/country-profile, accessed on 10 July 2022.

M Peneder 'Digitisation and the evolution of money as a social technology of account' (2022) 32 *Journal of Evolutionary Economics* 175.

R Pomeroy, C Arango, C G Lomboy & S Box 'Financial inclusion to build economic resilience in small-scale fisheries' (2020) 118 *Marine Policy* 103982.

S K Prathap *Financial Inclusion of Fisher Households in Coastal Kerala - Role of Micro-Finance* (Doctor of Philosophy degree, Cochin University of Science and Technology, 2011) 79 .

C Robino, C Trivelli, C Villanueva, F C Sachetti, H Walbey & L Martinez 'Financial inclusion for women: A way forward' 2020, available at https://www.g20-insights.org/policy_briefs/financial-inclusion-for-women-a-way-forward/, accessed on 5 July 2022.

A Salman & K Nowacka *Innovative Financial Products and Services for Women in Asia and the Pacific* (Asian Development Bank Sustainable Development working paper series no. 67, April 2020) 3.

B Saskia, S Schneider & D WeBels 'The Kiel maturity model as a future-oriented mindset for sustainable knowledge management processes' (2016) 8 *International Journal of Sustainable Economy* 312.

J Sklair & P Gilbert 'Giving as "de-risking": Philanthropy, impact investment and the pandemic response, public' (2022) 4 *Anthropologist* 51.

G Soderberg *Behind the Scenes of Central Bank Digital Currency: Emerging Trends, Insights, and Policy Lessons, FinTech Note/2022/004, International Monetary Fund, Publication Services* (2022).

O A Stopler & A Walter 'Financial literacy, financial advice, and financial behaviour' (2017) 87 *Journal of Business Economics* 581.

L Tay, H Tai & G Tan 'Digital financial inclusion: A gateway to sustainable development' (2022) 8 *Heliyon* 1.

The Wall Street Journal 'Paul Volker: Think more boldly' 2009, available at https://www.wsj.com/articles/SB10001424052748704825504574586330960597134, accessed on 5 July 2022.

The World Bank 'Poverty reduction in practice: How and where we work' 2013, available at https://www.worldbank.org/en/news/feature/2013/02/05/poverty-reduction-in-practice, accessed on 6 July 2022.

The World Bank 'Poverty and health' 2014, available at https://www.worldbank.org/en/topic/health/brief/poverty-health, accessed on 6 July 2022.

The World Bank 'In Kenya, uplifting the poor and vulnerable through a harmonised national safety net system' 2019, available at https://www.worldbank.org/en/results/2019/04/18/in-kenya-uplifting-the-poor-and-vulnerable-through-a-harmonized-national-safety-net-system, accessed on 6 July 2022.

The World Bank 'UFA2020 overview: Universal financial access by 2020' 2020, available at https://www.worldbank.org/en/topic/financialinclusion/brief/achieving-universal-financial-access-by-2020, accessed on 7 July 2022.

The World Bank 'The Global Findex Database 2021: Financial inclusion, digital payments, and resilience in the age of covid-19' 2021, available at https://globalfindex.worldbank.org/basic-page-overview, accessed on 6 July 2022.

The World Bank 'Financial inclusion: Financial inclusion is a key enabler to reducing poverty and boosting prosperity' 2022, available at https://www.worldbank.org/en/topic/financialinclusion/overview, accessed on 8 July 2022.

J P Tiefenbacher (ed.) 'Environmental management – Pollution, habitat, ecology, and sustainability', available at https://www.intechopen.com/books/10765, accessed on 13 July 2022.

UN 'Remittances and the SDGs' 2022, available at https://www.un.org/en/observances/remittances-day/SDGs, accessed on 6 July 2022.

UN Department of Economic and Social Affairs 'Sustainable development', available at https://sustainabledevelopment.un.org/sdgs, accessed on 7 July 2022.

UNCDF 'Financial inclusion for what?' 2020, available at https://www.financedigitalafrica.org/2020/03/02/financial-inclusion-for-what/, accessed on 10 July 2022.

UNCDF 'Women's empowerment to strengthen food security' n.d., available at https://www.uncdf.org/f4f/womens-empowerment, accessed on 8 July 2022.

United Nations 'Transforming our world: The 2030 agenda for sustainable development' n.d., available at https://sdgs.un.org/2030agenda, accessed on 10 July 2022.

United Nations Capital Development Fund 'Financial inclusion and the SDGs' n.d., available at https://www.uncdf.org/financial-inclusion-and-the-sdgs, accessed on 11 July 2022.

United Nations Capital Development Fund 'What is the last mile finance trust fund - UN Capital Development Fund (UNCDF)' n.d., available at https://www.uncdf.org/lmftf/what-is-the-last-mile-finance-trust-fund, accessed on 11 July 2022.

United Nations Conference on Trade and Development *Access to Financial Services as a Driver for the Post-2015 Development Agenda* (Policy brief no. 35, September 2015). Access to Financial Services as a Driver for the Post-2015 Development Agenda (unctad.org), accessed on 8 July 2022.

United Nations Development Programme 'Corporate, investment leaders review SDG impact plans' 2019, available at https://www.undp.org/stories/corporate-investment-leaders-review-sdg-impact-plans, accessed on 10 July 2022.

United Nations International Children's Emergency Fund 'Goal 4: Quality education' 2018, available at https://data.unicef.org/sdgs/goal-4-quality-education/, accessed on 6 July 2022.

D Vorisek & S Yu *Understanding the Cost of Achieving the Sustainable Development Goals* (Policy research working paper no. 9146, 2020) 1.

Y Wang, B M Lucey, S A Vigne & L Yarovaya 'The effects of central bank digital currencies news on financial markets' (2022) 180 *Technological Forecasting and Social Change* 121715.

2 South Africa's initial implementation of the Financial Action Task Force's customer identity verification standards

Perspectives and reflection on regulatory processes and approaches

Louis de Koker

2.1 Introduction

In 1998, the G7 established a temporary task force to investigate the means to protect the financial systems of G7 members against the proceeds of crime. This step was taken in support of the then-new anti-money laundering measures embodied in the 1988 United Nations Convention against Illicit Traffic in Narcotic Drugs and Psychotropic Substances. The task force, known as the Financial Action Task Force (FATF), compiled a set of 40 recommendations on steps countries and financial institutions could take to increase their resilience against money laundering abuse.[1] Over time, these recommendations hardened into international standards that countries and an increasing number of regulated institutions are expected to meet, while the FATF became recognised and formalised as the global intergovernmental anti-money laundering and counter-terrorist and proliferation financing standard-setting body.

Countries are assessed by their peers for their technical compliance with standards as well as the effectiveness with which these standards are implemented. Failure to meet minimum standards may result in the grey listing or even the blacklisting of a jurisdiction by the FATF. Such a listing holds the potential for negative economic impact on a country.[2] The risk of such negative impact has been sufficient for most countries to improve levels of compliance.

One of the key objectives of the FATF is to increase financial transparency. During the latter part of the 20th century, organised criminals developed various ways to hide their transactions and wealth using the shield of bank secrecy. The standards required countries to introduce a range of customer due diligence obligations for banks and other regulated institutions, including the duty to identify and verify the identity of each customer. Over time, wide-scale implementation of the new customer due diligence measures, and especially the duty to verify the identity of customers, became problematic as it undermined the ability of people who lacked the necessary identity credentials to access formal financial services.

DOI: 10.4324/9781003369400-2

This chapter reviews and reflects on the initial implementation of South Africa's identity verification responses to the FATF standards. The emphasis will fall on the identification of individuals within the context of financial inclusion. It draws on research undertaken by the author since 1996, including analysis and texts in articles and a book published since 1999 and updated annually.[3]

2.2 FATF's pre-2012 identity verification standards

The original 1990 version of the FATF's 40 recommendations[4] set out a range of customer identification measures. These are relevant to a discussion of South African implementation of the standards as the original FICA and the FICA regulations were mainly drafted to respond to this version of the standards.

Three recommendations, Recommendations 12, 13 and 14, addressed customer identification and record-keeping. Recommendation 12 determined that financial institutions should not keep anonymous accounts or accounts in obviously fictitious names. They should be required (whether by law, by regulations, by agreements between supervisory authorities and financial institutions or by self-regulatory agreements among financial institutions) to identify, on the basis of an official or other reliable identifying document, and record the identity of their clients, either occasional or usual, when establishing business relations or conducting transactions (in particular, opening of accounts or passbooks, entering into fiduciary transactions, renting of safe deposit boxes and performing large cash transactions).

Recommendation 13 required financial institutions to take reasonable measures to obtain information about the true identity of the person(s) on whose behalf an account was to be opened or a transaction conducted if there were any doubts as to whether the clients or customers were not acting on their own behalf.

Recommendation 14 required financial institutions to maintain, for at least five years, all necessary records on transactions, both domestic and international, to enable them to comply swiftly with information requests from competent authorities. Such records had to be sufficient to permit the reconstruction of individual transactions (including the amounts and types of currency involved if any) so as to provide, if necessary, evidence for the prosecution of criminal behaviour. Financial institutions had to keep records on customer identification (such as copies or records of official identification documents like passports, identity cards, driving licenses or similar documents), account files and business correspondence for at least five years after the account was closed. These documents should be available to domestic competent authorities in the context of relevant criminal prosecutions and investigations.

The FATF Recommendations did not define "identity" or prescribed how a person should be identified, that is, the information that should be collected to uniquely individualise a particular customer. At that stage, they did not yet distinguish between identification (the collection of identifying particulars) and verification of identity (the verification of some or all of the relevant identifiers). From the language used ("identify, on the basis of an official or other reliable identifying document" and "official identification documents like passports, identity cards, driving licenses or similar documents"), it was clear that they were focused on a person's identity as known to the state, that is, a person's bureaucratic or official identity. This created tensions to be navigated in relation to persons who were not holders of official identity credentials, although these were probably not foreseen by the government representatives and experts of developed economies who drafted the standards.

The recommendations were extensively revised in 2003. The phrase "identify, on the basis of an official or other reliable identifying document" was changed to "[i]dentifying the customer and verifying that customer's identity using reliable, independent source documents, data or information" in Recommendation 5. This change reflected an improved understanding of the distinction between identification and verification of identity.[5] In practice, however, many FATF stakeholders did not fully embrace this distinction until the 2012 standards were drafted. The new phrase also allowed non-documentary means of identity verification. That change was, however, not fully complete as the record-keeping standard (Recommendation 10) still referenced retention of copies or records of documents (" copies or records of official identification documents like passports, identity cards, driving licenses or similar documents").

Importantly, a voluntary risk-based approach to customer due diligence (CDD) was introduced in Recommendation 5:

> Financial institutions should apply each of the CDD measures … but may determine the extent of such measures on a risk sensitive basis depending on the type of customer, business relationship or transaction. The measures that are taken should be consistent with any guidelines issued by competent authorities. For higher risk categories, financial institutions should perform enhanced due diligence. In certain circumstances, where there are low risks, countries may decide that financial institutions can apply reduced or simplified measures.

Simplified or reduced CDD measures were further discussed in interpretive note 9 to the Recommendations. It made it clear that such measures may be considered where the risk of money laundering or terrorist financing was lower, where information on the identity of the customer and the beneficial owner of a customer was publicly available or where adequate checks and controls existed elsewhere in national systems. The note provided a range of examples of such lower-risk cases, for example:

- Financial institutions that are subject to requirements to combat money laundering and terrorist financing consistent with the FATF Recommendations and are supervised for compliance with those controls.
- Public companies that are subject to regulatory disclosure requirements.
- Government administrations or enterprises.

It also listed examples of products or transactions that may potentially be lower risk:

- Life insurance policies where the annual premium is no more than US$/EUR1000 or a single premium of no more than US$/EUR2500.
- Insurance policies for pension schemes if there is no surrender clause and the policy cannot be used as collateral.
- A pension, superannuation or similar scheme that provides retirement benefits to employees, where contributions are made by way of deduction from wages and the scheme rules do not permit the assignment of a member's interest under the scheme.

While the general risk-based principles were potentially helpful to address the plight of financially excluded persons, none of the examples listed were relevant to poor, undocumented persons and the services that they required. The risk-sensitive framework provided principles that could empower financial inclusion, but they were not interpreted by FATF to extend to low-value transactions. At that stage, in the aftermath of the 9/11 attacks, there was in fact an elevated concern about the terrorist financing risks that small transactions may pose.

2.3 Basel Committee on Banking Supervision

FATF is often accused of erecting financial inclusion barriers by setting customer due diligence standards that many people cannot meet. As pointed out earlier, the FATF set the requirement that customers have to be identified and their identities verified but did not prescribe how that should be done. National regulators set those requirements and often created unnecessary barriers to financial inclusion. They in turn were often informed by steps taken by other leading developed economies. In some cases, guidance issued by another financial standard-setting body, the Basel Committee on Banking Supervision (BCBS) may also have influenced overdesigned identity verification requirements.

In February 2003, the BCBS issued its *General Guide to Account Opening and Customer Identification*. This guide supplemented its 2001 paper entitled *Customer Due Diligence for Banks*.[6] The guide addressed identification requirements in respect of a host of customers. In respect of natural persons, it required the following information to be obtained, where applicable:[7]

- legal name and any other names used (such as maiden name);
- correct permanent address (the full address should be obtained; a Post Office box number is not sufficient);
- telephone number, fax number, and e-mail address;
- date and place of birth;
- nationality;

- occupation, public position held and/or name of employer;
- an official personal identification number or other unique identifier contained in an unexpired official document (e.g. passport, identification card, residence permit, social security records, driving licence) that bears a photograph of the customer;
- type of account and nature of the banking relationship;
- signature.

The guide required banks to verify the par 10 information by at least one of the following methods:[8]

- confirming the date of birth from an official document (birth certificate, passport, identity card, social security records);
- confirming the permanent address (utility bill, tax assessment, bank statement, a letter from a public authority);
- contacting the customer by telephone, by letter or by e-mail to confirm the information supplied after an account has been opened (a disconnected phone, returned mail or incorrect e-mail address should warrant further investigation);
- confirming the validity of the official documentation provided through certification by an authorised person (e.g. embassy official, notary public).

This information was viewed as baseline information to open a bank account. The financial institution had to use this information to make an initial assessment of a customer's risk profile. Particular attention needed to be focused on those customers identified thereby as having a higher risk profile. Additional inquiries made or information had to obtained in respect of those customers, for example, evidence of an individual's permanent address could be sought through a credit reference agency search or through independent verification by home visits; a personal reference could be obtained, for example, from a current customer of the same institution.[9]

The guide did reflect sensitivities to the plight of people who may experience these requirements as a barrier. It advised that it "is important that the customer acceptance policy is not so restrictive that it results in a denial of access by the general public to banking services, especially for people who are financially or socially disadvantaged".[10] While this statement was helpful, it did not have much effect in practice. In essence, the guide reflected the best practices of the large global banks in relation to high-net-worth clients. It set very high baseline expectations of client identification processes to be adopted. Many regulators and smaller banks looked to the example of these banks and the Basel guidance to inform the design of their own processes. In the rush to design and implement new, compliant processes, the plight of financially or socially disadvantaged persons was not often considered and given due weight.

2.4 FICA and the Money Laundering Control Regulations[11]

South Africa was an early adopter of money laundering legislation.[12] In 1992, it adopted its first statutory money laundering offences aimed at the proceeds of drug trafficking as part of the Drugs and Drug Trafficking Act 140 of 1992. In 1996, it broadened the scope of the money laundering provisions to the proceeds of all crimes in the Proceeds of Crime Act 76 of 1996. It enhanced its measures against organised crime and addressed flaws in the Proceeds of Crime Act[13] by adopting the Prevention of Organised Crime Act 121 of 1998. These Acts only created offences and law enforcement powers and not the money laundering control obligations envisaged by the FATF standards.

In August 1996 when the South African Law Commission published a Money Laundering Control Bill as part of a report entitled *Money laundering and related matters*.[14] The government was, however, slow to act on the report. South African business leaders and academics, at that stage deeply involved in Business Against Crime and other public-private crime combating partnerships with the government, put increasing pressure on the government to adopt money laundering control laws.[15] Eventually, in 2001, the Financial Intelligence Centre Act 38 of 2001 (FICA) was adopted. This Act created the Financial Intelligence Centre as well as the main anti-money laundering obligations.

Section 21(2) of FICA determined that an "accountable institution may not establish a business relationship or conclude a single transaction with a client unless the accountable institution has taken the prescribed steps ... to establish and verify the identity of the client".

Section 21(2) determined that if an accountable institution had established a business relationship with a client before the Act took effect, the accountable institution may not conclude a transaction in the course of that business relationship unless the accountable institution has taken the prescribed steps to establish and verify the identity of the client. The AML provisions of FICA commenced on 1 July 2003, but the commencement of section 21(2) was delayed by another year.

Originally, the FICA Bill allowed accountable institutions "a reasonable period" to establish the identity of their existing customers. A few stakeholders requested parliament to provide more certainty to the business community about the period of time allowed. In response, parliament removed the reference to "a reasonable period" on the understanding that the Ministry of Finance would allow a delayed commencement of one year.

Insufficient thought was given to whether this time period would suffice to convince millions of South Africans to present their identity credentials to their financial institutions. Major concerns arose when the year started to run out and it was clear that millions of clients would not meet the deadline. This left banks with the obligation to freeze the majority of active accounts in South African on 1 July 2004. Such actions would have caused a financial meltdown. As a consequence, the Minister of Finance was forced to introduce a risk-based exemption that allowed for tiered, managed identity verification of customers over a longer period of time.

2.4.1 Money Laundering Control Regulations

While FICA required that customers had to be identified and their identities verified, it did not prescribe how customers had to be identified. The relevant measures had to be detailed in the Money Laundering Control Regulations to be made by the Minister of Finance under FICA after consultation with the Financial Intelligence Centre and the Money Laundering Advisory Council, established by FICA.

The Council consisted of representatives of key government agencies, regulated institutions and academia. It provided a forum for a robust discussion of appropriate regulations.

The drafting of the Money Laundering Control Regulations took place against the background of heightened concerns to ensure compliance with the FATF standards. After the 9/11 attacks, the FATF's scope was broadened to terrorist financing. Compliance with the full set of standards was viewed as crucial to mitigate the risks of terrorism globally. Furthermore, the FATF launched its Non-Compliant Countries or Territories (NCCT) programme in 2001, publicly listing countries that it assessed as not sufficiently compliant with its standards.[16] There were concerns that South Africa may be listed because it had not yet adopted legislation to comply with the standards. Apart from potential negative concerns that may be linked to an NCCT listing, it would also impact on South Africa's ability to join FATF as its first African member. These concerns often informed a more conservative regulatory design approach by government officials.

Towards the end of 2002, the FIC provided a draft text of the Regulations, and this was exhaustively discussed and amended during several Council engagements before the publication of the Regulations on 20 December 2002.

The relevant identification and verification requirements were set out in Regulations 3 and 4 of the Money Laundering Control Regulations. In essence, accountable institutions had to obtain the following information about a customer who was a South African citizen or resident and who did not require legal assistance and was not aiding another:

Full name
Date of birth
Identity number
Residential address.[17]

The person's full name, date of birth and identity number had to be verified by comparing them with an identification document of the person (defined in relation to a South African citizen or resident as an official identity document). If the person was, for a reason which was acceptable to the bank, unable to produce an identity document, another document was acceptable to the bank (taking into regard any guidance notes that may be applicable) and which had a photograph of the person; the person's full names or initials and surname; the person's date of birth; and the person's identity number. If it was believed to be necessary, considering any relevant guidance notes, any of these particulars must be compared with information obtained from any other independent source.

The residential address had to be compared to information that could reasonably be expected to achieve verification of the particulars and could be obtained by reasonably practical means (taking into regard any relevant guidance notes).

When these measures were discussed prior to the finalisation of the text of the Regulations, academic concerns were about unintended negative impact on persons who lacked a formal verifiable address. According to the 2001 census, nearly a third of South African households did not have formal addresses; 30% of the approximately then 9.1 million households in South Africa lived in either traditional dwellings or informal structures.[18] They often lacked official documents or other information that can be used to verify their informal residential addresses.

South Africans are issued with a unique identity number, and it was argued in 2002 that a person's name and this number would suffice for identification purposes, while residential address information would add little value as an identifier.[19] The Ministry of Finance was, however, concerned about the general integrity of South Africa's national identification system and the quality of the national identification data. Various projects to overhaul the system had failed and there was evidence that the integrity of the system was undermined by corruption. The ministry, therefore, believed that residential address information was an important secondary identifier that had to be obtained and verified to achieve appropriate identity verification.

This approach enjoyed the support of law enforcement agencies. In principle, these agencies could obtain address information from the Department of Home Affairs, but the department was slow to respond to such requests and the information they provided was often dated. If accountable institutions were compelled to collect the data, the agencies believed it would provide a faster avenue to access up-to-date information.

Given the concerns about the negative impact on persons with informal residences and informal residential addresses, it was decided to address the issue with an exemption from address requirements and address verification for persons using lower-value products. The exemption was closely reviewed by bank representatives who were viewed as the leading experts on the design of such an exemption.

The exemption, Exemption 17, primarily relieved banks from collecting and verifying residential address information in respect of every business relationship with a natural person who was a citizen of, or resident in, South Africa, in terms of which that person held an account which:

a) enabled the account holder to withdraw or transfer or make electronic payments from that account to an amount not exceeding R15,000.00 over a 24-hour period;
b) enabled the account holder to receive a deposit, or a series of deposits over a period of 24 hours, into that account not exceeding on more than one occasion in a calendar month, an amount of R5,000.00; and at any time, an amount of R20,000.00;

c) enabled the account holder to maintain a balance in that account not exceeding R25,000.00; and
d) did not enable the holder of that account to transfer funds out of that account to any destination outside South Africa, subject to the conditions that such an account did not remain dormant for a period exceeding 180 days and that the same person did not hold more than one such account with the same institution at any time.

This exemption was intended to address the negative FICA identification impact on the vast majority of low-income persons. As soon as the FICA obligations took effect on 1 July 2003, it became clear, however, that the exemption provided little value. The conditions imposed by the exemption either ran counter to the needs of the low-income market or conflicted with the optimal product design of low-cost products.[20] For example, most of the mass-market products at that stage utilised internationally branded debit cards with cross-border functionality. Such products fell outside the ambit of the exemption. The 180-day dormancy cut-off was an unrealistic requirement for seasonal and other workers without a regular income. All of the conditions had to be met before an institution could rely on the exemption and that happened in a very limited number of cases. Many banks lacked the ability to quickly implement systems that would correctly impose the conditions to ensure compliance with the exemption. The exemption furthermore focused on business relationships and did not extend to single transactions.

The earliest study of Exemption 17 by Bester, De Koker and Hawthorne in 2003 identified these challenges but also pointed out that the design failed to mitigate financial crime risks appropriately:[21]

> If the transactions product anticipated by the exemption is used to its fullest extent, a client can deposit and withdraw up to R165 000 per month through the account. (The primary restriction is the amount that can be deposited in the account. The maximum is 29 × R5 000 + R20 000 = R165 000 per month.) This is well in excess of the US$15 000 threshold for occasional transactions suggested by the FATF.

The design failure of the exemption stemmed mainly from a lack of understanding of the unbanked and underbanked communities by both government and bank drafters of the exemption. Most of the experts involved in the drafting process were primarily money laundering and compliance experts rather than development experts who understood the practical challenges faced by vulnerable and excluded communities.

2.5 Residential address verification challenges and solutions

The difficulties regarding the verification of residential addresses created predicaments for all accountable institutions, but financial institutions faced a particular dilemma in this regard. Financial institutions committed in the 2003 Financial

Sector Charter to purposefully and substantially increase access to financial services. They agreed to meet certain targets and deadlines in respect of the provision of certain financial services to segments of the population that lacked adequate access.[22] These commitments were given against the backdrop of the then government's commitment to Black economic empowerment and its policy to increase access to financial services. Strict compliance with FICA impacted the ability of the industry to meet these commitments and comply with government policy in this regard.

As the implications of FICA identity verification requirements became clear, the banking industry took several steps to increase process efficiencies. The industry was already working closely to ensure the effective and efficient implementation of FICA. They agreed, for example, to collaborate on FICA training of staff members and, with BANKSETA support and working with academia, they developed standardised training for more than 140,000 employees in the industry. The leading banks furthermore agreed to collaborate by pooling their customer data in one central database of an industry-controlled utility where one bank would not be able to access the customer data of another bank, but the utility would be able to facilitate customer due diligence measures and the consistency of customer data across all participating institutions. Their collaboration in such a utility was however conditional on FIC support. The FIC's compliance division unfortunately declined to support such collaboration. It preferred each bank to build its own systems and conduct its own processes. Support for the proposed model would have put South Africa in the lead regarding the development of so-called KYC utilities globally.

The negative impact of the strict identity verification requirements was becoming clear in practice as banks were having to turn away clients who could not produce the prescribed documents. The government was, however, slow to respond to the problem. On 18 July 2003, therefore, the Banking Council South Africa, later known as "The Banking Association South Africa" issued practice notes relating to FICA procedures.[23] The notes were published to assist banks to comply with FICA and reduce the arbitrage between banks in this regard.[8] One of the practice notes addressed the so-called "mass market clients".

The practice note defined a mass market client as "an individual account holder with a net income per month (income into the bank account) of less than R5 000". The note allowed a more relaxed identification and verification procedure in relation to savings accounts, transaction accounts, investments and deposits in relation to the mass market. It stipulated that the identity of a person in this sector should be determined by means of an identity document and that the bank should request details regarding the client's physical address and the source of income or of the funds being deposited. With regard to residential address verification for mass market clients, practice note 2.4 required banks to request proof of residential address. However, if the client "responds that he does not have any, and the bank is reasonably satisfied with that answer (the physical address details are consistent with such an answer), the answer should be noted and the account pened/transaction concluded".

This practice note reflected a frustration with the impracticality of Exemption 17 and a concern about the impact of the regulations on access to financial services in South Africa. The practice that was envisaged did not, however, comply with FICA and the regulations. According to FICA, read with the regulations, an account could not be opened until the address particulars were verified as prescribed. The practice note envisaged circumstances where a bank would do its best to comply with the law but would open an account despite not having verified the particulars as set out in the regulations. This extraordinary approach apparently received moral support from the Registrar of Banks. In December 2003, the Registrar was reported as having acknowledged that banks were not fully complying with FICA, saying that the Act was proving impossible to implement.[24]

The matter became politically critical when it transpired that banks were unable to use the old Exemption 17 framework to launch the Mzansi account. This was a new basic low-cost bank account that the major banks developed to increase financial access and which they wished to launch in October 2004. It was, however, not feasible to launch within the framework of the existing requirements. The easiest way to resolve the problem was to redraft the Exemption. This time round the drafting process engaged development and business experts who could assist with the drafting of an improved exemption, and it drew on FinMark Trust-funded research regarding the flaws of the old Exemption 17.[25]

After extensive consultation with representatives of the financial services community and civic representatives, the Minister of Finance therefore repealed the old Exemption 17 and replaced it with a new Exemption 17.[26]

The new Exemption 17 exempted primarily banks from compliance with requirements to obtain and verify, as part of the customer identity verification, the income tax details and residential address particulars of South African citizens and residents. Unlike the old Exemption 17, it also extended to single transactions.

The new exemption extended to all business relationships and single transactions that:

- enabled the client to withdraw or transfer or make payments of an amount not exceeding R5000.00 per day and not exceeding R25,000.00 in a monthly cycle; and
- did not enable the client to effect a transfer of funds to any destination outside South Africa, except for a transfer as a result of a point-of-sale payment or a cash withdrawal in a country in the Rand Common Monetary Area.

The exemption was subject to a number of conditions. If the business relationship entailed the holding of an account:

- the balance maintained in that account could not exceed R25,000.00 at any time; and
- the same person could not simultaneously hold two or more accounts that met the criteria referred to above and were similar in nature to the same institution.

If any of the conditions were breached, no debit from that account could be realised before the standard customer identity verification and record-keeping processes were completed.

The publication of the new Exemption 17 made it possible for banks to launch the Mzansi bank account. Although the amendment was only formally made in November 2004, the banks were allowed to successfully launch the account at the end of October 2004.

The Mzansi project initially appeared very successful. Within the first seven months of the project, more than one million new accounts were opened. According to the Banking Association of South Africa, this rose to more than 3.2 million by June 2006. Many of these were however existing clients who switched accounts to benefit from the cheaper service fees of the Mzansi account. The account failed to deliver on key financial inclusion targets and was later abandoned in favour of more targeted initiatives of individual banks. These initiatives, however, mainly utilised the Exemption 17 framework. The new Exemption 17, therefore, proved effective in supporting access to lower-value products and services.

Exemption 17 proved valuable even though it did not remove all the obstacles that the customer identity verification requirements posed to financial access. The FICA scheme, read with the new Exemption 17, still required a prospective customer to prove their identity by furnishing an official identity document or a similar document if they had an acceptable reason for not being able to furnish an official document.[13] The *FinScope South Africa 2004* study found that 19% of South Africans did not have a formal identity document.[14] In addition, the identity verification requirements placed obligations on financial institutions that were expensive to meet. To the extent that such expenses were reflected in increased costs of services, a financial barrier to access was raised.

The new Exemption 17 had, however, addressed major obstacles regarding address verification. In 2005, the FIC signalled a further softening of the regulatory approach to address verification in guidance note 3.

2.5.1 Guidance note 3

In July 2005, the FIC issued its non-binding guidance note 3 (*guidance for banks on customer identification and verification and related matters*) to provide general guidance to banks on customer identification and verification and related matters. The guidance specifically addressed residential address verification.[27]

According to the guidance note, the most secure way of verifying a residential address was for a staff member and/or agent of the bank to visit the residential address of the person to confirm that the person resided at the particular residential address. In most instances, however, it would be sufficient to review the original document and obtain a copy of a document that offered a reasonable confirmation of the information in question. Since the documentation must be current, a good practice would be to require documentation that was less than three months old.

The guidance note provided a list with examples of documents that may, depending on the circumstances, offer confirmation of a residential address. This list was not exhaustive and other forms of documentation could be used in the verification process. Decisions as to how residential addresses are to be verified should be based on a bank's customer due diligence risk framework. The following documents were listed:

- a utility bill reflecting the name and residential address of the person;
- a bank statement from another bank reflecting the name and residential address of the person if the person previously transacted with a bank registered in terms of the Banks Act and that bank had confirmed the person's particulars;
- a recent lease or rental agreement reflecting the name and residential address of the person;
- municipal rates and taxes invoice reflecting the name and residential address of the person;
- mortgage statement from another institution reflecting the name and residential address of the person;
- telephone or cellular account reflecting the name and residential address of the person;
- valid television licence reflecting the name and residential address of the person;
- a recent long-term or short-term insurance policy document issued by an insurance company and reflecting the name and residential address of the person; or
- recent motor vehicle license documentation reflecting the name and residential address of the person.

If the recent utility bill did not identify the physical street address of the property owner (for instance, if the bill was sent to a postal address), the bill could still be used for the purposes of verification provided that it reflected the customer's name, the erf or stand number and township details. In such a case, the guidance note advised, the customer's physical address, erf or stand number and township details should be recorded, and the township should be cross-referenced to the suburb in which the customer resides. If there was any doubt thereafter about the customer or the physical address of the customer, the erf or stand number and the township details should be verified by reference to the records of the Deeds Office.

If none of the above was available, the guidance note advised banks to explore other means to verify a client's address. This could include considering an affidavit that contains the following particulars from a person co-habiting with the client or an employer of the client:

- name, residential address, identity number of the client and the deponent of the affidavit;
- relationship between the client and the deponent of the affidavit; and
- confirmation of the client's residential address.

The guidance note was helpful but banks remained cautious to implement it in full. Unlike FICA and the Regulations, the guidance was non-binding. Furthermore, the decisions as to which documents would be acceptable were left to banks who had to make judgement calls based on their customer due diligence risk frameworks. Compliance officers tended to be risk-averse and opted to only accept official documents.[28] The biggest problem, however, was that the guidance note was risk-based while FICA and the Regulations did not allow for a risk-based approach. Until the FICA was amended to allow for such an approach, any institution relying on non-binding guidance was at risk of regulatory enforcement action and even prosecution for non-compliance with the FICA.

Ironically, many of the documents that the FIC used as examples of residential address verification documents were not particularly reliable and could be generated through self-declaration of the information.[29] This gave rise to fraud and money laundering risks for banks and allowed space for prosecution if their systems were abused by criminals.

2.5.2 *Bank circular 6/2006*[30]

The Exemption 17 framework was taken a step further when AML/CFT controls for mobile phone bank account origination had to be designed. South African banks have offered mobile phone-based banking services for some time. These services supported the use of accounts that were opened in the traditional manner after contact with a representative of a bank. However, Standard Bank entered into a partnership with MTN, a major mobile phone service provider, to provide a banking service where accounts could be opened and activated via the phone without personal contact with the bank or a representative of the bank. The product was launched without consultation with the FIC and their initial response was one of alarm. After urgent ministerial intervention over the weekend, the Registrar of Banks was requested to regulate the client identity verification requirements of this new type of service.

The Money Laundering and Terrorist Financing Control Regulations allowed business to be conducted without personal contact with the customer as long as the bank took reasonable steps to verify the identity of the customer. The Registrar of Banks issued bank circular 6/2006 to provide greater clarity about the measures that would be regarded as reasonable in relation to mobile phone bank account origination.

Circular 6/2008 was limited to products that fall within the parameters of Exemption 17 and could be obtained via a non-face-to-face process. The Registrar approved non-face-to-face customer registration in this case, provided that the bank offering the product took adequate steps to verify the identity of the customer, including cross-referencing the prospective customer's identity number against an acceptable third-party database.[31] In addition, the following key conditions were set:

a) The bank could not allow customers who obtain the facility in a non-face-to-face manner to transact against their accounts for more than R1000 a day.

b) The bank could not open more than one such account for a customer.
c) The bank had to apply enhanced measures to monitor the account for suspicious activity.

The circular provided a helpful extension of Exemption 17. It prepared the groundwork for a framework for mobile banking in South Africa. Initial efforts to establish a vibrant mobile banking model in South Africa, however, met with limited commercial success, in part due to a complex regulatory environment, institutional constraints, product design flaws and clients who preferred standard financial services.[32]

2.5.3 Refugees

While AML/CFT regulatory support for financial inclusion in South Africa has increased since 2002, this support was not always consistent.

In May 2010, for example, the FIC issued a public compliance communication advising banks that they may not regard the section 22 permit and section 24 certificate issued by the South African government in terms of the Refugees Act 130 of 1998 to asylum-seekers to evidence their asylum applications as identification documents for purposes of the FICA.[33]

This meant that accountable institutions could not use these documents to allow asylum seekers to open new accounts, conclude single transactions or even operate pre-existing accounts. The announcement essentially prevented affected account holders from accessing and withdrawing their funds. In December 2010, after litigation against some banks and the FIC by organisations representing asylum-seekers who were unable to withdraw their savings from pre-existing accounts, the FIC introduced an interim measure.[34] In terms of this measure, banks could rely on such a permit and certificate but first had to verify the document by faxing or emailing a copy of it to the Department of Home Affairs before they could use it for FICA verification purposes. Existing clients could withdraw funds from pre-existing accounts but could not deposit funds until such verification was done.

The FIC furthermore advised that for purposes of FICA, accounts could only be opened for refugees on the strength of the maroon refugee identity document issued in terms of section 29 of the Refugees Act or a United Nations certified travel document. Once a maroon refugee identity document was issued (and probably also after a United Nations travel document was provided), a refugee should be identified and verified as a South African citizen or resident.[35] The communication also introduced the principle that the document used for identification purposes must remain current when the account is open:[36]

> However, accountable institutions need to take note that the refugee identity document is temporary in nature in that it is valid for 2 (two) years. The document is, however, renewable. Accountable institutions should therefore have internal controls in place to periodically monitor such accounts to ensure that

on the expiry of the 2- (two) year period, these accounts are suspended/frozen to prevent any transactions occurring on these accounts. Once the identity document has been renewed the hold can be lifted.

The FIC did not extend this principle to the use of other documents that are temporary in nature, for instance, passports. The principle that the identification document must remain current for the duration of the business relationship has not been part of general compliance requirements or practices in the past. In 2014, the FIC formally stepped away from the currency requirement, allowing identity verification measures to stand as long as the documents were valid when the processes were initially performed.[37]

The 2010 treatment of refugee identity verification came as a surprise and indicated that the FIC had not yet fully considered the impact of FICA identity verification requirements on vulnerable users and the unbanked, despite grappling with these issues since 2003. The measures envisaged by the FIC were surprisingly bureaucratic and created unnecessary and very harmful barriers for refugees.

2.6 Internationalisation of the Exemption 17 model

South African challenges with the FATF-related customer identity verification measures led to research engagements that ultimately informed a more supportive FATF approach to financial inclusion.

Multidisciplinary research on this topic was initially sponsored by FinMark Trust. FinMark Trust was set up by the then UK Department for International Development (DFID) and the Banking Council of South Africa to advance financial inclusion. The first study in 2003 focused on legislative and regulatory obstacles to mass banking, essentially to inform discussions of a regulatory framework that would support the later Mzansi account.[38] In its analysis of the challenges in South Africa, this report considered the impact of the FATF standards and South African AML/CFT laws, and unpacked the Basel account opening guidance of 2003 as well as UK measures to facilitate access to financial services. This report was recently described as the first study to uncover customer due diligence barriers to opening a bank account.[39] It is probably more correct to describe it as the first of its nature that addressed the impact of the FATF standards and the Basel guidance on financial inclusion in developing economies.

The report resonated with DFID, which commissioned a further FinMark Trust paper to be included in the papers for the G7's 2004 summit.[40] These reports identified inclusion challenges posed by AML/CFT measures but also steps that FATF could take to explicitly extend its lower-risk CDD measures to low-value products and services that advance financial inclusion.

However, the international policy environment was not supportive of views that lower-value transactions could pose a lower risk. In the immediate post-9/11 years, government agencies in South Africa and within the FATF consistently emphasised that disastrous terrorist attacks can be low budget and that smurfing, splitting or structuring of large transactions into small transactions can evade and undermine controls based on transaction values.[41]

The 2003 and 2004 studies enjoyed DFID support but DFID advised that a financial inclusion study reaching beyond South Africa will be required to engage the international policy framework and gain FATF traction. Funding for such a study was challenging to obtain. In the post-2001 period, there was a reluctance to be associated with any study that appeared to be critical of FATF and especially of its CFT standards. In addition, a prevailing view was that the FATF standards had no negative impact on inclusion. While the search for funding for such a study continued, ongoing policy research was conducted on South African challenges and solutions to identity verification responses,[42] calling, for example, for more research about the profile and needs of the financially excluded to inform regulatory decisions.

After two years of funding discussions and with the post-2001 tensions relaxing, the Financial Sector Reform and Strengthening Initiative (FIRST), managed by the World Bank, agreed in October 2005 to fund a five-country study (South Africa, Indonesia, Kenya, Mexico and Pakistan) by Genesis Analytics to investigate the impact of FATF standards on financial inclusion. When the initial findings of the study were disseminated globally in 2006 and 2007, and finally published in 2008, evidence was available that FATF standards indeed impacted on financial inclusion and related policy and regulatory decisions.[43] The report argued that:[44]

> **The pursuit of financial inclusion and the pursuit of an effective AML/CFT regime are complementary and not conflicting financial sector policy objectives**. The objective with financial inclusion is that individual clients, particularly low-income clients currently excluded from using formal financial services, must be able to access and on a sustainable basis use financial services that are appropriate to their needs and provided by registered financial service providers. Without a sufficient measure of financial inclusion, a country's AML/CFT system will thus safeguard the integrity of only a part of its financial system – the formally registered part – leaving the informal and unregistered components vulnerable to abuse. Measures that ensure that more clients use formal financial services therefore increase the reach and effectiveness of the AML/CFT controls.
>
> **The imposition of AML/CFT controls can and did have an impact on access to and usage of financial services in the countries concerned**. The most vulnerable clients are those who lack the prescribed identification documents, undocumented migrants and clients of institutions (such as money services businesses) whose links with formal financial institutions are severed for AML/CFT reasons. AML/CFT controls also tend to increase transaction costs which can cause financial institutions to withdraw from low-value

transactions and client markets using these. Impact differed from country to country depending on the design of the national AML/CFT framework.

CGAP, the leading financial inclusion think tank housed at the World Bank, played a major role to ensure that the "complementarity" message was conveyed to key regulators and standard-setters, including the FATF.[45]

On 21 August 2009, the Dutch president of FATF embraced the findings and language of the report when he held in Lesotho an address to the ESAAMLG Ministers:[46]

> I do believe that the pursuit of financial inclusion and the pursuit of an effective AML/CFT regime are complementary; they are by no means conflicting financial sector policy objectives. Without a sufficient degree of financial inclusion, a country's AML/CFT system will safeguard the integrity of only a part of its financial system – the formally registered part – leaving the informal and unregistered components vulnerable to abuse. Measures that ensure that more clients use formal financial services therefore enlarges the legitimate financial sector. A robust financial sector, including effective AML/CFT controls, are important ingredients for aspiring members of the global financial community.

Michael Pisa credited this speech as "the first public indication of a shift in thinking within the FATF" and linked the language it used to the Genesis Analytics report.[47] It also signalled dedicated action by the Dutch presidency of the FATF to address the financial inclusion concerns that were highlighted.

The Genesis Analytics study led to engagements with Mexico, Pakistan and later Nigeria, who were considering adopting the Exemption 17 model but expanding it to more levels. These models, known as tiered-based CDD models,[48] essentially allow for minimal identity verification where very basic financial services are accessed and increased functionality of products where increased verification requirements can be met. These Exemption 17-inspired models have proven to be very helpful to advance inclusion in a range of other countries, although it was never further pursued by South African authorities.

The Dutch presidency of FATF's actions led to a decision by the FATF to issue guidance on how best to advance financial inclusion within its standards framework. This 2011 guidance, drafted by a working group that included academic representation, informed the drafting of the 2012 revised standards of the FATF. The 2012 standards provided an important breakthrough as they specifically linked simplified customer due diligence measures, including simplified customer identity verification, to financial inclusion objectives. This set of standards also introduced a mandatory risk-based approach to AML/CFT, requiring scarce compliance and supervisory and enforcement resources to be focused on higher risks. While the FATF's risk-based approach did not solve all of the challenges posed by its customer due diligence measures, it did provide an improved framework that allowed countries to address the challenges more effectively.[49]

2.7 The repeal of Exemption 17

South Africa's FICA framework primarily responded to FATF's 1990 standards, as revised in 1996. From the start, the statutory framework was out of step with the more risk-sensitive approach embodied in the 2003 version of the standards. While FICA itself did not refer to a risk-sensitive approach to AML compliance, the FIC attempted to support risk-based compliance measures by means of non-binding guidance notes, and later, non-binding public compliance communications.

After the 2012 changes to the FATF standards and especially the introduction of the mandatory risk-based approach, the gap between the design of the FICA framework and the standards of the FATF broadened even further. The gap was eventually narrowed by the adoption of the Financial Intelligence Centre Amendment Act 1 of 2017, which introduced a mandatory risk-based approach to AML/CFT. This set the context for the repeal of the rule-based compliance regulations and exemptions., allowing accountable institutions to determine how best to mitigate the higher and lower risks that they identified in their own risk assessment processes.

As a consequence of the adoption of a comprehensive risk-based approach to FICA compliance, the customer-specific identification and verification requirements of the Money Laundering and Terrorist Financing Control Regulations were repealed and all of the exemptions that were in force on 2 October 2017 were withdrawn. Some provisions of the Amendment Act entered into effect on 13 June 2017 and others on 2 October 2017 while a further set came into effect on 1 April 2019.[50]

The risk-based approach to compliance was supported by guidance notes issued by the FIC. Financial inclusion is also referenced in the FIC's 2017 guidance note 7,[51] where it is indicated that the risk-based approach to AML/CFT affords accountable institutions the flexibility to use a range of mechanisms to establish and verify the identities of their clients, creating opportunities for accountable institutions to explore more innovative ways of offering financial services to a broader range of clients and bringing previously excluded sectors of society into the formal economy. Where the risk-based approach is applied correctly, it will improve the efficacy of measures to combat ML/TF while promoting financial inclusion without undermining AML/CFT objectives.

The indications are that most of the large banks adopted internal risk-based measures that allowed for simplified CDD to advance financial inclusion. These measures, in turn, have been informed by South African experiences with Exemption 17 since 2003.

2.8 Reflection

Although FATF is often accused of setting identity verification standards that were unrealistic, this chapter has shown that such critique is not founded. FATF set the principle of customer identification and verification but did not prescribe how that should happen. That decision was left to national regulators.

Many of the national regulators were concerned about NCCT-listing for non-compliance by FATF, especially in the immediate aftermath of 9/11. They drew on examples of developed countries and large, global banks when designing their own regulatory responses. This often resulted in overdesigned regulatory requirements. International regulatory consultants who supported regulators from lower-capacity jurisdictions to draft and implement their FATF-compliant laws also contributed to this trend. They tended to be from G7 countries and drew on experiences in their own jurisdictions that often had very different identification mechanisms compared with the jurisdiction they were advising. These consultants were often law enforcement experts rather than regulatory experts on financial inclusion.

In South Africa, further factors were at play. South Africa had a well-developed national identity system. The integrity of the data was, however, questioned by the Ministry of Finance. They insisted on including residential address verification requirements to bolster the effectiveness of the FICA identity verification processes. They enjoyed the support of law enforcement agencies who believed it would be easier for them to access residential address information from banks than from the Department of Home Affairs. They realised the address verification requirements would impact negatively on vulnerable South Africans but believed that an appropriate exemption would relieve their plight.

Looking back at the decisions in 2002, the major views regarding the integrity of the national identity database and frustrations with accessing information held by the Department of Home Affairs were honestly held but not informed by research or a cost-benefit analysis. The design of the first version of Exemption 17 failed for the same reason. It reflected the views of bankers on the needs of the unbanked and mirrored law enforcement concerns of the key officials involved in the drafting process.

When it became clear that the old Exemption 17 was not going to address the unintended consequences of the identity verification rules that were adopted, the regulators failed to respond timeously. This forced the banking industry into a measure of civil disobedience to enable them to continue to advance the government's policy objectives on financial inclusion. Rigorous debate at the Money Laundering Advisory Council was suppressed when the Ministry opted not to call regular meetings. The Council was further weakened by the Ministry's decision not to fill the position of chair of the Council.

The major financial inclusion improvements in the regulatory framework came about as a result of multidisciplinary research on an appropriate financial inclusion regulatory framework. The emphasis on, and interest in, financial inclusion policies at that time, combined with the discussions about the Mzansi account that the banking industry wanted to launch, provided a policy environment that enabled the uptake of the research. This resulted in the improved 2004 version of Exemption 17. As a result of the better understanding of the needs of the unbanked and how products should be allowed to be designed to meet these needs, the 2004 version of Exemption 17 was far more effective in its support of financial inclusion.

Multidisciplinary research, this time across a range of jurisdictions, also helped to convince the FATF to be more sensitive about unintended consequences that the implementation of its standards may hold for financial inclusion. From its initial recognition of the challenges in this regard in 2009, and the drafting of its initial 2011 financial inclusion guidance, the FATF has been prepared to consider financial inclusion impact in its work, in those cases where it identified potential relevance. However, this was not necessarily consistent, as reflected when it published its 2020 proposals for changes to its proliferation financing standards.[52]

Progress in this space in South Africa has, however, not been linear. Despite developing an understanding of the key issues, the FIC's 2010 guidance on the management of refugee documents was unduly harsh and impacted on their financial inclusion. The general regulatory trend has, nevertheless, been positive.

What is clear from this case study of South Africa's implementation of the FATF's customer identity verification standards is the positive role that multidisciplinary research can play to inform regulatory design and compliance practices. Much in this space is still driven by broader political considerations and personal views of experts and officials involved in the relevant processes. Even at an international level, the FATF has not adopted regulatory impact and cost-benefit analysis to inform the design of changes to its standards.[53] There is much to be gained by all involved in these processes – and by the community at large – if appropriate multidisciplinary research is undertaken and incorporated into these important decision-making processes.

Much multidisciplinary research remains to be done by researchers, collaborating closely with industry and regulatory bodies, to inform regulatory solutions that will advance policy objectives effectively and efficiently, with minimal unintended consequences.

Notes

1 For the history of the FATF, see L de Koker and M Turkington, 'Anti-Money Laundering Measures and the Effectiveness Question' in BAK Rider (ed), *Research Handbook on International Financial Crime* (Edward Elgar Publishing, 2015) 520.

2 See, for example, RT Kurdrle, 'Did Blacklisting Hurt the Tax Havens?' (2008) 12.1 *Journal of Money Laundering Control* 33; JC Morse, *The Bankers' Blacklist: Unofficial Market Enforcement and the Global Fight Against Illicit Financing* (Cornell University Press, 2022); MT Nance, 'Naming and Shaming in Financial Regulation: Explaining Variation in the Financial Action Task Force on Money Laundering' in HR Friman (ed), *The Politics of Leverage in International Relations*' (Palgrave Macmillan, 2015) 123; M Ricardi, '*Money Laundering Blacklists* (Routledge, 2022).

3 The book (L de Koker, *KPMG Money Laundering Control Service,* Butterworth Lexis) first appeared in 1999. Since 2011 it was published as L de Koker, *South African Money Laundering and Terrorist Financing Law*, Butterworths LexisNexis). Since 2017 the book appeared as L de Koker, M Basson, P Smit and J Symington De Koker L, Basson M, Smit P, J Symington, *Money Laundering and Terror Financing – Law and Compliance in South Africa* (LexisNexis).

4 Financial Action Task Force, *The Forty Recommendations of the Financial Action Task Force* (FATF, 1990) https://www.fatf-gafi.org/media/fatf/documents/recommendations/pdfs/FATF%20Recommendations%201990.pdf. Accessed on 3 October 2022.

5 See, for example, PL Chatain, et al., *Protecting Mobile Money Against Financial Crimes: Global Policy Challenges and Solutions* (The World Bank, 2011) 77.

6 Basel Committee on Banking Supervision *Customer Due Diligence for Banks* (Bank for International Settlements, 2001).

7 Basel Committee on Banking Supervision, BCBS *General Guide to Account Opening and Customer Identification* (Bank for International Settlements, 2003) par 10.

8 Basel Committee on Banking Supervision, BCBS *General Guide to Account Opening and Customer Identification (*Bank for International Settlements, 2003) par 11. Par 12 stated that these examples are not the only possibilities. In particular jurisdictions, there may be other documents of an equivalent nature that may be produced as satisfactory evidence of customers' identity.

9 Basel Committee on Banking Supervision, BCBS *General Guide to Account Opening and Customer Identification (*Bank for International Settlements, 2003) par 14.

10 Basel Committee on Banking Supervision, BCBS *General Guide to Account Opening and Customer Identification* (Bank for International Settlements, 2003) par 16.

11 Money laundering Control Regulations, GN.1595 of 20 December 2002.

12 See L de Koker, M Basson, P Smit and J Symington De Koker L, Basson M, Smit P, J Symington, *Money Laundering and Terror Financing – Law and Compliance in South Africa* (LexisNexis, 2021) chapter 2.

13 See, for example, L de Koker and JL Pretorius, 'Confiscation Orders in terms of the Proceeds of Crime Act: Some Constitutional Perspectives (Part 1)' (1998) 1 *South African Journal of Law* 39; (Part 2) (1998) 2 *South African Journal of Law* 277; (Part 3) (1998) 3 *South African Journal of Law* 467.

14 South African Law Commission, *Money laundering and Related matters* Project 104 (SALC, 1996). See P Smit, 'Proposed Measures to Control Money Laundering" in L de Koker & JJ Henning (eds), *Money Laundering Control in South Africa* 30 Tran CBL (UFS, 1998).

15 See, in general, L de Koker, 'Money Laundering Control in South Africa: A South African Response to an American Comment' (2001) 1.3 *Financial Crime Review* 9.

16 Financial Action Task Force, *Report on Non-Cooperative Countries or Territories* (FATF, 2002) https://www.fatf-gafi.org/media/fatf/documents/reports/Initial%20Report%20on%20NCCTs%2002_2000.pdf. Accessed on 10 August 2022.

17 The list also included the income tax number to be verified against a document issued by SARS. Complexity regarding the ability of SARS and taxpayers to provide such documents led to a general exemption (Exemption 6(2)) from this duty.

18 H Bester, L de Koker and R Hawthorne, *Access to Financial Services in South Africa: A Brief Case Study of the Effect of the Implementation of the Financial Action Task Force Recommendations* (Genesis Analytics for FinMark Trust, 2004) par 6.1; L de Koker, 'Money Laundering Control and Suppression of Financing of Terrorism: Some Thoughts on the Impact of Customer Due Diligence Measures on Financial Exclusion' (2006) *Journal of Financial Crime* 26.

19 For an overview of the arguments that I raised as a member of the Money Laundering Advisory Council, see L de Koker, 'Client Identification and Money Laundering Control: Perspectives on the Financial Intelligence Centre Act 38 of 2001' (2004) 4 *Journal of South African Law* 715.

20 H Bester, L de Koker and R Hawthorne, *Legislative and Regulatory Obstacles to Mass Banking* (Genesis Analytics for FinMark Trust, 2003) pars 6.6 and 9.1. See also South African Banking Council, *Practice Notes: Implementation of the FIC Act* (SABC, 2003): "The savings product exemption (No.17) is proving unworkable as the various restrictions are difficult to implement, monitor and manage, and because the customer often requires additional products (eg an investment)".

21 H Bester, L de Koker and R Hawthorne, *Legislative and Regulatory Obstacles to Mass Banking* (Genesis Analytics for FinMark Trust, 2003) par 9.1

22 Cl 8 of the Financial Sector Charter http://www.treasury.gov.za/comm_media/press/2003/2003101701.pdf. Accessed on 3 October 2022.
23 South African Banking Council *Practice Notes: Implementation of the FIC Act* (SABC, 2003).
24 R Rose "Money laundering laws impossible" *Business Day* 12 December 2003 1. As banks came under increasing pressure to meet the 30 June 2004 deadline for re-identification of current clients, many banks appeared to be either following the Banking Council's practice notes or a version of the old Exemption 17 that was re-interpreted in view of the Council's practice notes. Comments by bank officials and press reports suggested that some banks were ignoring the conditions of the old Exemption 17 and applied it to all current clients who maintained credit balances of less than R25,000 and whose monthly deposits were less than R5000. See, for example, R Stovin-Bradford "Banks in race to verify client details" *Sunday Times Business Times* 2 May 2004 4.
25 H Bester, L de Koker and R Hawthorne, *Legislative and Regulatory Obstacles to Mass Banking* (Genesis Analytics for FinMark Trust, 2003); H Bester, L de Koker and R Hawthorne, *Access to Financial Services in South Africa: A Brief Case Study of the Effect of the Implementation of the Financial Action Task Force Recommendations* (Genesis Analytics for FinMark Trust, 2004).
26 'Exemption in terms of the Financial Intelligence Centre Act, 2001' R 1353 published in *Government Gazette* 27011 of 19 November 2004.
27 Financial Intelligence Centre, *Guidance Note 3: Guidance for banks on customer identification and verification and related matters* (FIC, 2015) https://www.gov.za/sites/default/files/gcis_document/201409/278030.pdf. Accessed on 2 October 2022 par 11.
28 L de Koker and J Symington, 'Conservative Corporate Compliance: Reflections on a Study of Compliance Responses by South African Banks' (2014) 30 *Law Context: A Socio-Legal Journal* 228.
29 See L de Koker, 'Client Identification and Money Laundering Control: Perspectives on the Financial Intelligence Centre Act 38 of 2001' (2004) 4 *Journal of South African Law* 715 731.
30 Registrar of Banks, "Banks Act Circular 6/2006: Cell-phone Banking' (South African Reserve Bank, 2006). This circular was withdrawn in 2008 when its text was issued as Guidance Note 6/2008 by the Registrar.
31 The database had to include information on the names and identity numbers of persons sourced from the Department of Home Affairs. According to the circular, the cross-referencing during the account-opening stage had enabled the bank to establish whether the identity number that was disclosed was valid and was linked to the name of the prospective client. The person to whom that number was linked should not have been deceased or have emigrated from South Africa. The name and the identity number must furthermore not have appeared on a database relating to fraud convictions. See Registrar of Banks, "Banks Act Circular 6/2006: Cell-phone Banking" (South African Reserve Bank, 2006) par 3.
32 FinMark Trust, *Research Report on Mobile Money in South Africa* (FinMark Trust, 2017).
33 Financial Intelligence Centre, *PCC03: Identification and Verification Matters Relating to Account Opening Procedures for Asylum Seekers and Refugees in Terms of the Financial Intelligence Centre Act 38 of 2001* (FIC, 2010). The following documentary scheme applied at that time under the Refugee Act: Upon application for refugee status, a permit was issued under section 22 of the Refugees Act 130 of 1998 (the asylum-seeker permit). This was valid for a limited time, normally one to three months at a time and is renewable. A refugee certificate (section 24 certificate) was issued when the asylum application was approved. This certificate was valid for two years and was also renewable. The holder of such a certificate could apply for a refugee identity document (maroon identity document), which was issued under section 29 of the Refugees Act and for a United Nations-issued travel docu-

ment. Five years after approval of the asylum application, the refugee may apply for permanent residency (section 27 of the Refugee Act) and, upon it being granted, for a green bar-coded identity document. See L de Koker, *Will RICA's Customer Identification Data Meet Anti-Money Laundering Requirements and Facilitate the Development of Transformational Mobile Banking in South Africa? An Exploratory Note* (Cenfri for FinMark Trust, 2010) https://cenfri.org/wp-content/uploads/2010/07/RICA-impact-on-financial-inclusion_FinMark-Trust_October-2010.pdf. Accessed on 3 October 2022.

34 Financial Intelligence Centre, *PCC03A: Supplementary Information Applicable to PCC03* (FIC, 2010).

35 Financial Intelligence Centre, *PCC03: Identification and Verification Matters Relating to Account Opening Procedures for Asylum Seekers and Refugees in terms of the Financial Intelligence Centre Act 38 of 2001* (FIC, 2010) 6.

36 Financial Intelligence Centre, *PCC03: Identification and Verification Matters Relating to Account Opening Procedures for Asylum Seekers and Refugees in terms of the Financial Intelligence Centre Act 38 of 2001* (FIC, 2010) 6.

37 Financial Intelligence Centre, *PCC27 Status of Expired Documents Relating to Client Identification and Verification Requirements for Asylum-seekers and Refugees in terms of the Financial Intelligence Centre Act 38 of 2001* (FIC, 2014).

38 H Bester, L de Koker and R Hawthorne, *Legislative and Regulatory Obstacles to Mass Banking* (Genesis Analytics for FinMark Trust, 2003) https://dro.deakin.edu.au/eserv/DU:30016861/dekoker-legislativeandregulatory-2003.pdf. Accessed on 3 October 2022.

39 B Cooper, M Ferreira and L Janse van Vuuren, *Digital Identity and Financial Inclusion: How Digitising Customer Due Diligence Can Strengthen Providers Curing COVID-19 and Beyond* (Cenfri, 2020) https://nextbillion.net/digital-identity-and-financial- inclusion/. Accessed on 3 October 2022: "One of the major barriers, originally uncovered by FinMark Trust in their research on obstacles to mass banking in 2003, was the customer due diligence (CDD) required to open a bank account – often associated with know-your-customer (KYC) requirements".

40 H Bester, L de Koker and R Hawthorne, *Access to Financial Services in South Africa: A Brief Case Study of the Effect of the Implementation of the Financial Action Task Force Recommendations* (Genesis Analytics for FinMark Trust, 2004), http://dro.deakin.edu.au/eserv/DU:30016860/dekoker-accesstofinancial-2004.pdf. Accessed on 3 October 2022.

41 For counter arguments, see L de Koker, "Aligning Anti-Money Laundering, Combating of Financing of Terror and Financial Inclusion: Questions to Consider when FATF Standards are Clarified", (2011) 18 *Journal of Financial Crime* 361.

42 See, for example, L de Koker, 'Client Identification and Money Laundering Control: Perspectives on the Financial Intelligence Centre Act 38 of 2001' (2004) 4 *Journal of South African Law* 715; L de Koker, 'Money Laundering Control and Suppression of Financing of Terrorism: Some Thoughts on the Impact of Customer Due Diligence Measures on Financial Exclusion' (2006) 13 *Journal of Financial Crime*, 13 (2006), 26 44.

43 H Bester et al., *Implementing FATF Standards in Developing Countries and Financial Inclusion: Findings and Guidelines* (FIRST Initiative, 2008) https://www.findevgateway.org/paper/2008/02/implementing-fatf-standards-developing-countries-and-financial-inclusion-findings-and. Accessed on 3 October 2022.

44 H Bester et al., *Implementing FATF Standards in Developing Countries and Financial Inclusion: Findings and Guidelines* (FIRST Initiative, 2008) https://www.findevgateway.org/paper/2008/02/implementing-fatf-standards-developing-countries-and-financial-inclusion-findings-and. Accessed on 3 October 2022 vi.

45 This was for example a core theme at CGAP's *Windsor Global Leadership Seminar on Regulating. Branchless Banking*. A strategically focused summary of the report (J Isern and L de Koker, 'AML/CFT: Strengthening Financial Inclusion

and Integrity' Focus Note 56 (CGAP, 2009, https://www.cgap.org/sites/default/files/CGAP-Focus-Note-AML-CFT-Strengthening-Financial-Inclusion-and-Integrity-Aug-2009.pdf) appeared in Arabic, English, French, Japanese, Russian and Spanish. Outreach was also undertaken by the authors and by members of the project steering committee. The committee consisted of representatives from the FIRST Management Unit (Subhrendu Chatterjee, Mark St Giles, Jayyad Malik and Rudi van der Bijl), World Bank (Latifah Merican Cheong and Raul Hernandez-Coss), International Monetary Fund (Chee Lee and Maud Bökkerink), the UK's Department for International Development (DFID) (Doug Pearce, Valsah Shah and Martin Alsop), the Consultative Group to Assist the Poor (CGAP) (Jennifer Isern and Tim Lyman), the South African National Treasury (Jonathan Dixon, Nkosana Mashiya and Raadhika Sookoo), FinMark Trust (Jeremy Leach) and Professor Nikos Passas.

46 L de Koker, 'Aligning Anti-Money Laundering, Combating of Financing of Terror and Financial Inclusion: Questions to Consider when FATF Standards are Clarified' (2011) 18 *Journal of Financial Crime* 361. See also M Pisa, 'Does the Financial Action Task Force (FATF) Help or Hinder Financial Inclusion? A Study of FATF Mutual Evaluation Reports' Centre for Global Development Policy Paper 143 (CGDev, 2019), https://www.cgdev.org/publication/does-financial-action-task-force-fatf-help-or-hinder-financial-inclusion-study-fatf. Accessed on 3 October 2022.

47 M Pisa, 'Does the Financial Action Task Force (FATF) Help or Hinder Financial Inclusion? A Study of FATF Mutual Evaluation Reports' Centre for Global Development Policy Paper 143 (CGDev, 2019), https://www.cgdev.org/publication/does-financial-action-task-force-fatf-help-or-hinder-financial-inclusion-study-fatf. Accessed on 3 October 2022n 25: "The first use of the "complementarity" frame appears to be: Bester, H., D. Chamberlain, L. de Koker, C. Hougaard, R. Short, A. Smith, and R. Walker. Implementing FATF Standards in Developing Countries and Financial Inclusion: Findings and Guidelines. The FIRST Initiative. Washington, D.C., May 2008".

48 Earlier called "progressive CDD". See, for example, PL Chatain et al., *Protecting Mobile Money Against Financial Crimes: Global Policy Challenges and Solutions* (The World Bank, 2011) 77.

49 For remaining questions and challenges, see, for example, L de Koker, The 2012 Revised FATF Recommendations: Assessing and Mitigating Mobile Money Integrity Risks within the New Standards Framework' (213) 8.3 *Washington Journal of Law, Technology & Arts* 165; L de Koker, 'The FATF's customer identification framework: fit for purpose?' (2014) 17.3 *Journal of Money Laundering Control* 281.

50 Commencement of the Financial Intelligence Centre Amendment Act No. 1 of 2017 Government Notice 563 published in *Government Gazette* 40916 of 13 June 2017. In terms of Commencement of Sections of the Financial Intelligence Centre Amendment Act No. 1 of 2017 Government Notice 519 published in *Government Gazette* 42360 of 29 March 2019 the following sections of the Amendment Act came into effect on 1 April 2019: ss 2(*a*) and (*c*), 3(*c*), 17, 20, 21(*b*), 24, 39 and 42.

51 Financial Intelligence Centre, *Guidance Note 7: Guidance on the Implementation of Various Aspects of the Financial Intelligence Centre Act, 2001 (Act 38 of 2001)* (FIC, 2017).

52 For concerns, see L de Koker, 'Financial Action Task Force Standards and Financial Inclusion: What Should Be Done – and What Should Not Be Done – to Improve the Alignment Between Integrity and Inclusion Policy Objectives? (SSRN, 2020) https://papers.ssrn.com/sol3/papers.cfm?abstract_id=3679779. Accessed on 3 October 2022.

53 See L de Koker, 'Editorial: Regulatory Impact Assessment: Towards a Better Approach for the FATF' (2021) 25.2 *Journal of Money Laundering Control* 265.

Bibiliography

Basel Committee on Banking Supervision *Customer Due Diligence for Banks* (Bank for International Settlements, 2001).

Basel Committee on Banking Supervision, BCBS *General Guide to Account Opening and Customer Identification* (Bank for International Settlements, 2003).

H Bester, L de Koker & R Hawthorne *Legislative and Regulatory Obstacles to Mass Banking* (Genesis Analytics for FinMark Trust, 2003).

H Bester, L de Koker & R Hawthorne *Access to Financial Services in South Africa: A Brief Case Study of the Effect of the Implementation of the Financial Action Task Force Recommendations* (Genesis Analytics for FinMark Trust, 2004).

H Bester et al. *Implementing FATF Standards in Developing Countries and Financial Inclusion: Findings and Guidelines* (FIRST Initiative, 2008) https://www.findevgateway.org/paper/2008/02/implementing-fatf-standards-developing-countries-and-financial-inclusion-findings-and, accessed on 3 October 2022.

P L Chatain et al. *Protecting Mobile Money Against Financial Crimes: Global Policy Challenges and Solutions* (The World Bank, 2011).

B Cooper, M Ferreira & L Janse van Vuuren *Digital Identity and Financial Inclusion: How Digitising Customer Due Diligence Can Strengthen Providers Curing COVID-19 and Beyond* (Cenfri, 2020) https://nextbillion.net/digital-identity-and-financial- inclusion/, accessed on 3 October 2022.

L de Koker 'Money laundering control in South Africa: A South African response to an American comment' (2001) 1.3 *Financial Crime Review* 1–50.

L de Koker 'Client identification and money laundering control: Perspectives on the financial intelligence centre act 38 of 2001' (2004) 4 *Journal of South African Law* 715–746

L de Koker 'Money laundering control and suppression of financing of terrorism: Some thoughts on the impact of customer due diligence measures on financial exclusion' (2006) *Journal of Financial Crime* 26–50.

L de Koker *Will RICA's Customer Identification Data Meet Anti-Money Laundering Requirements and Facilitate the Development of Transformational Mobile Banking in South Africa? An Exploratory Note* (Cenfri for FinMark Trust, 2010) https://cenfri.org/wp-content/uploads/2010/07/RICA-impact-on-financial-inclusion_FinMark-Trust_October-2010.pdf, accessed on 3 October 2022.

L de Koker 'Aligning anti-money laundering, combating of financing of terror and financial inclusion: Questions to consider when FATF standards are clarified' (2011) 18 *Journal of Financial Crime* 361–386

L de Koker 'The 2012 revised FATF recommendations: Assessing and mitigating mobile money integrity risks within the new standards framework' (2013) 8.3 *Washington Journal of Law, Technology & Arts* 165–196

L de Koker 'The FATF's customer identification framework: Fit for purpose?' (2014) 17.3 *Journal of Money Laundering Control* 281–295

L de Koker *Financial Action Task Force Standards and Financial Inclusion: What Should Be Done – And What Should Not Be Done – To Improve the Alignment between Integrity and Inclusion Policy Objectives?* (SSRN, 2020) https://papers.ssrn.com/sol3/papers.cfm?abstract_id=3679779, accessed on 3 October 2022.

L de Koker 'Editorial: Regulatory impact assessment: Towards a better approach for the FATF' (2021) 25.2 *Journal of Money Laundering Control* 265–267.

L de Koker, M Basson, P Smit & J Symington *Money Laundering and Terror Financing – Law and Compliance in South Africa* (LexisNexis, 2021).

L de Koker & J L Pretorius 'Confiscation orders in terms of the proceeds of crime act: Some constitutional perspectives (Part 1)' (1998) 1 *South African Journal of Law* 39; (Part 2) (1998) 2 *South African Journal of Law* 277; (Part 3) (1998) 3 *South African Journal of Law* 467.

L de Koker & J Symington 'Conservative corporate compliance: Reflections on a study of compliance responses by South African banks' (2014) 30 *Law Context: A Socio-Legal Journal* 228–256.

L de Koker & M Turkington 'Anti-money laundering measures and the effectiveness question' in B A K Rider (ed) *Research Handbook on International Financial Crime* (Edward Elgar Publishing, 2015) 520.

Financial Action Task Force *The Forty Recommendations of the Financial Action Task Force* (FATF, 1990) https://www.fatf-gafi.org/media/fatf/documents/recommendations/pdfs/FATF%20Recommendations%201990.pdf, accessed on 3 October 2022.

Financial Action Task Force *Report on Non-Cooperative Countries or Territories* (FATF, 2002) https://www.fatf-gafi.org/media/fatf/documents/reports/Initial%20Report%20on%20NCCTs%2002_2000.pdf, accessed on 10 August 2022.

Financial Intelligence Centre *PCC03: Identification and Verification Matters Relating to Account Opening Procedures for Asylum Seekers and Refugees in Terms of the Financial Intelligence Centre Act 38 of 2001* (FIC, 2010).

Financial Intelligence Centre *PCC03A: Supplementary Information Applicable to PCC03* (FIC, 2010).

Financial Intelligence Centre *PCC27 Status of Expired Documents Relating to Client Identification and Verification Requirements for Asylum-seekers and Refugees in Terms of the Financial Intelligence Centre Act 38 of 2001* (FIC, 2014).

Financial Intelligence Centre *Guidance Note 3: Guidance for Banks on Customer Identification and Verification and Related Matters* (FIC, 2015) https://www.gov.za/sites/default/files/gcis_document/201409/278030.pdf, accessed on 2 October 2022.

FinMark Trust *Research Report on Mobile Money in South Africa* (FinMark Trust, 2017).

J Isern & L de Koker 'AML/CFT: Strengthening financial inclusion and integrity' Focus Note 56 (CGAP, 2009), https://www.cgap.org/sites/default/files/CGAP-Focus-Note-AML-CFT-Strengthening-Financial-Inclusion-and-Integrity-Aug-2009.pdf.

R T Kurdrle 'Did blacklisting hurt the tax havens?' (2008) 12.1 *Journal of Money Laundering Control* 33.

J C Morse *The Bankers' Blacklist: Unofficial Market Enforcement and the Global Fight Against Illicit Financing* (Cornell University Press, 2022).

M T Nance 'Naming and shaming in financial regulation: Explaining variation in the financial action task force on money laundering' in H R Friman (ed) *The Politics of Leverage in International Relations* (Palgrave Macmillan, 2015) 123.

M Pisa 'Does the Financial Action Task Force (FATF) help or hinder financial inclusion? A study of FATF mutual evaluation reports' Centre for Global Development Policy Paper 143 (CGDev, 2019) https://www.cgdev.org/publication/does-financial-action-task-force-fatf-help-or-hinder-financial-inclusion-study-fatf, accessed on 3 October 2022.

M Ricardi *Money Laundering Blacklists* (Routledge, 2022).

Registrar of Banks 'Banks Act Circular 6/2006: Cell-phone Banking' (South African Reserve Bank, 2006).

R Rose 'Money laundering laws impossible' *Business Day* 12 December 2003 1.

P Smit 'Proposed measures to control money laundering' in L de Koker & J J Henning (eds) *Money Laundering Control in South Africa* 30 Tran CBL (UFS, 1998).

South African Banking Council *Practice Notes: Implementation of the FIC Act* (SABC, 2003).

South African Law Commission *Money Laundering and Related Matters* Project 104 (SALC, 1996).

R Stovin-Bradford 'Banks in race to verify client details' *Sunday Times Business Times* 2 May 2004 4.

3 Financial inclusion or exclusion

A British perspective on poor underwriting questions in insurance law

Neels Kilian

3.1 Introduction

In the financial industry, a person's inclusion or exclusion may be viewed from different perspectives. One such perspective is the law of insurance, where an insurer or insurance company may refuse to accept the insured as a policyholder and/or refuse to settle any claims the policyholder submits.[1] The inclusion or exclusion of a person as a policyholder is therefore dependent on the rules of insurance law.[2] In this chapter, we will not focus on any relevant legislation, rather we will focus on the practices used by insurers to include or exclude a policyholder from participating in the insurance industry.[3] One should also be aware that the acceptance of a person as a policyholder is no guarantee of financial inclusion.[4]

Generally speaking, there are two forms or stages of underwriting relevant to the law of insurance. The first stage occurs when a person applies for insurance. Based on the person's risk profile, the insurer may then either accept or reject the risk; in other words, accept or reject the application for insurance. This is probably the best example to observe financial exclusion or inclusion. The second underwriting stage occurs during the claim stage.[5] Here, the insurer will compare the policyholder's responses provided on the application form with the latter's true circumstances. For example, the insurer will compare these responses with those received previously by other insurers in the past as a way of verifying the correctness of the answers received.[6] If the answers differ widely from previous answers, the insurer will simply reject any claim submitted by the policyholder – another example to observe financial exclusion.[7] This chapter will focus on this scenario – what is considered a good underwriting question to prevent financial exclusion? In order to do so, the following case law example is relevant to our discussion.

3.2 *Ristorante Limited t/a Bar Massimo v Zurich Insurance Plc* Case No BL-2020-MAN-000035 Manchester Circuit Commercial Court (QBD) as an example of financial inclusion

In the Ristorante case, the plaintiff applied to the court for a declaratory order, asking the court whether the defendant, Zurich Insurance, would be entitled to

DOI: 10.4324/9781003369400-3

avoid or reject the insurance contract based on a truthful response to an underwriting question.[8] The plaintiff also asked the court whether the defendant would be entitled to question the correctness of the response provided since the underwriting question on the application form for insurance was very clear, precise or specific. In other words, there was no misrepresentation on the part of the insured. The underwriting of the risk was done by an electronic platform, Z-Trade, which used an algorithm designed to understand the risk profile of a prospective policyholder without human intervention.[9] As a result of the dropdown menu used in the Z-Trade software program, responses to the underwriting questions used on this platform could only be provided in the form of either "agree" or "disagree". The facts of the case were that the plaintiff traded as a restaurant and the directors and shareholders of the company were a Mr Lilli, a Mr Dalsasso and a Mr Stefano Dalsasso, all of whom were part of other companies that had, at one point or another, either been voluntarily or compulsorily liquidated. When applying for the insurance, one of the underwriting questions simply required the prospective policyholder to state whether any directors had not been part of a business that had previously been subjected to a winding-up or liquidation order. The plaintiff answered the question as "agree".[10] The defendant continued to defend his case by relying on other statements that were part of the underwriting process, namely, that the plaintiff had a duty to disclose all material information; if not, the defendant was entitled to reject the policy or any claim submitted under the policy.[11] In addition, the defendant also relied on another underwriting statement that the plaintiff has a duty to give a fair presentation of the risk to the insurer; if not, the insurer or defendant is entitled to reject the claim submitted under the policy.[12] The statement continued, mentioning that if the insured was in doubt as to whether all material information had been provided, it would be advisable to disclose all relevant information.[13] Finally, another statement was included exhorting the applicant to make sure that all questions had been answered correctly on the application form.[14] Needless to say, when the plaintiff submitted a claim for fire damage to the restaurant, the insurance company rejected the claim owing to the undisclosed insolvency events relating to the directors/shareholders of the restaurant business.[15] Zurich argued that these undisclosed facts amounted to material non-disclosure since, where previous liquidations had occurred, it would not have taken on the risk. Accordingly, the Z-Trade platform would not have generated a quote; in other words, the system would have automatically rejected the application for insurance.[16]

3.3 Three key issues for financial inclusion

Before we focus on the three key issues of relevance here, it should be pointed out that irrespective of the correctness of the responses given, financial exclusion can occur either during the insurance application process or when submitting a claim – the disclosure of previous liquidations would have allowed the system to reject the application and/or the provision of an answer deemed unacceptable by the system would have resulted in the rejection of the claim. Be that as it may, the plaintiff focused on the following three key issues, deemed to be logical and straightforward, as to why the defendant should be liable for settling the claim:[17]

a) Issue one, was there an unfair representation of the risk or misrepresentation of the risk (previous liquidations)?
b) Issue two, did the defendant waive any entitlement to additional information (pertaining to the previous liquidations)?
c) Issue three, did the defendant avoid or reject (repudiate) the contract of insurance?

If the answer to the first key issue were "yes", it would mean that the defendant was entitled to additional information; however, no additional information was communicated, allowing the defendant to avoid the contract and the submitted claim. This logic is subject to whether the key issue was addressed correctly. In order to understand the correctness of the underwriting question pertaining to previous liquidations, the court referred to *Wood v Capita Insurance Services Ltd* [2017] AC 1173 10-13, in which the task of any court would have been to establish the objective meaning of the language chosen by the parties to express their consensus or intention clearly on an application form for insurance.[18] In order to understand the objectiveness of the language, the court had to consider all the relevant clauses of the contract or policy to reach such an opinion or conclusion. The quality of the underwriting question is of the utmost importance here: a poorly drafted question could lead to circumstances that – with hindsight – would not be in the interests of the policyholder.[19] In addition, the court had to consider the possibility of whether the underwriting question had been drafted in such a way that it elicited precise or specific information from the applicant (i.e. the plaintiff). The underwriting question that was posed on the Z-Trade platform read as follows:[20]

> No owner, director, business partner, or family member involved in the business – has ever been the subject of a winding-up order or company/individual voluntary arrangement with creditors, or has been placed into administration, administrative receivership or liquidation.

The intention of the parties must be evident from the language used in the contract or underwriting questions that form part of the contract of insurance. This is applicable to any kind of contract too, for example, a contract of sale. In considering this underwriting question at claim stage, it may be said that it could have been expressed in more precise terms, for example, by asking the applicant to supply the dates of previous liquidations.[21] However, the Z-Trade platform merely required the response "agree" or "disagree", giving no option to provide relevant dates. Since the question could have been formulated better and in more precise terms (specific question), it is obvious that the insurer had no true intention of establishing or requesting additional information pertaining to any previous liquidations – from the owner, director, business partner and so on. Objectively, it is even possible to argue that since the underwriting question was poorly drafted (above), the defendant or insurer waived his right to acquire additional information from the plaintiff.[22] The underwriting question could have been made more precise or specific by asking in which court – when and where – a liquidation order had been obtained in terms of either a voluntary or compulsory liquidation – from the owner, director, business partner and so on. In brief, it would have been possible to design this question in more precise terms so as to establish the true intention of the insurer pertaining to the liquidation or the winding-up (or previous winding-up) of a company, where the owner, director and business partner were part thereof.

3.4 Subjective understanding of the underwriting question and financial inclusion

The underwriting question and how it should be understood by a policyholder or prospective policyholder is not subjective.[23] In other words, how a policyholder or prospective policyholder understands the question is irrelevant; the way the underwriting question should be understood by any current or prospective policyholder is always subjected to an objective test. However, if the underwriting question causes doubt or leads to ambiguity, the court should interpret such a question and its meaning so that it is most relevant from a common-sense business perspective.[24] This requirement regarding how a court should interpret an underwriting question is only relevant if there is indeed ambiguity. If one considers the above underwriting question in paragraph three above pertaining to previous liquidations, it is possible to argue that the question is imprecise or vague, which results in ambiguity – a court should follow the principle of common sense; that is, how it should be understood (objectively) in practice. Nevertheless, since the question is not formulated precisely, it is possible to conclude on the basis of common sense, that the insurer had no intention to request further information (relevant to liquidations or previous liquidations of other companies) since the insurer did not consider it to be important or relevant to the business of a restaurant. On the other hand, if an underwriting question could elicit two diverse answers, then the court must choose the answer (on the basis of common sense) that is in favour of the plaintiff or policyholder.[25] This is based on the reasonable person test that holds that if the answer is answered truthfully – irrespective of whether the question is precise or not – the answer cannot amount to misrepresentation should a reasonable person have answered it in the same way (promotes financial inclusion).[26] It would appear from the plaintiff's response to the question that the answer provided on the application form was true. To understand why the question was answered truthfully, the underwriting question should have read as follows (the missing words have been inserted to indicate why the question was deemed inadequate):[27]

> No owner, or director (*or any company in which any owner or director has been involved*), and no business partner or family member involved in with business … has ever been the subject of (*any*) winding-up order or company/individual voluntary arrangement with creditors, or has been placed into administration, administrative receivership or liquidation.

Subsequent to responding to the above question with "agree", the defendant could then have been asked for the relevant dates of the previous liquidations. The difference between the two underwriting questions is therefore clear (the question quoted in paragraph three above and the question quoted above which includes the missing words) since the above question requests a response to "any company in which the owner or director has been involved" and relates clearly to previous liquidations. Without these words, the original underwriting question (in paragraph three) relates to liquidations or winding-ups to the restaurant business only, and whether liquidation or winding-up has ever happened to that business.[28] Therefore, objectively, the plaintiff provided the correct answer relevant to the original underwriting question since neither he nor any other director had ever been involved in liquidation or winding-up procedures relevant to the restaurant business. In other words, the words "no owner, director, business partner or family member involved with the business" clearly define the business to which the notion of liquidation is linked – the restaurant business only (the words "involved with the business"). This question also defines the business to which the underwriting question relates; that is, the business of the restaurant only. Based on the nature of the underwriting question, the plaintiff did not realise that the defendant/insurer was interested in other companies and liquidation processes relevant to the partners/shareholders in the restaurant business. The court clearly emphasised in this regard that the underwriting question related to the owner/director of the applicant company only, that is, the restaurant business only.[29]

3.5 Is there a duty on the insurer to know case law to promote financial inclusion?

Most insurance companies have a dedicated legal department. Therefore, one may assume that any legal department would consider the underwriting question (in paragraph three) in light of previous cases or case law.[30] In the *Ristorante* case, the court held that the defendant should have had knowledge of the *Doheny v New India Assurance* [2005] 1 All ER (Comm) 382 (CA) and *R&R Developments v Axa Insurance UK plc* [2010] 2 All EW (Comm) 521 cases to understand the meaning and relevance of the missing words (in paragraph four) "or any company in which any owner or director have been involved". Clearly, the defendant did not compare these case law conclusions to their own underwriting question (as discussed earlier).[31] If they had been aware of these case law, they or the defendant would have changed the underwriting question – an action that would have taken just a few minutes after reading the relevant cases (for financial inclusion). In this regard, one may assume that insurers should be aware of the importance of case law and amend their underwriting questions appropriately to reflect a better, more precise or specific underwriting question that is not contrary to these case law – *Doheny* and *R& R Development* cases.[32] Obviously, this approach was not followed by the defendant and the underwriting question was as a result, very vague, as discussed earlier.

3.6 Policyholder's or prospective policyholder's duty of disclosure to prevent financial exclusion

The court held that the duty to disclose additional information or material information could be waived by the insurer, depending on the wording of the underwriting question; for example, have you been in an accident in the last three years?[33] This question requires only the disclosure of accidents that have occurred in the preceding three years and does not require comprehensive disclosure of all accidents experienced in the lifetime of the policyholder/prospective policyholder.[34] The same rationale applies, to some extent, to the original underwriting question (in paragraph three) pertaining to liquidations relevant to the restaurant business only. On the basis of the unique formulation of the original underwriting question, no duty was placed on the plaintiff or insured to explain all the liquidations of all the directors, business partners, and so on, involved to the defendant (financial inclusion). Accordingly, the court held that the defendant had to settle the claim submitted by the plaintiff.[35] Based on the discussion above, it is clear that financial inclusion was obtained owing to the poor wording of the original underwriting question. However, the same did not apply in the following matter, which was decided by the South African Ombudsman for Short-Term Insurance.

3.7 The South African Ombudsman and financial exclusion

In South Africa, the Insurance Ombudsman is a qualified lawyer and/or advocate. In *Swanepoel v Brolink* S638/18F, the facts of the matter were very straightforward. Mr Swanepoel was a policyholder of OUTsurance Insurance Company who submitted a claim to OUTsurance. OUTsurance responded with a letter informing Mr Swanepoel that the claim had been cancelled owing to fraud on 17 November 2009.[36] Subsequently, the state attempted to prosecute Mr Swanepoel for fraud. This resulted in the court issuing a *nolle prosequi* in 2012 after finding no evidence of fraud.[37] On 14 May 2015, Mr Swanepoel obtained insurance from Brolink, a type of binder holder that can by law act as an insurer without an insurance licence under specific circumstances.[38] On 8 April 2019, the insured caused a motor vehicle collision and the vehicle was subsequently written off. On investigating the claim, Brolink found that the insured, Mr Swanepoel, had answered "no" to the following question:

> Have you, or any other person that will be covered by this insurance, ever had an application for insurance declined or has any insurer ever cancelled your policy or refused to renew your insurance or imposed special terms or conditions on your insurance cover? [the applicant answered "no"].[39]

Regarding this underwriting question, Brolink argued that the negative response was in fact the incorrect answer because OUTsurance cancelled the previous policy owing to fraud. What is interesting about this matter is the term "cancellation". While cancellation is a remedy for breach of contract, it is clear that the insured was not guilty of such an act.[40] Had fraud been committed, then the policy would simply have been suspended or terminated, depending on the choice of words used by the insurer.[41] Obviously, the insurer did not suspend or terminate the policy since the policy did not continue after the *nolle prosequi* judgment. Mr Swanepoel explained to Brolink and to the Assistant Ombudsman that fraud had never been committed and that OUTsurance had used incorrect legal terminology in cancelling the contract/policy.[42] Hence, no fraud was committed, and no cancellation occurred in the law – the question therefore was answered correctly (without any misrepresentation) as "no". The words "refused to renew your insurance or imposed special terms or conditions on your insurance cover" were not part of the Brolink investigation and, since OUTsurance did not refuse to renew the insurance or to impose special terms on the policy, the OUTsurance policy was cancelled on the basis of fraud only. In view of the judgment in *Ristorante Limited t/a Bar Massimo v Zurich Insurance Plc*, it is clear that the Brolink underwriting question is only relevant to cancellations and/or previous cancellations in this regard. In addition, the question (above) is vague and lacks specificity since it does not make a distinction between a voided policy (as a result of fraud) and a cancelled policy.[43] For this reason, we may assume that Brolink waived any additional information since there was no specific question that required an explanation or an answer to questions relevant to *nolle prosequi* judgments or requesting additional information pertaining to cancellations.[44] Brolink also relied on a very vague, imprecise underwriting question, namely:

> The insurer or binder holder could repudiate a claim if they find that the information given was incorrect. Can you please confirm that all of the information you have supplied pertaining to this application for insurance is correct and that you do not know of any reason why an insurer should not grant you cover for the property to be insured? [the applicant answered "no"][45]

In considering the above underwriting question, the Ombudsman, Deanne Wood, did not put an emphasis on *nolle prosequi* and its consequences.[46] In her opinion, *nolle prosequi* was irrelevant, and for all practical circumstances, fraud had been committed.[47] In addition, the Ombudsman held that the difference between specific and non-specific questions should not play a significant role in South Africa, but rather whether a reasonable person would have disclosed (additional) information or not. In this instance, an imprecise question (from a South African perspective) for the reasonable person test indicates which additional information should have been disclosed to Brolink or the defendant Mr Swanepoel or insurer.[48] (Please contact the author for a copy of this judgment.) In *Ristorante Limited t/a Bar Massimo v Zurich Insurance Plc*, the court quoted a similar imprecise or vague question – "we may remind you that you have a duty to disclose all material facts: that is, those facts that would influence an insurer in the acceptance of assessment of the risk".[49] One must keep in mind that the policyholder/prospective policyholder is not superhuman and cannot decide on behalf of an insurer whether certain information is relevant or not for the purposes of insurance.

Therefore, the importance of drafting proper and precise underwriting questions cannot be overstated (to prevent financial exclusion).[50] The Ombudsman and Assistant Ombudsman focused on the above underwriting questions (vague and imprecise underwriting questions), and in their opinion, Mr Swanepoel had answered this vague question incorrectly – Mr Swanepoel committed misrepresentation. In addition, fraud is an offence in criminal law and clearly a *nolle prosequi* judgment does not support the fact that fraud was committed – it would thus be unfair to assume that fraud existed, keeping in mind that a *nolle prosequi* certificate exists.[51] Nevertheless, it is clear that neither fraud nor cancellation exists in the law. However, the Ombudsman and Assistant Ombudsman explained that a reasonable person would have answered the above underwriting questions in such a way as to explain *nolle prosequi* to Brolink.[52] One should keep in mind here that insurance law in the United Kingdom requires that underwriting questions be formulated precisely in order to avoid the consequence of being "void for vagueness". Mr Swanepoel argued that the "any reason" as part of an underwriting question is not a specific question in the law. Subsequently, the Ombudsman and Assistant Ombudsman did not express any opinion on the differences between precise and imprecise questions and held that a reasonable person would have disclosed *nolle prosequi* on the application form – the rejected claim was therefore upheld by the Ombudsman.

In view of the above, it is clear that reliance on imprecise or vague underwriting questions can lead to financial exclusion in South Africa. Because, objectively, no fraud and/or cancellation had occurred in the law, why should any reasonable person (objectively) have disclosed this to an insurer – surely it could not affect the applicant's risk profile?[53] Or to explain it differently, would an insurer have rejected an application for insurance that disclosed no previous fraud and/or cancellation? Brolink argued that if they had known about a *nolle prosequi* and cancellation, they would not have insured Mr Swanepoel.[54] It is possible to take another point of view here: if *nolle prosequi* is considered to be so important, surely the insurer would have formulated a precise underwriting question where the applicant would have been required to explain *nolle prosequi* in detail and the same would apply to cancellation.[55] Needless to say, Mr Swanepoel appealed the judgment to the chairman of the Appeal Board for Short-term Insurance, a retired Constitutional Court Judge, Justice Sandile Ngcobo. Justice Ngcobo delivered his judgment in two pages, confirming that no court would reach a different conclusion from the Ombudsman and Assistant Ombudsman regarding the above factual circumstances.[56] It is possible to argue that South Africa tends to ride roughshod over the principles of insurance in understanding the importance of specific underwriting questions – in principle, there is no difference between precise and imprecise questions in South Africa – focusing solely on the reasonable person test to produce a disclosure of relevant information, which Mr Swanepoel neglected to do (financial exclusion).[57] In this case, the Ombudsman's reasoning is arbitrary in terms of the scientific explanation of the meaning and purpose of precise questions when one considers the importance of specific underwriting questions as was held by *Ristorante Limited t/a Bar Massimo v Zurich Insurance Plc*.[58]

3.8 Financial inclusion perspectives for South Africa

To understand the legal difference between precise and imprecise underwriting questions in the law, and how the answers given to imprecise questions may not be considered misrepresentation when applying the reasonable person test at claim stage, the *Swanepoel v Brolink* case should be considered with reference to *Ristorante Limited t/a Bar Massimo v Zurich Insurance Plc*.[59] While both Mr Swanepoel and Bar Massimo answered imprecise questions truthfully, the end result for both cases was different.[60] Mr Swanepoel had his arguments rejected by an informal tribunal (the Ombudsman), while Bar Massimo's arguments were upheld by a court. This cannot be explained by saying that an informal tribunal has lesser standing in the law, since such a tribunal includes lawyers and retired judges and is funded by insurers in South Africa. Nevertheless, in light of the judgment delivered in the *Ristorante Limited t/a Bar Massimo v Zurich Insurance Plc* case, it remains unclear how the informal tribunal in the Swanepoel case reached its conclusion – it would appear that there is no need to distinguish between poorly phrased – imprecise and precise questions – in South Africa.[61] This is unfortunate and could be used opportunistically by the informal tribunal (Ombudsman office) or insurer, for example, the application of incorrect legal principles to factual circumstances could promote financial exclusion in South Africa – to the financial detriment of policyholders.[62] In addition, the procedure to appeal to the Appeal Board lacks transparency. All relevant documents are simply forwarded to the Appeal Board for a judgment and plaintiffs such as Mr Swanepoel are not given the opportunity to draft additional documents to present to the Appeal Board. In brief, the process of approaching the Assistant Ombudsman, the Ombudsman and then the Appeal Board results in unnecessary delays in resolving such an uncomplicated matter. It is time that clear rules be formulated for the Short-Term Ombudsman (as a form of informal tribunal). These rules should be disclosed on the website so that a complainant knows what to expect and how disputes are resolved in practice: first, the Assistant Ombudsman, then the Ombudsman and lastly the Appeal Board.[63]

3.8.1 Financial inclusion perspectives for High Court litigation in South Africa

Contrary to the *Ristorante Limited t/a Bar Massimo v Zurich Insurance Plc* it seems that the High Court in South Africa is not concerned with the wording of underwriting questions, or it could be that attorneys/advocates are not concerned with how to argue the differences between specific and unspecific underwriting questions. In *Mignon Adelia Steyn v Profmed Medical Scheme* Western Cape Division (case 23378/2018), the High Court nor the full bench High Court of Appeal in *Profmed Medical Scheme v Mignon Adelia Steyn* (case A 171/ 2021) considered the importance of the wording of underwriting questions. In these cases, the insurer or Profmed continued with additional information as to what a reasonable person would have disclosed to the insurer – initially, it was wrist pains, hip problems, gastritis and breast aspiration as non-disclosures, and adding later heart murmur and kidney stones, to reject a claim submitted by the plaintiff.[64] We assume the above non-disclosures result from a question similar to "you do not know of any reason why an insurer should not grant you cover" for any medical condition. The courts, in the above two cases, did not indicate whether an underwriting question was answered incorrectly, thereby contributing to misrepresentation of the risk profile of the insured, for example, do you suffer from kidney stones – agree or disagree? The courts tried to argue why a reasonable person would have disclosed the above, keeping in mind that wrist pains are not equal to osteoarthritis, hip problems are not equal to hip replacements, gastritis is not equal to gastritis ulcers, kidney stones are not equal to kidney replacements, a heart murmur is not equal to heart failure, and probably most women will be examined for breast aspiration at least once in their lifetime. The insurer could not argue the underwriting weight (or risk) to be attached to the above medical conditions. Needless to say, the full bench held that only the non-disclosed ulcer renders the policy voidable, allowing the insurer an opportunity to reject the policy (financial exclusion).[65] The court did not indicate how long ago the insured received treatment for an ulcer – it could be ten years ago or even longer.[66] Nevertheless, one can argue that the mere fact that there were no specific underwriting questions indicates that the insurer did not consider these medical conditions as severe – the insurer, therefore, waived the right to obtain information about these conditions.[67] For this reason, the insurer should have settled the insured's claim, if one follows the reasoning of *Ristorante Limited t/a Bar Massimo v Zurich Insurance Plc* (financial inclusion).

Notes

1 *Swanepoel v Brolink* S638/18F. Contact the author for copies of the Assistant Ombudsman's judgment, the Ombudsman's judgment and the Appeal Board judgment.
2 *Ristorante Limited t/a Bar Massimo v Zurich Insurance Plc* Case No: BL-2020-MAN-000035 Manchester Circuit Commercial Court (QBD).
3 See, for example, section 53(1) of the Short-Term Insurance Act 53 of 1998 (South African legislation) which requires a statutory disclosure of material facts; *Regent Insurance Company Ltd v King's Property Development (Pty) Ltd* [2004] ZASCO (176) 21 November 2014 para 21; *Clifford v Commercial Union Insurance Co of SA Ltd* 1998 (4) SA 150 (SCA) for a clear discussion of the differences between material and non-material disclosures; *Mutual and Federal Insurance Co Ltd v Oudtshoorn Municipality* 1985 (1) SA 419 (A) 435; *Qilingele v South African Mutual Life Assurance Society* 1993 (1) SA 69 (A).
4 See, in general, *Ristorante Limited t/a Bar Massimo v Zurich Insurance Plc* Case No: BL-2020-MAN-000035 Manchester Circuit Commercial Court (QBD).
5 Ibid.
6 *Mahadeo v Direct Insurance Ltd* 2008 (4) SA 80 (W) paras 17 and 18; *Regent Insurance Co Ltd v King's Property Development (Pty) Ltd t/a King's Prop* 2015 (3) SA 85 (SCA) paras 24 and 25.
7 See, in general, *Mignon Adelia Steyn v Profmed Medical Scheme* Western Cape Division (case 23378/2018); *Profmed Medical Scheme v Mignon Adelia Steyn* (case A 171/ 2021). Profmed relied on an application form submitted to Momentum to understand the relevant non-disclosures.

8 *Ristorante Limited t/a Bar Massimo v Zurich Insurance Plc* Case No: BL-2020-MAN-000035 Manchester Circuit Commercial Court (QBD) 2–5.
9 Ibid, 2.
10 Ibid, 5.
11 Ibid, 5–7.
12 Ibid, 5–7.
13 Ibid, 4.
14 Ibid, 4; *Wood v Capita Insurance Services Ltd* [2015] EWCA Civ 389 [2017] UKSC 24 para 10.
15 Ibid, 5.
16 See, in general, *Regent Insurance Company Ltd v King's Property Development (Pty) Ltd* [2004] ZASCO (176) 21 November 2014 para 25.
17 *Ristorante Limited t/a Bar Massimo v Zurich Insurance Plc* Case No: BL-2020-MAN-000035 Manchester Circuit Commercial Court (QBD) 5.
18 Ibid, 5 and 7.
19 Ibid, 9.
20 Ibid, 7.
21 Ibid, 8–9.
22 Ibid, 13.
23 Ibid, 6.
24 Ibid, 7.
25 Ibid, 7.
26 Ibid.
27 Ibid. My emphasis.
28 Compare to *Swanepoel v Brolink* S638/18F. Contact the author for copies of the Assistant Ombudsman's judgment, the Ombudsman's judgment and the Appeal Board judgment.
29 *Ristorante Limited t/a Bar Massimo v Zurich Insurance Plc* Case No: BL-2020-MAN-000035 Manchester Circuit Commercial Court (QBD) 9.
30 Ibid, 15.
31 Ibid.
32 *Swanepoel v Brolink* S638/18F incorrect legal terminology used by OUTsurance to communicate with Mr Swanepoel. Surely, an insurer with a legal department should be using the correct legal phrases and terminology when communicating with their policyholders.
33 *Ristorante Limited t/a Bar Massimo v Zurich Insurance Plc* Case No: BL-2020-MAN-000035 Manchester Circuit Commercial Court (QBD) 13.
34 Ibid, 13–15.
35 Ibid, 15.
36 *R&R Developments Limited v Axa Insurance UK Plc* [2009] EWHC 2429 (Ch) 5. In the presence of ambiguity pertaining to "cancellation", the court held as follows: "representations are often made in response to questions asked by the insurer, from which the replies take their colour. If true in the sense in which it is reasonably intended as an answer to a question in the proposal form, the proposer's statement is true in law, for any ambiguity in the question results in the construction of the question against the insurer",
37 *S v Swanepoel* (Gauteng Regional Court Division) (unreported case 44/07/2011).
38 Amended by Short-Term Insurance Act 53 of 1998 under section 70, GN 34877 in GG 1076, of 23 December 2011 for an explanation of a binder holder.
39 Please ask the author for a copy of the judgment.
40 *Wood v Capita Insurance Services Ltd* [2015] EWCA Civ 389 [2017] UKSC 24 para 10 to establish the objective meaning of words used in questions.
41 *Regent Insurance Company Ltd v King's Property Development (Pty) Ltd* [2004] ZASCO (176) 21 November 2014 para 18 uses the term "void".

42 Ibid, para 18. South African court cases can be criticised for the fact that actual underwriting questions are not quoted in judgments, making it difficult to distinguish between specific and unspecific questions.
43 Ibid, para 20.
44 Ibid.
45 Please ask the author for a copy of the judgment.
46 *R&R Developments Limited v Axa Insurance UK Plc* [2009] EWHC 2429 (Ch) 32 the grammar and syntax of the question pertaining to cancellations are very similar to the *Swanepoel v Brolink* matter. Subjectively, how this question should be understood does not play a role; objectively, the term "cancellations" should be assigned as to what is held in the law – remedy for breach of contract. It is clear that Mr Swanepoel did not commit breach of contract when submitting his claim. The true reason why the policy was "cancelled" – or terminated to be more accurate – was as a result of fraud. OUTsurance is a well-known South African insurance company with a legal department but nevertheless made use of incorrect legal terminology.
47 *Doheny v New India Assurance Company Ltd* Case No: 2004 1215 A3 Court of Appeal 15 December 2004 5 held: "These extracts only show that different judges sometimes formulate the same concept in somewhat different terms. In that particular case none of the lords justices had any difficulties in deciding that, whatever the words of the declaration, they did not excuse the failure to disclose a criminal conviction. Taking into account the different formulations in that case … I see no reason to qualify the test". In this regard, criminal conviction should be disclosed, but perhaps not *nolle prosequi* since it is not a conviction per se; *Schooman v Hall* [1951] 1 Lloyds Rep 139; even if one argues that the duty of disclosure is regulated in the Short-Term Insurance Act 53 of 1998, the court in Doheny also held the following on 5: "It is unquestionably plain that questions in a proposal form may be so framed as necessary to imply that the underwriter only wants information on certain subject matters, or that within a particular subject-matter their desire for information is restricted within the narrow limits indicated by the question, and in such a case, they may pro tanto dispense the proposer from what otherwise at common law would have been a duty to disclose everything material".
48 *Mahadeo v Direct Insurance Ltd* 2008 (4) SA 80 (W) paras 17 and 18.
49 *Ristorante Limited t/a Bar Massimo v Zurich Insurance Plc* Case No: BL-2020-MAN-000035 Manchester Circuit Commercial Court (QBD) 3.
50 JP van Niekerk, 'Good Bye to the Duty of Disclosure in Insurance Law: Reasons, to Rethink, Restrict Reform or Repeal the Duty' (2005) *South African Mercantile Law Journal* 150.
51 *R&R Developments Limited v Axa Insurance UK Plc* [2009] EWHC 2429 (Ch) 32 the court has a duty to correct incorrect and poorly drafted questions – the court will generally follow questions in a policy unless the court is satisfied that "something has gone wrong with the language". The ombud Deanne Wood did not consider whether something was wrong with the word "cancellation" and/or the word "fraud" and the actual truthful facts of the case.
52 Van Niekerk (n 50) 150–160.
53 HE Raynes, *A History of British Insurance Law* 2ed (Pitman 1964) 161.
54 *Regent Insurance Company Ltd v King's Property Development (Pty) Ltd* [2004] ZASCO (176) 21 November 2014 paras 25–27 and 47 the test for inducement. In this case, the building contained highly flammable products and should have been disclosed to the insurer. In the Swanepoel matter, fraud was not committed, hence it should not have affected Swanepoel's risk profile; *Pan Atlantic Co Ltd v Pine Top Insurance Co Ltd* [1995] 1 AC 501 (HL) 506 "Once materiality has been established, the insured is likely to face an uphill struggle in trying to demonstrate that his non-disclosure or misrepresentation bearing this stamp had no effect".
55 *Regent Insurance Company Ltd v King's Property Development (Pty) Ltd* [2004] ZASCO (176) 21 November 2014 para 25.

56 Please ask the author for a copy of the judgment.
57 Van Niekerk (n 50) 150.
58 *Wise (Underwriting Agency) v Oceanus* [1984] 1 Lloyds Rep 476 511. Failure on the part of an insurer to ask a question could be an indication that it has waived its right to information, unless a suspicion exists that the insured must disclose such information to the insurer; *Mahadeo v Dial Direct Insurance Ltd* 2008 (4) SA 80 (W) 83. In this case, a blatantly incorrect answer was supplied to a specific question – the insured previously submitted a claim for pothole repairs and when asked by a consultant about any previous claims, the insured answered no.
59 *Regent Insurance Company Ltd v King's Property Development (Pty) Ltd* [2004] ZASCO (176) 21 November 2014 para 45. In this case, the insurer was required to conduct a survey before the policy was accepted. As the insurer never conducted a survey, the insured relied on estoppel to prevent the rejection of the submitted claim.
60 See, in general, Van Niekerk (n 50) 53 footnote 18.
61 *Mignon Adelia Steyn v Profmed Medical Scheme* Western Cape Division (case 23378/2018); *Profmed Medical Scheme v Mignon Adelia Steyn* (case A 171/ 2021); these cases can be criticised for not listing the underwriting questions in their judgments, making it impossible to distinguish between specific and non-specific questions and to which one the judgments relate to. As an example, please see *R&R Developments Limited v Axa Insurance UK Plc* [2009] EWHC 2429 (Ch) 2–3 where the court clearly quoted the relevant questions.
62 See, in general, Van Niekerk (n 50) 154 special circumstances or special facts should be disclosed – those facts would increase the monthly premium.
63 Short-Term Ombud "Appeal Mechanism Rules 2022" https://www.osti.co.za/media/1010/the-appeal-mechanism.pdf, accessed 5 May 2022.
64 *Mignon Adelia Steyn v Profmed Medical Scheme* Western Cape Division (case 23378/2018) paras 6 and 15.
65 *Profmed Medical Scheme v Mignon Adelia Steyn (*case A 171/ 2021) para 32. In the *Mignon Adelia Steyn v Profmed Medical Scheme* Western Cape Division (case 23378/2018), the court held that there was no duty to disclose all information to Profmed – it was based on a technical argument presented by the advocate, for example, the informal tribunals did not comply with the law of evidence.
66 *Profmed Medical Scheme v Mignon Adelia Steyn (*case A 171/ 2021) para 26.
67 Ibid, para 20; see *Ristorante Limited t/a Bar Massimo v Zurich Insurance Plc* Case No: BL-2020-MAN-000035 Manchester Circuit Commercial Court (QBD) 2–10.

Bibiliography

Amended by Short-Term Insurance Act 53 of 1998 under section 70, GN 34877 in GG 1076, of 23 December 2011.
Clifford v Commercial Union Insurance Co of SA Ltd 1998 (4) SA 150 (SCA).
Doheny v New India Assurance Company Ltd Case No: 2004 1215 A3 Court of Appeal 15 December 2004.
Mahadeo v Direct Insurance Ltd 2008 (4) SA 80 (W).
Mignon Adelia Steyn v Profmed Medical Scheme Western Cape Division (case 23378/2018).
Mutual and Federal Insurance Co Ltd v Oudtshoorn Municipality 1985 (1) SA 419 (A) 435.
Pan Atlantic Co Ltd v Pine Top Insurance Co Ltd [1995] 1 AC 501 (HL) 506.
Profmed Medical Scheme v Mignon Adelia Steyn (case A 171/ 2021).
Qilingele v South African Mutual Life Assurance Society 1993 (1) SA 69 (A).
H E Raynes *A History of British Insurance Law* 2 ed (Pitman, 1964) 161.

Regent Insurance Company Ltd v King's Property Development (Pty) Ltd [2004] ZASCO (176) 21 November 2014.

Ristorante Limited t/a Bar Massimo v Zurich Insurance Plc Case No: BL-2020-MAN-000035 Manchester Circuit Commercial Court (QBD).

R&R Developments Limited v Axa Insurance UK Plc [2009] EWHC 2429 (Ch) 5.

S v Swanepoel (Gauteng Regional Court Division) (unreported case 44/07/2011).

Schooman v Hall [1951] 1 Lloyds Rep 139.

Short-Term Insurance Act 53 of 1998 (South African legislation).

Short Term Ombud 'Appeal mechanism rules 2022' https://www.osti.co.za/media/1010/the-appeal-mechanism.pdf, accessed 5 May 2022.

Swanepoel v Brolink S638/18F (Assistant Ombudsman, contact author for copy of judgment).

Swanepoel v Brolink S638/18F (Appeal Board, contact author for copy of judgment).

Swanepoel v Brolink S638/18F (Ombudsman, contact author for copy of judgment).

J P van Niekerk 'Good bye to the duty of disclosure in insurance law: Reasons, to rethink, restrict reform or repeal the duty' (2005) 17(2) *South African Mercantile Law Journal* 150.

J P Van Niekerk 'Good bye to the duty of disclosure in insurance law: Reasons, to rethink, restrict reform or repeal the duty part 1' (2005) *South African Mercantile Law Journal* 150–169.

Wise (Underwriting Agency) v Oceanus [1984] 1 Lloyds Rep 476.

Wood v Capita Insurance Services Ltd [2015] EWCA Civ 389 [2017] UKSC 24.

4 "Shareholder capitalism" or an all-inclusive stakeholder model

What is the preferred corporate governance model for South Africa?

Jean Jacques du Plessis

4.1 Introduction

This chapter is based on the keynote address delivered at the North West University's (NWU) first virtual Annual Conference on Corporate and Financial Markets Law. The two-day Conference dealt with several issues of primary interest. The Conference Programme reflected the richness of topics divided into 12 session themes with a highly contemporary title, "Confronting the Effects of the Covid-19 Pandemic on Corporate Governance, Corporate Insolvency and Financial Education Measures in Practice". It brought together academics from different jurisdictions and had a truly international flavour to it. The conference theme and conference programme covered some very exciting topics. The primary focus on Covid-19 made it particularly relevant and the papers provided several important suggestions on how the future of corporate governance, corporate insolvency and financial markets would be shaped by the Covid-19 pandemic. Covid-19 has been a game-changer that exposed many cracks in the widely adopted corporate law and corporate governance models in the entire world. It resulted in a fresh and critical look at many aspects that were considered to be holy cow principles, but their true nature was far from perfect, in fact, they were the very cause of serious negative impacts on societies and the environment.

In section 4.2 of this chapter, the merits of the South African Companies Act 71 of 2008 (SACA) and the approach adopted in the King Reports on corporate governance will be evaluated. Section 4.3 will delve deeper into the historical developments of the stakeholder debate and some recent corporate governance debates in the United States. The impact of Covid-19 on employee interests is the focus of section 4.4, while the protection of and remedies provided to employees under South African law are touched upon in section 4.5. Some concluding remarks will be made in section 4.6.

4.2 The South African Companies Act 71 of 2008 and the corporate governance approach adopted in the King Reports

I strongly suggest that there is no need in South Africa to re-invent the wheel as far as the South African Companies Act 71 of 2008 (SACA) is concerned. It

DOI: 10.4324/9781003369400-4

has a very solid and flexible legal basis for refinement and is one of the most modern pieces of company law legislation in the world.[1] The SACA contains unique legislative approaches to issues like directors' statutory duties; an all-inclusive safe-harbour provision for directors when they perform acts and exercise their duties as directors; a unique statutory derivative action, also providing standing for employees to bring such actions on behalf of the company; an advanced and modern application of the "solvency and liquidity test"; and special rights of employees during business rescues and insolvency procedures, to name but a few. That certain provisions in the SACA serve as trend-setting statutory provisions is illustrated by the protection provided for directors, called the "business judgment rule" in other jurisdictions, in the SACA 2008. In Australia, a so-called statutory business judgment rule is contained in section 180(2) and (3) of the Australian Corporations Act, 2001 (Cth) (ACA 2001). However, because of the narrow nature of the rule, it has widely been considered to be a very poor form of protection for directors.[2] Based on this view, several attempts were made to reform the Australian statutory business judgment rule.[3] As part of the discussion on such law reforms, the South African approach has been proposed as a basis for law reform in Australia.[4] Although no law reform to sections 180 (2) and (3) of the ACA 2001 has been proposed to Parliament, as recently as 2021, the proposed amendment based on the South African protective rule has again been considered seriously[5] in an attempt to create greater legal certainty to directors regarding their protection when acting in their capacity as directors and when exercising their powers and performing the functions of directors.

Since 1994, the South African King Reports adopted a very sensible approach of not only focusing on the financial bottom line, but on a triple bottom line approach, where economic, social *and* governance issues were focused on. This formed the basis of an all-inclusive stakeholder approach adopted by later King Reports, and, different from most other jurisdictions, the South African Courts embraced the South African Corporate Governance Code as providing guiding principles to interpret the blackletter law of the SACA and common law. The unique approach of South Africa is illustrated very well by Dr Helena Stoop, in her PhD Thesis, "The Role of Voluntary Corporate Governance Codes in the Interpretation and Application of the Statutory and Common Law Duties of the Company Director: A South African Perspective".[6] There might well be some concerns regarding the legal basis of such an approach if compared with other jurisdictions,[7] but it is submitted that the approach by the South African Courts is realistic and in line with a contemporary approach to statutory interpretation. In addition, it reflects the important role voluntary Corporate Governance Codes play in the many countries that have adopted such Codes as part of their corporate law and corporate governance models.

The approach that King IV (2016) adopted to directors' duties, and the interests of all company stakeholders, is based on sound theoretical foundations of the legal nature of a company as a separate legal entity and a Code adopting an all-inclusive stakeholder approach. As a basis, King IV recognises the company as a separate legal entity, with directors having to fulfil their duties to the company as a separate legal entity, but, in fulfilling their duty to act in the best interests of the company, the directors must, and I want to emphasise must, balance the interests of all stakeholders, and not only act in the best interests of the shareholders. And, I want to emphasise again, directors, under South African company law, cannot only act in the best interests of the shareholders:

> The position taken in King IV is that [quoting Esser and Du Plessis (2007 article, SA Merc LJ)][8] "directors owe their duties to the company and the company alone as the company is a separate legal entity from the moment it is registered until it is deregistered … The company is represented by several interests and these include the interests of shareholders, employees, consumers, the community and the environment. Thus, requiring directors to act in good faith in the interests of 'the company' cannot nowadays mean anything other than a blend of all these interests, but first and foremost they must act in the best interest of the company as a separate legal entity … An interest that may be primary at one particular point in time in the company's existence may well become secondary at a later stage".

Based on the current approach by South African courts to rely on the principles of the King Corporate Governance Code to guide them in interpreting the SACA, it can be expected that the courts will also use this position taken by King IV in determining the standards of directors' conduct when expected to act "in the best interests of the company" (s 76(3)(b) of the SACA 2008):

> Standards of directors' conduct.
>
> …
>
> (3) Subject to subsections (4) and (5), a director of a company, when acting in that capacity, must exercise the powers and perform the functions of director—
>
> (a) in good faith and for a proper purpose;
> (b) in the best interests of the company; and
> (c) with the degree of care, skill and diligence that may reasonably be expected of a person—
>   (i) carrying out the same functions in relation to the company as those carried out by that director; and
>   (ii) having the general knowledge, skill and experience of that director.

Based on the position taken by King IV, many of the complexities associated with the common law meaning of "the company", in the phrase "best interests of the company", can be avoided.[9] It might require a slight change of mindset for directors who, incorrectly, see the shareholders as the "owners" of the company and, again incorrectly, considering their primary duty to be "maximise profits for the shareholders" – these myths have been debunked and do not form part of the South African company law any longer.[10] What is important is that institutes like the Institute of Directors in Southern Africa (IoDSA) and the South African

Institute of Chartered Accountants (SAICA) keep on emphasising the significance of the approach adopted by King IV (2016) during their training, education and continuing professional development courses, programmes and seminars. Without a constant reminder, and explanation of the practical consequences of the approach adopted by King IV, directors and senior managers may fall back on bad old habits and the illusion that profit maximisation for shareholders is the primary purpose of companies.

As will be seen from the discussion below, in the United States of America (USA), the all-inclusive stakeholder approach, already adopted in South Africa several years ago, only started to get serious traction, from a practical point of view, since about 2018. It means that South Africa saw the light several years before the USA and for this, Professor Mervyn King should get all the credit. His vision and close involvement in the corporate governance reform in South Africa from King I (1994) until King IV (2016) as Chair of the King Committee ensured continuity and South Africa also stayed with the pack as far as other contemporary corporate governance developments were concerned. His most recent involvement with the integrated reporting (IR) initiative had an enormous impact internationally, especially now that the International Integrated Reporting Council (IIRC) and the Sustainability Accounting Standards Board (SASB) have merged into the Value Reporting Council (VRC).

The current unstoppable momentum of the IR initiative is further illustrated by the announcements made by the IFRS Foundation at the COP 26 Conference in Glasgow, to form an International Sustainability Standards Board (ISSB) in the first half of 2022. It also announced an intention to merge the Value Reporting Foundation, itself the result of the 2021 merger of the International Integrated Reporting Council and Sustainability Accounting Standards Board, into the IFRS Foundation. It means that the IFRS Foundation will oversee standard setting for both financial (IASB) and sustainability (ISSB) standards.[11] In November 2021, the IFRS Foundation released a prototype climate reporting standard, which is expected to be the basis of the ISSB's standard.[12] It is now for countries around the world to decide how to adopt this global infrastructure and standards in their own markets.[13]

4.3 Historical developments of the stakeholder debate and recent debates in the USA[14]

There is no need to go back in history to revisit in detail some of the most influential debates in the USA in corporate law during the 1930s,[15] but one can hardly avoid referring to one of the most often referred to trends identified by Berle and Means in the 1930s, namely the trend that in large public companies, there was a "separation between ownership and control".[16] Berle's assumption was very clearly one that shareholders were the "owners" of the company[17] and Berle and Means based this assumption on the fact that the shareholders were, after all, the suppliers of capital.[18] In other words, it was assumed that if the shareholders did not provide the "share capital", which was essential for the commercial endeavours of the company, there would be no company. To a certain extent this is true, but giving the shareholders "ownership" of the company based on the fact that they are the providers of share capital, has been exposed as incorrect by looking at the legal nature of a company: a company is a separate legal entity,[19] a legal or juristic person or body corporate, and as natural persons cannot be "owned", neither can these "creatures of statute" be "owned". Furthermore, there is a growing trend to recognise other forms of capital apart from financial capital, namely manufactured, intellectual, social and relationship, human and natural capital.[20]

Before moving on to focus on later developments regarding the stakeholder or pluralistic model of corporate law, it should be mentioned that although the American debate was dominated by the shareholder primacy approach to corporate law, there was always a very deep appreciation of the significance of the role that other stakeholders play in public companies. As Berle and Means put it:[21]

> The large public corporation] involves the interrelation of a wide diversity of economic interests, – those of the "owners" who supply capital, those of the workers who "create", those of the consumers who give value to the products of enterprise, and above all those of the control who wield power.

Thus, although Dodd conceded, after a long public debate with Berle,[22] that there were some legal and practical issues in treating directors as trustees for employees, consumers and other interest groups, rather than only as trustees for shareholders,[23] it did not mark the end of the stakeholder debate. In fact, since the early 1980s, the stakeholder or pluralistic theory of corporate law received in-depth analysis, most notably with the well-argued article by Freeman and Reed in 1983[24] and the later work by Donaldson and Preston.[25] In the United States, the approach to corporate governance formed the focus of a comprehensive restatement of the principles of corporate governance by the American Law Institute between 1982 and 1992.[26] The all-inclusive stakeholder approach received considerable attention in other parts of the world, but suffice just to refer to a few quite significant recent initiatives in this regard.[27] The focus was now on sustainability, longtermism and a serious concern that more fundamental change is required, and not only focusing on the behaviour and practices in individual companies. Paul Hawken summarises a more holistic approach very well:[28]

> To create an enduring society, we need a system of commerce and production where each and every act is inherently sustainable and restorative. Business will need to integrate economic, biologic, and human systems to create a sustainable method of commerce. As hard as we may try to become sustainable on a company-by-company level, we cannot fully succeed until the institutions surrounding commerce are redesigned.

A more general, and publicly expressed, recognition of the all-inclusive stakeholder model started again in the USA roughly in the mid-2000s, but it was embraced more specifically, and publicly, in 2018. Note the year (2018) and note that it was before there was any Covid-19 pandemic. Larry Fink, the CEO of one of the largest investment corporations in the world, BlackRock, started to send out letters to all CEOs (since 2014) in which BlackRock invests at the end of each year.[29] In 2018, his letter signalled one of the most significant deviations from the traditional shareholder-primacy-based corporate law model of the United States since the early 1930s. In this 2018 letter, he warned the CEOs of the companies in which BlackRock invests as follows, and it is quoted verbatim because of the important moment it marks as far as the prevailing views of capitalism were concerned. For many decades, the Milton Friedman form of capitalism, based solely on profit maximisation for shareholders, dominated. However, Fink realised that other demands, and other interests, necessitated a different focus:[30]

> Society is demanding that companies, both public and private, serve a social purpose. To prosper over time, every company must not only deliver financial performance, but also show how it makes a positive contribution to society. Companies must benefit all of their stakeholders, including shareholders, employees, customers, and the communities in which they operate. [C]ompanies must be able to describe their strategy for long-term growth. I want to reiterate our request, outlined in past letters, that you publicly articulate your company's strategic framework for long-term value creation and explicitly affirm that it has been reviewed by your board of directors. This demonstrates to investors that your board is engaged with the strategic direction of the company. When we meet with directors, we also expect them to describe the Board process for overseeing your strategy.

He guided companies by requesting companies to ask the following vital questions:[31]

> What role do we play in the community? How are we managing our impact on the environment? Are we working to create a diverse workforce? Are we adapting to technological change? Are we providing the retraining and opportunities that our employees and our business will need to adjust to an increasingly automated world? Are we using behavioral finance and other tools to prepare workers for retirement, so that they invest in a way that will help them achieve their goals?

In 2019, he drew companies' attention to the true "purpose" of corporations, and emphasised that it was not only to maximise profits for shareholders, but that an all-inclusive stakeholder approach should become the norm and again a long quote is justifiable because of the emphasis in the quote and the pertinent mention of all stakeholders, not only shareholders:[32]

> **Profits are in no way inconsistent with purpose – in fact, profits and purpose are inextricably linked.** Profits are essential if a company is to effectively serve all of its stakeholders over time – not only shareholders,

> but also employees, customers, and communities. Similarly, when a company truly understands and expresses its purpose, it functions with the focus and strategic discipline that drive long-term profitability. Purpose unifies management, employees, and communities. It drives ethical behavior and creates an essential check on actions that go against the best interests of stakeholders. Purpose guides culture, provides a framework for consistent decision-making, and, ultimately, helps sustain long-term financial returns for the shareholders of your company. (Emphasis in bold was emphasised in the original letter)

The letter of Larry Fink was sent to CEOs in early 2019. Probably based on that letter, the influential American Business Roundtable (ABR) mirrored the sympathies of Fink, and for the first time ever, moved away from endorsing a shareholder primacy model in favour of an all-inclusive stakeholder approach. In a statement signed by 181 CEOs, this new direction was announced under the heading, "Business Roundtable Redefines the Purpose of a Corporation to Promote 'An Economy That Serves All Americans'". The ABR and those signing the letter committed to:

- Delivering value to our customers.
- Investing in our employees.
- Dealing fairly and ethically with our suppliers.
- Supporting the communities in which we work.
- Generating long-term value for shareholders.

It goes without saying that customers are important because they generate business and allow for profit-making. Companies can hardly exist without employees who manufacture goods and provide services to customers. Dealing fairly and ethically with suppliers is critical in a globalised world where multinational corporations rely heavily on supply chains. Communities in which corporations conduct business are directly affected by corporations and a healthy and responsible relationship with these communities is of great importance to companies. Last, but surely not least, the shareholders often provide financial capital to allow corporations to invest, grow and innovate, but their interests become submerged in the interests of all the other stakeholders and should not be considered to be dominant or superior to the interests of all the other stakeholders. Striving to achieve a balance between all these interests is core to a sustainable and long-term future of the company as a separate legal entity. That is pivotal to an all-inclusive stakeholder corporate governance model.

Larry Fink's 2020 letter to CEOs was the first one sent out after the immense impact the Covid-19 pandemic had globally – impacting corporations probably just as much, or even more severely, than any previous depressions or crashes of the financial markets, including the Global Financial Crisis (GFC) of 2007–2008. It was to be expected that Larry Fink mentioned the Covid-19 pandemic and its impact, but he did not abandon his consistent views of the importance of all stakeholders,[33] again mentioning the benefits when companies "create enduring, sustainable value for *all* of [the companies'] stakeholders" ("all" italicised in the Fink letter).[34] He did, however, also emphasise the threats the globe faces because of climate change:[35]

> [O]ver the past year, we experienced something even more far-reaching [than the 2008 GFC] – a pandemic that has enveloped the entire globe and changed it permanently … [T]he pandemic has presented such an existential crisis – such a stark reminder of our fragility – that it has driven us to confront the global threat of climate change more forcefully … [T]he pandemic … has reminded us how the biggest crises … demand a global and ambitious response.

There is no doubt that there is a shift in approach away from pure profit maximisation for shareholders in the USA towards a more stakeholder-orientated model of corporate governance. In this regard, the approach in South Africa, having adopted an all-inclusive stakeholder approach several years ago, is to be commended and illustrates that South Africa has in fact been ahead of other jurisdictions as far as corporate governance is concerned.

4.4 The Covid-19 pandemic and employee interests

The Covid-19 pandemic probably had a greater impact on society than any other event since World War II. Its impact was, and still is (December 2021), felt at every level of society. Affecting the fundamentals like personal and family relationships, causing the personal suffering of millions of people worldwide, not just for those who survived after being infected and for all those close to them, but also the indescribable suffering for millions of people close to people who died because of the coronavirus. In addition to the personal and emotional suffering of millions, the Covid-19 pandemic also rocked the economic foundations of the world. It revealed some serious cracks in probably the most dominant economic form, namely capitalism.[36] It is a significant issue, and requires discussion in a separate contribution, but for current purposes, it could just be mentioned that employees suffered tremendously. Millions of people lost their jobs, and the majority were left in the cold, not even receiving any government support as the magnitude of the economic crisis was such that governments could not step in. However, that is not the point as the question is why could corporations simply neglect their employees, the core corporate stakeholder. In a very powerful attack on the terrible neglect of social responsibilities of corporations, Strine and Lund drill down to the real impact on employees and ask fundamental questions about irresponsible and short-term, and short-sighted, approaches and behaviour of corporations during several years of huge economic growth for many American companies. They opined as follows:[37]

> After a 10-year economic expansion that led to record increases in earnings, plus huge corporate tax relief, American corporations should have had substantial cash reserves to sustain them during a short period without revenue. But many did not, and instead were highly leveraged, lacked adequate reserves and lived paycheck to paycheck, so to speak. What happened to that cash? Much of it was returned to shareholders in dividends and stock buybacks … At the same time, American corporations weakened the traditional gain-sharing between the workforce and stockholders that characterized the post-World War II era. During that period, when corporate profits went up, workers shared equitably in the gains. Not anymore.

The fundamental change in responsible profit-sharing by large corporations since the 1970s has been commented on in 2015 by the influential economist and former Chief Economist of the Bank of England, Andy Haldane. He pointed out that in 1970 only 10% of company profits were paid to shareholders as dividends. In 2015, the estimate was that 60%–70% of company profits were paid to shareholders as dividends.[38] A similar trend has been noticed by several studies into capital allocation of large public companies, with all concluding that a disproportionate percentage of company profits and financial resources available to companies are channelled to shareholders, either by way of dividend payments or share/stock buybacks by companies from their own shareholders.[39] All these studies illustrated one point very clearly, and that is that employees progressively were given shorter ends of the stick, with shareholders, directors and executives claiming longer ends of the stick.[40]

This resulted in a renewed interest in, and critical evaluation of, responsible capital allocation of large public companies.[41] In 2019, it was illustrated that American companies spend on average 61% of their tax savings on shareholders by way of dividend payments and share/stock buybacks, while only 6% of it is invested in employees.[42]

Even before Covid-19, the former Chief Justice of Delaware, Leo S. Stine, published an insightful paper on some of the most serious corporate law challenges we face this century. Under the insightful title, "A New Deal for This New Century: Making Our Economy Work for All", he makes out a convincing case for law reform, focusing on the neglected interests of workers/employees, the disproportionate gainsharing between employees and shareholders and why a drastic change is required to ensure sustainable long-term growth for corporations.[43]

For purposes of South African employee interests and how employee interests are acknowledged and protected through legal remedies is important, especially as through law reform proposals there are continuous efforts to provide more recognition and ways to ensure employee interests are not neglected. In the following part, the focus will be on employee interests in South Africa through the lens of corporate law and corporate governance. The protection of individual employee rights through individual contractual arrangements, collective bargaining, general labour legislation and Black economic empowerment (BEE) fall outside the scope of this chapter.

4.5 Employee interests in South Africa

It cannot be disputed that there is a particular problem regarding inequality and the huge gap between the rich and the poor in South Africa. According to the Gini Index, measuring the inequality between the income of the top-earning individual and the lowest-earning income groups, South Africa has the highest inequality coefficients in the world.[44] The most recent effort to accentuate this problem is a proposed amendment to the SACA that will require certain companies to disclose publicly the mean income of the highest-remunerated individuals and the mean remuneration of the lowest-paid employees.[45] It will have to be seen whether disclosure of this information will be enough to address the underlying problems caused by these inequalities of income or whether more drastic measures, at a national level, involving government involvement and initiatives will be required.

There are indeed some unique ways in which employee interests are protected under South African company law, including the right of employees to bring a statutory derivative action on behalf of the company for breaches of directors' duties or breaches of provisions of the SACA; employees' rights during liquidations, administration and rescue schemes; and the application by unions and employees to get directors declared "delinquent" or "under probation" and employees' rights to be informed about significant transactions and where the "insolvency and liquidity test" will find application, including loans and related party transactions to directors, to name but a few.[46]

In addition, companies can adopt employee shareholder schemes, and as part of the all-inclusive stakeholder approach of the King Reports, employee interests and informing employees are central in South Africa. Taken together, all these mechanisms catering for, and protecting employee interest, make South Africa a country where employees are indeed seen as a central part of corporations, and they have a place comparable to that of shareholders under South African company law and principles applicable to corporate governance. The South African Corporate Governance Code (King (I–IV) Reports) is an exemplar and envy of the world regarding an all-inclusive and deeply embedded stakeholder approach, including employee interests.

4.6 Conclusion and recommendations

South Africa has already made a choice in favour of an all-inclusive stakeholder corporate governance model and moved away from "shareholder capitalism" as it was seen in the past. It is recommended that by involving all stakeholder-orientated organisations and institutions, there is a concerted effort made to ensure all South African corporations are focused on the long-term and sustainable future of corporations.

From a distance, it seems as if organisations representing the interests of employees, shareholders, directors, customers, businesses and the community are all focusing on their own agendas. This silo-approach should be replaced by a harmonised, all-inclusive stakeholder approach. It will require that all parties should be brought together under an umbrella body to stimulate collaboration, rather than pulling in different directions. Such a combative approach is not in the best interests of all stakeholders, and it is not in the best interest of corporate South Africa, and neither is it in the best interest of the South African economy.

It seems, again from a distance, that the King Committee is an excellent starting point to promote the collaboration mentioned, but it will require an all-representative organisation (body), not dominated by, for instance, the Institute of Directors in Southern Africa NPC, to take ownership of such an initiative in the future. It is to be hoped that this challenge will be taken seriously and that steps will be taken to ensure the formation of such a representative body to oversee corporate governance on a continuous basis in South Africa.

Notes

1 Jean J du Plessis 'Company Law Developments in South Africa: Modernisation and Some Salient Features of the Companies Act 71 of 2008' (2012) 27 *Australian Journal of Corporate Law* 46.
2 Jean J du Plessis and Jim A Mathiopoulos 'Defences and Relief from Liability for Company Directors: Widening Protection to Stimulate Innovation' (2016) 31 *Australian Journal of Corporate Law* 287 295 and 297–299.
3 Ibid, 299–305.
4 Ibid, 305–309.
5 Nicholas Todd 'The Future of the Statutory Business Judgment Rule – Balancing Accountability and Protection' (2021) 38 *Company and Securities Law Journal* 515, 532–533.
6 Helena Stoop *The Role of Voluntary Corporate Governance Codes in the Interpretation and Application of the Statutory and Common Law Duties of the Company Director: A South African Perspective*. PhD, Thesis Law School Durham University (2019).
7 RP Austin 'What is Corporate Governance? Precepts and Legal Principles' (2005) *New Zealand Law Review* 335, 347–354.
8 I Esser and JJ du Plessis 'The Stakeholder Debate and Directors' Fiduciary Duties' (2007) 19 *South African Mercantile Law Journal* 346, 359–360.
9 Jean J du Plessis 'Directors' Duty to Act in the Best Interests of the Corporation: "Hard Cases Make Bad Law"' (2019) 34 *Australian Journal of Corporate Law* 3–26.
10 Jean J du Plessis 'Chapter 3: Some Myths and Fallacies Regarding Corporate Law and Corporate Governance: Have they Been Debunked in South Africa?' in Hermie Coetzee and Carika Fritz (eds) *De Serie Legenda, Developments in Commercial Law, Entrepreneurial Law* (Volume III) 40–61.
11 See https://www.ifrs.org/news-and-events/news/2021/11/ifrs-foundation-announces-issb-consolidation-with-cdsb-vrf-publication-of-prototypes/.
12 See https://www.ifrs.org/news-and-events/news/2021/11/ifrs-foundation-announces-issb-consolidation-with-cdsb-vrf-publication-of-prototypes/ and https://www.ifrs.org/content/dam/ifrs/groups/trwg/trwg-climate-related-disclosures-prototype.pdf.
13 I would like to thank Michael Bray, Professor of Practice, Deakin Business School, Deakin University, for helping me to draft this paragraph and making me aware of the latest developments from July–November 2021.
14 This part is based on Jean Jacques du Plessis 'Shareholder Primacy and other Stakeholder Interests' (2016) 34 *Company and Securities Law Review* 238–242.
15 A list of references, in chronological order, to some of the interesting debates and issues of the day in the early 1930s is useful as they are a scattered and diverse contribution.

AA Berle 'Corporate Powers as Powers in Trust' (1931) 2 *Harvard Law Review* 1049; E Merrick Dodd 'For Whom are Corporate Managers Trustees? (1932) *Harvard Law Review* 1145; AA Berle 'For Whom Corporate Managers Are Trustees: A Note' (1932) 45 *Harvard Law Review* 1365; AA Berle and GC Means *The Modern Corporation and Private Property* (1932); E Merrick Dodd, 'Book Review' (1933) *University of Pennsylvania Law Review* 782; EM Dodd 'Book Review' (1942) 9 *University of Chicago Law Review* 538.

16 AA Berle and GC Means (n 15)) 352–353.

17 Berle (n 15) 1365–1372.

18 Berle and Means (n 15) 352–353.

19 Illustrated so clearly by the classic case of *Salomon v Salomon & Co Ltd* [1897] AC 22.

20 See International Integrated Reporting Council, *The International IR Framework* (IIRC, 2013), http://integratedreporting.org/wp-content/uploads/2013/12/13-12-08-THE-INTERNATIONAL-IR-FRAMEWORK-2-1.pdf 2, 12–13.

21 Berle and Means (n 15) 352–353.

22 Berle (n 15) 1365–1372.

23 EM Dodd Book Review on ME Dimock & HK Hyde *Bureaucracy and Trusteeship in Large Corporations* (1940) in (1942) 9 *University of Chicago Law Review* 538 at 547.

24 Edward Freeman and David L Reed 'Stockholders and Stakeholders: A New Perspective on Corporate Governance' (1983) 26 *California Management Review* 88.

25 Thomas Donaldson and Lee E Preston 'The Stakeholder Theory of the Corporation: Concepts, Evidence, and Implications' (1995) 20(1) *The Academy of Management Review* 65.

26 See, in particular, the American Law Institute's *Principles of Corporate Governance and Structure: Restatement and Recommendations* Tentative Draft No 1 (1982); *Principles of Corporate Governance: Analysis and Recommendations* Tentative Draft No. 10 (1990) and *Principles of Corporate Governance: Analysis and Recommendation* Tentative Final Draft (1992), adopted and promulgated by the American Law Institute on 13 May 1992.

27 Frank Bold *The Modern Corporation: Statement on Company Law* (2014) http://www.purposeofcorporation.org/modern-corporation-statements.pdf; Jeroen Veldman, Filip Gregor and Paige Morrow *Corporate Governance for a Changing World: Report of a Global Roundtable Series* (2016) https://papers.ssrn.com/sol3/papers.cfm?abstract_id=2805497; Beate Sjåfjell *Companies, Markets and Sustainability* (2017) https://www.jus.uio.no/english/research/areas/companies/; and Beate Sjåfjell *SMART Project (Sustainable Market Actors for Responsible Trade)* (2016–2020) https://www.smart.uio.no/.

28 Paul Hawken *The Ecology of Commerce* (2010) at xii.

29 See https://www.blackrock.com/corporate/investor-relations/larry-fink-ceo-letter# and scroll down to the bottom of the page to get access to all the letters of Larry Fin since 2012.

30 Larry Fink 'A Sense of Purpose' (2018) *Letter to CEOs of Corporations in Which Blackrock Invested* https://www.blackrock.com/corporate/investor-relations/2018-larry-fink-ceo-letter.

31 Ibid.

32 Larry Fink 'A Sense of Purpose' (2019) *Letter to CEOs of Corporations in Which Blackrock Invested* https://www.blackrock.com/corporate/investor-relations/2019-larry-fink-ceo-letter.

33 See https://www.blackrock.com/corporate/investor-relations/larry-fink-ceo-letter and, in particular, video-link to interview with Fink on his 2020 letter to CEOs.

34 See https://www.blackrock.com/corporate/investor-relations/larry-fink-ceo-letter.

35 Ibid.

36 The British Academy *Future of the Corporation – Purpose Summit* (22 and 23 June 2020) https://www.thebritishacademy.ac.uk/programmes/future-of-the-corporation/#:~

:text=Purpose%20Summit&text=The%20Future%20of%20the%20Corporation,senior%20business%20and%20policy%20leaders.&text=The%20COVID%2D19%20pandemic%20has,the%20fault%2Dlines%20across%20society. (accessed on 24 November 2021).

37 Leo S Strine Jr. and Dorothy S Lund 'How to Restore Strength and Fairness to our Economy', New York Times (10 April 2020). For more sensationalised comment on the sad state of affairs, see Bruce MacEwen 'Leo Strine has a Few Thoughts on How We Screwed Up Corporate Governance' https://adamsmithesq.com/2020/04/leo-strine-has-a-few-thoughts-on-how-we-screwed-up-corporate-governance/ (accessed 24 November 2021).

38 Mentioned in Weldon 'Shareholder Power "Holding Back Economic Growth"', BBC (Online, 24 July 2015).

39 Jeff Desjardins 'The Controversy Around Stock Buybacks Explained', Visual Capitalist (online, 1 March 2019) https://www.visualcapitalist.com/stock-buybacks-explained/ (accessed on 24 November 2021); George Dallas 'COVID-19 and Capital Allocation, Harvard Law School Forum on Corporate Governance' Posted on 3 May 2020 https://drive.google.com/file/d/1Fi_MYOehZVdScUHiRd6mViyJz4fzDaqV/view (accessed on 24 November 2021).

40 Wolf Richter 'Intel & TSMC on Chip Shortage: After Blowing $84 Billion on Share Buybacks Since 2011 and Now Woefully Behind, Intel Clamors for $50 Billion in Subsidies for US Chip Industry', Wolf Street, May 3, 2021 https://wolfstreet.com/2021/05/03/intel-tsmc-on-chip-shortage-after-blowing-84-billion-on-share-buybacks-since-2011-and-now-woefully-behind-intel-clamors-for-50-billion-in-subsidies-for-us-chip-industry/ (accessed on 24 November 2021); Lawrence Mishel and Jessica Schieder 'CEO Compensations Surged in 2017' https://www.epi.org/publication/ceo-compensation-surged-in-2017/ (accessed 24 November 2021); John Shields, Michael O'Donnell & John O'Brien 'The Bucks Stops Here: Private Sector Executive Remuneration in Australia' Labor Council of NSW, https://www.researchgate.net/publication/242042789_The_Bucks_Stop_Here_Private_Sector_Executive_Remuneration_in_Australia (accessed 24 November 2021).

41 Dallas (n 39).

42 Desjardins (n 39).

43 Leo E Strine, Jr 'A New Deal for This New Century: Making Our Economy Work for All' (3–4 October 2019) https://www.law.nyu.edu/sites/default/files/Fair%20and%20Sustainable%20Capitalism%20Proposal%20-%20White%20Paper_09.26.19%20FINAL_0.pdf (accessed on 28 November 2021).

44 https://upload.wikimedia.org/wikipedia/commons/b/b1/GINI_index_World_Bank_up_to_2018.svg. See generally https://en.wikipedia.org/wiki/Gini_coefficient for other Gini comparative statistics.

45 See explanatory memorandum to the South African Company Amendment Bill, 2021 http://www.thedtic.gov.za/wp-content/uploads/Revised_Companies_Amendment_Bill-1_October2021.pdf par 2.2.2 and Part 5.

46 For more comprehensive discussion of these unique South African approaches to employee protection rights and employee interests, see Du Plessis (n 10) 40–61; Jean J du Plessis 'The South African Statutory Derivative Action: Background, Comparisons and Application' in *Jopie: Jurist, Mentor, Supervisor and Friend: Essays on the Law of Banking, Companies and Suretyship* (ed Chris Nagel), Juta (2017) at 261–281; Du Plessis (n 1) 46; and JJ du Plessis and PA Delport 'Delinquent Directors' And "Directors Under Probation": A Unique South African Approach Regarding Disqualification of Company Directors' (2017) 134 *South African Law Journal* 274–295.

Bibiliography

American Law Institute *Principles of Corporate Governance and Structure: Restatement and Recommendations* Tentative Draft No 1 (1982).

American Law Institute *Principles of Corporate Governance: Analysis and Recommendations* Tentative Draft No. 10 (1990).

R P Austin 'What is corporate governance? Precepts and legal principles' (2005) 3 *New Zealand Law Review* 335–364.

A A Berle 'Corporate powers as powers in trust' (1931) 2 *Harvard Law Review* 1049.

A A Berle 'For whom corporate managers are trustees: A note' (1932) 45 *Harvard Law Review* 1365.

A A Berle & G C Means *The Modern Corporation and Private Property* (1932).

B Bold *The Modern Corporation: Statement on Company Law* (2014) http://www.purposeofcorporation.org/modern-corporation-statements.pdf.

G Dallas 'COVID-19 and capital allocation, Harvard Law School forum on corporate governance' 3 May 2020 https://drive.google.com/file/d/1Fi_MYOehZVdScUHiRd6mViyJz4fzDaqV/view (accessed on 24 November 2021).

J Desjardins 'The controversy around stock buybacks explained' Visual Capitalist (online, 1 March 2019) https://www.visualcapitalist.com/stock-buybacks-explained/ (accessed on 24 November 2021).

E M Dodd 'Book review' (1933) 81(6) *University of Pennsylvania Law Review* 782.

E M Dodd 'For whom are corporate managers trustees?' (1932) 45 *Harvard Law Review* 1145.

E M Dodd 'Book review on ME Dimock & HK Hyde bureaucracy and trusteeship in large corporations' (1940) in (1942) 9 *University of Chicago Law Review* 538.

T Donaldson & L E Preston 'The stakeholder theory of the corporation: Concepts, evidence, and implications' (1995) 20.1 *The Academy of Management Review* 65.

J J Du Plessis 'Chapter 3: Some myths and fallacies regarding corporate law and corporate governance: Have they been debunked in South Africa?' in H Coetzee and C Fritz (eds) *De Serie Legenda, Developments in Commercial Law, Entrepreneurial Law (Volume III)* 40–61, 2019.

J J Du Plessis 'Company law developments in South Africa: Modernisation and some salient features of the Companies Act 71 of 2008' (2012) 27 *Australian Journal of Corporate Law* 46.

J J Du Plessis 'Directors' duty to act in the best interests of the corporation: "Hard cases make bad law"' (2019) 34 *Australian Journal of Corporate Law* 3–26.

J J Du Plessis 'The South African statutory derivative action: Background, comparisons and application' in Chris Nagel (ed) *Jopie: Jurist, Mentor, Supervisor and Friend: Essays on the Law of Banking, Companies and Suretyship* (Juta, 2017).

J J Du Plessis & P A Delport 'Delinquent directors' and "directors under probation": A unique South African approach regarding disqualification of company directors' (2017) 134 *South African Law Journal* 274–295.

J J Du Plessis & J A Mathiopoulos 'Defences and relief from liability for company directors: Widening protection to stimulate innovation' (2016) 31 *Australian Journal of Corporate Law* 287–299.

I Esser & J J Du Plessis 'The stakeholder debate and directors' fiduciary duties' (2007) 19 *South African Mercantile Law Journal* 346.

Explanatory Memorandum to the South African Company Amendment Bill, 2021 http://www.thedtic.gov.za/wp-content/uploads/Revised_Companies_Amendment_Bill-1_October2021.pdf.

F Fink 'A sense of purpose' 2019 Letter to CEOs of corporations in which BlackRock invested https://www.blackrock.com/corporate/investor-relations/2019-larry-fink-ceo-letter

L Fink 'A sense of purpose' 2018 Letter to CEOs of corporations in which BlackRock invested https://www.blackrock.com/corporate/investor-relations/2018-larry-fink-ceo-letter

E Freeman & D L Reed 'Stockholders and stakeholders: A new perspective on corporate governance' (1983) 26 *California Management Review* 88.

P Hawken *The Ecology of Commerce* (Harper Collins, 2010).

https://en.wikipedia.org/wiki/Gini_coefficient.

https://upload.wikimedia.org/wikipedia/commons/b/b1/GINI_index_World_Bank_up_to_2018.svg.

https://www.blackrock.com/corporate/investor-relations/larry-fink-ceo-letter#.

https://www.blackrock.com/corporate/investor-relations/larry-fink-ceo-letter.

https://www.ifrs.org/news-and-events/news/2021/11/ifrs-foundation-announces-issb-consolidation-with-cdsb-vrf-publication-of-prototypes/.

https://www.ifrs.org/news-and-events/news/2021/11/ifrs-foundation-announces-issb-consolidation-with-cdsb-vrf-publication-of-prototypes/.

International Integrated Reporting Council The International IR Framework (IIRC, 2013), http://integratedreporting.org/wp-content/uploads/2013/12/13-12-08-THE-INTERNATIONAL-IR-FRAMEWORK-2-1.pdf.

King IV Report on Corporate Governance for South Africa 2016 (King IV), 1 November 2016.

B MacEwen 'Leo Strine has a few thoughts on how we screwed up corporate governance' https://adamsmithesq.com/2020/04/leo-strine-has-a-few-thoughts-on-how-we-screwed-up-corporate-governance/.

L Mishel & J Schieder 'CEO compensations surged in 2017' https://www.epi.org/publication/ceo-compensation-surged-in-2017/ (accessed on 24 November 2021).

Principles of Corporate Governance: Analysis and Recommendation Tentative Final Draft (1992).

W Richter 'Intel & TSMC on chip shortage: After blowing $84 billion on share buybacks since 2011 and now woefully behind, intel clamors for $50 billion in subsidies for US chip industry' *Wolf Street* 3 May 2021 https://wolfstreet.com/2021/05/03/intel-tsmc-on-chip-shortage-after-blowing-84-billion-on-share-buybacks-since-2011-and-now-woefully-behind-intel-clamors-for-50-billion-in-subsidies-for-us-chip-industry/ (accessed on 24 November 2021).

J Shields, M O'Donnell & J O'Brien 'The bucks stops here: Private sector executive remuneration in Australia' Labor Council of NSW, PDF downloadable at https://www.researchgate.net/publication/242042789_The_Bucks_Stop_Here_Private_Sector_Executive_Remuneration_in_Australia (accessed on 24 November 2021).

B Sjåfjell *Companies, Markets and Sustainability* (2017) https://www.jus.uio.no/english/research/areas/companies/.

B Sjåfjell *SMART Project (Sustainable Market Actors for Responsible Trade)* (2016–2020) https://www.smart.uio.no/.

H Stoop *The Role of Voluntary Corporate Governance Codes in the Interpretation and Application of the Statutory and Common Law Duties of the Company Director: A South African Perspective* (PhD Thesis Law School Durham University, 2019).

Jr L S Strine & D S Lund 'How to restore strength and fairness to our economy' *New York Times* 10 April 2020.
Jr L E Strine 'A new deal for this new century: Making our economy work for all' (3–4 October 2019) https://www.law.nyu.edu/sites/default/files/Fair%20and%20Sustainable%20Capitalism%20Proposal%20-%20White%20Paper_09.26.19%20FINAL_0.pdf (accessed on 28 November 2021).
The British Academy *Future of the Corporation – Purpose Summit* (22 and 23 June 2020) https://www.thebritishacademy.ac.uk/programmes/future-of-the-corporation/#:~:text=Purpose%20Summit&text=The%20Future%20of%20the%20Corporation,senior%20business%20and%20policy%20leaders.&text=The%20COVID%2D19%20pandemic%20has,the%20fault%2Dlines%20across%20society.
N Todd 'The future of the statutory business judgment rule – Balancing accountability and protection' (2021) 38 *Company and Securities Law Journal* 515.
J Veldman, F Gregor & P Morrow *Corporate Governance for a Changing World: Report of a Global Roundtable Series* (2016) https://papers.ssrn.com/sol3/papers.cfm?abstract_id=2805497.

5 Impact of financial education on financial literacy and financial inclusion in Namibia

Eukeria Wealth, Tendai D. Svotwa and Charles Makanyeza

5.1 Introduction

The dawn of the global financial crisis has brought to light the importance of financial inclusion (FI). Financial inclusion deals with the quality and availability of financial products on offer as well as equality of opportunities to access these financial services timeously.[1] Financial inclusion has been identified as an important tool not only to curtail the global financial crisis effects but to the realisation of the United Nations' Sustainable Development Goals (SDGs). It has been associated with high economic growth and poverty reduction,[2] a macro-economic fundamental that most African states are battling with. The literature concedes on the undeniable benefits of financial inclusion in socio-economic development.[3] These include improved financial attitude and financial behaviour that translates to the increased usage of financial products and a stable financial system.[4] Despite the optimism regarding the effects of FI on socio-economic development, it has remained very low in Africa[5] with levels as low as 23%.[6] This was further buttressed by scholars who reported uptake levels of basic financial products in Sub-Saharan Africa to be as low as 10%.[7] In a survey conducted between 2008 and 2012, Namibia scored lowest at 4% financial inclusion compared with a cohort of its African counterparts.[8] Such a paltry level of financial inclusion implies that the bulk of Namibia's population is financially excluded from the country's financial system, which also suggests relatively lower levels of economic growth and that the country is not anywhere close to achieving the poverty alleviation goal.

A significant number of adults (37%) aged 15 years and above were reported to have professed ignorance about money and finance, with 68% remaining unbanked and only 43% banked (have/use bank products with traditional banks) in Namibia.[9] Unbanked consumers refer to businesses and individuals who are served by other regulated financial institutions such as credit providers, microfinance banks and other institutions' insurance companies.[10] This reveals a need for policymakers, the government and academics to take responsibility and consider the implications of this status quo for the country. One way is to identify drivers of financial inclusion in order to inform policy and produce strategies that improve financial inclusion for the 96% financially excluded Namibian population. While the literature suggests numerous drivers of financial inclusion such

DOI: 10.4324/9781003369400-5

as ICT,[11] banking services,[12] the internet and mobile phones,[13] political will[14] and the regulatory framework and physical infrastructure,[15] the importance of financial education is emphasised.[16] The Organisation for Economic Cooperation and Development (OECD) defines financial education as the process by which individuals gain an understanding of financial products and concepts, and through information, instruction and advice develop skills and confidence to become more conscious of financial risks and opportunities to make informed judgements to improve financial security.[17]

Four benefits of financial education to financial inclusion include minimising demand-side barriers to financial inclusion, empowering consumers in managing personal resources, relevancy for SMEs and improved financial market efficiency.[18] With all these anticipated benefits, financial education has been described as low in underdeveloped countries, including in Africa. While the formulation of national strategies by governments is commendable, research argues that their impact remains anecdotal, thus making this study an important tool for policymakers.[19] Research on financial inclusion in Namibia is scant, and the few available studies[20] have concentrated on the supply side of financial inclusion, neglecting the demand-side such as the level of education, which is central to this chapter.

This chapter, therefore, seeks to assess the effects of financial education on the financial inclusion of vulnerable groups specifically in Namibia, a Southern African country whose financial inclusion levels are very low, financial education efforts have been handicapped by an unclear policy framework and financial literacy programmes have been excluded from the formal education system (Namibia Financial Sector Strategy NFSS, 2011). There is a lack of evidence of the effects of financial education on financial inclusion, especially in the Namibian context, thus, this chapter will help policymakers devise strategies that address their specific needs for improved financial inclusion. With the current global financial crisis, the need for financial education for the average person and society at large cannot be overemphasised.

5.2 Financial inclusion and financial education in Namibia

Poverty is a common phenomenon in Namibia. Despite several interventions that have been proposed to alleviate poverty in Namibia, more efforts are required. High poverty levels have been inter alia attributed to low levels of education and limited access to financial services.[21] The Covid-19 pandemic has caused a further strain on the already affected Namibian population. The situation deteriorated for most people, especially the vulnerable who were financially excluded. Financial exclusion levels deepened with the lockdowns, loss of income and so on, as many became more distant from financial tools, products and services. This is sad, especially when there is compelling evidence that financial inclusion reduces poverty and income inequality.[22] A study that focused particularly on Namibia has shown that financial inclusion assuages poverty by creating wealth through increased access to financial products and improved financial attitude and behaviour.[23] A positive financial attitude and behaviour have been found to be demonstrated by financially literate individuals. The bulk of the Namibian populace remains unbanked as a result of its ignorance of financial products and financial management.[24] Not only that, outstanding debts and poor savings have become common problems in Namibia. High attrition rates have also been experienced in higher learning institutions as parents are heavily indebted and the Namibia Students Financial Assistance Fund (NSFAF) cannot sponsor everyone. All this has led to the establishment of intervention programmes by various stakeholders.

The Ministry of Finance Bank of Namibia and Namibia Financial Institutions Supervisory Authority (NAMFISA) embarked on financial literacy programmes in order to financially educate and promote financial inclusion of its vulnerable population groups. The initiatives were targeted at training and empowering youths, pupils, SMEs and low-income earners on budgeting, saving, borrowing and making financial decisions. However, the financial inclusion levels of Namibia have remained very low, the literacy programmes were fragmented, uncoordinated, duplicated and short of a clear teaching and learning framework (Namibia financial sector strategy 2011–2021). Since the inception of the financial literacy programmes, formative and summative assessments are barely conducted. This has implications for the identification of areas of deviation and the possibility of taking corrective action.

Learning institutions from elementary levels to higher levels have barely any financial education programmes yet financial education is a major driver of financial literacy. The non-inclusion of financial literacy courses in Namibian formal schools and higher learning institutions precludes learners from becoming financially literate. This has really affected young people and youth who are often faced with complex financial decisions and responsibilities such as debt management and student loan management. This is a major economic challenge as young people may carry their family's financial struggles into adulthood. Unfortunately, Namibia has no legislation in place to ensure consumers are educated on financial products. Through financial education, one is expected to gain financial literacy that has some level of awareness, knowledge, attitude, skill and behaviour. A combination of these is envisaged to improve the financial welfare of individuals, families and society at large. Although other studies argue that financial inclusion is more likely to be found in people with basic education than financial education.[25]

Financial education at school may serve as a strategy to thwart youth from making grave financial decisions and help them manage global financial crises. However, the Namibian education system is faced with a plethora of challenges, which include weak policies, a lack of infrastructure and a lack of teacher capacity. The literature emphasises the need to distinguish between perceived and actual competencies of being financially literate and being sufficiently financially literate to teach financial education-related topics.[26] Some studies affirm the deficiencies in teacher proficiencies to teach financial education, with findings revealing that more than 60% of teachers fail to meet the minimum scores of financial attitude and depict a lack of subject-matter knowledge and skills, thus causing scepticism in their ability to impart the same on students.[27] Furthermore, the educational programmes, pedagogical approaches and teaching methodologies and aids are not harmonised. Other scholars stress that financial education initiatives need to be coordinated and tailor-made to suit the information needs of targeted groups such as young adults.[28] A cross-country analysis using Programme for International Student Assessment (PISA) data revealed that financial literacy is enhanced when financial education courses are taught by industry experts and non-governmental organisations rather than school teachers.[29]

Namibia is also blamed for its lack of up-to-date national baseline data, which compromises proper assessment of financial education efforts. The weak and fragmented policy framework stalls the effective implementation of programmes that capacitate individuals in terms of financial knowledge and management. The financial landscape has changed drastically with completely new and complex financial products such as cryptocurrencies, complex insurance products and so on, so a lack of financial knowledge makes life difficult for most people, especially the vulnerable. Financial education is a continuum that provides individuals with continuous updates on the financial landscape that is relentlessly evolving. It exposes them to financial knowledge, awareness and skills for the purposes of making financial plans and judgements concerning four financial elements; (i) debt, (ii) income, (iii) expenses and (iv) assets, which are often misunderstood and mismanaged. Consumers require information relating to risk management and protection since they are vulnerable to financial insecurities due to the complexity and dynamism of financial products. A study conducted in Namibia found that policies that improve education levels, financial knowledge and access to financial products of vulnerable groups enhance financial inclusion.[30]

Financial education plays a key role in fostering financial literacy, yet it remains fragmented and polarised in Namibia. Namibia is among the African countries that have deficient policies, relatively low school enrolment ratios, high student attrition rates, high income inequalities and low financial inclusion and literacy levels. A study conducted in Namibia has shown that there is a lack of harmony between policies and students' learning experiences, thus hindering inclusive education.[31] Another study revealed that limited government support and a lack of financial and marketing skills negatively affect women entrepreneurs in Namibia.[32] This problem is not peculiar to Namibia but has been confirmed in many African states as it hinders financial literacy of the thriving sector of SMEs.[33] Financial education requires concerted efforts from all stakeholders such as institutions of higher learning and financial institutions as well as political will. Support from banking institutions is necessary to complement educational programmes with financial education courses from primary level to tertiary level as well as school leavers and entrepreneurs. Financial inclusion remains low in Namibia, while financial literacy levels are very low and financial education underdeveloped.

5.3 The relationship between financial education, literacy and financial inclusion

Financial inclusion has several drivers. However, surveys have revealed that financial illiteracy is the main obstacle to financial inclusion in Africa.[34] Financial illiteracy is widespread with only one out of three adults being financially literate worldwide. Financial literacy refers to the knowledge and understanding of financial matters, risks and concepts and the ability to apply such knowledge in real-life financial decision-making processes.[35] Financial literacy is the primary goal of financial education. Financial education helps consumers to handle financial matters. This includes the ability to manage personal finances and make shrewd financial decisions as well as plan for future financial needs. The literature explains how financial inclusion without financial education is risky as policies that focus on the supply side of financial services while neglecting the demand side leave vulnerable groups uninformed and reluctant to participate in financial markets.[36] Financial inclusion entails access to financial products, financial knowledge, the right financial attitude and behaviour and the ability to make sound financial decisions concerning savings and debt management. Most of these behaviours and financial dispositions are modelled by financial literacy, which is a product of financial education. The literature provides a wealth of evidence on the relationship between these elements. Heuristic research has found a significant positive association between financial literacy and financial inclusion and that financial education improves financial literacy.[37]

Financial education enhances financial literacy by building consumer confidence to select financial services suitable for them and managing their spending, saving and borrowing abilities.[38] It is through financial education that consumers learn about investment, risk diversification, debt management, complex financial products, compound interest, homeownership and retirement savings. Even women in entrepreneurship are positively influenced by financial training programmes.[39] Financial education programmes can be delivered through platforms such as workshops, social networks, seminars, radio, television and online lectures. The benefits of multiple learning platforms and different learning methods are manifold as they cater for diverse groups of consumers. Exploring various teaching styles and learning modes is important since the efficacy of teaching methods has shown inconsistent results,[40] for example, Kenya's classroom training on saving, targeted at school children, has proved to be ineffective. While South Africa's debt management on low-income households through a soap opera has proved effective and Uganda's financial education results administered through seminars remained inconclusive. South Africa has placed a legal obligation on financial institutions and the regulatory board (South African Financial Services Board) to educate and inform consumers.[41] Namibia's policies need to be responsive to financial literacy needs. There is an undisputed need for financial education programmes that offer differentiated learning styles and custom-made content for specific audiences.[42] Nonetheless, it is essential to note that financial education can be attained in various settings such as parental or family interactions, workplaces, church attendance and academic or professional modes.[43] All these modes have the potential to reinforce financial attitudes and behaviours.

Research has shown that a properly designed financial education programme significantly improves financial knowledge and behaviour such as saving and spending habits of students and citizens.[44] Financial education courses and topics such as money management, money saving, debt management, personal banking and financial planning are crucial to empower young people, entrepreneurs and adults to make prudent financial decisions that ultimately transform their financial well-being. However, other scholars believe that financial literacy does not improve simply by attending a money management course unless money management principles are embedded in another course.[45] All stakeholders in Namibia's financial inclusion have to draw lessons from other countries and incorporate various strategies in their financial education programmes that empower both the young and the poor in the short and long term.

While others opine that financial literacy has no impact on financial inclusion, illiterate communities in Namibia remain marginalised and impoverished. Illiteracy is detrimental to consumers as they fail to identify financial opportunities and appreciate the risks involved in financial transactions and their rights as consumers. Financial education is essential for consumers to remain informed and guided. Studies have shown that financial education has a positive impact on financial knowledge and behaviour.[46] The pillars of financial education include (i) building bank-mindedness; (ii) building public awareness of financial products and consumer rights; and (iii) building risk consciousness. These pillars help regulate the behaviour of consumers and flexibly manage their finances and improve their financial well-being.[47] Financial education answers financial illiteracy problems.

Similarly, financial literacy is positively correlated to financial inclusion. Individuals who received financial education scored higher in financial literacy, and consumers with low financial literacy ratings were found to be demonstrating undesirable financial behaviour compared with those with high ratings.[48] Financial literacy involves two main dimensions, which are financial knowledge (understanding) and application of this knowledge, and these can only be attained through educating consumers.[49] A complete understanding of financial matters will result in the appropriate application of the knowledge to challenging financial puzzles and the ultimate financial wellness of consumers. Substantial evidence confirms that those who receive financial education are less likely to struggle with debts, be it student loans, business loans or consumer loans.[50] Financial inclusion is close to impossible without proper financial literacy.[51]

Financial literacy is an essential competence that enables both the young and the elderly to participate in financial markets. It stimulates demand for financial products, thus accelerating financial inclusion. As consumers become aware of financial products and start appreciating financial risks and consumer rights, the higher the chances for them to consume financial services. A study has confirmed a significant positive impact of financial literacy on small enterprises and financial inclusion.[52] Another study found increased financial literacy in young people arising from financial education,[53] on the contrary, others found financial education in higher learning institutions not advantageous to those without such education.[54] Financial literacy is expected to prepare consumers for dire financial situations by equipping them with financial tools that help them make wise credit decisions, acquire assets and insurance as well as conduct budgeting and saving for

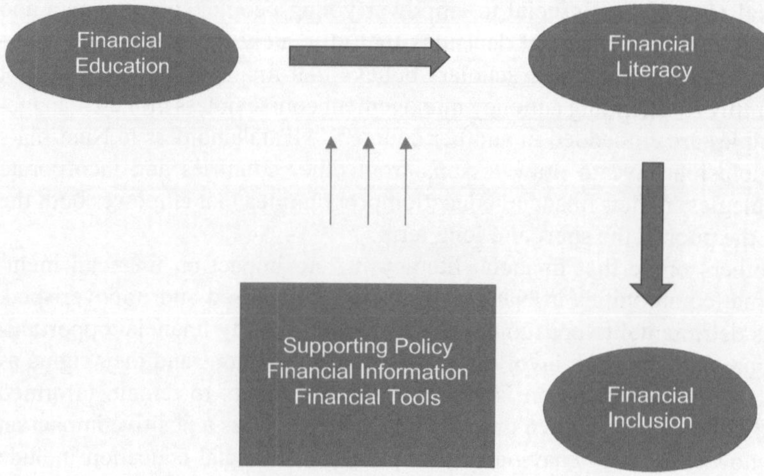

Figure 5.1 Conceptual framework own compilation (2021).

the future. One study argues that the higher the financial education and income level, the higher the financial knowledge.[55] The knowledge forges a certain financial behaviour in consumers that includes settlement of debts on time, investing, accumulating savings and financial risk mitigation.

The major determinant of financial literacy is the quality of financial education where the effectiveness is influenced by the strength of the existing policies, the availability of financial tools and the quality of financial information. Financial education is a potent tool for improving planning and managing savings and spending. The relationship among these elements is illustrated in Figure 5.1.

5.4 Conclusion

Financial inclusion has attracted global attention, and Namibia has very low levels of financial inclusion that continue to aggravate inequality levels among the citizens. The literature has shown that financial literacy is a major determinant of financial inclusion. This chapter sought to assess the impact of financial education on financial literacy and financial inclusion. The chapter revealed that while there are conflicting views regarding the efficacy of education in influencing financial literacy and financial inclusion, many authors concede that they are positively correlated. The disparities are largely explained by the strength of supporting policies, the type of financial education programmes, the learning styles applied, teacher capabilities and the teaching channels employed. The chapter also revealed that financial illiteracy remains a major obstacle to financial inclusion in Namibian as the financial education system is fragmented and highly uncoordinated among stakeholders. This is mainly attributed to weak policies and the non-existence of a teaching and learning framework. Teachers are also not capacitated to impart financial knowledge and skills sufficient to influence the desired financial literacy levels and ultimately financial inclusion.

Namibia can draw lessons from other success stories of effective teaching strategies such as South Africa's soap opera as well as legislating the duty to educate consumers about NAMFISA. Such informal education channels, including family, workplace and church interactions, should not be neglected as they complement formal education programmes since they are not motivated by pervasive academic grades.[56] South Africa also introduced other initiatives such as developing learning resources for grade 10–12 teachers called "Managing your money" and financial literacy workshops between tertiary institutions and the Department of Higher Education[57]. Certain financial education practices such as the timing of financial education programmes are crucial. Namibia can learn from scholarly work[58] that advocates for the incorporation of financial education curriculum in elementary schools as this is envisaged to shape personal behaviours and yield a saving culture, high credit scores, lower levels of non-performing loans and financial stability in the future. With high student attrition in Namibia, delaying financial education has negative ramifications as many will miss the opportunity to be financially literate.

This chapter is important in the context of expanding financial education interventions in the face of dwindling savings, complex financial systems, over-indebtedness and heterogeneous financial education systems. There is a need for well-coordinated financial education programmes entrenched with tailor-made content and teaching strategies that promote financial literacy to marginalised population groups within Namibia. This requires concerted efforts by stakeholders such as the Ministry of Education, financial institutions, the Ministry of Finance, parents and employers. Financial institutions should also complement formal financial programmes with just-in-time training such as debt therapy, retirement savings and so on for teachers and consumers. Both national and institutional strategies should be structured in a manner that arrests financial ignorance and financial exclusion. One effective way to produce results would be to adopt what South Africa did and legislate the duty to educate consumers on the regulatory board. Financial education is essential in that it is the foundation for financial literacy and virtually all financial inclusion efforts, hence the need to increase financial literacy in Namibia should be underscored.

Notes

1 A Grohmann et al. 'Does Financial Literacy Improve Financial Inclusion? Cross Country Evidence' (2018) *World Development Discussion Paper No. 95* 84–96.
2 P Mader 'Contesting Financial Inclusion' (2018) *Development and Change* 461–483.
3 PK Ozili 'Financial Inclusion Research Around the World: A Review' (2020) *Forum for Social Economics* 1 2. See also A Zins and L Weill 'The Determinants of Financial Inclusion in Africa' (2016) 6 *Review of Development Finance* 1 2.
4 MK Refera et al. 'Financial Literacy for Developing Countries in Africa: A Review of Concept, Significance and Research Opportunities' (2016) *Journal of African Studies and Development* 1–12.

5 T Chinoda and F Kwenda 'Do Mobile Phones, Economic Growth, Bank Competition and Stability Matter for Financial Inclusion in Africa?' (2019) 7 *Cogent Economics & Finance* 1–21.
6 O Evans 'The Effects of Economic and Financial Development on Financial Inclusion in Africa' (2015) 1 *Review of Economic and Development Studies* 17–25.
7 L Xu and B Zia 'Financial Literacy Around the World: An Overview of The Evidence With Practical Suggestions for the Way Forward' (2012) *The World Bank Policy Research Working Paper 6107* 1–56; J Kendall et al. 'Measuring Financial Access Around the World' (2010) *World Bank Policy Research Working Paper 5253* 1–65.
8 LO Oyelami et al. 'Determinants of Financial Inclusion in Sub-Sahara African Countries' (2017) 8 *Covenant Journal of Business & Social Sciences* 104–116
9 FinMark Trust 'FinScope Consumer Survey Namibia' (2012) http://www.finmark. Org .za/publication/finscope-consumer-surveynamibia-2011. Accessed May 2021.
10 SADC 'Financial Inclusion Strategy 2016–2021' (2016) 12.
11 S Bisht and V Mishra 'ICT-Driven Financial Inclusion Initiatives for Urban Poor in a Developing Economy: Implications for Public Policy' (2016) 35 *Behaviour & Information Technology* 817–832.
12 T Lal 'Impact of Financial Inclusion on Poverty Alleviation through Cooperative Banks' (2018) 45 *International Journal of Social* 808–828.
13 E Olaniyi 'Connecting the Poor: The Internet, Mobile Phones and Financial Inclusion in Africa' (2018) 20 *Digital Policy Regulation and Governance* 568–581.
14 RM Sahay 'Financial Inclusion: Can it Meet Multiple Macroeconomic Goals?' (2015) *IMF Staff Discussion Note*.
15 World Bank 'UFA2020 Overview: Universal Financial Access by 2020' (2018).
16 MK Refera et al. 'Financial Literacy for Developing Countries in Africa: A Review of Concept, Significance and Research Opportunities' (2016) Journal of African Studies and Development 1–12; A Atkinson and F Messy 'Promoting Financial Inclusion through Financial Education: OECD/INFE Evidence, Policies and Practice' (2013) *OECD Working Papers on Finance Insurance and Private Pensions, No. 34* 1–55.
17 OECD 'Improving Financial Literacy: Analysis of Issues and Policies' (2005) OECD Publishing 1–180.
18 FA Messy and C Monticone 'The Status of Financial Education in Africa' (2012) *OECD Working Papers on Finance Insurance and Private Pensions No. 25* 1–93.
19 PK Ozili 'Financial Inclusion Research Around the World: A Review' (2020) *Forum for Social Economics* 1–23.
20 NS Shaninga *Poverty Reduction through Access to Financial Services in Rural Areas of Namibia: A Case study of Omusati Region* (Masters Dissertation, University of Capetown, 2018); C Samundengu *Supply-Side Data and Measurement for Financial Inclusion: A Case Study of Namibia* (Masters Dissertation, UNAM 2014) and LJ Tshoopara *Problems Affecting the Growth of Microfinance Institutions In Namibia: An Operational, Regulatory And Legislative Perspective* (master's dissertation, UKZN, 2012).
21 Shaninga (master's dissertation, University of Cape Town, 2018).
22 MA Omar and K Inaba 'Does Financial Inclusion Reduce Poverty and Income Inequality in Developing Countries? A Panel Data Analysis' (2020) 9 *Journal of Economic Structures* 1 1; EA Özşuca 'Does Financial Inclusion Affect Poverty and Income Inequality? Evidence from Emerging and Developing Countries' in K Natsuda et al. *Globalisation and Public Policy* (2019) 63.
23 E.T Hasheela *Access to Finance and Financial Inclusion in Namibia* (master's thesis, University of Stellenbosch, 2013) 12.
24 FinScope 'Consumer Survey Namibia' (2011).
25 P Kostov et al. 'Access to Financial Services: The Case of the 'Mzansi' Account in South Africa' (2015) *Review of Development Finance* 32.
26 KD Bekker et al. 'The Capabilities of Secondary School Teachers to Provide Financial Education' (2019) 18(2) *Citizenship, Social and Economics Education* 66–81.

27 D Otter *Teaching Financial Literacy in K-12 Schools: A Survey of Teacher Beliefs and Knowledge* (PhD Thesis, The University of New Mexico, 2010). See also Bekker et al. (2019) Citizenship, Social and Economics Education 66–81.

28 W Walstad et al. 'Perspectives on Evaluation in Financial Education: Landscape, Issues, and Studies' (2017) *The Journal of Economic Education* 93–112.

29 JM Cordero et al. 'Financial Education and Student Financial Literacy: A Cross-Country Analysis Using PISA 2012 Data' (2020) *The Social Science Journal* 1–19.

30 A Mukong et al. 'A Decomposition of the Gender Gap in Financial Inclusion: Evidence from Namibia African' (2020) 15 *Journal of Business and Economic Research* 149–169.

31 C Kaliinasho et al. 'Inclusive Education Policies versus Practices: Exclusion of the Included' (2019) *Journal for Studies in Humanities and Social Sciences* 141–170.

32 E Madalena and M Semente 'Women Entrepreneurship in Namibia: Challenges and Prospects International' (2019) 6 *Journal of Applied Management Sciences and Engineering* 1–14.

33 HA Abubakar 'Entrepreneurship Development and Financial Literacy in Africa' (2015) 11 *World Journal of Entrepreneurship, Management and Sustainable Development* 281–294.

34 Messy and Monticone (2012) *OECD Working Papers on Finance Insurance and Private Pensions No. 25* 1–93; See also S Chikalipah 'What Determines Financial Inclusion in Sub-Saharan Africa?' (2017) 8(1) *African Journal of Economic and Management Studies* 8–18.

35 P PISA 'PISA 2015 Results (Volume IV): Students' Financial Literacy' (2017) *Paris: OECD Publishing.* See also N Fabris and R Luburić 'Financial Education of Children and Youth' (2016) 5(2) *Journal of Central Banking Theory and Practice* 65–79.

36 A Atkinson and F Messy 'Assessing Financial Literacy in 12 OECD Countries AN OECD Exercise' (2011) *Journal of Pension Economics & Finance* 657–665; I Peña-López 'Financial Literacy Framework' in *OECD, PISA 2012 Assessment and Analytical Framework: Mathematics, Reading, Science, Problem Solving and Financial Literacy* (2012) OECD Publishing.

37 A Grohmann et al. 'Does Financial Literacy Improve Financial Inclusion? Cross Country Evidence' (2018) *Discussion Paper, No. 95* 84–96; R Mindra et al. 'Financial Self-Efficacy: A Determinant of Financial Inclusion' (2017) 35 *International Journal of Bank Marketing* 338–353.

38 A Mehrotra and J Yetma 'Financial Inclusion Issues for Central Banks' (2015) *BIS Quarterly Review* 83–96. See also T Kaiser and L Menkhoff 'Does Financial Education Impact Financial Literacy and Financial Behavior, and If So, When?' (2017) World Bank Report https://openknowledge.worldbank.org/handle/10986/31469.

39 N Baporikar and S Akino 'Financial Literacy Imperative for Success of Women Entrepreneurship' (2020) 11 *International Journal of Innovation in the Digital Economy* 1–21.

40 MF Pang 'Enhancing the Financial Literacy of Young People: A Conceptual Approach Based on the Variation Theory of Learning' (2016) *International Handbook of Financial Literacy* 587–602.

41 G Pearson et al. 'Balancing Responsibilities – Financial Literacy' (2017) 20 *Potchefstroom Electronic Law Journal* 1–55.

42 A Lusardi 'Financial Literacy and the Need for Financial Education: Evidence and Implications' (2019) 155 *Swiss Journal of Economics and Statistics* 1–8.

43 L Fan and S Chatterjee 'Financial Socialization, Financial Education, and Student Loan Debt' (2019) *Journal of Family and Economic Issues* 74–75; SM Danes et al. 'Evaluation of Financial Literacy Development of High School Students: A Longitudinal Mixed Methods Study' (2016) *International Handbook of Financial Literacy* 425–447.

44 CJ Asarta et al. 'The Features and Effectiveness of the Keys to Financial Success Curriculum' (2014) 16 *International Review of Economics Education* 39–50; DW Rothwell and S Wu 'Exploring the Relationship between Financial Education and Financial Knowledge and Efficacy: Evidence from the Canadian Financial Capability Survey' (2019) *The Journal of Consumer Affairs* 1725–1727.

45 J Farinella et al. 'The Impact of Financial Education on Financial Literacy and Spending Habits' (2017) 11 *International Journal of Business, Accounting, and Finance* 1–12; JM Cordero and F Pedraja 'The Effect of Financial Education Training on the Financial Literacy of Spanish Students in PISA' (2019) 51 *Applied Economics* 1679–1693.

46 K.D Bekker et al. 'The Capabilities of Secondary School Teachers To Provide Financial Education' (2019) 18 *Citizenship, Social and Economics Education* 66–68; JJ Xiao and B O'Neill B 'Consumer Financial Education And Financial Capability' (2016) 40 *International Journal of Consumer Studies* 712–721; and JM Cordero et al. 'Financial Education and Student Financial Literacy: A Cross-Country Analysis Using PISA 2012 Data' (2020) *The Social Science Journal* 1–19.

47 A Antonietti et al. 'A Metacognitive Approach to Financial Literacy' (2016) *International Handbook of Financial Literacy, Springer* 57; U Singh 'Financial Literacy and Financial Stability are Two Aspects of Efficient Economy' (2014) *Journal of Finance, Accounting and Management* 59–76.

48 JJ Xiao and B O'Neill B 'Consumer Financial Education and Financial Capability' (2016) 40 International Journal of Consumer Studies 712–721.

49 K.D Bekker et al. 'The Capabilities of Secondary School Teachers to Provide Financial Education' (2019) 18 *Citizenship, Social and Economics Education* 66–67.

50 L Fan and S Chatterjee 'Financial Socialization, Financial Education, and Student Loan Debt' (2019) *Journal of Family and Economic Issues* 74–75.

51 V S Dube and P Asthana 'A Comparative Study on Financial Literacy of Uttar Pradesh with Central Zone States in India' (2017) 19 *Journal of Business and Management* 22–27.

52 P A Sanistasya et al. 'The Effect of Financial Literacy and Financial Inclusion on Small Enterprises Performance in East Kalimantan' (2019) 14 *Jurnal Economia* 48.

53 M Brown et al. 'Financial Education and the Debt Behavior of The Young' (2016) 29 *The Review of Financial Studies* 2490–2522.

54 L Mandell & KO Hanson 'The Impact of Financial Education in High School and College on Financial Literacy and Subsequent Financial Decision Making' (2009) *American Economic Association Meetings* 1–38.

55 S Heenkkenda 'Inequalities in the Financial Inclusion in Sri Lanka: An Assessment of the Functional Financial Literacy' (2015) *MPRA Paper No. 67293* 35 https://mpra.ub.uni-muenchen.de/67293/.

56 V Frisancho 'The Impact of Financial Education for Youth' (2019) *IDB Working Paper Series No. IDB-WP-1038.*

57 G Pearson et al. (2017) 20 *Potchefstroom Electronic Law Journal* 1–55.

58 JM Collins and E Odders-White 'Framework for Developing and Testing Financial Capability Education Programs Targeted to Elementary Schools' (2015) 46 *The Journal of Economic Education* 105–120.

Bibliography

H A Abubakar 'Entrepreneurship development and financial literacy in Africa' (2015) 11 *World Journal of Entrepreneurship, Management and Sustainable Development* 281–294.

A Antonietti, A Borsetto & P Iannello 'A metacognitive approach to financial literacy' in *International Handbook of Financial Literacy* (2016) 57–68.

C J Asarta, A T Hill & B T Meszaros 'The features and effectiveness of the keys to financial success curriculum' (2014) 16 *International Review of Economics Education* 39–50.

A Atkinson & F A Messy 'Assessing financial literacy in 12 OECD countries an OECD exercise' (2011) *Journal of Pension Economics & Finance* 657–665.

A Atkinson & F A Messy *Promoting Financial Inclusion Through Financial Education: OECD/INFE Evidence, Policies and Practice* (OECD working papers on finance insurance and private pensions, no. 34, 2013) 1 at 55.

N Baporikar & S Akino 'Financial literacy imperative for success of women entrepreneurship' (2020) 11 *International Journal of Innovation in the Digital Economy* 1 at 21.

S S Bisht & V Mishra 'ICT-driven financial inclusion initiatives for urban poor in a developing economy: Implications for public policy' (2016) 35 *Behaviour & Information Technology* 817 at 832.

M Brown, J Grigsby, W Van Der Klaauw, J Wen & B Zafar 'Financial education and the debt behavior of the young' (2016) 29 *The Review of Financial Studies* 2490 at 2522.

S Chikalipah 'What determines financial inclusion in Sub-Saharan Africa?' (2017) 8 *African Journal of Economic and Management Studies* 8 at 18.

T Chinoda & F Kwenda 'Do mobile phones, economic growth, bank competition and stability matter for financial inclusion in Africa?' (2019) 7 *Cogent Economics & Finance* 1 at 21.

J M Collins & E Odders-White 'Framework for developing and testing financial capability education programs targeted to elementary schools' (2015) 46 The Journal of Economic Education 105 at 120.

J M Cordero, M Gil-Izquierdo & F Pedraja-Chaparro 'Financial education and student financial literacy: A cross-country analysis using PISA 2012 data' (2020) *The Social Science Journal* 1 at 19.

J M Cordero & F Pedraja 'The effect of financial education training on the financial literacy of Spanish students in PISA' (2019) 51 *Applied Economics* 1679 at 1693.

S M Danes, V Deenanath & Y Yang 'Evaluation of financial literacy development of high school students: A longitudinal mixed methods study' (2016) *International Handbook of Financial Literacy* 425 at 447.

K De Beckker, B Compen, D De Bock & W Schelfhout 'The capabilities of secondary school teachers to provide financial education' (2019) 18 *Citizenship, Social and Economics Education* 66 at 81.

V S Dube & P K Asthana 'A comparative study on financial literacy of Uttar Pradesh with central zone states in India' (2017) 19 *Journal of Business and Management* 22 at 27.

O Evans 'The effects of economic and financial development on financial inclusion in Africa' (2015) 1 *Review of Economic and Development Studies* 17 at 25.

N Fabris, R N Fabris & R Luburić 'Financial education of children and youth' (2016) 5 *Journal of Central Banking Theory and Practice* 65 at 79.

L Fan & S Chatterjee 'Financial socialization, financial education, and student loan debt' (2019) *Journal of Family and Economic Issues* 74 at 85.

J Farinella, J Bland & J Franco 'The impact of financial education on financial literacy and spending habits' (2017) 11 *International Journal of Business, Accounting, and Finance* 1 at 12.

FinMark Trust 'FinScope consumer survey Namibia' 2012, available at http://www.finmark.org.za/publication/finscope-consumer-surveynamibia-2011, accessed May 2021.

V Frisancho *The Impact of Financial Education for Youth* (IDB working paper series no. IDB-WP-1038, 2019).

Government of the Republic of Namibia 'Namibia Financial Sector Strategy 2011-2021: A Sector Development Document Towards Achieving Vision 2030' (2011), available at https://www.bon.com.na/CMSTemplates/Bon/Files/bon.com.na/e7/e7e69c6d-b02b-4109-8d3d-5b41a79f9d89.pdf.

A Grohmann, T Klühs & L Menkhoff *Does Financial Literacy Improve Financial Inclusion? Cross Country Evidence* (World Development discussion paper no. 95, 2018) 84 at 96.

E T Hasheela *Access to Finance and Financial Inclusion in Namibia* (Master of Business Administration thesis, University of Stellenbosch, 2013).

S Heenkkenda *Inequalities in the Financial Inclusion in Sri Lanka: An Assessment of the Functional Financial Literacy* (MPRA paper no. 67293 35, 2015), available at https://mpra.ub.uni-muenchen.de/67293/.

T Kaiser & L Menkhoff 'Does financial education impact financial literacy and financial behavior, and if so, when?' (2017) *The World Bank Economic Review* 611 at 630.

C Kaliinasho, S G Moshana & P D Kandjii 'Inclusive education policies versus practices: Exclusion of the included' (2019) *Journal for Studies in Humanities and Social Sciences* 141 at 170.

J Kendall, N Mylenko & A Ponce *Measuring Financial Access Around the World* (World Bank Policy research working paper 5253, 2010) 1 at 65.

P Kostov, T Arun & S Annim 'Access to financial services: The case of the 'Mzansi' account in South Africa' (2015) *Review of Development Finance* 34 at 42.

T Lal 'Impact of financial inclusion on poverty alleviation through cooperative banks' (2018) 45 *International Journal of Social* 808 at 828

A Lusardi 'Financial literacy and the need for financial education: Evidence and implications' (2019) 155 *Swiss Journal of Economics and Statistics* 1 at 8.

E Madalena & M Semente 'Women entrepreneurship in Namibia: Challenges and prospects international' (2019) 6 Journal of Applied Management Sciences and Engineering 1 at 14

P Mader 'Contesting financial inclusion' (2018) *Development and Change* 461 at 483.

L Mandell & K O Hanson 'The impact of financial education in high school and college on financial literacy and subsequent financial decision making' (2009) *American Economic Association Meetings* 1 at 38.

A N Mehrotra & J Yetman 'Financial inclusion-issues for central banks' (2015) *BIS Quarterly Review* 83 at 96.

F A Messy and C Monticone *The Status of Financial Education in Africa* (OECD working papers on finance insurance and private pensions no. 25, 2012) 1 at 93.

R Mindra, M Moya, L T Zuze & O Kodongo 'Financial self-efficacy: A determinant of financial inclusion' (2017) 35 *International Journal of Bank Marketing* 338 at 353.

A Mukong, N Shiwayu & T Kaulihowa 'A decomposition of the gender gap in financial inclusion: Evidence from Namibia African' (2020) 15 *Journal of Business and Economic Research* 149 at 169.

OECD *Improving Financial Literacy: Analysis of Issues and Policies* (2005) 1 at 180.

E Olaniyi 'Connecting the poor: The internet, mobile phones and financial inclusion in Africa' (2018) 20 Digital Policy Regulation and Governance 568 at 581.

M A Omar & K Inaba 'Does financial inclusion reduce poverty and income inequality in developing countries? A panel data analysis' (2020) 9 *Journal of Economic Structures* 1 at 25.

D Otter *Teaching Financial Literacy in K-12 Schools: A Survey of Teacher Beliefs and Knowledge* (PhD thesis, The University of New Mexico, 2010)

L O Oyelami, O M Saibu & B S Adekunle 'Determinants of financial inclusion in Sub-Sahara African countries' (2017) 8 *Covenant Journal of Business & Social Sciences* 104 at 116.

Ozili 'PK financial inclusion research around the world: A review' (2020) *Forum for Social Economics* 1 at 23.

E A Özşuca 'Does financial inclusion affect poverty and income inequality? Evidence from emerging and developing countries' in K Natsuda (ed) *Globalisation and Public Policy* (2019).

M F Pang 'Enhancing the financial literacy of young people: A conceptual approach based on the variation theory of learning' (2016) *International Handbook of Financial Literacy* 587 at 602.

G Pearson, P N Stoop & M Kelly-Louw 'Balancing responsibilities – Financial literacy' (2017) 20 *Potchefstroom Electronic Law Journal* 1 at 55.

I Peña-López 'Financial literacy framework' in *OECD, PISA 2012 Assessment and Analytical Framework: Mathematics, Reading, Science, Problem Solving and Financial Literacy* (2012).

M K Refera, N K Dhaliwal & J Kaur 'Financial literacy for developing countries in Africa: A review of concept, significance and research opportunities' (2016) *Journal of African Studies and Development* 1 at 12.

D W Rothwell & S Wu 'Exploring the relationship between financial education and financial knowledge and efficacy: Evidence from the Canadian financial capability survey' (2019) 53 *The Journal of Consumer Affairs* 1725 at 1727.

R M Sahay 'Financial inclusion: Can it meet multiple macroeconomic goals?' (2015) *IMF Staff Discussion Note.*

Samundengu C *Supply-Side Data and Measurement for Financial Inclusion: A Case Study of Namibia* (master's dissertation, UNAM, 2014).

P A Sanistasya, K Raharjo & M Iqbal 'The effect of financial literacy and financial inclusion on small enterprises performance in East Kalimantan' (2019) 14 *Jurnal Economia* 48 at 59.

N S Shaninga *Poverty Reduction Through Access to Financial Services in Rural Areas of Namibia: A Case Study of Omusati Region* (master's dissertation, University of Capetown, 2018).

U Singh 'Financial literacy and financial stability are two aspects of efficient economy' (2014) 5 *Journal of Finance, Accounting and Management* 59 at 76.

L J Tshoopara *Problems Affecting the Growth of Microfinance Institutions in Namibia: An Operational, Regulatory and Legislative Perspective* (master's dissertation, UKZN, 2012).

W Walstad, C J Urban, C Asarta, E Breitbach, W Bosshardt, J Heath, B O'Neill, J Wagner & J J Xiao 'Perspectives on evaluation in financial education: Landscape, issues, and studies' (2017) 48 *The Journal of Economic Education* 93 at 112.

J J Xiao & B O'Neill 'Consumer financial education and financial capability' (2016) 40 *International Journal of Consumer Studies* 712 at 721.

L Xu & B Zia *Financial Literacy Around the World: An Overview of the Evidence with Practical Suggestions for the Way Forward* (The World Bank Policy Research working paper 6107, 2012) 1 at 56.

6 The role of trade finance in promoting the financial inclusion of small and medium enterprises and the poor in South Africa

Howard Chitimira and Friedrich Hamadziripi

6.1 Introduction

The term "trade finance" has been traditionally used in the context of international trade to refer to bank products that are specifically linked to underlying international trade transactions involving either the exporting or importing of goods.[1] Employed this way, trade finance facilitates international trade through bank-issued letters of credit.[2] However, the term "trade finance" could also refer to a form of micro-credit asset-backed funding provided by local banks or other financial institutions to domestic businesses or individuals to mainly purchase new stock or raw materials.[3] It is this latter form of trade finance that is discussed in this chapter. Unlike other forms of micro-credit, trade finance takes the form of goods rather than cash.[4] For example, trade financiers may provide seeds, agricultural tools and machinery, fertilisers and pesticides to poor people living in rural areas. In return, the beneficiaries of trade finance would be obliged to repay by selling their agricultural produce to the trade financiers at below-the-market prices.[5] Trade financiers usually resell these agricultural outputs to urban markets where prices, for example, for fresh produce, are higher than in remote areas.[6] In South Africa, the provision of trade finance has been largely left to the private sector. Banks and other private institutions remain key players in the financial inclusion of SMEs in South Africa through the provision of micro-credit.[7] However, this chapter advocates for a public-private partnership between the government and private financial institutions such as banks to champion the financial inclusion of the poor and small to medium enterprise (SME) owners in South Africa.

Regardless of the pivotal role that financial inclusion plays in poverty alleviation, financial inclusion remains an under-researched topic in South Africa.[8] This chapter contributes to the existing body of literature on financial inclusion in South Africa in several ways. First, of the existing literature that has been authored on financial inclusion, very little has been written on the financial inclusion of the poor who live in rural areas and SMEs.[9] The possibility of complete financial exclusion of people who live in rural areas is very high because they are usually unemployed, very poor and unbanked.[10] The plight of SME owners requires attention, especially considering contemporary challenges to accessing financial products and services that have been aggravated by the coronavirus disease (Covid-19). Most SMEs fail to secure credit from commercial

DOI: 10.4324/9781003369400-6

banks because they are regarded as not creditworthy.[11] SMEs in more urbanised provinces of South Africa such as Gauteng have relatively better access to formal credit than their counterparts in what are regarded as rural provinces like the Eastern Cape and KwaZulu-Natal.[12] Second, most of the academic literature on financial inclusion in South Africa does not include any elaborate theoretical framework.[13] This has led to financial inclusion being portrayed as a mere social responsibility that the government and other role-players fulfil for the poor.[14] The principles underlying financial inclusion need to be ascertained to understand how to achieve it and efficiently determine the beneficiaries of financial inclusion.[15] These principles or propositions are called theories. The discussion in this chapter integrates a theoretical framework for financial inclusion in South Africa. Lastly, most studies on financial inclusion in South Africa have been restricted to "cash" forms of micro-credit financing and unconsciously neglected the role of asset-based funding in promoting financial inclusion. Very little has been written on trade finance as a way of promoting financial inclusion in South Africa.[16] The authors of this chapter argue that trade finance offers an alternative to the traditional means of micro-credit financing to promote the financial inclusion of the poor, especially those living in rural areas and SME owners in South Africa.

6.2 Definition of key terms

The term financial inclusion is defined in section 1 of the Financial Sector Regulation Act[17] (FSRA) to refer to a state whereby all persons have timely and fair access to appropriate, fair and affordable financial products and services. A myriad of academics and commentators have defined financial inclusion to mean the development and provision of appropriate and affordable financial products and services sustainably to all persons in a country by the government, banks and other role-players.[18] Although the scope of financial inclusion initiatives and programmes includes everyone,[19] the main target population groups are marginalised people. In South Africa, these people include the youths, women, the elderly, rural dwellers, the disabled and owners of SMEs because they usually have limited or no access to financial services and products.[20] Additionally, financial inclusion entails that members of the society have access to affordable credit, insurance services and banking services.[21] In the context of this chapter, financial inclusion entails that SMEs and the poor, especially those dwelling in rural areas of South Africa, have access to trade finance. On the other hand, financial exclusion entails the failure, reluctance or inability of certain persons to access mainstream financial products and services, in this context, trade finance, at affordable costs.[22] In that regard, it is important to note that there is voluntary and involuntary financial exclusion.[23] Voluntary financial exclusion takes place when individuals willingly decide not to access financial products and services for religious or cultural reasons and a lack of confidence or trust in the banking sector.[24] Involuntary financial exclusion takes place when financial consumers fail to access certain financial products and services either because they do not meet some of the stringent requirements or because the bank charges are unaffordable.[25]

Another important distinction that needs to be highlighted is between formal and informal channels of providing financial products and services.[26] Formal financial inclusion refers to the provision of financial products and services through banks and other regulated financial institutions.[27] Informal financial inclusion takes place when financial consumers access financial products and services from unregulated providers such as private money lenders.[28] Examples of informal micro-financing schemes include but are not limited to interpersonal borrowing (money from friends or family members), private money houses, pawnshops and community cooperatives.[29]

There is no legislation that expressly defines poverty in South Africa. However, the Department of Statistics of South Africa (Stats SA) constructed three different categories of poverty thresholds known as national poverty lines (NPLs) to objectively determine and define a poor person. The first NPL is known as the food poverty line (FPL). This is the most extreme poverty line. According to the FPL, a poor person will earn a maximum of R585 per month.[30] This amount is just enough for a person to buy food to acquire the minimum amount of energy required daily. The second NPL is known as the lower-bound poverty line (LBPL), according to which a poor person earns a maximum of R840 per month.[31] A poor person in this category can afford to buy food to acquire the minimum amount of energy required daily plus a few other basic non-food items. The last NPL is known as the upper-bound poverty line (UBPL), according to which a poor person earns R1268 per month.[32] In this chapter, the UBPL will be adopted to define a poor person in South Africa because people need more than just food to survive.

6.3 Theoretical framework for financial inclusion in South Africa

A good financial inclusion theoretical framework should provide an outline of ideas to explain financial inclusion objectives and outcomes.[33] Most academic literature discusses the financial inclusion of the poor in South Africa as a social responsibility initiative by the government, banks and other role-players without an elaborate theoretical framework.[34] The authors argue that the lack of a theoretical framework on financial inclusion literature has led to uncertainty about whether financial inclusion, particularly through trade finance, is part of the South African government's responsibility.

Three theories underpin the discussions in this chapter. The first theory is the asymmetric information theory or the financial literacy theory of financial inclusion. According to this theory, the lack of correct information regarding financial products and services such as trade finance could lead to financial exclusion.[35] The free flow of information from trade financiers and other role-players to financial consumers is a major component of financial inclusion.[36] A financial consumer is financially literate when he/she is able to exercise discretion to make well-informed decisions pertaining to personal financial management for both short- and long-term objectives, taking into account any foreseeable changes in the socio-economic and political landscape.[37] A financial consumer is financially illiterate when he/she lacks the primary skills, knowledge and understanding of the accessible financial products and services to make informed decisions pertaining to his/her finances.[38] Financial literacy could increase poor people and SME owners' willingness to participate in the formal financial sector by making them aware of financial products and services that are available to them, which include trade finance.[39] It is argued that it could be more economical for the South African government to implement robust financial literacy programmes for the poor than to support them through social grants.[40]

In this chapter, information asymmetry could take place in two main ways. First, information tends to be asymmetric when a trade financier such as a bank or any other financial institution possesses more information about a financial product or service, in this case, trade finance, than the financial consumer.[41] This form of information asymmetry could be a natural result of the financial illiteracy of most poor people and SME owners in South Africa. Most poor people, especially those dwelling in rural areas, and SME owners are financially illiterate and are not aware of trade finance.[42] The second form of information asymmetry happens when a financial consumer such as a potential borrower provides untrue, insufficient or misleading information to a trade financier regarding his/her creditworthiness.[43] Information asymmetry could lead to an unfair distribution of financial products and services such as trade finance in South Africa in that financial institutions will become extra vigilant and tighten their know-your-customer (KYC) and customer due diligence (CDD) requirements.[44] Ultimately, financial consumers such as the poor and SME owners in South Africa who would otherwise qualify for various financial products and services such as trade finance could become unfairly excluded due to stringent KYC and CDD rules.

The second theory of financial inclusion that has influenced this chapter is called the vulnerable group theory. According to this theory, South Africa's financial inclusion programmes should prioritise vulnerable demographic groups such as the poor, young people, women and the elderly.[45] These are the people who are most adversely affected by economic hardship and crises.[46] Accordingly, it is pertinent to examine South Africa's financial inclusion programmes such as trade finance for the poor and SMEs considering the socio-economic setback occasioned by the Covid-19 pandemic. The vulnerable group theory of financial inclusion attempts to reduce the financial exclusion of the poor and SME owners by targeting them for financial inclusion and ensuring that they have access to the formal financial sector.[47] Additionally, employing the vulnerable group theory could enable the government of South Africa and other financial institutions providing trade finance to focus their efforts on identifying the financially excluded members of the population.[48] The level of vulnerability of members of the South African population could be determined by various considerations such as income level, education, gender, age and other characteristics.[49] The poor, especially those living in rural areas, are vulnerable because most of them are unemployed and generally unbanked. The vulnerability of SMEs stems from their limited financial clout that prohibits them from accessing formal financial products and services such as trade finance. The authors argue that it is economical to target only the vulnerable groups for financial inclusion initiatives such as trade finance than attempting to achieve financial inclusion for the entire population at once.[50]

The vulnerable group theory is complemented by the special agent theory of financial inclusion. According to the special agent theory of financial inclusion, the delivery of financial inclusion to excluded communities can be affected by "complex issues and technicalities" relating to the nature of the community or the geography.[51] To this end, it is pertinent to engage the services of "specialised agents" to deliver financial inclusion to excluded communities such as the poor and SME owners.[52] The special agent theory establishes a principal-agent relationship. In this chapter, the principal is the government and the special agents that deliver trade finance are banks and any other competent financial institutions. Application of the special agent theory of financial inclusion could relieve the government of the burden to deliver financial inclusion services through trade finance and instead allows it to focus on other important issues.[53] The special agent theory could also guarantee efficient financial inclusion programmes in South Africa since there is generally a higher level of confidence in a specialised agent than in government bureaucracy.[54]

6.4 The financial exclusion of SMEs and the poor in South African rural communities

Most SMEs and poor people in South Africa are financially excluded due to a lack of proper documentation, financial illiteracy, high bank charges and a poor legislative framework on financial inclusion.[55] As a result, most SME owners in South Africa end up applying for predatory loans with unreasonably high interest rates from "loan sharks". Unfortunately, most SMEs in South Africa collapse in their infancy stage due to over-indebtedness as they fail to pay back the high interest loans from private moneylenders.[56] On the other hand, rural dwellers mostly access credit through informal means such as stokvels and from family members and friends.[57] Apart from the challenge of non-regulation of these informal means of credit, the services offered on the informal financial market are unsustainable and insufficient for SMEs and the poor to escape poverty and long-term over-indebtedness. This puts SMEs and poor people in South Africa in an unenviable dilemma that makes them susceptible to financial exclusion. According to the vulnerable group theory, SMEs and poor people in South Africa need to be prioritised to receive trade finance. On one hand, SMEs and poor people in South Africa mostly do not qualify for formal access to credit.[58] On the other hand, although SMEs and the poor can access the informal credit market, it does not satisfy their needs and is characterised by higher interest rates.[59] The difference between the amount of informal funding available to SMEs and the poor and what they actually need results in what is known as the "credit gap".[60]

Some of the government's initiatives that were meant to improve the financial inclusion of the poor in South Africa, especially rural dwellers, were unsuccessful.[61] This could be attributed to several reasons such as corruption, lack of infrastructure and failure to communicate effectively with the intended beneficiaries.[62]

Most of these programmes benefited the institutions that were supposed to provide financial products and services to the poor.[63] Regrettably, the poor became poorer and more indebted.[64] Fairly recently, financial inclusion initiatives such as the Mzansi account and M-Pesa have also failed.[65] The government of South Africa has traditionally employed social security grants and other temporary initiatives such as the Expanded Public Works Program (EPWP), Recapitalisation and Development Programme (RADP) and the Comprehensive Rural Development Programme (CRDD) as rural poverty alleviation schemes.[66]

Most rural people are excluded from formal channels of micro-financing because they fail to meet micro-financiers' burdensome formalities and documentation. Most financial institutions have rigorous KYC and CDD requirements. Most poor people, especially those living in rural areas, lack proper documentation to satisfy these requirements. However, vulnerable people such as the poor from rural areas and SME owners might have been relieved by the court's judgment in *Truworths Limited and others v Minister of Trade and Industry and others* (*Truworths case*).[67] The implication of the judgment in the *Truworths* case is that poor people and SME owners can now apply for formal credit without payslips, bank statements and financial statements.[68] However, it must be pointed out that the relaxation of prospective borrowers' credit assessment requirements does not automatically improve the financial inclusion of rural people and SME owners.[69] In fact, the relaxation of credit lending assessment is one of the major causes of over-indebtedness.[70]

Another influential factor in the financial exclusion of rural people is the lack of collateral security when applying for credit.[71] Since most rural people are poor, they lack the relevant assets or property that they can use as collateral security when applying for formal credit. Land and houses built in rural areas are usually cheaper than those in urban areas. As a result, rural land and houses will generally not suffice as collateral security for rural people. Regardless of the efforts that have been made to establish whether rural land and houses may be formally used as collateral, it must also be noted that title to such property is usually unwarranted since land in rural areas is communally owned.

Additionally, most rural people's income is seasonal because they rely on agricultural activities to earn a living. Apart from this, the other form of income for poor rural people in South Africa is remittances from their relatives employed in urban areas. Additionally, most rural people are financially excluded because they lack credit history, which makes it difficult, if not impossible, for formal micro-financiers to conduct effective credit lending assessment procedures. These factors make poor people dwelling in rural areas vulnerable to financial exclusion. Consequently, these financial consumers should be prioritised for financial inclusion initiatives such as trade finance according to the vulnerable group theory.

One of the reasons that has not received wide academic coverage regarding why some SME owners are financially excluded is informal intermediation. Informal intermediation takes place when businesses (intermediaries) that satisfy the stringent KYC and CDD requirements because of their good credit score borrow money from formal micro-finance providers and then lend either a fraction or the entire loan to other SMEs who do not qualify, especially due to a lack of proper documentation.[72] Consequently, having access to formal, low-interest micro-finance creates opportunities for informal intermediation among entrepreneurs.[73] In some cases, these informal intermediaries have complex operations that generate multiple revenue streams. This makes it difficult for formal lenders to thoroughly screen them to ensure that the loans are used consistently with financial inclusion objectives.[74] Most money lenders do not have structures to check whether the borrowers used the money for the intended objectives. Most moneylenders are only worried about the borrower's ability to repay them and their credit score.[75] This demonstrates the need to incorporate "specialised agents", as per the special agent theory, to deliver trade finance to SMEs and the poor in South Africa. The emergence of informal intermediaries could be attributed to the availability of formal low-interest micro-financing and information asymmetry.[76] These informal intermediaries have superior information through business relations and social networks.[77] According to the asymmetric information theory, financial literacy programmes could be employed as a tool to promote the financial inclusion of the poor and SMEs through trade finance.

6.5 Trade finance and the financial inclusion of SMEs and the poor in South Africa

In the case of farmers, trade financiers usually have flexible payment terms. Trade financiers can even go to the extent of offering additional loans in instances where the borrowers' crops fail due to natural causes and they can also provide practical help during harvesting time.[78] Although some borrowers recognise that larger loans are available through traditional formal micro-finance channels, trade finance could be more attractive to rural farmers because most trade financiers are friendly to rural people and communicate in languages they understand.[79] For example, substantial trust is involved during the harvesting, transportation and weighing of the products. Sometimes farmers and trade financiers trust each other to weigh the agricultural products correctly without both parties present.[80] Consequently, borrowers view trade financiers as genuinely supportive.[81]

Additionally, the value of the "loan amounts" accessed through trade finance is often significantly bigger than those from private moneylenders.[82] Moreover, trade finance allows SMEs to secure stock without immediately using their cash reserves and paying later.[83] This allows SME owners to use their cash reserves to pay for other immediate and fixed expenses like salaries and rentals without the risk of a cash crisis.[84] This is one of the major reasons why the government of South Africa should consider resorting to trade finance to promote financial inclusion because it solves SMEs' liquidity problem by allowing SME owners to secure productive goods without using their cash.[85] Most SMEs in South Africa have liquidity problems.[86] Trade finance will relieve SME owners of the burden to pay for productive goods using cash. This could present an opportunity for SMEs to save their cash and grow.

Trade finance could also mitigate the payment risk of rural people and SME owners.[87] Payment risk refers to the possibility of a debtor failing to fully pay back a creditor within the agreed timeframe. Most micro-finance providers are hesitant to extend credit to rural people and SME owners because they are usually poor and lack the appropriate collateral security.[88] Consequently, in a bid to reduce the payment risk, micro-finance providers end up either charging exorbitant interest rates or imposing rigorous credit lending assessment measures.[89] This has resulted in the involuntary financial exclusion of most poor people and SME owners in South Africa. However, trade finance could reduce payment risk since the beneficiaries do not have to repay in cash. For example, if poor rural farmers benefit from trade finance through the provision of agricultural inputs such as seeds, fertilisers and chemicals, they will repay by selling the products to the trade financiers at a reasonably low price. This arrangement also provides a guaranteed market for rural people's agricultural products. Poor rural people usually struggle to reach the urban market due to, *inter alia*, transport costs and fear. Trade finance could address all these concerns as rural people do not have to travel to urban areas to sell their products. Therefore, trade finance provides working capital while guaranteeing trade markets for rural farmers' produce.[90]

Another advantage of trade finance is that the substitution of cash for productive goods or stock makes it not to be perceived as a loan.[91] Due to the exorbitant interest rates and stringent KYC and CDD requirements that are associated with cash loans, most poor people in rural areas and other SME owners in South Africa have avoided formal means of micro-financing. However, poor people and SME owners could be more inclined to use trade finance since there is no visible interest. The total cost of the loan will be calculated or factored into the selling price of the goods. By building trust and confidence in poor people and SME owners, trade finance could improve the financial inclusion of rural people and SME owners in South Africa.[92]

However, regardless of all the possibilities of improving the financial inclusion of the poor and SME owners in South Africa through trade finance, there are a few obstacles that may need to be addressed. For example, about half of South Africa's adult population is financially illiterate and therefore not familiar with trade finance as a form of credit.[93] The granting of credit to the poor and illiterate rural dwellers could be tantamount to financial exclusion as it could increase their indebtedness.[94] There is a need for the poor and SME owners to receive financial education before they are assisted through trade finance.

Furthermore, there is no specific legislation that is dedicated to the promotion of financial inclusion in South Africa.[95] Although the Financial Sector Regulation Act[96] (FSRA) provides that the Financial Sector Conduct Authority (FSCA) should promote financial inclusion in South Africa, there are inadequate measures to practically fulfil this objective.[97] As a result, the FSCA cannot effectively promote the financial inclusion of rural dwellers and SMEs.[98]

6.6 Concluding remarks

It is submitted that trade finance could play a pivotal role in improving the financial inclusion of the poor, especially those in rural areas and SME owners in South Africa, because it is a relatively cheaper way of accessing credit, it can be accessed by unbanked people, less documentation is required to apply for it, it has a very low payment risk and borrowers do not usually need to provide collateral security.[99] The vulnerable group theory of financial inclusion was used to identify the poor and SME owners as groups that need to be prioritised by the government of South Africa in terms of financial inclusion programmes. The asset-based nature of trade finance makes it a potential channel for improving the financial inclusion of the poor and SME owners in South Africa. However, for rural people and SME owners in South Africa to fully benefit from trade finance as a tool that improves financial inclusion, the following recommendations need to be considered.

First, since it has been highlighted that most financial consumers are not aware of trade finance as a form of micro-credit, it is submitted that there is a need for various financial education initiatives targeting poor people and SME owners.[100] Well-informed financial consumers tend to make better decisions regarding the available financial products and services.[101] Financial education programmes will allow rural financial consumers in South Africa to consider trade finance as a possible micro-financing option. It is recommended that the FSCA should play a major role in enhancing the financial literacy of rural people and SME owners in South Africa. This can be done through radio shows, seminars and workshops targeting rural people and SME owners. The FSCA could also make use of social media platforms, which have become a powerful communication tool. This recommendation is inspired by the asymmetric information theory or the financial literacy theory of financial inclusion discussed previously.

Second, it is recommended that the South African legislature enact legislation that is specifically dedicated to the promotion of financial inclusion. Third, to counter government bureaucracy and the profit motive of private financial institutions that could make financial inclusion initiatives expensive to the beneficiaries, the authors of this chapter recommend that there be a public-private partnership in the provision of financial products and services to rural people and SME owners in South Africa. This could be achieved through the government of South Africa incentivising the providers of financial products and services. This will relieve the government of the pressure to be the main provider of financial products and services to rural people and SME owners. Additionally, a public-private partnership will also ensure that rural people and SME owners benefit from the specialised knowledge of private financial products providers. This is inspired by the special agent theory of financial inclusion.

Notes

1 M Kohler and A Saville 'Measuring The Impact of Trade Finance on Country Trade Flows: A South African Perspective' (2011) 14(4) *South African Journal of Economic and Management Sciences* 466 466–476; M Auboin, 'Improving the Availability of

Trade Finance in Low-Income Countries: An Assessment of Remaining Gaps' 2015 31(4) *Oxford Review of Economic Policy* 379, 380–381; see also related discussion by S Boshoff, G van Vuuren and W Viviers, 'Identifying the Drivers of Trade Finance in South Africa' (2020) 44(3) *Studies in Economics and Econometrics* 139 140–141.

2 Kohler and Saville (note 1 above) 469; Auboin (note 1 above) 380–381; also see related discussion by Boshoff, van Vuuren and Viviers (note 1 above) 140–141.

3 F Arp, A Ardisa and A Ardisa, 'Microfinance for Poverty Alleviation: Do Transnational Initiatives Overlook Fundamental Questions of Competition and Intermediation?' (2017) 24(3) *Transnational Corporations* 103 110; Merchant Factors, 'Trade finance in South Africa: Finding the Right Finance Partner' (2015) Merchant Factors, Cape Town https://www.mfactors.co.za/insights_trade_finance_sa.php, accessed on 07 May 2021.

4 Arp, Ardisa and Ardisa (note 3 above) 110.

5 Ibid.

6 Ibid.

7 See related discussion by RC Daniels, 'Financial Intermediation, Regulation and the Formal Microcredit Sector in South Africa' (2004) 21(5) *Development Southern Africa* 831 838–841.

8 V Matsebula and D Yu, 'An Analysis of Financial Inclusion in South Africa African' (2020) 12(1) *Review of Economics and Finance* 171, 171–172; D Mhlanga, SH Dunga and T Moloi, 'Understanding the Drivers of Financial Inclusion in South Africa' (2021) 14(1) *Journal of Economic and Financial Sciences* 1 2; see related discussion by P Shipalana, 'Digitising Financial Services: A Tool for Financial Inclusion in South Africa?' (2019) *South African Institute of International Affairs Occasional Paper* 1 2. See also World Bank (2018) Universal financial access initiative 2020 available at World Bank, 'Universal Financial Access Initiative 2020' (October 2018) The World Bank Group https://www.worldbank.org/en/topic/financialinclusion/brief/achieving-universal-financial-access-by-2020, accessed on 05 February 2021.

9 L Louis and F Chartier 'Financial Inclusion in South Africa: An Integrated Framework for Financial Inclusion of Vulnerable Communities in South Africa's Regulatory System Reform' (2017) 1(1) *Journal of Comparative Urban Law and Policy* 170, 172–173 noted the scarceness of academic literature on financial inclusion initiatives and the integration of vulnerable communities into the mainstream domestic financial services sector in South Africa. However, Chitimira and Ncube have made some notable pioneering contributions on access to formal financial products and services by the poor. For example, see H Chitimira and M Ncube 'Legislative and Other Selected Challenges Affecting Financial Inclusion for the Poor and Low-Income Earners in South Africa' (2020) 64(3) *Journal of African Law* 337, 338; H Chitimira and M Ncube 'Overview Legislative Flaws Hampering the Promotion of Financial Inclusion for the Poor and Low-Income Earners in South Africa' (2021) 10(1) *Interdisciplinary Journal of Economics and Business Law* 67, 68. See related discussion by Mhlanga, Dunga and Moloi (note 8 above) 2.

10 Matsebula and Yu (note 8 above) 172, 173; TA Kasali, SA Ahmad and LH Ean, 'Does Microfinance Operation Have Effect on Poverty Alleviation in Nigeria?' (2015) 2(2) *European Journal of Contemporary Economics and Management* 54, 58; see related discussion by Mhlanga, Dunga and Moloi (note 8 above) 2.

11 Matsebula and Yu (note 8 above) 173; see related discussion by Auboin (note 1 above) 386 and 391; see further related discussion by Boshoff, van Vuuren and Viviers (note 1 above) 141.

12 Matsebula and Yu (note 8 above) 179.

13 PK Ozili, 'Theories of financial inclusion' (2020) *Munich Personal RePEc Archive* 2.

14 Louis and Chartier (note 9 above) 173.

15 Ozili (note 13 above) 2, 3.

16 See related discussion by Boshoff, van Vuuren and Viviers (note 1 above) 141 and 144.

17 Nine of 2017.
18 Chitimira and Ncube (note 9 above) 67, 68; H Chitimira and M Ncube 'The Role of Regulatory Bodies and Other Role-Players in the Promotion of Financial Inclusion in South Africa' (2020) 16(1) *Acta Universitatis Danubius Juridica* 7, 15; Louis and Chartier (note 9 above) 182; Matsebula and Yu (note 8 above) 174; Chitimira and Ncube (note 9 above) 338; Ozili (note 13 above) 3. See also Shipalana (note 8 above) 4.
19 This is in line with the United Nations (UN) 2030 Sustainable Development Goals (SDGs) available at United Nations Capital Development Fund, 'Financial Inclusion and the SDGs' (2020) UNCDF, New York https://www.uncdf.org/financial-inclusion-and-the-sdgs, accessed on 28 March 2021, which seeks to *inter alia* achieve gender equality and mobilise savings for investment. See also Chitimira and Ncube (note 9 above) 338; Ozili (note 13 above) 3.
20 Chitimira and Ncube (note 9 above) 68; Ozili (note 13 above) 5; see related discussion by Auboin (note 1 above) 386.
21 Chitimira and Ncube (note 9 above) 68; Louis and Chartier (note 9 above) 182. See related discussion by Shipalana (note 8 above) 5.
22 Chitimira and Ncube (note 9 above) 68; Chitimira and Ncube (note 18 above) 25; Louis and Chartier (note 9 above) 173.
23 Matsebula and Yu (note 8 above) 174.
24 Matsebula and Yu (note 8 above) 174; Chitimira and Ncube (note 9 above) 339.
25 Ibid.
26 F Allen, Q Meijun and X Jing 'Understanding Informal Financing' (2019) 39 *Journal of Financial Intermediation* 19 19; Matsebula and Yu (note 8 above) 176.
27 Matsebula and Yu (note 8 above) 175, 176.
28 Matsebula and Yu (note 8 above) 176; Allen, Meijun and Jing (note 26 above) 19.
29 Allen, Meijun and Jing (note 26 above) 19.
30 Statistics South Africa, 'National Poverty Lines 2020' (August 2020) http://www.statssa.gov.za/publications/P03101/P031012020.pdf, accessed on 5 July 2021; Statistics South Africa, 'Poverty in Perspective' (June 2020) https://www.parliament.gov.za/storage/app/media/1_Stock/Events_Institutional/2020/womens_charter_2020/docs/05-03-2021/StatsSa_presentation.pdf, accessed on 5 July 2021. It is noteworthy that these figures were officially released to the public on 13 August 2020. At the type of writing this chapter, the revised 2021 figures were not yet published/accessible by the authors.
31 Statistics South Africa (June 2020) https://www.parliament.gov.za/storage/app/media/1_Stock/Events_Institutional/2020/womens_charter_2020/docs/05-03-2021/StatsSa_presentation.pdf, accessed on 5 July 2021; Statistics South Africa (June 2020); https://www.parliament.gov.za/storage/app/media/1_Stock/Events_Institutional/2020/womens_charter_2020/docs/05-03-2021/StatsSa_presentation.pdf, accessed on 5 July 2021.
32 Ibid.
33 Ozili (note 13 above) 3.
34 See related discussion by Louis and Chartier (note 9 above) 173.
35 Matsebula and Yu (note 8 above) 176, 177; Ozili (note 13 above) 12; see related discussion by A Zait and PE Bertea, 'Financial Literacy – Conceptual Definition and Proposed Approach for a Measurement Instrument' 2014 4(3) *Journal of Accounting and Management* 37, 39, 40.
36 E Aryeetey, 'Informal Finance for Private Sector Development in Sub-Saharan Africa' (2005) 7(1) *Journal of Microfinance* 1, 25.
37 Chitimira and Ncube (note 9 above) 342; Zait and Bertea (note 35 above) 38; H Coetzee, 'An Opportunity for No Income No Asset (NINA) Debtors to get out of check? – An Evaluation of the Proposed Debt Intervention Measure' (2018) 81 *THRHR* 593, 609.
38 Chitimira and Ncube (note 9 above) 342; also see related discussion by JR Behrman, OS Mitchell, CK Soo et al., 'How Financial Literacy Affects Household Wealth Accumulation' (2012) 102(3) *American Economic Review* 300, 300–304.

39 Ozili (note 13 above) 12; Zait and Bertea (note 35 above) 38; also see related discussion by Behrman, Mitchell, Soo et al. (note 38 above) 300–304; see further related discussion by Auboin (note 1 above) 386, 387.
40 See related discussion by Ozili (note 13 above) 12.
41 Matsebula and Yu (note 8 above) 177; Allen, Meijun and Jing (note 26 above) 19; Aryeetey (note 36 above) 18.
42 Chitimira and Ncube (note 9 above) 342.
43 Matsebula and Yu (note 8 above) 177.
44 Ibid.
45 Ozili (note 13 above) 7; Ozili PK, 'Theories of Financial Inclusion', in Ozen E and Grima S (ed) *Uncertainty and Challenges in Contemporary Economic Behaviour* (Emerald Publishing Limited 2020) 98, 99.
46 Ozili (note 13 above) 7; Ozili (note 45 above) 98, 99.
47 Ozili (note 13 above) 8; Ozili (note 45 above) 99.
48 Ibid.
49 Ibid. See related discussion by Mhlanga, Dunga and Moloi (note 8 above) 6, 7.
50 See related discussion by Ozili (note 13 above) 8.
51 Ozili (note 13 above) 11; Ozili (note 45 above) 103.
52 Ozili (note 13 above) 11; Ozili (note 45 above) 103.
53 Ozili (note 13 above) 11; Ozili (note 45 above) 103, 104.
54 Ozili (note 13 above) 12.
55 Chitimira and Ncube (note 9 above) 339; Matsebula and Yu (note 8 above) 176; see related discussion by Boshoff, van Vuuren and Viviers (note 1 above) 141.
56 See related discussion by B Bushe 'The Causes and Impact of Business Failure among Small to Micro and Medium Enterprises in South Africa' (2019) 7(1) *Africa's Public Service Delivery and Performance Review* 1, 8.
57 Kasali, Ahmad and Ean (note 10 above) 64; D Makina 'Financial Access for Migrants and Intermediation of Remittances in South Africa' (2013) 51(1) *International Migration* 133, 134; Matsebula and Yu (note 8 above) 176.
58 Chitimira and Ncube (note 9 above) 348; Allen, Meijun and Jing (note 26 above) 20; see related discussion by Auboin (note 1 above) 386.
59 Kasali, Ahmad and Ean (note 10 above) 64; Makina (note 57 above) 134; Aryeetey (note 36 above) 19.
60 Aryeetey (note 36 above) 24.
61 Matsebula and Yu (note 8 above) 178.
62 Daniels (note 7 above) 840; ZE Mfusi and KK Govender, 'Alleviating Poverty in South Africa – A Theoretical Overview of the Expanded Public Works Program' (2015) 6(2) *Journal of Economics* 118, 119; Kasali, Ahmad and Ean (note 10 above) 56.
63 Matsebula and Yu (note 8 above) 178; Chitimira and Ncube (note 9 above) 346.
64 Ibid.
65 Louis and Chartier (note 9 above) 184. See also VA Lawack 'Mobile Money, Financial Inclusion and Financial Integrity: The South African Case' (2013) 8(13) *Washington Journal of Law, Technology & Arts* 317, 321; Matsebula and Yu (note 8 above) 175 states that the Mzansi account initiative was unsuccessful as it failed to meet the demands of the financial consumers it was directed to.
66 Some of these social security grants include the Child Support Grant, the Foster Child Grant and the Care Dependency Grant, the Older Persons grant and the Coronavirus disease (Covid-19) Relief Grant. See South African Government, 'Government Programmes, Projects and Campaigns' (2020) https://www.gov.za/about-government/government-programmes/projects-and-campaigns#, accessed on 05 March 2021; Mfusi and Govender (note 62 above) 119. An example of a grant that is tailor-made for rural people is the Comprehensive Agricultural Support Programme (CASP).
67 2018 (3) SA 558 (WCC).

68 *Truworths case* para 45; Chitimira and Ncube (note 9 above) 72; T Wazvaremhaka and P Osode, 'The implications of Truworths Limited v Minister of Trade and Industry 2018 (3) SA 558 (WCC) for access to credit by historically disadvantaged and low-income consumers' (2019) 23 *Law, Democracy & Development* 2, 8.
69 Chitimira and Ncube (note 9 above) 72.
70 Ibid.
71 Wazvaremhaka and Osode (note 68 above) 4.
72 Arp, Ardisa and Ardisa (note 3 above) 111.
73 Arp, Ardisa and Ardisa (note 3 above) 111.
74 Ibid.
75 Ibid.
76 Allen, Meijun and Jing (note 26 above) 19.
77 Ibid.
78 Arp, Ardisa and Ardisa (note 3 above) 110, 111.
79 Arp, Ardisa and Ardisa (note 3 above) 110.
80 Ibid.
81 Ibid.
82 Arp, Ardisa and Ardisa (note 3 above) 110.
83 Merchant Factors (note 3 above).
84 Ibid.
85 Ibid.
86 Ibid.
87 Ibid; also see related discussion by Auboin (note 1 above) 381.
88 See related discussion by Wazvaremhaka and Osode (note 68 above) 4.
89 See related discussion by Bushe (note 56 above) 8; Kasali, Ahmad and Ean (note 10 above) 64; Makina (note 57 above) 134; Aryeetey (note 36 above) 19.
90 Merchant factors (note 3 above).
91 See related discussion by Arp, Ardisa and Ardisa (note 3 above) 112.
92 See related discussion by Auboin (note 1 above) 390.
93 See related discussion by EL Nanziri and M Leibbrandt, 'Measuring and profiling financial literacy in South Africa' (2018) 21(1) *South African Journal of Economic and Management Sciences* 1, 6.
94 Chitimira and Ncube (note 9 above) 73.
95 Chitimira and Ncube (note 9 above) 68; Chitimira and Ncube (note 18 above) 25.
96 Nine of 2017.
97 Section 58(1)(e) of the FSRA; Chitimira and Ncube (note 9 above) 68 and 80; Chitimira and Ncube (note 18 above) 27.
98 Chitimira and Ncube (note 9 above) 81.
99 See related discussion by Auboin (note 1 above) 380, 381; Arp, Ardisa and Ardisa (note 3 above) 111 and Wazvaremhaka and Osode (note 68 above) 4.
100 Chitimira and Ncube (note 9 above) 82; Chitimira and Ncube (note 18 above) 27; also see related discussion by Auboin (note 1 above) 386, 387.
101 Louis and Chartier (note 9 above) 182, 183.

Bibliography

F Allen, Q Meijun & X Jing 'Understanding informal financing' (2019) 39 *Journal of Financial Intermediation* 19 at 33.

F Arp, A Ardisa & A Ardisa 'Microfinance for poverty alleviation: Do transnational initiatives overlook fundamental questions of competition and intermediation?' (2017) 24(3) *Transnational Corporations* 103 at 117.

E Aryeetey 'Informal finance for private sector development in Sub-Saharan Africa' (2005) 7(1) *Journal of Microfinance* 1 at 26.

M Auboin 'Improving the availability of trade finance in low-income countries: An assessment of remaining gaps' (2015) 31(4) *Oxford Review of Economic Policy* 379 at 395.

J R Behrman, O S Mitchell, C K Soo & D Bravo 'How financial literacy affects household wealth accumulation' (2012) 102(3) *American Economic Review* 300 at 304.

S Boshoff, G van Vuuren & W Viviers 'Identifying the drivers of trade finance in South Africa' (2020) 44(3) *Studies in Economics and Econometrics* 139 at 162.

B Bushe 'The causes and impact of business failure among small to micro and medium enterprises in South Africa' (2019) 7(1) *Africa's Public Service Delivery and Performance Review* 1 at 26.

H Chitimira & M Ncube 'Legislative and other selected challenges affecting financial inclusion for the poor and low-income earners in South Africa' (2020) 64(3) *Journal of African Law* 337 at 355.

H Chitimira & M Ncube 'Overview legislative flaws hampering the promotion of financial inclusion for the poor and low-income earners in South Africa' (2021) 10 Interdisciplinary Journal of Economics and Business Law 67 at 87.

H Chitimira & M Ncube 'The role of regulatory bodies and other role-players in the promotion of financial inclusion in South Africa' (2020) 16(1) *Acta Universitatis Danubius Juridica* 7 at 20.

H Coetzee 'An opportunity for no income no asset (NINA) debtors to get out of check? – An evaluation of the proposed debt intervention measure' (2018) 81 *THRHR* 593 at 611.

R C Daniels 'Financial intermediation, regulation and the formal microcredit sector in South Africa' (2004) 21(5) *Development Southern Africa* 831 at 849.

Financial Sector Regulation Act 9 of 2017.

T A Kasali, S A Ahmad & L H Ean 'Does microfinance operation have effect on poverty alleviation in Nigeria?' (2015) 2(2) *European Journal of Contemporary Economics and Management* 54 at 69.

M Kohler & A Saville 'Measuring the impact of trade finance on country trade flows: A south African perspective' (2011) 14(4) *South African Journal of Economic and Management Sciences* 466 at 478.

V A Lawack 'Mobile money, financial inclusion and financial integrity: The south African case' (2013) 8(13) *Washington Journal of Law, Technology & Arts* 317 at 346.

L Louis & L Chartier 'Financial inclusion in South Africa: An integrated framework for financial inclusion of vulnerable communities in South Africa's regulatory system reform' (2017) 1(1) *Journal of Comparative Urban Law and Policy* 170 at 196.

D Makina 'Financial access for migrants and intermediation of remittances in South Africa' (2013) 51(1) *International Migration* 133 at 147.

V Matsebula & D Yu 'An analysis of financial inclusion in South Africa African' (2020) 12(1) *Review of Economics and Finance* 171 at 202.

Merchant Factors 'Trade finance in South Africa: Finding the right finance partner' (2015) Merchant Factors, Cape Town, available at https://www.mfactors.co.za/insights_trade_finance_sa.php, accessed on 7 May 2021.

Z E Mfusi & K K Govender 'Alleviating poverty in South Africa – A theoretical overview of the expanded public works program' (2015) 6(2) *Journal of Economics* 118 at 127.

D Mhlanga, S H Dunga & T Moloi 'Understanding the drivers of financial inclusion in South Africa' (2021) 14(1) *Journal of Economic and Financial Sciences* 1 at 8.

E L Nanziri & M Leibbrandt 'Measuring and profiling financial literacy in South Africa' (2018) 21(1) *South African Journal of Economic and Management Sciences* 1 at 17.

P K Ozili 'Theories of financial inclusion' (2020) *Munich Personal RePEc Archive* 1 at 24.

P K Ozili 'Theories of financial inclusion', in E Ozen & S Grima (eds) *Uncertainty and Challenges in Contemporary Economic Behaviour* (2020) 89–115.

P Shipalana 'Digitising financial services: A tool for financial inclusion in South Africa?' (2019) *South African Institute of International Affairs Occasional Paper* 1 at 36.

South African Government 'Government programmes, projects and campaigns' (2020), available at https://www.gov.za/about-government/government-programmes/projects-and-campaigns#, accessed on 5 March 2021.

Statistics South Africa 'National poverty lines 2020' (August 2020), available at http://www.statssa.gov.za/publications/P03101/P031012020.pdf, accessed on 5 July 2021.

Statistics South Africa 'Poverty in perspective' (June 2020), available at https://www.parliament.gov.za/storage/app/media/1_Stock/Events_Institutional/2020/womens_charter_2020/docs/05-03-2021/StatsSa_presentation.pdf, accessed on 5 July 2021.

Truworths Limited and Others v Minister of Trade and Industry and Other 2018 (3) SA 558 (WCC).

United Nations Capital Development Fund 'Financial inclusion and the SDGs' (2020) UNCDF, New York, available at https://www.uncdf.org/financial-inclusion-and-the-sdgs, accessed on 28 March 2021.

T Wazvaremhaka & P Osode 'The implications of Truworths Limited v Minister of Trade and Industry 2018 (3) SA 558 (WCC) for access to credit by historically disadvantaged and low-income consumers' (2019) 23 *Law, Democracy & Development* 2 at 17.

World Bank 'Universal financial access initiative 2020' (October 2018). The World Bank Group, available at https://www.worldbank.org/en/topic/financialinclusion/brief/achieving-universal-financial-access-by-2020, accessed on 5 February 2021.

A Zait & P E Bertea 'Financial literacy – Conceptual definition and proposed approach for a measurement instrument' (2014) 4(3) *Journal of Accounting and Management* 37 at 42.

7 Mobile money

A double-edged sword to financial inclusion and Covid-19 prevention in Botswana

Olipha Mpofu and Nednah Maraga

7.1 Introduction

In the past decades, technology has been evolving at a rapid pace in most sectors, including the financial sector, where it has emerged as "financial technology" (FinTech).[1] The development of FinTech has resulted in greater connectivity among people within and across borders.[2] Evidently, the financial industry is the most regulated sector in any economy to ensure financial stability.[3] This is premised on the fact that financial instability has a disruptive impact on an economy and can have lasting negative impacts on economic activities.[4] Most governments in the developing economies of Africa and Asia tend to enforce large regulatory burdens on banks and this impedes them from promoting innovativeness. Emerging technologies in FinTech have changed this financial landscape[5] as mobile network operators (MNOs) do not suffer the same regulatory burden; therefore, they are free to innovate new products that are client-oriented. Although cash is the most preferred method of payment accepted by the majority,[6] the rapid evolution of technology[7] and the spread of transmissible diseases[8] such as Covid-19 has accelerated the rise and use of cash alternatives like mobile money (MM) to make payments.[9]

On the other hand, globalisation has led to a high demand for the quick and safe completion of international transactions. For instance, remittance of cash from Botswana to Zimbabwe can be done by using Orange Money in Botswana and received through EcoCash in Zimbabwe.[10] In addition, high levels of financial exclusion due to high costs, rigorous know-your-client (KYC) requirements and collateral demands[11] have pushed customers to demand financial products that they perceive as user-friendly, convenient and less costly.[12] Moreover, in developing economies, banks are normally located in urban areas, thus posing proximity challenges to the majority.[13] Against these backdrops, MM provides solutions by offering financial products that are less costly, convenient and safe. While the MNOs are mobilising a new niche market by providing client-oriented products, the traditional financial institution (TFI) system has also acknowledged the need to improve its services.

MM has become a powerful technological means to achieve an expansion of access to finance and sustainable development.[14] In 2020, global MM accounts

DOI: 10.4324/9781003369400-7

increased by 12.7% to 1.2 billion accounts. The growth of the MM sector has been attributable to Covid-19 protocols that have compelled the majority of the populace to resort to MM use as an alternative to cash.[15] Furthermore, stronger partnerships augmented the shift to digital as governments and non-governmental organisations partnered with mobile money operators (MMOs) to disburse social and humanitarian payments quickly, securely and efficiently.[16] Although MM uptake growth can be traced back to the early 2000s, it took a decade (2006 to 2016) to reach 100 million monthly active MM accounts while the subsequent 200 million monthly active accounts were achieved in less than five years between 2016 and December 2020.[17] In 2017, the Global System for Mobile Communications (GSMA)[18] recorded 276 MM services and 689 million registered accounts globally. Similarly, the IMF[19] reported that deposit accounts from the TFI were twice as much as MM accounts in 2012, however, by 2015, MM accounts had surpassed traditional deposits.[20]

Figure 7.1 illustrates the aforementioned global trend of MM accounts and TFI accounts from 2012 to 2015. It shows that MM accounts are increasing at a faster rate compared with TFI.

MM has been widely acknowledged as a global leader in accelerating financial inclusion (FI) and this is attributable to the success story of M-PESA Kenya.[21] Developing economies, particularly in Africa,[22] have experienced an acceleration in MM use in the last few decades. The World Bank reported that in Africa,

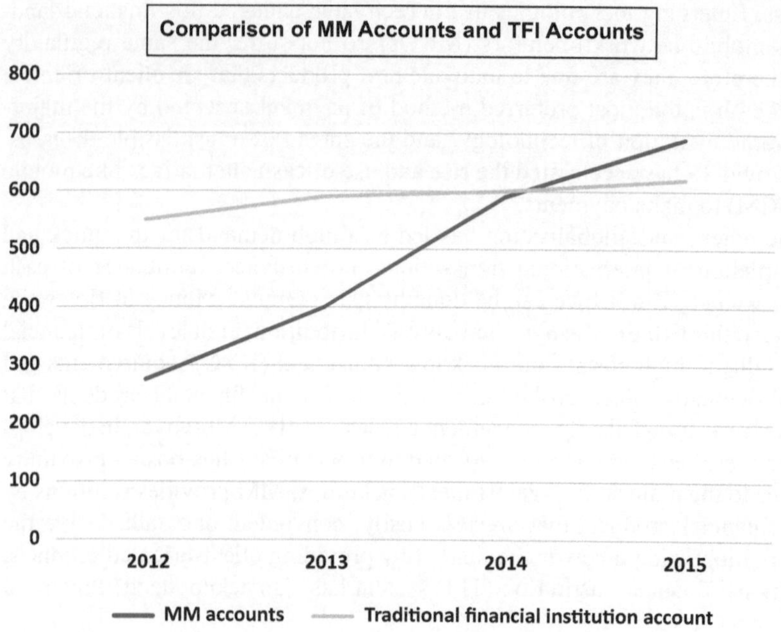

Figure 7.1 MM accounts versus TFI accounts. Source: International Monetary Fund (IMF) Financial Access Survey.

many people own an MM account than a bank account.[23] GSMA regards Sub-Saharan Africa (SSA) as the enduring epicentre of MM, having registered 50 million accounts in 2019.[24] It has also been ranked as one of the highest in terms of mobile internet penetration rate[25] and this is possibly the reason why MM use is high in the region. Several empirical studies[26] on the effects of MM on FI of an unbanked population denote that mobile phones have become a powerful means to achieve FI.[27] This is because financial services have been taken to remote areas through mobile phones where TFIs have been physically absent.[28] Studies have invariably shown that ownership of an MM account is necessitated by an increase in ownership of a mobile handset[29] and a high mobile penetration rate is more than 100 mobile cellular subscriptions per 100 people in most SSA countries.

Figure 7.2 shows the trend for mobile cellular subscriptions per 100 people for a few selected Southern African Development Community (SADC) countries for the period between 2012 and 2018.

Arguably, a high mobile penetration rate can reflect the high level of adoption of MM. Considering that Botswana is one of the countries with the highest rate of mobile penetration, it is a reasonable expectation to have a high level of MM usage in Botswana. Moreover, as a result of the global pandemic (Covid-19), MM usage is expected to achieve the smooth running of daily business operations with minimised direct contacts, while ensuring that everyone is participating in the financial system. This chapter, therefore, seeks to analyse the level of MM usage

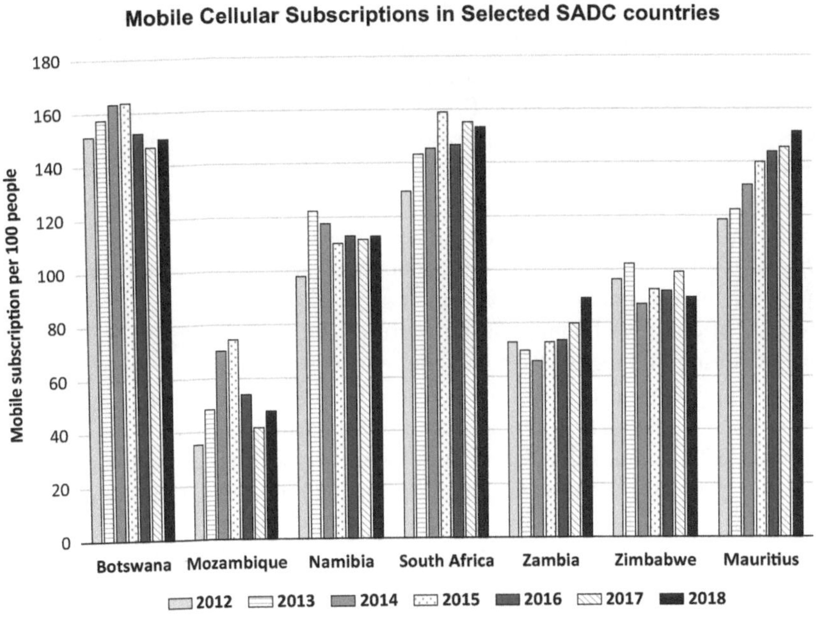

Figure 7.2 Mobile cellular subscriptions per 100 people. Source: International Telecommunication Union (ITU) 2018.

in Botswana, the challenges of implementing MM services and barriers to its adoption in its role of achieving FI and Covid-19 prevention. It is envisaged that the study will show policymakers how to enhance MM to improve FI, prevent the spread of Covid-19 and ultimately achieve sustainable development.

7.2 Financial inclusion

Financial inclusion (FI) has topped the developmental agenda in most economies, particularly developing countries, as a means of tackling poverty[30] and addressing the needs of the unbanked and underbanked.[31] The African Development Bank defined FI as all the initiatives making formal financial services available, accessible and affordable to all segments of the population.[32] The World Bank Group further stated that FI should equally relate to the usefulness of financial products and services to meet individual and business needs and should be delivered in a responsible and sustainable manner.[33]

In a Botswana context, FI is achieved when consumers across the income spectrum can access and sustainably use financial services that are affordable and appropriate to their needs.[34] Growing empirical evidence[35] has established that FI promotes the participation of marginalised segments of the population in the financial system, thus reducing poverty and income inequalities and ultimately enhancing economic growth.[36] For instance, economies with higher levels of FI experience greater economic growth, as better access to financial services encourages the majority of the population to engage in entrepreneurial activities.[37]

In SSA, the share of the adult population having accounts or borrowing from TFIs remains low compared with other developing regions.[38] Despite intensified FI initiatives and campaigns, most developing countries still struggle to achieve the objectives set in their national FI strategies.[39] SADC[40] noted that a lack of business incentives and effective infrastructure to extend financial products to low-income clients is one of the greatest barriers to FI.[41] Generally, most African economies are characterised by poor and insufficient telecommunication, physical and financial infrastructure.[42] The situation is worse in rural areas[43] where the majority of the population has no TFI accounts as access to finance is predominantly by the middle and upper-working class residing in urban areas.[44]

The lack of effective financial infrastructure leads to inefficiency in financial systems, resulting in a loss of trust and confidence by consumers.[45] Similarly, the regulatory framework also affects the levels of FI.[46] If the framework is perceived to be protecting consumers, more consumers will participate in the financial system. On the other hand, a regulatory framework supporting innovativeness will result in the production of a wider range of financial products. Empirical studies have established that financial illiteracy is one of the factors of financial exclusion[47] as the literate often participate in financial markets.[48] Furthermore, KYC requirements coupled with high costs are the major obstacles to getting more customers into the financial system, particularly the unemployed population, as they cannot provide the required documents such as pay slips.[49] Similarly, Finscope[50] also highlighted that affordability is a source of financial exclusion as bank charges tend to be out of reach for the low-income population. In addition to high costs, banks also tend to request collateral security for managing default risks.

7.2.1 The current status of financial inclusion in Botswana

In Botswana, about 68% of the population has access to financial services and this is in line with 65% of the population residing in urban areas.[51] FI is part of Botswana's transformational agenda of becoming a high-income economy by 2036.[52] Although Botswana has experienced rapid growth in the financial sector over the past two decades, it has not managed to maximise the full potential of FI as only 51% of the population owns a TFI account and the majority of the financially excluded reside in rural areas.[53] The Botswana Financial Inclusion Roadmap and Strategy (2015–2021)[54] identifies six priority strategies to promote FI. They include the development of a payments ecosystem, facilitation of low-cost and accessible savings products, the development of accessible risk mitigation products, improvement in the workings of the credit market, consumer protection and empowerment and lastly national coordination.

Similar to many other developing economies,[55] Botswana is also affected by limited financial infrastructure. Compared with developed economies like the United States, Botswana has limited financial access points. For instance, Botswana has 45 automated teller machines (ATMs) for every 100,000 people compared with the United States with 174 ATMs for 100,000 people.[56] A limitation of access to finance is dominant in rural areas with only 25% of TFI branches and 20% of ATMs.[57] Unlike in developed countries, Botswana's credit bureaus are ineffective as no legal framework governing credit providers exists.[58] The inefficiency of the credit bureaus limits the ability of financial institutions to assess the creditworthiness of potential borrower(s). Nevertheless, the Credit Information Bill 2021 has been tabled in parliament to provide for the regulation of the credit reporting system and the licensing and supervision of credit bureaus. The enactment of this Bill will help fill the aforementioned gap in credit worthiness assessment.

Participation in the financial system is mostly by the working class, however, the youth are the most affected by financial exclusion[59] due to high levels of unemployment (20%).[60] This is in line with the level of totally excluded people (23%).[61] One major barrier to FI in Botswana is excessive bureaucracy in financial institutions due to collateral security and rigorous KYC requirements.[62] Although there has been development and innovation in the payment ecosystem, FI would be enhanced if the payment ecosystem is improved through the adoption of various technologies.

7.3 Mobile money in Botswana

The IMF defined MM as a pay-as-you-go digital medium of exchange and store of value using mobile applications.[63] Similarly, Donovan[64] described it as the provision of financial services through a mobile device. In the Botswana context, MM is a technology that allows customers to receive, store and spend money using a mobile phone.[65] Although Donovan included banking services in the definition, the IMF differentiated MM from mobile banking and wallet by stating that MM is not linked to a traditional bank account. MM services are normally offered by MNOs,[66] however, TFIs can equally partner with them.[67]

7.3.1 Status of mobile money in Botswana

SSA has indisputably embraced the development of FinTech, particularly MM, and Botswana is not an exception.[68] The MM market in Botswana started in June 2011 with a value of BWP175 million in Orange Money, and by 2014, it had increased to BWP1 billion.[69] Currently, Botswana has four MM services, which are Smega by Botswana Telecommunications Corporation (BTC), Poso Money by Botswana Post, Orange Money by Orange Botswana and Myzaka by Mascom.[70] In recognition of the importance of MM, TFIs partnered with MNOs and FinTech companies to provide digital financial services that can be extended to the non-banked population.[71] Due to Covid-19, the Bank of Botswana (BoB) encouraged MNOs to increase their daily limits and reduce the charges for digital payments in an attempt to facilitate payment and settlement.[72] This led to an increase in domestic MM transfers by 95.7% from March 2020 to September 2020.[73]

Figure 7.3 shows the trend of MM accounts in Botswana between 2018 and 2021. It shows that MM accounts remained stagnant between 2018 and 2020 (pre-Covid-19), however, a slight increase of 0.4% occurred post-Covid-19 (between 2020 and 2021).

Although 60 million new MM accounts were opened globally during the Covid-19 era, it is worth noting that Botswana's trend remained stagnant at 24%[74] despite almost doubling the total value of MM transactions in six months (March to September 2020). This reflects MM account holders in Botswana managing to utilise the use of MM services, while those who did not have accounts prior to Covid-19 not adopting the services.

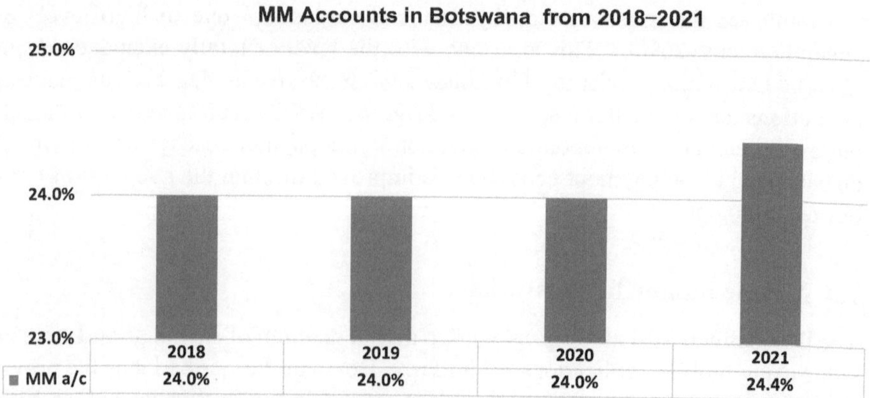

Figure 7.3 MM trends in Botswana. Source: Statista (2021).

7.3.2 Regulation of mobile money in Botswana

The success of MM is evident where an enabling regulatory environment exists. MM regulation is often complex as it veers across various regulatory domains,[75] thus policy and regulations should focus on licensing, consumer protection,[76] promoting FI, integrity and economic growth as well as bridging the economic inequalities gap.[77] The Mobile Money Regulatory Index scores[78] show that high MM adoption and use in most SSA countries indicate the enactment of MM regulatory frameworks.[79]

The regulatory framework on electronic payment services providers (EPSPs) such as MMOs in Botswana is managed by the BoB through the Bank of Botswana Act[80] and other pieces of legislation such as the National Clearance and Settlement Systems (NCSS) Act,[81] the Bills of Exchange Act,[82] the Electronic Communications and Transactions Act and the Electronic Records (Evidence) Act.[83] The Electronic Records (Evidence) Act, 2014, provides for the admissibility of electronic records as evidence in legal proceedings and authentication of the records while the Electronic Communication and Transactions Act, 2014, provides for the facilitation and regulation of electronic communications and transactions, and specifically for electronic commerce by providing the scope of electronic transactions and payments using MM.

In 2019, the BoB, in its oversight function of payment systems,[84] introduced the Electronics Payment Services (EPS) Regulations[85] to promote an enabling environment for innovation in financial service delivery channels. They establish a legal framework for electronic payment services (EPS) such as MM by providing for the market conduct, regulation and licensing[86] of EPSPs. The regulations introduce new operating requirements such as operating in a safe, secure and sound manner,[87] with the necessary infrastructure, operational arrangements[88] and capital[89] to ensure that EPS are provided in tandem with BoB. The regulations have been hailed as progressive as the implementation necessitates the introduction of functional regulation within the national payment system (NPS).[90]

The Data Protection Act, 2018, based on the consent model of data protection, protects the EPS user's privacy and personal data by providing a legal framework for data collection, processing, sharing and localisation. This reduces the risks as data protection is vital in maintaining the market integrity and confidence of EPSs.[91] At first glance, the regulations are a salvation for the MM industry in Botswana, however, it is worth noting that the provisions are mostly EPSP-centred and not customer-centred. This is postulated on the position that the regulations do not provide any provision on market price regulation, thus cannot protect MM consumers from exorbitant charges from MMOs. The consent model of data protection is an insufficient tool for data protection as some consumers are illiterate or do not understand the terms and conditions.[92] Amending the regulations to encompass MM users' needs on EPS price regulation would enhance FI, increase the use and demand of MM through cashless services and ultimately reduce the spread of Covid-19.

7.3.3 Benefits of mobile money

FinTech has proven to offer solutions to the high-cost challenges posed by TFIs.[93] MM increases the ability to access finance[94] by providing proximity and convenience, thus eliminating costs and time of travelling to make payments. It further reduces the risks and burdens associated with handling cash.[95] Similarly, MM in Botswana has enabled the majority (unbanked) to send and receive money anywhere in and outside Botswana, thus closing the financial exclusion gap[96] as only 51% of the populace has a TFI account.[97] Botswana being a host to a large percentage of foreigners,[98] there is a need for the expatriates to remit funds back home, which can be undertaken by MM as it is cost-effective and solves distance barriers.

Also, Botswana MM services allow the payment of bills, and this brings about convenience, prevents queuing and reduces costs and time associated with travelling. Due to convenience and the proximity of mobile products, customers are lured to make more transactions, thus increasing revenue. On the other hand, the costs of offering the services are reduced through the elimination of physical infrastructure barriers, resulting in an increase in operational effectiveness.[99] For example, Orange Money has partnered with different supermarkets and outlets such as Choppies, Sefalana and Spar stores to improve proximity and convenience.[100] However, a reduction in costs from the MMOs has a spillover effect on consumers as the products become affordable and accessible. In addition, MNOs have managed to increase their reputation and investment opportunities as well as widen their range of products and ultimately their revenues in the financial sector.[101]

7.3.4 Challenges of mobile money in Botswana

In relation to MM, Botswana faces challenges such as high operational and implementation costs, poor connectivity, incompatibility with other financial facilities, low cash limits and cyber security issues. Tangirala and Nlondiwa in their study on the effect of MM on small and medium enterprises in Botswana established that the high costs of MM charges are the major barrier to the use of MM.[102] For example, the cost of transactions using MyZaka is as much as BWP99 for withdrawing less than BWP4000.[103] Notwithstanding the reduced cost of running MM services, Botswana's mobile application industry is young and lacks funding[104] because the initial implementation is very costly for developing countries as the acquisition of ICT infrastructure is a great challenge.

Apart from the challenges faced in implementation, a poor and inconsistent network[105] also affects MM operations.[106] In addition, unreliable information systems result in conflict between stakeholders.[107] For instance, MM agents could have repeated system malfunction challenges and inadequate cash and e-floats for withdrawing large sums. Tangirala and Nlondiwa established that the daily set limit of BWP4000 is not enough to facilitate daily operations.[108] Botswana is equally guilty of network challenges and unaffordable access to broadband speeds for internet connections[109] as they rely on obsolete technology. Due to lagging in technology, management information systems are normally unreliable and this impedes rapid service.[110]

In developing economies, conducive regulatory environments are necessary for two purposes; first, to promote innovation and foster customer adoption/usage. Second, to protect consumers from the risks associated with using the new products.[111] Arguably, EPS regulation in Botswana is not client-centred as it does not provide regulation on the pricing of MM services to protect consumers. Similarly, Bizah posits that a lack of a clear regulatory framework on MM between finance and telecommunications poses challenges to consumers as they become exposed to abuse from service providers.[112]

Security issues are the other challenge for the adoption of MM usage in Botswana.[113] MM use has affected financial risk management requirements and the transaction policy control environment. The bare minimum requirements of a personal identity (ID) card and a subscriber identity module (SIM) card for registration as an MM user bring about security gaps[114] as it attracts fraudsters[115] and cyber attackers.[116] Considering that Botswana is a technophobic nation,[117] the population is still sceptical about using MM services, particularly in terms of revealing their private information to MNOs. These perceived risks by consumers affect the rate of MM adoption in Botswana.[118]

A lack of knowledge[119] and trust in MM services affects MM adoption as the amount of information received by consumers has a positive impact on attitudes towards adoption. MNOs should inform consumers of changing technologies in MM that are compatible with their lifestyle, values and needs as well as other MM services apart from remittances. Therefore, as a result of Covid-19, where there is a need to tweak lifestyles to accommodate the new normal, the adoption of MM should be a panacea to facilitate the remote operations of businesses.

7.4 Mobile money and Covid-19

Covid-19 has severely and negatively impacted economies and people's lives. The financial sector has equally been affected as it undermined global financial stability and brought about new data needs such as the use of digital financial services.[120] Governments, in an effort of curbing and preventing the spread of Covid-19, advocated for the adoption of various measures such as contactless interactions.

The MM industry did not slack or hesitate, they responded promptly, embraced the change, leveraged digital technologies, built resilience and worked towards penetrating the market through a digitalised system.[121] MM has seen a rapid uptake and use as mobile technology and IT became a necessary need.[122] MNOs and MMOs through their services and products have become a critical and integral part of the Covid-19 task force. They partnered with governments and other TFIs to offer a financial approach that is convenient, fast, efficient, safe and minimises direct contact from person to person (P2P), thus ensuring and promoting social distancing.[123] The use of MM is a preferred and powerful response tool[124] to diseases subject to international health regulations (IHR)[125] and governments have been encouraging its use through various measures such as an easement of the requirements needed to open up an MM account.[126]

Globally, governments like India,[127] Bangladesh, Japan[128] and Brazil have embraced digital technology and expanded payments using digital services like MM to offer wage payment, social assistance and emergency relief services.[129] In Indonesia and Paraguay, governments used mobile payments to disperse social aid transfers to the low-income populace.[130] In Africa, MM was turned to as a public health tool to curb Covid-19 and its effects.[131] The Kenyan and Ghanaian governments advocated for MM usage to reduce the risk of spreading the virus through the physical handling of cash and this led to a reduction of MM transaction fees.[132] Countries like South Africa, Rwanda, Togo and Namibia instituted P2P social measures and transfers using MM to cushion the social and economic impacts of the pandemic.[133] This is premised on the position that social distancing and contactless and cashless modes of payment remain among the most useful methods of reducing the rate of transmission of Covid-19.[134] All these efforts spur digital and financial inclusion in the Covid-19 era.[135]

The Global Findex and GSMA illustrate a paradigm shift from cash to digital transactions as MM use for payments and international remittances has intensified.[136] In 2020, international remittance services via MM in SSA increased by 52%, reaching a total of US$10 billion and is expected to be higher in 2021. According to IMF's Financial Access Survey (FAS), MM use in the Covid-19 era increased significantly in low and middle-income economies like India, Kenya, Ghana and Myanmar, even surpassing traditional banking services. By the end of 2020, SSA topped the MM index globally, accounting for 64% of all MM value transactions. The surge in MM use in SSA was necessitated by various government measures such as the imposition of lockdowns and restrictions in movement,[137] cuts in P2P transaction fees (Mozambique), cuts in digital payment fees (Rwanda)[138] and easing of KYC requirements (Ghana).[139] Further to that is the notion that handling hard cash was considered riskier.[140] Countries like Nigeria,[141] Kenya and Namibia advocated for cashless transactions and contactless modes of payment as a monetary policy lever to combat the spread of Covid-19.[142] MMOs and banks halted MM transfer charges[143] while other countries, like Ghana, classified MM agents and their supply chains as essential service workers to ensure the continuity of the service and increase the flow of funds.[144] This resulted in an increase in MM use in SSA.[145]

GSMA notes that in 2020, MM was considered a safe option for carrying out financial transactions and SSA was at the forefront with 43% of all new accounts. It indicates that the number of MM registered accounts grew by 12.7% globally to 1.21 billion accounts (double the forecasted growth rate) and the number of monthly active MM accounts topped 300 million, having grown at a rate of 17% year on year. Further to that, GSMA notes that the Southern Africa region recorded the fastest growth of 24% year on year and this is evidenced by an increase in MM value transactions in Botswana.

As the pandemic accelerated a digital shift, companies globally and regionally experienced huge growth.[146] Digital remittances through MM in Botswana increased as MNOs made money transfers easier by introducing new digital remittance services. MyZaka introduced MM services across borders, allowing its customers to send money to the neighbouring countries of Malawi, Mozambique, Tanzania, Zambia and Zimbabwe. This limited access to traditional remittance service providers like banks, thus reducing the spread of Covid-19. Traditional MM remittance services have equally partnered with MMOs for faster, more convenient and more efficient services.[147] MoneyGram remittance senders can send money that can be received via M-PESA, an MM service in Kenya and Tanzania as well as through Ecocash in Zimbabwe and Vodafone Cash in Ghana.[148] This has cut the cost and interaction of middlemen such as agents who need to be visited to receive remittance. These MM services have thus prevented the spread of Covid-19 as they promote adherence to Covid-19 health protocols, standards and regulations.[149] MM trends in Botswana during lockdown indicate an increase in the value of domestic MM transfers. This shows that MM played a significant role in ensuring a smooth flow of payment systems and ultimately Covid-19 prevention.

Despite coming with unprecedented challenges, uncertainties and turmoil, Covid-19 has been a saviour to the MM industry as it has acted as a catalyst for MM growth in Botswana. Overall, the pandemic has spurred the increased use of MM by showing that MM is indeed a key element in the financial industry in achieving FI and helping to curb/prevent the spread of Covid-19. MM has brought about and increased the delivery of safe, secure and efficient financial services and has helped reach the unserved and underserved population(s). This is through the increase in the numbers of MM customers and transactions globally, regionally and locally (Botswana).

7.5 Conclusion

MM has proved to be an enabler of FI and Covid-19 prevention. This is premised on the position that MM accounts and transactions increased globally, which is attributable to the call and adherence to Covid-19 protocols. In Africa, SSA is the enduring epicentre of MM owing to the success story of M-PESA, while having the highest mobile internet penetration rate and MM accounts as opposed to TFI accounts.

Botswana has managed to enhance its FI levels by embracing MM as part of its strategy of achieving the transformational agenda of becoming a high-income economy by 2036. Notwithstanding the other motivational factors (which include the high levels of financial exclusions by TFIs, advancement of technology, increase in globalisation and changing consumer preference), Covid-19 has also contributed to an increase in the uptake of MM transactions. Against the backdrops of various Covid-19 protocols, MM has become a boon and double-edged sword to FI and Covid-19 prevention in Botswana. This is because of its attributes of agility, convenience and enabler of minimised direct contact. Although MM transactions increased tremendously, doubling the total value during the Covid-19 era, the number of MM accounts in Botswana remained stagnant. This reflects that MM account holders utilised the service as a safer option for carrying out financial transactions, while those who did not have an account prior to Covid-19 did not adopt the service.

Considering the growing recognition of the importance of MM use, the challenges affecting the adoption of MM in Botswana cannot be ignored. The challenges unravelled are twofold: first, the implementation by providers, and second, the barriers to adoption by consumers. The MM industry in Botswana is still young and growing. However, a lack of adequate funding and limited expertise in mobile application technology brings about challenges to its implementation. Poor connectivity levels, high costs, inadequate daily limits, a lack of compatibility with other banking services and perceived risks affect the rate of adoption by consumers. Although the EPS regulations were introduced in 2019, there is a need to implement an effective regulatory and legislative framework that is client-centred to ensure consumer protection and awareness. On the other hand, the framework should promote and nurture innovativeness in the financial sector. In addition, there must be a collaboration of various stakeholders, including but not limited to government, TFIs and the private sector, to implement an efficient and up-to-date MM infrastructure and management information system.

Notes

1 R Alt, R Beck and MT Smits 'FinTech and the Transformation of the Financial Industry' (2018) 28 *Electronic Markets* 235–243.

2 P Gomber, JA Koch and M Siering, 'Digital Finance and FinTech: Current research and Future Research Directions' (2017) 87(5) *Journal of Business Economics* 537–580.

3 M Pelaelo (Governor Bank of Botswana), Keynote Address at the 'Fintech, Payments and Financial Inclusion Workshop–Gaborone' https://www.bankofbotswana.bw/sites/default/files/speech-documents/Keynote%20Address%20for%20Fintech%20Workshop%20-%20July%2010%202018.pdf, accessed on 22 September 2021.

4 Ibid.

5 D Dhingra, V Agarwal and S Ashok, 'Emerging Technologies in Financial Services' in *Disruptive Technology and Digital Transformation for Business and Government* (2021) IGI Global 323–347.

6 ML Bech, U Faruqui, F Ougaard and C Picillo 'Payments are A-Changin 'But Cash Still Rules' (2018) *BIS Quarterly Review* 67–80.

7 KK Ferguson, L Soutter and M Neubert 'Digital Payments in Africa-How Demand, Technology, and Regulation Disrupt Digital Payment Systems' (2019) 10(4) *International Journal of Teaching and Case Studies* 319–340.

8 E Angelakis, EL Azhar, F Bibi, M Yasir, AK Al-Ghamdi, AM Ashshi and D Raoult 'Paper Money and Coins as Potential Vectors of Transmissible Disease' (2014) 9(2) *Future Microbiology* 249–261.

9 V Kameswaran and S Hulikal Muralidhar, 'Cash, Digital Payments and Accessibility: A Case Study from Metropolitan India' (2019) 3 *Proceedings of the ACM on Human-Computer Interaction* 1–23.

10 Orange Money Botswana offers international money transfer services regionally and globally. See https://www.orange.co.bw/en/om-money-transfer/international-money-transfer-service.html?utm_source=onsite-search, accessed on 03 September 2021.

11 M Mazanai and O Fatoki 'Access to Finance in the SME Sector: A South African Perspective' (2012) 4(1) *Asian Journal of Business Management* 58–67.
12 J Springford 'A Confidence Crisis? Restoring Trust in Financial Services' (2011) *Social Market Foundation* 1 90–98.
13 D Mhlanga and V Denhere 'Determinants of Financial Inclusion in Southern Africa' (2020) 65(3) *Studia Universitatis Babeş-Bolyai Oeconomica* 39–52. See also S Chikalipah, 'What Determines Financial Inclusion in Sub-Saharan Africa?' (2017) 8(1) *African Journal of Economic and Management Studies* 8–18.
14 K Donovan 'Mobile Money for Financial Inclusion' (2012) 61(1) *Information and Communications for Development* 61–73. See also E Eilu and TO Auma 'Mobile Money Services as a Panacea to Financial Inclusion in Sub-Saharan Africa: The Case of Uganda' (2017) 8(4) *International Journal of Technology Diffusion* 77–88.
15 Z Kazzaz 'Emergency Disbursements During COVID-19: Regulatory Tools for Rapid Account Opening and Oversight' (2020).
16 GSMA 'State of the Industry Report on Mobile Money' (2021).
17 Ibid.
18 GSMA, 'State of the Industry Report on Mobile Money' (2017).
19 IMF *International Monetary Annual Report* 2016.
20 IMF *Financial Access Survey* 2017.
21 L Klapper, S Ansar, J Hess and D Singer 'Sub-Saharan Africa Series: Mobile Money and Digital Financial Inclusion' (2019) *Development Research Group, The World Bank.*
22 The economies include Kenya, Botswana, Ghana, South Africa and Angola.
23 A Demirguc-Kunt, L Klapper, D Singer and PV Oudheusden 'The Global Findex Database 2014: Measuring Financial Inclusion Around the World' (2015) *World Bank Policy Research Working Paper 7255* 1–97.
24 GSMA 'State of the Industry Report on Mobile Money' (2019) 6.
25 GSMA 'State of the Mobile Money Industry in Sub-Saharan Africa 2018' (2019).
26 S Mago and S Chitokwindo 'The Impact of Mobile Banking on Financial Inclusion in Zimbabwe: A Case for Masvingo Province' (2014) 5(9) *Mediterranean Journal of Social Sciences* 221.
27 M Chibba 'Financial Inclusion, Poverty Reduction and the Millennium Development Goals' (2009) 21(2) *European Journal of Development Research* 213–230.
28 T Dube and BZ Chummun 'Mobile Money Access and Usage among the Rural Communities in Zimbabwe' (2019) *Munich Personal RePEc Archive No. 97578*; J Frydrych and H Aschim, 'Extending Reach: Mobile Money in Rural Areas Findings based on the State of the Industry Report' (2014) *GSMA Mobile Money for Unbanked Series* 1–9.
29 S Aggarwal and L Klapper 'Designing Government Policies to Expand Financial Inclusion: Evidence from Around the World' (2013) *World Bank Working Paper* https://citeseerx.ist.psu.edu/viewdoc/download?doi=10.1.1.594.9694andrep=rep1andtype=pdf, accessed on 21 July 2021.
30 Chibba (2009) 21(2) *European Journal of Development Research* 213–230.
31 A Demirguc-Kunt, L Klapper and D Singer 'Financial Inclusion and Inclusive Growth – A Review of Recent Empirical Evidence' (2017) *World Bank Policy Research Working Paper No. 8040* 1–27.
32 African Development Bank Group 'African Economic Outlook 2018' (2018).
33 World Bank 'Financial Inclusion Overview' (2018) World Bank, Washington, DC.
34 Ministry of Finance & Economic Development 'Botswana Demand, Supply, Policy and Regulation Diagnostic Report' (2015) 1–132.
35 MA Omar and K Inaba 'Does Financial Inclusion Reduce Poverty and Income Inequality in Developing Countries? A Panel Data Analysis' (2020) 9(1) *Journal of Economic Structures* 1–25; CY Park and JR Mercado 'Financial Inclusion, Poverty, and Income Inequality' (2018) 63(1) *The Singapore Economic Review* 185–206.

36 A Demirguc-Kunt and LF Klapper 'Financial Inclusion in Africa: An Overview' (2012) *World Bank Policy Research Working Paper No.6088* 1–20; See also M Duvendack and P Mader 'Impact of Financial Inclusion in Low- and Middle-Income Countries: A Systematic Review of Reviews' (2019) 15(1–2) *Campbell Systematic Review* 1–57.
37 D Sharma 'Nexus Between Financial Inclusion and Economic Growth: Evidence from the Emerging Indian Economy' (2016) 8(1) *Journal of Financial Economic Policy* 13–36.
38 M Mlachila, D Dykes, S Zajc, PH Aithnard, T Beck, M Ncube and O Nelvin 'Banking in Sub-Saharan Africa: Challenges and Opportunities' (2013) *The European Investment Bank Report* 1–118.
39 T Inoue and S Hamori 'Financial Access and Economic Growth: Evidence from Sub-Saharan Africa' (2016) 52 *Emerging Markets Finance and Trade* 743–753.
40 SADC 'Financial Inclusion Strategy 2016–2021' (2015).
41 Ibid.
42 O Kabakova and E Plaksenkov 'Analysis of Factors Affecting Financial Inclusion: Ecosystem View' (2018) 89 *Journal of Business Research* 198–205.
43 VS Tchamyou, G Erreygers and D Cassimon 'Inequality, ICT and Financial Access in Africa' (2019) 139 *Technological Forecasting and Social Change* 169–184.
44 W Munyanyi 'Women Financial Inclusion in Zimbabwe: A Descriptive Comparison of Rural and Urban Populaces' (2014) 2(6) *International Journal of Education and Research* 255–266.
45 A Zins and L Weill 'The Determinants of Financial Inclusion in Africa' (2016) 6(1) *Review of Development Finance* 46–57.
46 O David-West, T Aluko and O Adetunji 'Mobile Money: A Panacea for Financial Exclusion in Emerging Markets' (2019) 8(1) *Journal of Banking* 27–55.
47 Z Brey, S Chisadza, A Ladin and M Stern 'Consumer Protection in SADC' (2016) *FinMark Trust Report* 1–36.
48 M Hasan, T Le and A Hoque 'How Does Financial Literacy Impact on Inclusive Finance?' (2021) 7(1) *Financial Innovation* 1–23.
49 A Grohmann and L Menkhoff 'The Relationship Between Financial Literacy and Financial Inclusion' (2020) *DIW Discussion Papers No. 1914* 1–25.
50 Finmark Trust 'Zimbabwe – FinScope MSME Survey 2012' (2012) *Finmark Trust Report* 1–12.
51 Making Access Possible 'Botswana Financial Inclusion Country Report' (2015).
52 See https://www.worldbank.org/en/country/botswana/overview, accessed on 23 July 2021
53 World Bank Group 'The Global Findex Database' (2018).
54 Ministry of Finance & Economic Development 'Botswana Financial Inclusion Roadmap and Strategy 2015–2021' (2020).
55 O Kabakova and E Plaksenkov (2018) 89 *Journal of Business Research* 198–205.
56 See World Bank 'World Economic Indicators' https://data.worldbank.org/indicator, accessed on 17 September 2021.
57 N Narayana and G Motlaleng 'Youth Unemployment and Vocational Training Strategies in Botswana' (2014) 11 *Journal of Social and Economic Policy* 13–20.
58 Making Access Possible 'Botswana Demand, Supply, Policy and Regulation Diagnostic Report' (2015) https://www.finance.gov.bw/images/publications/fin/ReportMAPBotswanaNovember2015.pdf, accessed on 5 July 2021.
59 Bank of Botswana 'Tsa Tuelano' (2020) 'The Botswana National Payments System Newsletter' https://www.bankofbotswana.bw/sites/default/files/publications/BOB%20Newsletter%202020.pdf, accessed on 5 July 2021.
60 World Bank 'Small and Medium Enterprises (SMEs) Finance: Improving SMEs Access to Finance and Finding Innovative Solutions to Unlock Sources of Capital' (2019) *The World Bank* 1–63.

61 Ibid.
62 Ibid.
63 IMF Annual Report (2019) https://www.imf.org/external/pubs/ft/ar/2019/eng/assets/pdf/imf-annual-report-2019.pdf, accessed on 6 July 2021.
64 Ibid.
65 Donovan (2012) 61(1) *Information and Communications for Development* 61–73.
66 K Shirono, MY Fan, B Das, MHC Villanova and ME Chhabra 'Is Mobile Money Part of Money? Understanding the Trends and Measurement' (2021) *IMF Working Paper WP/21/177* 1–41. In Kenya, M-PESA is operated by the MNO Safaricom, while in Botswana, MyZaka is offered by Mascom, OrangeMoney by Orange and Smega by BTC Mobile.
67 AB Makulilo, 'Privacy in Mobile Money: Central Banks in Africa and their Regulatory Limits' (2015) 23(4) *International Journal of Law and Information Technology* 372–391. In Kenya, Safaricom has partnered with the Commercial Bank of Africa to offer credit services to MM users.
68 See GSMA 'Mobile Money Accounts Grow to 1.2 Billion in 2020' https://www.gsma.com/newsroom/press-release/mobile-money-accounts-grow-to-1-2-billion-in-2020/, accessed on 15 September 2021
69 Mmegi Online 'BOB Takes Over Multi-Billion Pula Mobile Money Market' (2020) https://www.mmegi.bw/business/bob-takes-over-multi-billion-pula-mobile-money-market/news, accessed on 14 July 2021.
70 The Botswana Gazette 'Exorbitant Mobile Money Fees: No End in Sight' (2020) https://www.thegazette.news/business-2/exorbitant-mobile-money-fees-no-end-in-sight/, accessed on 14 July 2021.
71 Bank of Botswana 'Tsa Tuelano' (2020) *The Botswana National Payments System Newsletter* https://www.bankofbotswana.bw/sites/default/files/publications/BOB%20Newsletter%202020.pdf, accessed on 05 July 2021.
72 Bank of Botswana 'Annual Report 2020' (2021) HTTPS://www.bankofbotswana.bw/sites/default/files/publications/BoB%202020%20Annual%20Report.pdf, accessed on 05 July 2021.
73 Ibid.
74 See Figure 7.3.
75 KK Toroitich, JM Jelaga and GA Omwono 'Factors Affecting Individuals to Adopt Mobile Banking in Kenya: A Case of Kenya Commercial Bank (KCB), Eldoret' (2016) *International Journal of Research in Business Studies and Management* 29–48.
76 A Pelletier, S Khavul and S Estrin 'Regulating Mobile Money, What's at Stake' (2019) *LSE Newsletter*.
77 GSMA 'GSMA Policy and Regulation- Mobile for Development' (2021) https://www.gsma.com/mobilefordevelopment/mobile-money/policy-and-regulation/, accessed on 3 July 2021.
78 GSMA 'Mobile Money Metrics-Regulatory Index' (2019) https://www.gsma.com/mobilemoneymetrics/#regulatory-index?y=2019, accessed on 3 July 2021.
79 L Katusiime 'Mobile Money Use: The Impact of Macroeconomic Policy and Regulation' (2021) 9(2) *Economies* 1–19.
80 Cap. 55:01.
81 Cap. 46:06.
82 Cap. 46:02.
83 Cap. 08:02.
84 Section 3 (3) of Cap. 46:06.
85 Statutory Instrument No.2.
86 Part II of the EPS Regulations.

87 Section 5 of the EPS Regulations.
88 Section 18 of the EPS Regulations.
89 Section 20 of the EPS Regulations.
90 See Bank of Botswana 'National Payments System Vision and Strategy 2020-2024' (2020) https://www.bankofbotswana.bw/publication/national-payments-system-vision-and-strategy-2020-2024, accessed on 7 July 2021.
91 GSMA 'Data Protection in Mobile Money' (2019) https://www.gsma.com/mobilefordevelopment/wp-content/uploads/2019/03/Data-Protection-in-mobile-money.pdf, accessed on 3 July 2021.
92 D Medine and G Murthy, 'Making Data Work for the Poor' (2020) *CGAP/World Bank* https://responsiblefinanceforum.org/wp-content/uploads/2020/01/2020_01_Focus_Note_Making_Data_Work_for_Poor-Jan2020.pdf, accessed on 7 July 2021.
93 SKA Rizvi, B Naqvi and F Tanveer, 'Mobile Banking: A Potential Catalyst for Financial Inclusion and Growth in Pakistan' (2017) 22 *The Lahore Journal of Economics* 251–281.
94 A Mugambi, C Njunge and SC Yang 'Mobile-Money Benefits and Usage: The Case of M-PESA' (2014) 16(3) *IT Professional* 16–21.
95 C Merritt, 'Mobile Money Transfer Services: The Next Phase in the Evolution of Person-to-Person Payments' (2011) 5(2) *Journal of Payments Strategy and Systems* 143–160.
96 Orange Money and Myzaka offer options to send money within Botswana and also to neighbouring countries like Zimbabwe, Kenya and Malawi, among others.
97 Ibid.
98 See Statistics Botswana 'Botswana Demographic Survey Report 2017' (2018) https://www.statsbots.org.bw/sites/default/files/publications/Botswana%20Demographic%20Survey%20Report%202017.pdf, accessed 14 September 2021.
99 Ibid.
100 See https://store.orange.co.bw/, accessed 19 September 2021.
101 EA Opare 'The Advantages and Disadvantages of Mobile Money on the Profitability of the Ghanaian Banking Industry' (2018) 4(2) *Texila International Journal of Management* 1–8.
102 S Tangirala and S Nlondiwa 'The Utilization of Mobile Money Services in Small Scale Enterprises: A Case Study' (2019) 4(6) *European Journal of Business and Management Research* 1–6.
103 See https://www.mascom.bw/about-mascom-myzaka/#2, accessed 24 September 2021.
104 A Nyamaka, A Botha, J Van Biljon and M Marais, 'Challenges Botswana's Mobile Application Developers Encounter: Funding, Commercial and Technical Support' (2018) *IST-Africa Week Conference (IST-Africa)* 1.
105 PN Makele and S Doss, 'Adoption of mMoney and mHealth in a Developing Country: An Assessment of the Network and Security Challenges in Botswana' (2017) 19(10) *IOSR Journal of Business and Management* 44–58.
106 SMDS Bizah 'Mobile Money Users Challenges: Evidence from Developing Countries' (2017) 5(11) *International Journal of Education and Research* 77–88.
107 Ibid.
108 Ibid.
109 K Maje 'BOFINET Takes No Blame Over Pricy, Poor Internet' (2019) https://www.mmegi.bw/news/bofinet-takes-no-blame-over-pricy-poor-internet/news, accessed 23 September 2021.
110 AH Ahmad, C Green and F Jiang 'Mobile Money, Financial Inclusion and Development: A Review with Reference to African Experience' (2020) 34(4) *Journal of Economic Surveys* 753–792.
111 Ibid.
112 Ibid.

113 Ibid.
114 A Harris, S Goodman and P Traynor 'Privacy and Security Concerns Associated with Mobile Money Applications in Africa' (2012) 8 *Washington Journal of Law, Technology and Arts* 245–263.
115 I Akomea-Frimpong, C Andoh, A Akomea-Frimpong and Y Dwomoh-Okudzeto 'Control of Fraud on Mobile Money Services in Ghana: An Exploratory Study' (2019) *Journal of Money Laundering Control* 300–317.
116 DM Sulieman and F Salleh 'Anti-Money Laundering Risk Posed by Mobile Money Services in Sub-Saharan Africa' (2020) 7(11) *Journal of Critical Reviews* 568–571.
117 Ibid.
118 R Makgosa and N Kootsholetse 'Exploring the Determinants of Cell Phone Banking Adoption in Botswana' (2012) 5(1) *Botswana Journal of Business* 34–42.
119 OC Otieno, S Liyala, BC Odongo and SO Abeka, 'Challenges facing the Use and Adoption of Mobile Phone Money Services' (2016) 4(1) *World Journal of Computer Application and Technology* 8–14.
120 J Fu and M Mishra 'Fintech in the Time of COVID-19: Trust and Technological Adoption During Crises' (2020) *Swiss Finance Institute Research Paper* 20–38.
121 SKA Manjang 'The Resilience of Mobile Money in Sub-Saharan Africa' (2021) https://www.findevgateway.org/blog/2021/08/resilience-mobile-money-sub-saharan-africa, accessed on 14 September 2021.
122 The Economist 'The COVID-19 Crisis is Boosting Mobile Money Middle East and Africa' (2020).
123 M Bazarbash, H Carcel-Villanova, E Chhabra, Y Fan, N Griffin, J Moeller and K Shirono, 'Mobile Money in the COVID-19 Pandemic' (2020) *IMF Special Series on COVID-19*.
124 IMF 'Digital Solutions for Direct Cash Transfers in Emergencies' (2020) *Special Series on Fiscal Policies to Respond to COVID-19*.
125 N Pandey and A Pal 'Impact of Digital Surge During Covid-19 Pandemic: A Viewpoint on Research and Practice' (2020) 55 *International Journal of Information Management* 102–171.
126 IMF *Financial Access COVID-19 Policy Tracker Statistics* (2020).
127 M Jakhiya, MM Bishnoi and H Purohit 'Emergence and Growth of Mobile Money in Modern India: A Study on the Effect of Mobile Money' (2020) *Advances in Science and Engineering Technology International Conferences (ASET)* 1–10.
128 H Fujiki, 'The Use of Noncash Payment Methods for Regular Payments and the Household Demand for Cash: Evidence from Japan' (2020) 71(4) *The Japanese Economic Review* 719–765.
129 A Gelb and A Mukherjee 'Digital Technology in Social Assistance Transfers for COVID-19 Relief: Lessons from Selected Cases' (2020) *CGD Policy Paper 181* 1–21.
130 Ibid.
131 J Bright 'Africa Turns to Mobile Payments as a Tool to Curb COVID-19' (2020) https://techcrunch.com/2020/03/25/african-turns-to-mobile-payments-as-a-tool-to-curb-covid-19/, accessed on 14 September 2021.
132 Ibid.
133 U Gentilini, M Almenfi, I Orton and P Dale 'Social Protection and Jobs Responses to COVID-19: A Real-Time Review of Country Measures' (2021) *Word Bank Series* 4–651.
134 T Ren and Y Tang, 'Accelerate the promotion of mobile payments during the COVID-19 epidemic' (2020) 1(2) *The Innovation* 1–2.
135 H Chen, W Engert, K Huynh, G Nicholls, M Nicholson and J Zhu 'Cash and COVID-19: The Impact of the Pandemic on the Demand for and Use of Cash' (2020) 6 *Bank of Canada Staff Discussion Paper No.2020-6* 1–22.

136 GSMA 'Mobile Money Accounts Grow to 1.2 Billion in 2020' https://www.gsma.com/newsroom/press-release/mobile-money-accounts-grow-to-1-2-billion-in-2020/, accessed on 15 September 2021.
137 S Davidovic, D Prady and H Tourpe 'You've Got Money: Mobile Payments Help People During the Pandemic' (2020) https://blogs.imf.org/2020/06/22/youve-got-money-mobile-payments-help-people-during-the-pandemic/, accessed on 15 September 2021.
138 I Carboni and H Bester 'When Digital Payment Goes Viral: Lessons from COVID-19's Impact on Mobile Money in Rwanda' (2020) https://cenfri.org/articles/covid-19s-impact-on-mobile-money-in-rwanda/, accessed on 19 September 2021.
139 Ibid.
140 B Gardner 'Dirty Banknotes May Be Spreading the Coronavirus, WHO Suggests' (2020) *Daily Telegraph* https://www.telegraph.co.uk/news/2020/03/02/exclusive-dirty-banknotes-may-spreading-coronavirus-world-health/, accessed on 4 September 2021.
141 T Obiezu 'Coronavirus Pandemic Fuels Mobile Money Transactions in Nigeria' (2020) https://www.voanews.com/a/covid-19-pandemic_coronavirus-pandemic-fuels-mobile-money-transactions-nigeria/6190756.html, accessed on 16 September 2021.
142 JB Nachega, R Leisegang, O Kallay, EJ Mills, A Zumla, and RT Lester 'Mobile Health Technology for Enhancing the COVID-19 Response in Africa: A Potential Game Changer?' (2020) 103(1) *The American Journal of Tropical Medicine and Hygiene* 3–5.
143 J Mutua 'Banks Now Halt Mobile Money Transfer Charges' (2020) *Business Daily Africa* https://www.businessdailyafrica.com/bd/corporate/companies/banks-now-halt-mobile-money-transfer-charges-2284304.Aaccessed on 7 September 2021.
144 AG Mora and M Rutkowski 'Remittances in Times of the Coronavirus-Keep Them Flowing' (2020) *World Bank Blogs* https://blogs.worldbank.org/psd/remittances-times-coronavirus-keep-them-flowing, accessed on 10 September 2021.
145 World Economic Forum 'West Africans are Switching from Cash to Mobile Money Because of COVID-19' (2020) https://www.weforum.org/agenda/2020/04/coronavirus-set-to-spur-mobile-money-growth-in-w-africa, accessed on 4 September 2021.
146 M Moeser 'Coronavirus- Driven Shift to Digital Remittances a Boon for Fintechs' (2020) https://www.americanbanker.com/payments/news/coronavirus-driven-shift-to-digital-remittances-a-boon-for-fintechs, accessed on 05 September 2021.
147 R Raithatha 'Mobile Money and International Remittances: Enabling Recovery During COVID-19' (2021) https://www.gsma.com/mobilefordevelopment/mobile-money-4/mobile-money-and-international-remittances-enabling-recovery-during-covid-19/, accessed on 10 September 2021.
148 See https://www.moneygram.com/mgo/us/en/m/send-to-kenya, accessed on 07 September 2021.
149 S Davidovic, S Nunhuck, D Prady, H Tourpe and E Anderson 'Beyond the COVID-19 Crisis: A Framework for Sustainable Government-to-Person Mobile Money Transfers' (2020) *IMF Working Paper WP/20/198* 1–38.

Bibliography

African Development Bank Group 'African economic outlook 2018' (2018).

S Aggarwal & L Klapper *Designing Government Policies to Expand Financial Inclusion: Evidence from Around the World* (World Bank working paper, 2013), available at https://citeseerx.ist.psu.edu/viewdoc/download?doi=10.1.1.594.9694andrep=rep1andtype=pdf, accessed on 21 July 2021.

A H Ahmad, C Green & F Jiang 'Mobile money, financial inclusion and development: A review with reference to African experience' (2020) 34(4) *Journal of Economic Surveys* 753 at 792.

I Akomea-Frimpong, C Andoh, A Akomea-Frimpong & Y Dwomoh-Okudzeto 'Control of fraud on mobile money services in Ghana: An exploratory study' (2019) 22 *Journal of Money Laundering Control* 300 at 317.

R Alt, R Beck & M T Smits 'FinTech and the transformation of the financial industry' (2018) 28 *Electronic Markets* 235 at 243.

E Angelakis, E L Azhar, F Bibi, M Yasir, A K Al-Ghamdi, A M Ashshi & D Raoult 'Paper money and coins as potential vectors of transmissible disease' (2014) 9(2) *Future Microbiology* 249 at 261.

Bank of Botswana 'Annual report 2020' (2021).

Bank of Botswana 'National payments system vision and strategy 2020–2024' 2020, available at https://www.bankofbotswana.bw/publication/national-payments-system-vision-and-strategy-2020-2024, accessed on 7 July 2021.

Bank of Botswana 'Tsa Tuelano' (2020) 'The Botswana national payments system newsletter', available at https://www.bankofbotswana.bw/sites/default/files/publications/BOB%20Newsletter%202020.pdf, accessed on 5 July 2021

M Bazarbash, H Carcel-Villanova, E Chhabra, Y Fan, N Griffin, J Moeller & K Shirono 'Mobile money in the COVID-19 pandemic' (*IMF Special Series on COVID-19*, 2020).

M L Bech, U Faruqui, F Ougaard & C Picillo 'Payments are A-changin 'but cash still rules' (2018) *BIS Quarterly Review* 67 at 80.

S M D S Bizah 'Mobile money users challenges: Evidence from developing countries' (2017) 5(11) *International Journal of Education and Research* 77 at 88.

Z Brey, S Chisadza, A Ladin & M Stern 'Consumer protection in SADC' (*FinMark Trust Report* 1-36, 2016).

J Bright 'Africa turns to mobile payments as a tool to curb COVID-19' (2020), available at https://techcrunch.com/2020/03/25/african-turns-to-mobile-payments-as-a-tool-to-curb-covid-19/, accessed on 14 September 2021.

I Carboni & H Bester 'When digital payment goes viral: Lessons from COVID-19's impact on mobile money in Rwanda' (2020), available at https://cenfri.org/articles/covid-19s-impact-on-mobile-money-in-rwanda/, accessed on 19 September 2021.

H Chen, W Engert, K Huynh, G Nicholls, M Nicholson & J Zhu *Cash and COVID-19: The Impact of the Pandemic on the Demand for and Use of Cash* (Bank of Canada Staff discussion paper no. 2020-6, 2020) 1 at 22.

M Chibba 'Financial inclusion, poverty reduction and the millennium development goals' (2009) 21(2) *European Journal of Development Research* 213 at 230.

S Chikalipah 'What determines financial inclusion in Sub-Saharan Africa?' (2017) 8(1) *African Journal of Economic and Management Studies* 8 at 18.

T A David-West & O Adetunji 'Mobile money: A panacea for financial exclusion in emerging markets' (2019) 8(1) *Journal of Banking* 27 at 55.

S Davidovic, S Nunhuck, D Prady, H Tourpe & E Anderson *Beyond the COVID-19 Crisis: A Framework for Sustainable Government-to-Person Mobile Money Transfers* (IMF Working Paper WP/20/198, 2020) 1 at 38.

S Davidovic, D Prady & H Tourpe 'You've got money: Mobile payments help people during the pandemic' 2020, available at https://blogs.imf.org/2020/06/22/youve-got-money-mobile-payments-help-people-during-the-pandemic/, accessed on 15 September 2021.

A Demirguc-Kunt & L F Klapper *Financial Inclusion in Africa: An Overview* (World Bank Policy Research working paper no. 6088, 2012) 1 at 20.

A Demirguc-Kunt, L Klapper & D Singer *Financial Inclusion and Inclusive Growth – A Review of Recent Empirical Evidence* (World Bank Policy Research working paper no. 8040, 2017) 1 at 27.

A Demirguc-Kunt, L Klapper, D Singer & P V Oudheusden *The Global Findex Database 2014: Measuring Financial Inclusion Around the World* (World Bank Policy research working paper 7255, 2015) 1 at 97

D Dhingra, V Agarwal & S Ashok 'Emerging technologies in financial services' in *Disruptive Technology and Digital Transformation for Business and Government* (2021) 323 at 47.

K Donovan 'Mobile money for financial inclusion' (2012) 61(1) *Information and Communications for Development* 61 at 73.

T Dube & B Z Chummun *Mobile Money Access and Usage Among the Rural Communities in Zimbabwe* (Munich personal RePEc archive no. 97578, 2019).

M Duvendack & P Mader 'Impact of financial inclusion in low- and middle-income countries: A systematic review of reviews' (2019) 15(1–2) *Campbell Systematic Review* 1 at 57.

E Eilu & T O Auma 'Mobile money services as a Panacea to financial inclusion in Sub-Saharan Africa: The case of Uganda' (2017) 8(4) *International Journal of Technology Diffusion* 77 at 88

K K Ferguson, L Soutter & M Neubert 'Digital payments in Africa - How demand, technology, and regulation disrupt digital payment systems' (2019) 10(4) *International Journal of Teaching and Case Studies* 319 at 340

Finmark Trust *Zimbabwe – FinScope MSME Survey 2012* (Finmark Trust Report, 2012) 1 at 12.

J Frydrych & H Aschim *Extending Reach: Mobile Money in Rural Areas Findings Based on the State of the Industry Report* (GSMA Mobile Money for Unbanked Series, 2014) 1 at 9.

J Fu & M Mishra *Fintech in the Time of COVID-19: Trust and Technological Adoption During Crises* (Swiss finance institute research paper, 2020) 20 at 38.

H Fujiki 'The use of noncash payment methods for regular payments and the household demand for cash: Evidence from Japan' (2020) 71(4) *The Japanese Economic Review* 719 at 765.

B Gardner 'Dirty banknotes may be spreading the coronavirus, WHO suggests' *Daily Telegraph* 2020, available at https://www.telegraph.co.uk/news/2020/03/02/exclusive-dirty-banknotes-may-spreading-coronavirus-world-health/, accessed on 4 September 2021.

A Gelb & A Mukherjee 'Digital technology in social assistance transfers for COVID-19 relief: Lessons from selected cases' (2020) 181 *CGD Policy Paper* 1 at 21.

U Gentilini, M Almenfi, I Orton & P Dale 'Social protection and jobs responses to COVID-19: A real-time review of country measures' (2021) *Word Bank Series* 4 at 651.

P Gomber, J A Koch & M Siering 'Digital finance and FinTech: Current research and future research directions' (2017) 87(5) *Journal of Business Economics* 537 at 580

A Grohmann & L Menkhoff *The Relationship Between Financial Literacy and Financial Inclusion* (DIW discussion papers no. 1914, 2020) 1 at 25.

GSMA 'Data protection in mobile money' 2019, available at https://www.gsma.com/mobilefordevelopment/wp-content/uploads/2019/03/Data-Protection-in-mobile-money.pdf, accessed on 3 July 2021.

GSMA 'GSMA policy and regulation - mobile for development' 2021, available at https://www.gsma.com/mobilefordevelopment/mobile-money/policy-and-regulation/, accessed on 3 July 2021.

GSMA 'Mobile money metrics-regulatory index' 2019, available at https://www.gsma.com/mobilemoneymetrics/#regulatory-index?y=2019, accessed on 3 July 2021.

GSMA 'State of the industry report on mobile money' (2017).

GSMA 'State of the industry report on mobile money' (2019).

GSMA 'State of the industry report on mobile money' (2021).

GSMA 'GSMA policy and regulation - Mobile for development' (2021).

A Harris, S Goodman & P Traynor 'Privacy and security concerns associated with mobile money applications in Africa' (2012) 8 *Washington Journal of Law, Technology and Arts* 245 at 263.

M Hasan, T Le & A Hoque 'How does financial literacy impact on inclusive finance?' (2021) 7(1) *Financial Innovation* 1 at 23.

IMF 'Digital solutions for direct cash transfers in emergencies' (2020) *Special Series on Fiscal Policies to Respond to COVID-19.*

IMF *Financial Access COVID-19 Policy Tracker Statistics* (2020).

T Inoue & S Hamori 'Financial access and economic growth: Evidence from Sub-Saharan Africa' (2016) 52 *Emerging Markets Finance and Trade* 743 at 753.

M Jakhiya, M M Bishnoi & H Purohit 'Emergence and growth of mobile money in modern India: A study on the effect of mobile money' (2020) *Advances in Science and Engineering Technology International Conferences (ASET)* 1 at 10.

O Kabakova & E Plaksenkov 'Analysis of factors affecting financial inclusion: Ecosystem view' (2018) 89 *Journal of Business Research* 198 at 205.

V Kameswaran & S Hulikal Muralidhar 'Cash, digital payments and accessibility: A case study from metropolitan India' (2019) 3 *Proceedings of the ACM on Human-Computer Interaction* 1 at 23.

L Katusiime 'Mobile money use: The impact of macroeconomic policy and regulation' (2021) 9(2) *Economies* 1 at 19.

Z Kazzaz 'Emergency disbursements during COVID-19: Regulatory tools for rapid account opening and oversight' (2020).

L Klapper, S Ansar, J Hess & D Singer *Sub-Saharan Africa Series: Mobile Money and Digital Financial Inclusion* (2019).

S Mago & S Chitokwindo 'The impact of mobile banking on financial inclusion in Zimbabwe: A case for Masvingo province' (2014) 5(9) *Mediterranean Journal of Social Sciences* 221 at 221.

K Maje 'BOFINET takes no blame over pricy, poor internet' (2019), available at https://www.mmegi.bw/news/bofinet-takes-no-blame-over-pricy-poor-internet/news, accessed on 23 September 2021.

P N Makele & S Doss 'Adoption of mMoney and mHealth in a developing country: An assessment of the network and security challenges in Botswana' (2017) 19(10) *IOSR Journal of Business and Management* 44 at 58.

R Makgosa & N Kootsholetse 'Exploring the determinants of cell phone banking adoption in Botswana' (2012) 5(1) *Botswana Journal of Business* 34 at 42.

'Making access possible 'Botswana Financial Inclusion Country Report' (2015).

A B Makulilo 'Privacy in mobile money: Central Banks in Africa and their regulatory limits' (2015) 23(4) *International Journal of Law and Information Technology* 372 at 391.

S K A Manjang 'The resilience of mobile money in Sub-Saharan Africa' 2021, available at https://www.findevgateway.org/blog/2021/08/resilience-mobile-money-sub-saharan-africa, accessed on 14 September 2021.

M Mazanai & O Fatoki 'Access to finance in the SME sector: A south African perspective' (2012) 4(1) *Asian Journal of Business Management* 58 at 67.

D Medine & G Murthy 'Making data work for the poor' 2020, *CGAP/World Bank*, available at https://responsiblefinanceforum.org/wp-content/uploads/2020/01/2020_01_Focus_Note_Making_Data_Work_for_Poor-Jan2020.pdf, accessed on 7 July 2021.

C Merritt 'Mobile money transfer services: The next phase in the evolution of person-to-person payments' (2011) 5(2) *Journal of Payments Strategy and Systems* 143 at 160.

D Mhlanga & V Denhere 'Determinants of financial inclusion in southern Africa' (2020) 65(3) *Studia Universitatis Babeș-Bolyai Oeconomica* 39 at 52.
Ministry of Finance & Economic Development 'Botswana demand, supply, policy and regulation diagnostic report' (2015) 1 at 132
Ministry of Finance & Economic Development 'Botswana financial inclusion roadmap and strategy 2015–2021' (2020).
M Mlachila, D Dykes, S Zajc, P H Aithnard, T Beck, M Ncube & O Nelvin 'Banking in Sub-Saharan Africa: Challenges and opportunities' (2013) *The European Investment Bank Report* 1-118.
Mmegi Online 'BOB takes over multi-billion Pula mobile money market' 2020, available at https://www.mmegi.bw/business/bob-takes-over-multi-billion-pula-mobile-money-market/news, accessed on 14 July 2021.
M Moeser 'Coronavirus-driven shift to digital remittances a boon for Fintechs' 2020, available at https://www.americanbanker.com/payments/news/coronavirus-driven-shift-to-digital-remittances-a-boon-for-fintechs, accessed on 5 September 2021.
A G Mora & M Rutkowski 'Remittances in times of the coronavirus-keep them flowing' *World Bank Blogs* 2020, available at https://blogs.worldbank.org/psd/remittances-times-coronavirus-keep-them-flowing, accessed on 10 September 2021.
A Mugambi, C Njunge & S C Yang 'Mobile-money benefits and usage: The case of M-pesa' (2014) 16(3) *IT Professional* 16 at 21.
W Munyanyi 'Women financial inclusion in Zimbabwe: A descriptive comparison of rural and urban populaces' (2014) 2(6) *International Journal of Education and Research* 255 at 266.
J Mutua 'Banks now halt mobile money transfer charges' *Business Daily Africa* 2020, available at https://www.businessdailyafrica.com/bd/corporate/companies/banks-now-halt-mobile-money-transfer-charges-2284304, accessed on 7 September 2021.
J B Nachega, R Leisegang, O Kallay, E J Mills, A Zumla & R T Lester 'Mobile health technology for enhancing the COVID-19 response in Africa: A potential game changer?' (2020) 103(1) *The American Journal of Tropical Medicine and Hygiene* 3 at 5.
N Narayana & G Motlaleng 'Youth unemployment and vocational training strategies in Botswana' (2014) 11 *Journal of Social and Economic Policy* 13 at 20.
A Nyamaka, A Botha, J Van Biljon & M Marais 'Challenges Botswana's mobile application developers encounter: Funding, commercial and technical support' (2018) *IST-Africa Week Conference (IST-Africa)*.
T Obiezu 'Coronavirus pandemic fuels mobile money transactions in Nigeria' 2020, available at https://www.voanews.com/a/covid-19-pandemic_coronavirus-pandemic-fuels-mobile-money-transactions-nigeria/6190756.html, accessed on 16 September 2021.
M A Omar & K Inaba 'Does financial inclusion reduce poverty and income inequality in developing countries? A panel data analysis' (2020) 9(1) *Journal of Economic Structures* 1 at 25.
E A Opare 'The advantages and disadvantages of mobile money on the profitability of the Ghanaian Banking Industry' (2018) 4(2) *Texila International Journal of Management* 1 at 8.
O C Otieno, S Liyala, B C Odongo & S O Abeka 'Challenges facing the use and adoption of mobile phone money services' (2016) 4(1) *World Journal of Computer Application and Technology* 8 at 14.
N Pandey & A Pal 'Impact of digital surge during Covid-19 pandemic: A viewpoint on research and practice' (2020) 55 *International Journal of Information Management* 102 at 171.

C Y Park & J R Mercado 'Financial inclusion, poverty, and income inequality' (2018) 63(1) *The Singapore Economic Review* 185 at 206.

M Pelaelo (Governor Bank of Botswana), keynote address at the 'Fintech, Payments and Financial Inclusion Workshop–Gaborone', available at https://www.bankofbotswana.bw/sites/default/files/speech-documents/Keynote%20Address%20for%20Fintech%20Workshop%20-%20July%2010%202018.pdf, accessed on 22 September 2021.

A Pelletier, S Khavul & S Estrin 'Regulating mobile money, what's at stake' (2019) *LSE Newsletter*.

R Raithatha 'Mobile money and international remittances: Enabling recovery during COVID-19' 2021, available at https://www.gsma.com/mobilefordevelopment/mobile-money-4/mobile-money-and-international-remittances-enabling-recovery-during-covid-19/, accessed on 10 September 2021.

T Ren & Y Tang 'Accelerate the promotion of mobile payments during the COVID-19 epidemic' (2020) 1(2) *The Innovation* 1 at 2.

S K A Rizvi, B Naqvi & F Tanveer 'Mobile banking: A potential catalyst for financial inclusion and growth in Pakistan' (2017) 22 *The Lahore Journal of Economics* 251 at 281.

D Sharma 'Nexus between financial inclusion and economic growth: Evidence from the emerging Indian economy' (2016) 8(1) *Journal of Financial Economic Policy* 13 at 36.

K Shirono, M Y Fan, B Das, M H C Villanova & M E Chhabra *Is Mobile Money Part of Money? Understanding the Trends and Measurement* (IMF working paper WP/21/177,2021) 1 at 41.

J Springford 'A confidence crisis? Restoring trust in financial services' (2011) *Social Market Foundation* 1 at 136.

D M Sulieman & F Salleh 'Anti-money laundering risk posed by mobile money services in Sub-Saharan Africa' (2020) 7(11) *Journal of Critical Reviews* 568 at 571.

S Tangirala & S Nlondiwa 'The utilization of mobile money services in small scale enterprises: A case study' (2019) 4(6) *European Journal of Business and Management Research* 1 at 6.

V S Tchamyou, G Erreygers & D Cassimon 'Inequality, ICT and financial access in Africa' (2019) 139 *Technological Forecasting and Social Change* 169 at 184.

The Botswana gazette 'Exorbitant mobile money fees: No end in sight' 2020, available at https://www.thegazette.news/business-2/exorbitant-mobile-money-fees-no-end-in-sight/, accessed on 14 July 2021.

K K Toroitich, J M Jelaga & G A Omwono 'Factors affecting individuals to adopt mobile banking in Kenya: A case of Kenya Commercial Bank (KCB), Eldoret' (2016) *International Journal of Research in Business Studies and Management* 29 at 48.

World Bank 'Small and medium enterprises (SMEs) finance: Improving SMEs access to finance and finding innovative solutions to unlock sources of capital' (2019) *The World Bank* 1 at 63.

World Bank 'World economic indicators', available at https://data.worldbank.org/indicator, accessed on 17 September 2021.

World Economic Forum 'West Africans are switching from cash to mobile money because of COVID-19' 2020, available at https://www.weforum.org/agenda/2020/04/coronavirus-set-to-spur-mobile-money-growth-in-w-africa, accessed on 4 September 2021.

A Zins & L Weill 'The determinants of financial inclusion in Africa' (2016) 6(1) *Review of Development Finance* 46 at 57.

8 Advancing financial inclusion for women in Botswana, Namibia, South Africa and Zimbabwe

Tendai D. Svotwa, Charles Makanyeza and Eukeria Wealth

8.1 Introduction

Financial inclusion has been the fulcrum of academic research and debate over the past two decades globally, with more pronouncements being placed on the financial inclusion of women. Financial inclusion has been defined from diverse angles, without any form of unanimity in its definition. The multiplicity of the definitions revolves around commonalities such as the accessibility of financial services to the populace and how the services are utilised, as well as the quality and cost of the financial services. However, financial inclusion has been defined as the process through which individuals, especially the poor, have access to basic financial services in the formal financial sector.[1]

In addition, financial inclusion has also been contextualised to refer to specific initiatives that are taken to make all formal financial services available, accessible and affordable to all the social strata of the population, with particular emphasis on women. A similar definition is also given which points out that financial inclusion refers to the delivery of financial services and products in a manner that is available, accessible and affordable to all segments of society and plays a critical role in combatting poverty and contributing to inclusive economic growth.[2] In a bid to have some form of convergence in terms of the workable definition of financial inclusion, certain parameters were laid out by the World Bank's 2014 Global Financial Development Report,[3] which posited that financial inclusion encompasses the proportion of individuals and firms that utilise financial services.

Generally, over the last decade, financial inclusion has been on an upward trajectory globally, and more specifically in Southern African Development Community (SADC) countries.[4] Prior studies by the International Monetary Fund (IMF) have shown that there has been a phenomenal growth in the proportion of the adult population holding a bank account, from a global average of 51% in 2011 to 69% in 2017[5] even though the same report shows an unbanked population of 1.7 billion adults globally without a bank account. Most of the unbanked population live in developing countries, and 56% of all unbanked adults are women.[6] These statistics, especially for the unbanked population, offer some opportunities for financial service providers to include some segments of society that have been marginalised for a long time, that is, women, so that they can contribute meaningfully, socially,

DOI: 10.4324/9781003369400-8

politically and economically within their respective societies. Research further confirms that the gender gap in Africa seems to be linked with women's participation outside the financial sector. Women are discriminated against in other areas of the economy, like formal employment, and African women are more likely to resort to informal financial services,[7] as opposed to formal services and products. Furthermore, research confirms that the poor, women, youth and rural residents tend to face greater barriers to accessing financial services.[8]

The Covid-19 pandemic from January 2020 ushered in unprecedented challenges globally in the financial services sector. Many countries instituted response measures to the pandemic, such as lockdowns and the observance of social distancing measures, to contain the virus, which has weakened many borrowers' ability to repay and, consequently, posed challenges for the survival of many financial institutions.[9] In light of the foregoing, women have not been spared from the brunt of the Covid-19 pandemic, with the closure of many firms, especially small businesses in which women are largely present, thus exacerbating the scourge of unemployment in the SADC region.

However, it has been evident that credit, savings, insurance, payment and mobile money are some of the financial inclusion products that have capacitated women entrepreneurs, especially start-ups.[10] Furthermore, research confirms that financial inclusion and financial systems have greatly enhanced the lives of women entrepreneurs and start-ups by improving their welfare, mitigating shocks and managing expenses, as well as performing daily transactions.[11] The preceding discussions attest to the fact that women should be part of the financial inclusion strategy of any nation, most especially in the SADC region. To capacitate women, some researchers[12] opine that Africa needs to define feasible financial inclusion strategies and interventions to exploit the vast potential of those women, and also women's businesses currently excluded from the formal financial sector, for their human and physical capital. Against this backdrop, this chapter focuses on the advancement of financial inclusion for women in the SADC region. A brief overview of the financial inclusion of women is provided in the first instance while the rationale and challenges of financial inclusion follow. Subsequently, the chapter focuses on country-specific financial inclusion strategies for women in the selected four countries within the SADC region, namely Botswana, Namibia, South Africa and Zimbabwe.

8.2 Overview of women's financial inclusion

Extant literature confirms that financial inclusion has multifarious benefits for the marginalised population, especially for women and poor adults in many countries, and governments globally have focused on financial inclusion as the key to economic empowerment and development and a solution to rising poverty levels.[13] In line with the assertion espoused previously, one could argue that through financial inclusion of women, the levels of social inclusion are likely to improve in societies within a country by targeting the formerly excluded women, thus addressing some of the United Nations' Sustainable Development Goals (SDGs), which promote and propagate gender equality in societies. Previous research confirms that women are still lagging behind men, although notable improvements are being evidenced in women's participation in financial inclusion, which has resulted in improved economic growth and better living standards in society.[14] Figure 8.1 highlights the gender disparities in developed and developing countries for account ownership, which has been used as one of the major measures for financial inclusion. The inequalities between men and women are quite pronounced in developing countries as compared with developed countries between 2011 and 2017. Gender disparities among developed countries are quite negligible (almost at par) as evidenced in Figure 8.1. Globally, women still lag in financial inclusion, which is the same scenario in developing country contexts, although at different magnitudes.

Figure 8.1 indicates that there is no gender balance in terms of account ownership, with women mostly being marginalised in developing countries. This violates women's rights and goes against the principles of the SDGs, especially SDG 5,[15] which advocates for the achievement of gender equality and empowerment of women and girls. All countries that are signatories to the United Nations (including the four SADC countries under study) need to ensure that women's rights are also protected, especially in the promulgation of policies that advance women's financial inclusion in the formal financial services sector.

While it is critical that women are not excluded in a country's financial system, it is imperative to have a cursory analysis of the reasons why women and other vulnerable members of society are excluded in most developing countries. Several reasons have been articulated, and from empirical literature, low-income individuals and/or households in marginal areas and activities taking place in areas such as rural areas, those in microenterprises and mostly the informal sector are negated by financial systems.[16] The fixed costs incurred by banks in advancing loans will not be offset by the low demand for financial services in remote, rural areas. Furthermore, compounding the issue of financial exclusion of women is the fact that empirical

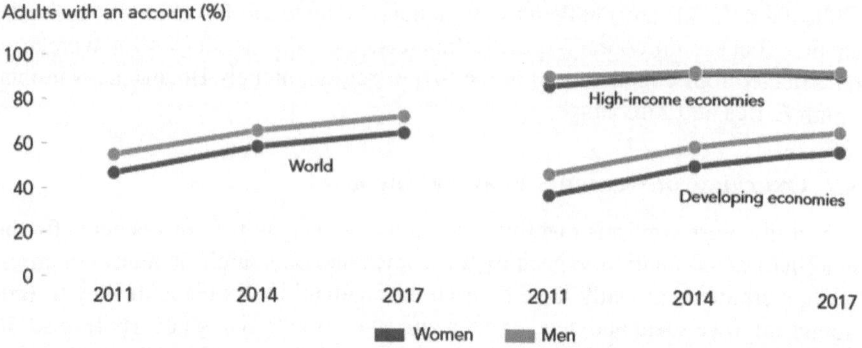

Figure 8.1 Gender gap in account ownership between developed and developing countries
Source: Demirgüç-Kunt et al. (2017) Global Findex Database. A Demirgüç-Kunt, L Klapper, D Singer, S Ansar and J Hess (2018) *World Bank* 1–113.

studies have shown that in the SADC region, the majority of commercial banks and financial institutions are situated in urban cities and towns, which present lucrative business opportunities, and high-income earners normally reside in these areas.[17] Resultantly, the majority of women, low-income earners, the poor and vulnerable members of society who reside mostly in the rural and farming communities are financially excluded.

Research further shows that the demands and requirements of commercial and financial institutions regarding minimum account balances to be maintained at banks,[18] certified copies of residential addresses and utility bills, monthly bank charges and low literacy, coupled with a great amount of paperwork preclude women from accessing financial services. Lastly, the cost of servicing customers in rural areas has been found to be astronomically high, unviable and not cost-effective for commercial banks to service the unbanked populace. The unbanked population mostly comprises low-income earners and the poor, and many women belong to this group, hence financial exclusion.

Most of the unbanked population and the small enterprises that they operate do not have a trading financial and business history/experience,[19] hence when it comes to borrowing, these groups find it extremely difficult to access loans in most instances and commercial banks are reluctant to advance credit to them. Coupled with the above, banks and financial institutions normally require collateral and security when they advance loans, and this is not readily available to marginalised members of society, the poor and women. Considering the preceding information, one could argue that many of the identified challenges vitiate the financial inclusion of women to a large extent. However, regardless of the noted glitches, these are not insurmountable for any government, which is propelled by the desire to achieve equality for all its citizenry in accessing financial services and products.

8.2.1 The rationale for financial inclusion

This section focuses on the rationale for financial inclusion in generic terms, which is also significant for the financial inclusion of women. While financial inclusion has been defined earlier, it is noteworthy to appreciate what financial exclusion entails to comprehend the distinction between the two terms. Financial exclusion refers to a situation where a significant proportion of a country's population has no access to the financial sector's services, products and systems. To some extent, financial exclusion may be described as a situation where some segments of the population, especially the poor and disadvantaged groups of society, are neglected from accessing formal financial services, and this is referred to as involuntary financial exclusion. Ultimately, this results in lower savings mobilisation and investment in a country. Voluntary financial exclusion normally arises when individuals voluntarily decide that they do not wish to utilise financial services and products, hence it is a matter of choice. However, the focus of this section is based on involuntary financial exclusion since it affects a larger proportion of the population in many countries.

In support of financial inclusion, empirical research has confirmed that financial inclusion is critical in a country for a variety of reasons,[20] as highlighted below, and that opportunities exist to provide financial services to the poor, and most importantly, to women.

Financial inclusion reduces transaction costs for households and individuals. This is evident in instances where commercial banks serve a large clientele, and thus benefit from economies of scale. The cost per unit of the transaction will be cheaper considering the large numbers of customers and transactions that will be processed.

Greater financial inclusion improves liquidity because the population of the unbanked will now shift their focus from mainly a consumptive behaviour to that one of saving. This will have a multiplier effect on the economy since savings will be pooled into investments. In this instance, the money market will be awash with cash as more customers will be participating in the financial system. On the other hand, credit will be readily available, especially for those customers who may need financial accommodation since the financial resources would be easily accessible.

Financial inclusion also promotes the creation of wealth on one hand and addresses income disparities for the unbanked segments of society. The creation of wealth is mainly a result of the process of financial intermediation that is played by commercial banks and financial institutions in the financial system of a country. Thus, there will be an efficient allocation of financial resources in the country.[21]

Financial inclusion reduces the levels of poverty in a country since income will be generated by the financial system where most people will have access to products and services in a country. This is premised on the fact that there are many participants in the financial services sector, inclusive of marginalised members of society. Consequently, this could lead to an amelioration of their financial well-being and living standards, which enables them to generate financial assets and income for their sustenance.[22]

Research also confirms that meaningful financial inclusion may positively contribute to reduced gender inequalities, especially in situations where women have access to bank accounts and other related services, and they would be able to manage their earnings. This implies that women would be able to make informed decisions about critical spending patterns daily.

In support of the above, other authors[23] echo the same sentiments by arguing that the achievement of financial inclusion can help boost inclusive growth and economic development, which is positive for businesses as reaching out and serving women can be profitable for the entirety of society. Several stakeholders stand to benefit from the financial inclusion of women, namely the communities, government and the providers of financial services, which results in robust financial systems.

In addition, financial inclusion assists governments in making social security payments such as old age pensions and child support grants, which are transferred to bank accounts through electronic transfers, for instance, the South African Social Security Agency (SASSA). SASSA is a government agency in South Africa that is mandated to meet the monthly financial needs of the aged, pensioners and children. In Zimbabwe, the National Social Security (NSSA) performs similar roles, but mostly for monthly pensioner payments. In this regard, financial inclusion aids in making funds available to vulnerable members of society. Without bank accounts, it would be practically impossible to come to the aid of deserving members in need of financial aid in society.

Furthermore, financial inclusion offers immense benefits to banks. The multiple, vast number of low-cost deposits will offer banks an opportunity to reduce their dependence on bulk deposits and help them to better manage both liquidity risks and asset-liability mismatches.[24] As a result of this, banks would be able to reduce concentration risk, since they could advance loans to different types of clients without focusing on a few selected clients in a specific sector.

An inclusive financial system has been found to reduce the proliferation of an informal source of funds, such as money lenders who have been found to be exploitative in charging exorbitant interest charges[25] on borrowings. Financial inclusion also results in a secure savings system that operates efficiently based on market forces. Borrowers will have the choice of accessing finance from the formal banking system without relying on these speculative sources of finance. To sum up, access to financial services is sacrosanct to the economic and social development of a country as shown from the evidence above. Hence, financial inclusion should be made a priority in policy pronouncements by governments around the globe since the benefits of financial inclusion far outweigh the costs of financial exclusion.

8.2.2 Challenges of financial inclusion

While it is evident and undeniable that the financial inclusion of women brings about innumerable benefits, there are challenges associated with the inclusion process as identified by researchers,[26] which include, among others:

a) Security: Commercial banks and financial institutions rely on technology in availing their products to customers. Security concerns have been raised regarding technology that includes hacking as well as cyber criminals who also commit fraudulent activities using other peoples' accounts. Such occurrences may result in the generality of the public not having confidence in the financial system, which may hinder the uptake of financial services by individuals who may become sceptical of the financial system.

b) Infrastructural limitations: The issues of network and power supply are important considerations, especially in SADC rural areas. Banking transactions are normally conducted on a real-time basis in cities and towns. However, in remote and rural areas of the SADC regions, issues of network and power supply are the major challenges, which make it extremely difficult to financially include women in the financial system.

c) Financial illiteracy: Lack of education militates against financial inclusion for women since some of them are not well conversant with the operations of financial markets as well as the availability of financial services. As a result, these women do not know the types of financial products available and do not appreciate the value of financial services. A lack of financial knowledge culminates in women being exposed to financial shocks and risks.

d) For the rural, remote poor women operating in villages, the cost of accessing financial services acts as a barrier for them to actively participate in the formal financial markets since they have constrained financial resources.
e) Related to the above, most rural women do not have a fixed income, while in other instances, the income levels would be very low. Therefore, it would be very difficult to integrate women who fall into this category into the mainstream financial system.
f) The geographical location of rural women: Since many women are residents in rural areas, the implication is that financial services can only be accessed either in cities or towns since that is where the commercial banks and financial institutions are located. In that regard, distance becomes a major consideration, hence women are financially excluded from the formal banking systems.

In addition, several business transactions are conducted in the informal sector, making it practically impossible to access formal financial services. Businesses in countries such as Zimbabwe, which now has a thriving informal economy due to the high unemployment rate, find it difficult to access formal financial services, hence many individuals will remain financially excluded. The continued use of only informal instruments implies that the poor are limited in their quest to make savings and manage risk appropriately.[27]

In addition, the implementation of an inclusive financial system that incorporates women is also prone to other limitations. Previous research confirmed that high transaction costs (especially in remote rural areas) make opening a bank branch or financial services point unprofitable. Hence, providing small services to the rural populace is very expensive, which explains why most commercial banks and financial service providers are in major towns and cities.

Furthermore, in developing or rural economies, the geographical dispersion of producers and the lack or bad condition of road networks contribute to very high transaction costs.[28] Taking note of the above, it becomes unviable economically for commercial banks and financial institutions to serve rural segments due to the high transaction costs involved. On a related matter, commercial banks and other financial service providers normally require collateral and security for loans and borrowings. Such products will not be within the reach of the marginalised poor, rural communities in which women are located.

8.3 Financial inclusion of women in the SADC region

The African continent exhibits varying degrees of financial inclusion among the 54 different member states. A review of the literature available confirms that all African countries have a high level of financially excluded people, and this is symptomatic of the lack of access to formal financial resources.[29] Consequently, this signifies that the level of financial inclusion is still very low on the African continent. The implication of this is a testament to the existence of an informal economy that serves the needs of most of the unbanked population, with the majority being women as articulated earlier. In Africa, it was established that approximate 500 million adults remain outside the formal financial system, while within SADC, 45 million people are financially excluded,[30] with women less likely to have an account than men,[31] thus compounding the problem of the exclusion of women from the financial system. To corroborate the fact above, research further confirms that women in developing economies are 20% less likely to have an account at a formal financial institution compared with men.[32] In SADC, 36% of women are financially excluded compared with 33% of men.[33] Figure 8.2 highlights the financial inclusion rates for selected countries in SADC and Kenya spanning from 2004 to 2015.

Generally, as presented in Figure 8.2, South Africa has the highest rates of financial inclusion, which indicate that it has more programmes that are meant to enhance the inclusion of people in accessing financial services and products. At the lower end of the continuum sits Zimbabwe, with plummeting financial inclusion rates between 2004 and 2011, which might be reflective of a plethora of social, political and economic problems that the country has been experiencing over the past two decades. Research confirms that women in SADC face barriers to financial access due to lower levels of education, a lack of formal employment and a lack of collateral requirements since they are not heading family households.[34] In comparison with other regions, for instance, in North, West and Central Africa, the literature confirms that the levels of financial inclusion for women are very low as compared with the SADC region. Countries such as Algeria, Cameroon, Burkina Faso and Nigeria exhibit a larger gender gap in terms of financial inclusion that militates against the respective countries' efforts in advancing women's financial inclusion.[35] West and Central Africa have been confirmed as the least

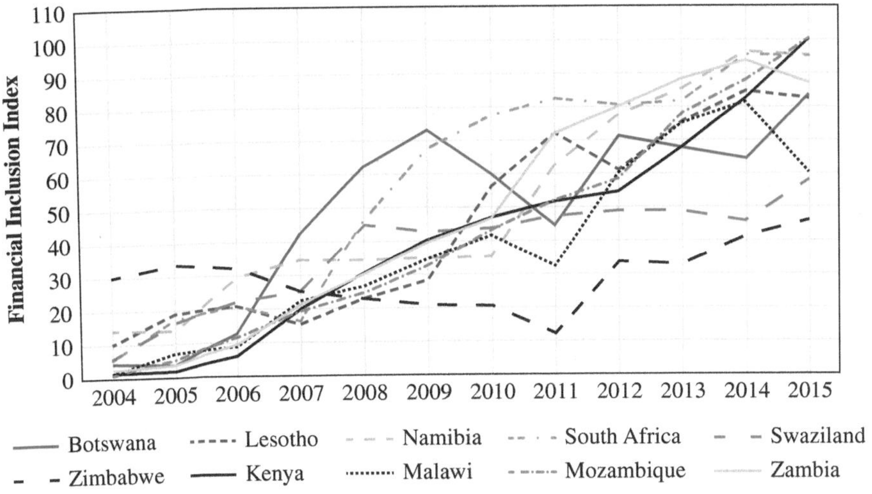

Figure 8.2 Within country indices of financial inclusion in SADC and Kenya. Source: Demirgüç-Kunt, L Klapper, D Singer, S Ansar and J Hess et al. (2018) *World Bank* 1–113.

financially inclusive regions in Africa, especially regarding women.[36] The West and Central African countries alluded to in the preceding discussion include Benin, Burkina Faso, Mali, Niger, Senegal, Togo, Ghana, Guinea, Nigeria, Sierra Leon, Cameroon, Congo, Gabon, Central African Republic, Chad and Burundi. The discussion below provides an analysis and synopsis of the level, extent and magnitude of financial inclusion for women in the SADC countries under study.

8.3.1 Financial inclusion of women in South Africa

South Africa has one of the most robust and sophisticated financial systems in Africa, as well as the SADC region, with a population of 59.62 million people constituted of 51.1% females, with the remainder being male.[37] In South Africa, the dimensions of financial inclusion are based on access, usage and quality of the financial products and services as presented in Figure 8.3. Financial inclusion is not only based on access to financial services but also considers the use and quality of those products and services.

In addressing all facets that are related to women, South Africa adopted the Millennium Development Goals (MDGs) in the early 2000s in collaboration with the United Nations. One of the MDGs has been the promotion of gender equality and the empowerment of women. South Africa adopted policies aimed at the regulation of the financial sector and the advancement of financial inclusion as a policy priority, which saw the introduction of the Financial Sector Regulation Act, 2017.[38] Results have shown that the policy pronouncements and initiatives have paid off as evidenced by a marked increase in financial inclusion from 61% in 2004 to 89% in 2016.[39]

In line with the above assertion, South Africa attained the National Development Plan goal of 90% financial inclusion by 2030 in 2019. In fact, among the SADC countries, South Africa is the only country that has managed to financially include most women in the financial services sector. These sentiments were echoed by other researchers who argued that financial inclusion may be reaching its saturation point in South Africa since more than 90% of females are financially included as compared with 84% of men.[40] In view of the above, South Africa has made

Access	Usage
"Access" refers to the ease with which a consumer can obtain a financial service and includes physical and electronic reach of service provisioning as well as the affordability of financial services	"Usage" refers to both the upake of appropriate and needed products and services as well as how the acquired services are being used after nitial acquisition
Quality	
"Quality" of financial services refers to the experience of the consumer, both when acquiring and during the use of financial services. This includes market conduct, treating customers fairly and equitably, as well as client awareness and financial literacy	

Figure 8.3 Dimensions of financial inclusion in South Africa Source: Financial Sector Conduct Authority. Financial Sector Conduct Authority 'Financial Inclusion Strategy' (2019) www.fsca.co.za, accessed on 8 February 2021.

considerable efforts and improvements in making sure that women access finance as compared with other countries in the SADC region, which is also confirmed in the extant literature.[41]

In concurrence with the above, some researchers investigated the state of financial inclusion in relation to the gender disparities in South Africa and found that women mainly used formal, transactional products and informal financial mechanisms, while men used formal credit and insurance. However, there were no noticeable differences in the welfare of financially included men and women;[42] the differences were not that significant. Currently, the focus for South Africa could possibly be related to the quality of products/services being offered by financial service providers since there is a saturation of financial inclusion. Considering the foregoing, one could argue that South Africa's situation presents a unique case, coupled with the fact that women are more financially included than men due to its well-established and well-advanced financial sector,[43] this is in contrast with the rest of Africa, where the rate of financial inclusion is very low.

8.3.2 Financial inclusion of women in Botswana

Botswana has been among the world's fastest-growing economies over the past 50 years, with the transition from being among the poorest to an upper middle-income status, consequently pulling the majority of Batswana out of abject poverty. Ironically, despite this major transition, many in Botswana are still poor, and the level of inequality is among the highest in the world.[44] As of 2020, Botswana had a population of 2,254,126, of which 51.64% were females. The country is classified as an upper-middle-income country.[45] The marked growth and development of Botswana over the last half a century has mainly been attributed to the sound democratic principles espoused by the country's leadership, and the prudent management of the country's mineral resources, which has culminated in the country being recognised on the continent as one of the beacons of democracy.

The promulgation of the National Development Plan 10 in 2007 highlights the serious commitment of the Botswana Government to its citizens having access to financial services. In support of the above fact, the Ministry of Finance and Economic Development (MFED) is mandated to implement the national financial inclusion programme with a budgetary allocation. In complementing the efforts of MFED, the Ministry of Investment, Trade and Industry provided budgetary support in two critical areas, namely credit market development and consumer protection and literacy, which were meant to enhance financial inclusion. Furthermore, the Botswana Financial Inclusion Roadmap 2015–2020 laid out Botswana's priorities for the enhancement of financial inclusion in the country. Five decades ago, the rate of financially excluded Batswana was approximately 96%, and the country registered a financial inclusion rate of 50% in 2014.[46] Despite some of these positives, research confirms that further progress in financial inclusion was hampered by several factors such as:[47]

a) A large informal sector. This implies that players in the informal sector trade within their sector, hence there is no need to be incorporated into the formal financial system.
b) A worry-free attitude, "no mathata" (meaning *no problem*) in terms of savings and borrowings of citizens and small, micro and medium enterprises.
c) Poor access to formal credit.
d) Market concentration – dominance of the retail financial sector by two banks and the widespread presence of monopolies or oligopolies in almost every sector of the economy.
e) Absence of, or very low presence of, formal financial institutions in both rural areas and small urban centres.
f) A weak enabling environment for private businesses.
g) Poor governance in areas such as monetary policy, land ownership, public sector agency governance, government procurement and the legal and regulatory framework.

The Government of Botswana set up the Citizen Entrepreneurial Development Agency (CEDA) with a mandate to help businesses grow through financial capacitation, which aids financial inclusion. Regardless of this positive move by the government in accelerating the levels of financial inclusion, accessing funds from CEDA is an uphill task for unemployed youths, the rural poor and women. As noted in prior studies, many Batswana have no access to financial services due to a lack of collateral demanded by formal banking institutions operating in the financial services sector. The problem is rife, mostly for women who cannot access the much-needed finance from the formal financial system due to the high levels of poverty. Therefore, the main challenge for Botswana is the lack of implementation of key strategies that are geared towards the reduction of financial exclusion to reduce poverty[48] and unemployment among vulnerable groups in society. To conclude, youths, the rural poor, women and those who are financially illiterate are mostly excluded from accessing finance from the formal banking system, which obliterates the Government of Botswana's efforts of increasing the levels of financial inclusion.

8.3.3 Financial inclusion of women in Namibia

Namibia is an upper-middle-income country with a population of about 2.5 million people, comprising 51.54% of women. The country's sound political stability and economic management have aided the leadership in containing the vagaries of poverty and unequal income distribution. The major segments of the population that are prone to poverty are female-headed households, the less educated, larger families, children, the elderly and labourers in subsistence farming. Coupled with all these challenges, unemployment is wreaking havoc among the youth at 43.4%, and 38.3% among women.[49] Covid-19 is also likely to have a negative impact on the mineral-rich country due to weak demand for minerals, which may hurt exports. Poverty levels among vulnerable groups may also rise due to the negative effects of the pandemic.

Since many women lack access to credit, they normally turn to the informal sector, and most women-headed households are greatly affected as compared with men because of being financially excluded.[50] The inability of women to access loans from banks and financial service providers means that they are constrained in terms of entrepreneurial projects they may wish to embark on. Such projects could benefit other people in the form of employment creation, thus alleviating unemployment and poverty.

However, Namibia's scenario is rather different from many African countries as regards women's financial exclusion. Namibia has done well in terms of financial inclusion, occupying number four within the SADC region, with women being more financially included than men, which suggests that most of the adults who are unbanked in Namibia are men. This is also a departure from global statistics[51] that indicate women fall into the majority of the unbanked. However, within the context of Namibia, the gender disparities are somehow skewed in favour of women. The 2017 financial inclusion report for Namibia highlights that 79.8% of eligible women are financially included, compared with 76.1% of eligible men.[52]

While disparities exist between men and women in terms of financial inclusion, it is noticeable that such disparities are not very significant as evidenced by the statistics presented above. On a positive note, lessons could be learned from the experiences of Namibia in how it has managed to financially include most women, which is not in tandem with trends on the African continent. Possibly one of the reasons could be related to the fact that Namibia has paid special attention to women's empowerment and gender equality, as enshrined in its constitution. Significant targets have been met, for instance, there has been a marked increase in the number of girls attending primary and secondary school. Namibia has also shown total commitment towards women's empowerment and ensuring women have access to services for education, health and employment.[53]

8.3.4 Financial inclusion of women in Zimbabwe

Zimbabwe is a low-income country that has a population of 14.6 million people, with women constituting 52.3% of the population.[54] Zimbabwe took a deliberate stance in 2016 in crafting a National Financial Inclusion Strategy (2016–2020) that was geared towards the promotion of access to and use of financial services by the country's unbanked individuals, coupled with enhancing financial inclusion of marginalised groups, including women. The National Financial Inclusion Strategy was in line with the SADC Financial Inclusion Strategy, 2016–2021. Women play a pivotal role in Zimbabwe's society in different facets such as leadership, entrepreneurship and service provision. Previous surveys[55] highlighted that while women own 57% of micro, small, and medium enterprises (MSMEs) in Zimbabwe, only 14% of MSMEs use banking services, confirming the fact that most of the women are not financially included in the formal financial system.

It is well-established that most women in Zimbabwe do not save with formal financial institutions, since some of the requirements for opening and maintaining bank accounts are prohibitive and very stringent. In addition, the high minimum balance requirements, as well as high bank charges, discourage women from opening and maintaining accounts with formal financial institutions. These commercial banks and other financial service providers do not adequately target women in their lending models.[56] In instances where commercial banks advance credit to women, they normally require collateral security, which could be in the form of title deeds that most women do not have access to. In trying to mitigate these problems, women resort to the informal sector where they "pool" small amounts together (Mukando) for personal and business needs.[57] The challenges faced by women in Zimbabwe cut across the globe in general and SADC in particular. Therefore, it is not very surprising that most women in Zimbabwe are financially excluded as it is a global trend.

Furthermore, previous research confirms that financial inclusion among women increased from 59% in 2011 to 76% in 2014, while among men, financial inclusion increased from 64% in 2011 to 79% in 2014.[58] Although the disparities are not that significant, it remains a fact that women are still lagging in terms of financial inclusion, despite the concerted efforts made by the Government of Zimbabwe in addressing the gender imbalances. While upper-middle-income countries, such as Namibia and South Africa, have high rates of financial inclusion that are driven by the financial services sector, countries such as Zimbabwe rely on both the formal sector and other channels such as mobile money and remittances.[59] In rural farming areas, women have limited access to loans advanced by commercial banks, thus further excluding women from the formal financial system.

8.4 Conclusion

This chapter focused on the importance of financial inclusion at a global level, which was narrowed to the SADC region. Evidence from previous research suggests that financial inclusion enhances economic development, promotes access to income and ameliorates the well-being of society. When women are denied access to loans and other financial products, it constrains their growth prospects and hinders their entrepreneurial intentions, which limits choices and exposes them to the vagaries of financial risks and shocks. As already noted, the major constraints to increased financial inclusion among women are lack of income, geographical distance to financial institutions, especially in rural areas, and weak financial literacy.

Some countries within the SADC region such as South Africa and Namibia have managed to financially include most women in the formal financial system, which is in contrast with global trends. This could be a learning curve, possibly for other countries with low inclusion rates like Zimbabwe and Botswana. At a national level, countries are encouraged to enact policies that address gender inequity, especially in terms of financial inclusion so that women can also have choices regarding savings, investments, access to credit and daily expenditures. Women's financial inclusion has been observed as a lever to advance gender equality.[60]

Commercial banks and other financial service providers should have policies that accommodate the needs of the poor and rural marginalised women in their lending criteria. Most importantly, banks and other financial service providers should not prescribe too many qualifying criteria for accessing loans that are prohibitive. As such, credit availability should be made easily accessible to women without the restrictive requirements of security. This also extends to the large volumes of paperwork that are associated with opening bank accounts, which should be eased. Financial institutions should be encouraged to educate potential customers, especially women, regarding finance since it was also identified as a constraint to accessing finance. Financial illiteracy contributes to a greater extent to the high levels of women's financial exclusion.

Regarding the issue of financial service providers being hesitant to set up branches in remote rural areas, governments could possibly offer tax incentives for those financial service providers that set up branches in rural areas to service the rural population. Such incentives could be related to granting a "grace period" for the payment of corporate tax, especially to those companies that decide to set up branches in rural areas serving women. This is the time when gender inequities should be addressed, otherwise, a greater proportion of women will be financially excluded from the formal banking systems in perpetuity, as if they are second-class citizens in various social strata.

Notes

1 PK Ozili 'Financial Inclusion Research Around the World: A Review' (2020) *Forum for Social Economics* 457–479.
2 Southern African Development Community 'SADC Financial Inclusion Strategy 2016–2021' (2016) 6–7.
3 World Bank 'Global Financial Report on Financial Inclusion' (2014) 2.
4 For the purposes of this study, SADC countries include Angola, Botswana, Comoros, Democratic Republic of Congo, Eswatini, Lesotho, Madagascar, Malawi, Mauritius, Mozambique, Namibia, Seychelles, South Africa, Tanzania, Zambia and Zimbabwe.
5 A Barajas, T Beck, M Belhaj and SB Naceur 'Financial Inclusion: What Have We Learned So Far? What Do We Have to Learn?' (2020) *International Monetary Fund Working Papers* 1–34.
6 A Demirgüç-Kunt, L Klapper, D Singer, S Ansar and J Hess 'The Global Findex Database 2017: Measuring Financial Inclusion and the Fintech Revolution' (2018) *World Bank* 1–113.
7 A Zins and L Weill 'The Determinants of Financial Inclusion in Africa' (2016) 6(1) *Review of Development Finance* 46-57.
8 World Bank 'Global Financial Report on Financial Inclusion' (2014) 3.
9 A Barajas, T Beck, M Belhaj and SB Naceur (2020) *International Monetary Fund Working Papers* 1–34.
10 JO Abebe, L Maina, J Ondiek and C Ogolla 'Background Paper Driving Gender-Responsive Financial Inclusion Models in Africa' (2017) *UN Women* 16.
11 Ibid.
12 Ibid.
13 PK Ozili (2020) *Forum for Social Economics* 457–479.
14 JO Abebe, L Maina, J Ondiek and C Ogolla (2017) *UN Women*' (2017) *UN Women* 11.

15 United Nations Sustainable Development Goals 'The 17 Goals' https://sdgs.un.org/goals, accessed 17 March 2021.
16 F Allen, E Carletti, R Cull, JQ Qian, L Senbet & P Valenzuela 'Improving Access to Banking: Evidence from Kenya' (2021) 25(2) *Review of Finance* 403-447; N Masiyandima, K Mlambo and S Nyarota 'Financial Inclusion and Quality of Livelihood in Zimbabwe' (2017) *14th African Finance Journal Conference-Africagrowth Institute* 1–38.
17 F Allen, E Carletti, R Cull, J Qian, LW Senbet and P Valenzuela 'Improving Access to Banking: Evidence from Kenya' (2014) *The World Bank Development Research Group* 30.
18 P Honohan 'Cross-Country Variation in Household Access to Financial Services' (2008) *Journal of Banking & Finance* 2493–2500.
19 N Masiyandima, K Mlambo and S Nyarota (2017) *14th African Finance Journal Conference-Africagrowth Institute* 1–38.
20 N Masiyandima, K Mlambo and S Nyarota (2017) *14th African Finance Journal Conference-Africagrowth Institute* 1–38.
21 Ibid.
22 Ibid.
23 Ibid.
24 P Shah and M Dubhashi 'Review Paper on Financial Inclusion – The Means of Inclusive Growth' (2015) *Chanakya International Journal of Business Research* 37–48.
25 M Sarma and J Pais 'Financial Inclusion and Development' (2011) *Journal of International Development* 613–628.
26 HR Khan 'Issues and Challenges in Financial Inclusion: Policies, Partnerships, Processes and Products' (2012) *RBI Monthly Bulletin* 1447–1457; CL Dhliwayo 'Initiatives to Promote Financial Inclusion for Women: The Case of Zimbabwe' (2016) *The Fletcher School Leadership Program for Financial Inclusion Policy Memoranda* 93–99.
27 K Donovan 'Mobile Money for Financial Inclusion' (2012) *Information and Communications for Development* 61–73.
28 MJR Garcia & M José 'Can Financial Inclusion and Financial Stability Go Hand in Hand?' (2016) *Economic Issues* 81–103.
29 CK Oji 'Promoting Financial Inclusion for Inclusive Growth in Africa' (2015) *South African Institute of International Affairs Occasional Paper 210* 1–18.
30 Finmark Trust 'Measuring Progress: Financial Inclusion in SADC' (2018) 7 https://finmark.org.za/system/documents/files/000/000/184/original/ME_Report.18.pdf?1601965010, accessed on 18 July 2021.
31 JO Abebe, L Maina, J Ondiek and C Ogolla (2017) *UN Women* 18.
32 Ibid.
33 Finmark Trust 'Measuring Progress: Financial Inclusion in Selected SADC Countries' (2019) *Finmark Trust Report* 17.
34 JO Abebe, L Maina, J Ondiek and C Ogolla (2017) *UN Women* 29.
35 A Demirguc-Kunt, L Klapper, D Singer, S Ansar and J Hess (2018) *The World Bank* 25-113. See also I Soumaré, F Tchana Tchana & TM Kengne 'Analysis of the Determinants of Financial Inclusion in Central and West Africa' (2016) *Transnational Corporations Review* 231–249.
36 A Demirguc-Kunt, L Klapper, D Singer, S Ansar and J Hess (2018) *The World Bank* 25–113.
37 Statistics South Africa 'Mid-Year Population Estimates 2020' (2020) http://www.statssa.gov.za/?s=mid-year+population+estimates&sitem=publicatic, accessed on 15 February 2021.
38 Ibid.
39 R Abrahams 'Financial Inclusion in South Africa: A Review of the Literature' (2017) *Southern African Accounting Association* 632–661.

40 P Shipalana 'Digitising Financial Services: A Tool for Financial Inclusion in South Africa?' (2019) *South African Institute of International Affairs Occasional Paper 301* 1–38.
41 JO Abebe, L Maina, J Ondiek and C Ogolla (2017) *UN Women* 27.
42 PK Ozili 'Financial Inclusion Research Around the World: A Review' (2020) *Forum for Social Economics* 457–479.
43 Finmark Trust 'Research Report on Mobile Money in South Africa' (2017) *Finmark Trust Report* 25.
44 World Bank 'Botswana Systematic Country Diagnostic' (2015) *The World Bank Group* vi.
45 A Barajas, T Beck, M Belhaj and SB Naceur (2020) *International Monetary Fund Working Papers* 1–34.
46 M Chibba 'Financial Inclusion, Poverty Reduction and the Millennium Development Goals' (2009) *The European Journal of Development Research* 213–230.
K Molefhi 'Financial Inclusion and its Impact on Employment Creation in Botswana' (2019) *Botswana Institute for Development Policy Analysis Working Paper 60* 1–28.
47 M Chibba (2009) *The European Journal of Development Research* 213–230.
48 PK Madigele and GEJ Mogomotsi 'Improving Financial Inclusion of the Socially and Economically Disadvantaged in Botswana Through the Grameen Bank Microcredit Model' (2016) 9(1) *Botswana Journal of Business* 55–65.
49 World Bank 'World Bank Namibia' (2020) https://www.worldbank.org/en/country/namibia/overview, accessed on 12 January 2021.
50 JH Kim 'A Study on the Effect of Financial Inclusion on the Relationship Between Income Inequality and Economic Growth' (2016) 52(2) *Emerging Markets Finance and Trade* 498–512.
51 A Mukong, N Shiwayu and T Kaulihowa 'A Decomposition of the Gender Gap in Financial Inclusion: Evidence from Namibia' (2020) 15 *African Journal of Business and Economic Research* 151.
52 Namibia Statistics Agency 'Namibia Financial Inclusion Survey' (2017) Financial Inclusion Report of Namibia 27.
53 UN Women Namibia 'Namibia Aims for Equal Access to Services, Roles for Women as Agents of Peace' (2015) https://www.unwomen.org/en/get-involved/step-it-up/commitments/namibia, accessed on 3 January 2021.
54 World Bank 'Zimbabwe' (2019) https://data.worldbank.org/country/ZW, accessed on 20 December 2019.
55 Finscope 'MSME Survey Zimbabwe 2012' (2012) http://www.finmark.org.za/wp-content/uploads/pubs/Finscope_Zimbabwe_Broch/3nfl.pdf, accessed on 18 November 2018.
56 CL Dhliwayo (2016) *The Fletcher School Leadership Program for Financial Inclusion Policy Memoranda* 93–99.
57 Ibid.
58 CL Dhliwayo (2016) *The Fletcher School Leadership Program for Financial Inclusion Policy Memoranda* 93–99.
59 SADC 'SADC Financial Inclusion Strategy (2016–2022)' (2016) *SADC* 16.
60 Bill and Melinda Gates Foundation 'A G7 Partnership for Women's Digital Financial Inclusion in Africa' (2019) *Bill and Melinda Gates Foundation* 16.

Bibliography

J O Abebe, L Maina, J Ondiek & C Ogolla 'Background paper driving gender-responsive financial inclusion models in Africa' (2017) *UN Women* 1 at 44.

R Abrahams 'Financial inclusion in South Africa: A review of the literature' (2017) *Southern African Accounting Association* 632 at 661.

F Allen, E Carletti, R Cull, J Q Qian, L Senbet & P Valenzuela 'Improving access to banking: Evidence from Kenya' (2021) 25(2) *Review of Finance* 403 at 447.

F Allen, E Carletti, R Cull, J Qian, L W Senbet & P Valenzuela 'Improving access to banking: Evidence from Kenya' (2014) *The World Bank Development Research Group* 1 at 53.

A Barajas, T Beck, M Belhaj & S B Naceur *Financial Inclusion: What Have We Learned So Far? What Do We Have to Learn?* (International monetary fund working papers, 2020) 1 at 34.

Bill and Melinda Gates Foundation 'A G7 partnership for women's digital financial inclusion in Africa' (2019) *Bill and Melinda Gates Foundation* 1 at 24.

M Chibba 'Financial inclusion, poverty reduction and the millennium development goals' (2009) *The European Journal of Development Research* 213 at 230.

A Demirgüç-Kunt, L Klapper, D Singer, S Ansar & J Hess 'The Global Findex database 2017: Measuring financial inclusion and the Fintech revolution' (2018) *World Bank* 1 at 113.

C L Dhliwayo 'Initiatives to promote financial inclusion for women: The case of Zimbabwe' (2016) *The Fletcher School Leadership Program for Financial Inclusion Policy Memoranda* 93 at 99.

K Donovan 'Mobile money for financial inclusion' (2012) *Information and Communications for Development* 61 at 73.

Financial Sector Conduct Authority 'Financial inclusion strategy' 2019, available at www.fsca.co.za, accessed on 8 February 2021.

Finmark Trust 'Measuring progress: Financial inclusion in SADC' 2018, available at https://finmark.org.za/system/documents/files/000/000/184/original/ME_Report.18.pdf?1601965010, accessed on 18 July 2021.

Finmark Trust *Measuring Progress: Financial Inclusion in Selected SADC Countries* (Finmark Trust Report 1-33, 2019).

Finmark Trust *Research Report on Mobile Money in South Africa* (Finmark Trust Report 1-75, 2017).

Finscope 'MSME survey Zimbabwe 2012' 2012, available at http://www.finmark.org.za/wp-content/uploads/pubs/Finscope_Zimbabwe_Broch/3nfl.pdf, accessed on 18 November 2018.

M J R Garcia & M José 'Can financial inclusion and financial stability go hand in hand?' (2016) *Economic Issues* 81 at 103.

P Honohan 'Cross-country variation in household access to financial services' (2008) *Journal of Banking & Finance* 2493 at 2500.

H R Khan 'Issues and challenges in financial inclusion: Policies, partnerships, processes and products' (2012) *RBI Monthly Bulletin* 1447 at 1457.

J H Kim 'A study on the effect of financial inclusion on the relationship between income inequality and economic growth' (2016) 52(2) *Emerging Markets Finance and Trade* 498 at 512.

P K Madigele & G E J Mogomotsi 'Improving financial inclusion of the socially and economically disadvantaged in Botswana through the grameen bank microcredit model' (2016) 9(1) *Botswana Journal of Business* 55 at 65.

N Masiyandima, K Mlambo & S Nyarota 'Financial inclusion and quality of livelihood in Zimbabwe' (2017) *14th African Finance Journal Conference-Africagrowth Institute* 1 at 38.

K Molefhi 'Financial inclusion and its impact on employment creation in Botswana' (Botswana Institute for Development Policy analysis working paper 60, 2019) 1 at 28.

A Mukong, N Shiwayu & T Kaulihowa 'A decomposition of the gender gap in financial inclusion: Evidence from Namibia' (2020) 15 *African Journal of Business and Economic Research* 149 at 164.

C K Oji 'Promoting financial inclusion for inclusive growth in Africa' (2015) 210 *South African Institute of International Affairs Occasional Paper* 1 at 18.

P K Ozili 'Financial inclusion research around the world: A review' (2020) *Forum for Social Economics* 457 at 479.

M Sarma & J Pais 'Financial inclusion and development' (2011) *Journal of International Development* 613 at 628.

P Shah & M Dubhashi 'Review paper on financial inclusion - The means of inclusive growth' (2015) *Chanakya International Journal of Business Research* 37 at 48.

P Shipalana 'Digitising financial services: A tool for financial inclusion in South Africa?' (2019) 301 *South African Institute of International Affairs Occasional Paper* 1 at 38.

I Soumaré, F Tchana & T M Kengne 'Analysis of the determinants of financial inclusion in central and West Africa' (2016) *Transnational Corporations Review* 231 at 249.

Southern African Development Community 'SADC financial inclusion strategy 2016 at 2021' (2016)

Statistics South Africa 'Mid-year population estimates 2020' 2020, available at http://www.statssa.gov.za/?s=mid-year+population+estimates&sitem=publicatic, accessed on 15 February 2021.

United Nations Sustainable Development Goals 'The 17 goals' available at https://sdgs.un.org/goals, accessed 17 March 2021.

United Nations Women Namibia 'Namibia aims for equal access to services, roles for women as agents of peace' 2015, available at https://www.unwomen.org/en/get-involved/step-it-up/commitments/namibia, accessed on 3 January 2021.

World Bank 'Botswana systematic country diagnostic' (2015) *The World Bank Group* 1 at 125.

World Bank 'Zimbabwe' 2019, available at https://data.worldbank.org/country/ZW, accessed on 20 December 2019.

A Zins & L Weill 'The determinants of financial inclusion in Africa' (2016) 6(1) *Review of Development Finance* 46 at 57.

9 Digital transformation strategies for financial inclusion in South African rural areas

Gertruida van Niekerk

9.1 Introduction

Previous studies have reported that financial inclusion improves the quality of life for poor people and low-income earners as it reduces poverty and inequality and increases economic growth and productivity.[1] When these individuals do not have access to a bank account, it consequently excludes them from access to other financial services, because a bank account is commonly the "gateway" to financial inclusion.[2] Without the use of a bank account, people find it problematic to enter into financial transactions without using cash.[3] Furthermore, it is difficult for the poor and low-income earners to save, borrow and invest and take out insurance if they do not have access to bank accounts.

During the apartheid regime in South Africa (SA), many people were financially excluded.[4] After SA became a democratic state in 1994, some of these inequalities were rectified. Much still has to be done to assist people who rely on the cash economy and subsequently on less-efficient, inadequate and high-risk financial services to become financially included.[5] Financial inclusion has the potential to impact people on a huge scale because it is a key aspect of uplifting previously disadvantaged people in SA, especially the poor and low-income earners.[6]

This chapter investigates whether digital financial inclusion of the poor and low-income earners in rural SA can be expanded through digital transformation. In particular, this chapter will examine whether such digital transformation will potentially decrease the number of individuals who rely on cash and as such have the effect that they use their bank accounts more often and be truly financially included.

Due to practical constraints, this chapter cannot analyse credit, insurance, savings products and remittances, but will only analyse access and usage of a bank account as the anchor product for individuals to participate in the economy and be financially included. It should be noted that digital transformation is a developing field, and therefore research for this chapter, apart from studying scholarly journal articles and books, made use of national and international policy documents and reports from, among others, the World Bank and the Group of Twenty (G20), to access the latest sources concerning digital financial inclusion of the poor and low-income earners.

DOI: 10.4324/9781003369400-9

9.2 Elucidating financial inclusion and digital financial inclusion

9.2.1 Financial inclusion: A global goal

Financial inclusion has been identified as an enabler for seven of the 17 sustainable development goals identified by the United Nations that are the blueprint to achieve a better and more sustainable future for all.[7] These goals address the global challenges that include poverty, inequality, climate change, environmental degradation, peace and justice.[8]

In 2013, the President of the World Bank Group, Dr Jim Y. Kim, set a goal of achieving universal financial access by 2020.[9] This universal financial access goal envisions that adults worldwide will be able to have access to an account or an electronic instrument to store money, send payments and receive deposits.[10]

The G20, an international forum representing the world's major developed and emerging economies, of which SA is a member, works to address key issues related to the global economy.[11] The G20 recognises the key role that financial inclusion plays to change the world economy to be inclusive of all people.[12] The G20 confirmed that digital financial inclusion is crucial in closing the remaining gaps in financial inclusion in the world and recognised the urgency thereof.[13] Digital financial services have the potential to award previously financially excluded people the chance to make payments, save for school fees, buy insurance or obtain a small business loan.[14] The G20 defined digital financial services as:

> financial products and services, including payments, transfers, savings, credit, insurance, securities, financial planning and account statements. They are delivered via digital/electronic technology such as e-money (initiated either online or on a mobile phone), payment cards and regular bank accounts.[15]

9.2.2 Defining financial inclusion and digital financial inclusion

Chitimira and Ncube define financial inclusion as the development and provision of affordable financial products and services to all members of society by the government, banks and other relevant role-players, such as financial services providers.[16] Matongela defines financial inclusion as the delivery of financial services at affordable costs to sections of disadvantaged and low-income segments of society.[17] The Centre for Financial Inclusion, an independent global think tank, defines full financial inclusion as a "state in which everyone who can use them has access to a full suite of quality financial services, provided at affordable prices, conveniently, with respect and dignity".[18]

For this chapter, financial inclusion means access for all persons to affordable and appropriate financial products and services such as payments, savings, credit and insurance responsibly and sustainably by various providers in a properly regulated environment. Digital financial inclusion in this chapter refers to the meaning attached to:

> Digital financial inclusion refers broadly to the use of digital financial services to advance financial inclusion. It involves the deployment of digital means to reach financially excluded and underserved populations with a range of formal financial services suited to their needs delivered responsibly at a cost affordable to customers and sustainable for providers.[19]

9.2.3 Financial inclusion in South Africa

In 2020, the National Treasury stated that:

> Appropriate access to financial services can empower individuals and entrepreneurs – particularly those with a lower income … to better integrate into the economy, actively engage in their development and protect themselves against economic shocks.[20]

Financial inclusion supports the alleviation of poverty by enabling poor people and low-income earners to invest in education and business.[21] In South Africa's National Development Plan, the transformative nature of financial inclusion is emphasised since it can exponentially increase economic growth and reduce income inequality.[22]

The Constitution of the Republic of South Africa, 1996, provides that no discrimination against any person on any ground is allowed and that everyone is equal before the law and has the right to equal protection and benefit of the law.[23] In the context of financial inclusion, this implies that no one should be deprived of financial access based on race, religion, gender, sex, marital status, ethnic or social origin and sexual orientation.[24] Equality can be either formal or substantive. Formal equality implies the sameness of treatment in that the law must treat individuals in similar circumstances alike.[25] On the other hand, substantive equality requires some tolerance of disparity of treatment to achieve equality of outcomes and thus closing the gap that might exist if one focuses strictly on formal equality.[26] Financial inclusion can be a formal and substantive equality tool to ensure financial access for everyone at all levels of society.

Financial inclusion in SA has risen from 61% in 2004[27] to 93% in 2018.[28] Or has it? The usage of bank accounts by clients of financial institutions affects whether a person is financially included. Considering that SA is an emerging economy, a high percentage of people in SA, namely 80%, have a bank account.[29] The problem though is that the quality of financial inclusion of banked people in SA is low since 7% of bank accounts are dormant and 33% are only used as a mailbox, where the account holder withdraws all the money in the bank account as soon as he/she receives it.[30] Thus, only 48% of people in SA who have a bank account use their bank account regularly.[31]

This chapter contests the claim that when an individual uses a bank account as a mailbox, such a person should be regarded as financially included. When an account holder only uses the bank account to receive money, but not to store it or to send payments and receive deposits, he/she does not facilitate the use of other financial products.[32] Despite the high number of bank account holders in SA, one can raise a question of whether these account holders are financially inclusive.

Many issues are preventing financial inclusion in SA. As mentioned previously, the mailbox phenomenon, as well as dormant bank accounts, resulted in 52% of adults in SA not being financially included. For the purposes of this chapter, the author will only analyse some of the issues that restrain individuals who have a bank account from using it regularly. Solving these issues will potentially lead to many more people being truly financially included.

In 2018, the World Bank found that cash remains the dominant payment method for a substantial segment of the population in SA, even for those that already have bank accounts.[33] The reasons for preferring cash to a bank account could be that access points are not readily available or the reluctance of respondents to adopt digital financial services.[34] The dependence on cash is the enemy of financial inclusion, as suggested by Alexandre and Eisenhart. [35]

The payments aspects of the Financial Inclusion Report found that for payment services to be effective, access points have to be nearby to the homes or places of work of customers using them.[36] In rural areas, people take twice as much or even more time to reach access points than people who live in urban areas.[37] The location of consumers may affect their access to financial services and therefore have to be brought closer to where customers live and work.[38] The cost involved for financial institutions in building and maintaining a brick-and-mortar can stand in the way of financial inclusion of the poor at affordable prices.[39] The effect of the high cost of buildings is that people in rural areas often do not have a bank nearby and consequently do not have access to financial services. A possible solution for this problem is the higher use of digital financial services since they can be used by customers without visiting a physical branch of a bank.

The National Treasury published a policy paper in February 2011 that sets out a new regulatory framework for the financial sector and wherein financial inclusion was identified as one of the key policy objectives.[40] Following this publication, just under ten years later, on 28 October 2020, the National Treasury published the first draft of a financial inclusion policy paper for public comments.[41] This policy document views financial inclusion as a tool for marginalised individuals and businesses to improve their involvement in the South African economy.[42]

In the draft financial inclusion policy, current prominent constraints to financial inclusion for individuals, based on their actual financial inclusion and how financial services and products are used, are set out.[43] These constraints inform the eight policy priorities. The first constraint mentioned is the inadequate use of bank accounts.[44] Policy priorities in the report applicable to this constraint are to promote the beneficial use of transactional accounts and build appropriate payment options to drive usage.[45] To expedite financial inclusion, more focus should be on the increased usage of dormant and mailbox bank accounts.

9.2.4 The Financial Sector Regulation Act of 2017

The Financial Sector Regulation Act 9 of 2017 (FSR Act) introduced the Twin Peaks approach to financial regulation in SA[46] and it embodies significant reforms to the South African financial regulatory architecture.[47] Financial inclusion is one of the objects of the Act.[48] Section 1 of the Act defines financial inclusion to mean that "all persons have timely and fair access to appropriate, fair and affordable financial products and services". The FSR Act established the Prudential Authority (PA)[49] and the Financial Sector Conduct Authority (FSCA).[50] The PA[51] and the FSCA[52] have to promote financial inclusion. The FSCA furthermore has to promote financial inclusion by developing and implementing strategies for the promotion of financial education to all persons in SA[53] and has to provide adequate financial education to all financial customers in SA.[54] Other authors demonstrate that the FSCA needs to take extra care to promote financial literacy and financial education programmes in SA, especially for poor and low-income earners in access to financial services and products.[55] Chitimira draws attention to the important issue that the regulators have to sufficiently enforce provisions in the FSR Act to limit the financial exclusion of the poor and low-income earners in SA.[56] Considering the provisions in the FSR Act, complete financial inclusion for clients of a bank in the 21st century should include a bank account that they use more than once a month.

Digital transformation, where people use digital technologies such as smartphones, websites, computers and automatic teller machines (ATMs) to modify existing processes in banking and finances, can have an impact on the problem of many people in SA having a bank account but not using it. Bearing in mind the increasing influence of the Fourth Industrial Revolution, the higher use of digital channels is important for banking services to remain relevant. [57]

9.3 Challenges and potential opportunities of digital transformation

The Covid-19 pandemic hit the world at the beginning of 2020 and severely affected SA. The South African government declared several lockdowns at various levels to curb the spread of the coronavirus.[58] This has slowed down the economy and left more people impoverished than before the pandemic. This is due to, among others, job losses of between 2.2 and 2.8 million between February and April 2020.[59] The National Treasury suggested in the 2020 Financial Inclusion Policy Paper that to mitigate the impact of the pandemic on financial inclusion in SA, an appropriate digital and payments ecosystem has to be built to deepen financial inclusion for individuals.[60] Digital transformation using digital transactions such as online and mobile banking and banking applications as well as contactless payments and POS devices became more important in this decade.[61] Digital innovation has the potential to fundamentally change the provision of financial services to the underserved through new technologies and alternative platforms, such as mobile phones and digital platforms, to reach financially excluded people in rural areas without the need for physical bank branches.[62]

In rural areas, many people are not aware of what digital financial services can offer them as they may either not be informed of other possibilities than transacting with cash or they may regard digital financial services as complex and difficult.[63] These individuals need more access to digital financial services and should not only rely on cash for all their transactions because that will keep them financially excluded.[64]

The accessibility of financial services is key to cultivating economic growth and reducing poverty,[65] but it is also a huge barrier to the financial inclusion of people in remote rural areas.[66] The accessibility of digital financial services can assist in improving earning capacity by enabling investments and boosting resilience to shocks such as disease and loss of employment.[67] Certain digital financial service models have proven to accelerate financial inclusion, including that of mobile banking, which enables customers to use their mobile phones as a channel for their banking services.[68]

Banks in SA follow the strategy to deliver banking services through digital channels, especially mobile-optimised services.[69] Since internet penetration plays an important role in banking,[70] banks worldwide reinvent themselves to be ready for the Fourth Industrial Revolution.[71] Louw and Niewenhuizen surveyed the South African banking environment and found that the trends in digital consumer services on offer from banks include those of web banking technologies (website and internet banking) and smartphone banking technologies (smartphone applications, mobile or unstructured supplementary service data (USSD) banking and zero-rated data).[72] Banks also offer services that facilitate process digitisation such as POS banking technologies (including smartphone POS and standard POS).[73] Banks provide their smartphone application as a zero-rated data application so that no data usage costs are incurred when the application is used.[74] This assists people to use their smartphone applications without being dependent on expensive data.[75]

A study by the Finmark Trust found that the use of mobile phones can expand financial services to the poor and low-income earners, but bank customers would need access to a smartphone to use banking applications.[76] Stumble blocks in digital transformation in SA are the cost of smartphones, being more than feature phones, and perceived complicated operation thereof that may be perceived as intimidating or overwhelming.[77] With the USSD service that banks offer, clients can access banking services with a more basic mobile phone by dialling dedicated mobile banking numbers and choosing from options available on their phones.[78] Louw and Niewenhuizen argued that "mobile- or smartphone-first banking does seem to be a strongly pursued component of the digital transformation trend in South African banks".[79] Louw also found in 2017 that smartphones are in the process of replacing traditional currency.[80]

The financial inclusion policy cautions that the availability of telecommunications infrastructure in rural areas does not support digital transformation in such areas.[81] Banking customers may require on-premises access to digital banking infrastructure.[82] Such access could be made available through affiliated supermarkets' premises.[83]

The major reasons for mobile banking adoption are "convenience, access to banking services at any time of the day or night and minimisation of effort, time and consultation costs".[84] According to Chigada and Hirschfelder, South African mobile banking improves banking skills and simplifies bank account maintenance and money transfers.[85] As customers of banks become accustomed to banking websites and mobile banking applications, they gain more confidence to do their banking independently from a consultant and this leads to improved banking skills.[86] Customers find it convenient and time-saving to be able to manage their finances at any time.[87] Sophisticated banking applications on smartphones and tablets are effective in improving the lives of customers.[88] Previously it took some effort for a sender to do money transfers with much paperwork and the receiver had to wait longer for the transaction to be completed.[89] With mobile or online banking, money transfers are simplified and the sender can complete it within a day.[90]

The G20 appealed for the digital financial services network and financial, information and communications technology infrastructure to be expanded in rural areas as that would promote digital financial inclusion.[91] Louis and Chartier found that incorporating mobile banking into the South African financial system would be an important step towards the financial inclusion of the poor.[92] It is vital to develop digital infrastructure through information and communication technology (ICT) where customers can make and receive efficient retail payments.[93] The implementation of ICT brings about organisational, environmental and individual changes.[94]

Chigada and Hirschfelder refer to Korpelainen, who identified the most cited theories for the adoption and acceptance of technology as the technology acceptance model (TAM), the theory of reasoned actions, diffusion of innovations and the theory of planned behaviour.[95] These theories mainly explore individual technology acceptance by analysing the organisation and implementation of ICT.[96] A discussion of these theories falls outside the limitations of this chapter. As TAM is the most widely accepted model in information system literature and a popular theory for the technology acceptance of mobile money,[97] Chigada and Hirschfelder use the TAM theory to illustrate that the rate of adoption of mobile banking in SA is relatively low, although there is a high number of mobile cellular phone users.[98] They show that resistance to the acceptance and use of technologies may negatively influence previously disadvantaged communities.[99]

The G20 indicated that the cost of digital platforms that are widely accessible would potentially reduce when more people use them for transactions.[100] They maintained that digital platforms should be employed to expand access points for customers and financial service providers including ATMs, POS devices, mobile phones and internet applications.[101]

9.4 Conclusion and recommendations

The research in this chapter has shown that digital transformation, specifically the use of digital financial services in banking, can assist poor and low-income earners living in rural areas in SA to become financially included. These poor and low-income earners are often too far away from big centres for convenient access to financial services and therefore have to rely on the cash economy. Through digital transformation, they will be able to use their dormant or infrequently used bank accounts regularly and become financially included. This move to digital financial services is viable since banks in SA increasingly offer services such as website and internet banking, smartphone applications with zero-rated data, mobile banking, USSD banking and POS banking technologies for use with smartphones.

The most obvious finding to emerge from this study is that effective digital transformation of banking services in rural areas is restrained by various factors. These factors are insufficient communications infrastructure, access to smartphones and cell phone data, the digital capability of individuals and the lack of digitising of informal trading. This finding implies that there is a definite need for accessibility of facilities through digital transformation in rural areas for poor and low-income earners.

Many rural villages and townships in SA have weak availability of telecommunications infrastructure[102] and therefore a drive from the government and private sector is necessary to provide sufficient infrastructure for these areas to support digital transformation. The author first recommends, as was also suggested by the G20,[103] that the broadband network and data coverage be expanded into underserved areas. This could be done by using policy mechanisms such as innovative public-private partnerships and incentives for shared infrastructure programmes.

Second, the author recommends that the retail payments infrastructure should be expanded and modernised by digitising informal trading. People in rural communities probably withdraw all their money from their bank account when they receive it because shops near their houses only accept cash. Make more POS technology available to informal vendors and spaza shops so that such businesses can connect with POS devices linked to smartphones, assisting to digitise informal trading. Paying digitally at the point where the sale takes place will contribute to owners of bank accounts using their bank accounts more often since the necessity then lessens to withdraw all their money to have cash available. When informal vendors and spaza shops that are currently not accepting digital payments are empowered to handle digital payments, people in rural areas could leave the money in their bank account until they need it and thus the mailbox effect of bank accounts will take hold.

In complying with the directions in the FSR Act, it should be practically feasible for all people in SA to have access to a bank account that they can use more than once a month. Finally, the author recommends that the PA and the FSCA exercise the powers vested in them to contribute to financial inclusion in SA.

Notes

1 A Zins and L Weill, 'The Determinants of Financial Inclusion in Africa' (2016) 6 *Review of Development Finance* 46-57, 49; T Beck, R Levine and N Loayza, 'Finance and the Sources of Growth' (2000) 58(1) *Journal of Financial Economics* 261-300, 261; G Clarke, C Xu and H Zou, 'Finance and Inequality: What Do the Data Tell Us?' (2006) 72(3) *Southern Economic Journal* 578-96, 578; T Beck, A Demirguc-Kunt and R Levine,

'Finance, Inequality, and the Poor' (2007) 12(1) *Journal of Economic Growth* 27-49, 27; A Demirgüc,-Kunt and L Klapper, 'Financial Inclusion in Africa. An Overview' (Policy Research Working Paper No. 6088 World Bank) 2; Department of Trade and Industry 'An Inclusive Financial Sector for All' known as Financial Inclusion Policy (2020) 8 http://www.treasury.gov.za/comm_media/press/2020/Financial%20Inclusion%20Policy%20-%20An%20Inclusive%20Financial%20Sector%20For%20All.pdf, accessed on 20 April 2021; A Demirguc-Kunt, L Klapper and D Singer 'Financial Inclusion and Inclusive Growth' (Policy Research Working Paper 8040 World Bank).

2 Financial Inclusion Policy (note 1 above) 11, 44.

3 Ibid, 44.

4 P Kostov, T Arun and S Annim, 'Access to Financial Services – The Case of the Mzansi Account in South Africa' (2015) 5 *Review of Development Finance* 34, 36.

5 V Matsebula and D Yu, 'An Analysis of Financial Inclusion in South Africa' (2020) 12(1) *African Review of Economics and Finance* 171-202, 172; Financial Inclusion Policy (note 1 above) 9; AS Ikdal et al., 'Improving Financial Inclusion in South Africa' (2017) https://www.bcg.com/publications/2017/globalization-improving-financial-inclusion-south-africa.aspx, accessed on 27 July 2021.

6 L Louis and F Chartier, 'Financial Inclusion in South Africa: An Integrated Framework for Financial Inclusion of Vulnerable Communities in South Africa's Regulatory System Reform' (2017) 1(1) *Journal of Comparative Urban Law and Policy* 170-196 182.

7 United Nations 'Sustainable Development Goals' (undated) https://www.un.org/sustainabledevelopment/sustainable-development-goals/, accessed on 16 July 2021; L Klapper, M El-Zoghbi and J Hess 'Achieving the Sustainable Development Goals: The Role of Financial Inclusion' 2016 (Consultative Group to Assist the Poor and United Nations Secretary General's Special Advocate for Inclusive Finance for Development 2016) 2.

8 World Bank, 'Financial Inclusion: Overview' (undated) http://www.worldbank.org/en/topic/financialinclusion/overview, accessed on 22 April 2021; United Nations (note 7 above).

9 World Bank, 'Achieving Effective Financial Inclusion in South Africa: A Payments Perspective' (2018) 18 http://www.treasury.gov.za/publications/other/Achieving%20Effective%20Financial%20Inclusion%20in%20South%20Africa.pdf, accessed on 6 September 2020.

10 Ibid.

11 G20 'About the G20' (undated) https://www.g20.org/, accessed on 23 July 2021; The Organisation for Economic Co-operation and Development (OECD) 'About the OECD' (undated) https://www.oecd.org/g20/about/, accessed on 23 July 2021.

12 G20 Ibid.

13 Global Partnership for Financial Inclusion (GPFI) 'G20 High-Level Principles for Digital Financial Inclusion' (2016) https://www.gpfi.org/publications/g20-high-level-principles-digital-financial-inclusion, accessed on 23 July 2021.

14 G20 (note 11 above); OECD (note 11 above) 1.

15 GPFI (note 13 above) 3.

16 H Chitimira and M Ncube 'Legislative and Other Selected Challenges Affecting Financial Inclusion for the Poor and Low-Income Earners in South Africa' (2020) 64(3) *Journal of African Law* 337-355, 338.

17 AM Matongela, 'Understanding the State of Financial Inclusion in Namibia' (2014) 5(23) *Research Journal of Finance and Accounting* 171-175, 171.

18 Centre for Financial Inclusion 'About' (undated) https://www.centerforfinancialinclusion.org/, accessed on 14 July 2021.

19 Global Partnership for Financial Inclusion (GPFI) 'Global Standard-Setting Bodies Financial Inclusions: The Evolving Landscape' (2016) 46 https://www.gpfi.org/sites/gpfi/files/documents/GPFI_WhitePaper_Mar2016.pdf, accessed on 20 April 2021.

20 Financial Inclusion Policy (note 1 above) 9.
21 Demirguc-Kunt, Klapper and Singer (note 1 above) 2.
22 Department of the Presidency Republic of South Africa 'National Development Plan 2030 – Our Future – Make it Work' (National Planning Commission 2012) 150.
23 S 9 of the Constitution (1) Everyone is equal before the law and has the right to equal protection and benefit of the law. (2) Equality includes the full and equal enjoyment of all rights and freedoms. To promote the achievement of equality, legislative and other measures designed to protect or advance persons, or categories of persons, disadvantaged by unfair discrimination may be taken. (3) The state may not unfairly discriminate directly or indirectly against anyone on one or more grounds, including race, gender, sex, pregnancy, marital status, ethnic or social origin, colour, sexual orientation, age, disability, religion, conscience, belief, culture, language and birth. (4) No person may unfairly discriminate directly or indirectly against anyone on one or more grounds in terms of subsection (3). National legislation must be enacted to prevent or prohibit unfair discrimination. (5) Discrimination on one or more of the grounds listed in subsection (3) is unfair unless it is established that the discrimination is fair.
24 S 9(5) read with s 9(3).
25 I Currie and J De Wall *Bill of Rights Handbook* 6th ed (2017) 213.
26 Ibid.
27 Finmark Trust 'Finscope South Africa 2014' (undated) http://www.finmark.org.za/wp-content/uploads/2016/08/FS-SA_2014-Brochure.pdf, accessed on 14 April 2020.
28 FinMark Trust 'FinScope SA 2018 Fact Sheet' (undated) https://www.finmark.org.za/finscope-south-africa-consumer-2018-results-factsheet/, accessed on 10 June 2019.
29 Ibid, 2.
30 Genesis Analytics 'Fintech Scoping in South Africa' (Genesis Analytics 2019) 39: FinMark Trust 'FinScope SA 2018' (note 28 above) 2; Ikdal (note 5 above); MG van Niekerk and NH Phaladi 'Digital Financial Services: Prospects and Challenges' (2021) 24 *PER/PELJ* 1-26, 8.
31 FinMark Trust 'FinScope SA 2018' (note 28 above) 2. This is calculated as follows: 80% of people are banked in SA, and only 60% of them use their bank account regularly. Of the other 40%, 7% of bank accounts are dormant and 33% are only used as mailboxes. Therefore, only 48% (80% banked × 60% regular users) of adult South Africans use their bank account regularly; Ikdal (note 5 above).
32 Financial Inclusion Policy (note 1 above) 21.
33 Ibid, 92.
34 World Bank (note 9 above) 92.
35 C Alexandre and LC Eisenhart, 'Mobile Money as an Engine of Financial Inclusion and Lynchpin of Financial Integrity' (2013) 8 *Washington Journal of Law, Technology and Arts* 285-302, 285.
36 World Bank (note 9 above) 68.
37 Ibid, 26.
38 Ibid, 92.
39 AB Fanta et al., 'The Role of Mobile Money in Financial Inclusion in the SADC Region – Evidence using FinScope Surveys' (Finmark Trust Policy research paper No. 03/2016) 1.
40 National Treasury, 'A Safer Financial Sector to Serve South Africa Better' (2011) 4 http://www.treasury.gov.za/twinpeaks/20131211%20%20Item%202%20A%20safer%20financial%20sector%20to%20serve%20South%20Africa%20better.pdf, accessed on 15 March 2017.
41 Financial Inclusion Policy (note 1 above).
42 Ibid, 8.
43 Ibid, 44.
44 Ibid.

45 Priority 1 and 2 in the policy.
46 G van Niekerk and C van Heerden, 'The Importance of a Legislative Framework for Co-operation and Collaboration in the Twin Peaks Model of Financial Regulation' (2020) 137(1) *SALJ* 108-144, 111.
47 AJ Godwin and AD Schmulow, 'The Financial Sector Regulation Bill in South Africa, Second Draft: Lessons from Australia' (2015) 132 *SALJ* 756-768, 756.
48 S 7(1)(f) of the FSR Act.
49 S 32(1) of the FSR Act.
50 S 56(1) of the FSR Act.
51 S 34(1)e) of the FSR Act.
52 S 58(1)(e) of the FSR Act.
53 S 58(1)(e) and (j) of the FSR Act.
54 S 57(b)(ii) of the FSR Act.
55 Chitimira and Ncube (note 16 above) 10.
56 H Chitimira, 'Historical Aspects of the Statutory Regulation of Financial Inclusion for the Poor and Low-Income Earners in South Africa' (2020) 16(5) *Acta Universitatis Danubius: Juridica* 269-284, 280.
57 C Louw and C Nieuwenhuizen, 'Digitalisation Strategies in a South African Banking Context: A Consumer Services Analysis' (2020) 22(1) *South African Journal of Information Management* 1-8, 1.
58 South African Government 'Let's grow South Africa Together' https://www.gov.za/covid-19/about/about-alert-system, accessed on 17 August 2021.
59 D Posel, A Oyenubi and U Kollamparambil (2021) 'Job Loss and Mental Health during the COVID-19 Lockdown: Evidence from South Africa' (2021) 16(3) *PLoS ONE* 1-15, 2.
60 Financial Inclusion Policy (note 1 above) 91.
61 Alexandre and Eisenhart (note 32 above) 288 and 294; Financial Inclusion Policy (note 1 above) 91.
62 JK Winn and L De Koker, 'Introduction to Mobile Money in Developing Countries: Financial Inclusion and Financial Integrity Conference Special Issue' (2013) 8(3) *Washington Journal of Law, Technology and Arts* 155-164, 159; A Demirguc-Kunt et al., 'The Global Findex Database 2017: Measuring Financial Inclusion and the Fintech Revolution' (International Bank for Reconstruction and Development/The World Bank 2018); L Kambale 'Digital Financial Services – A Case of Malawi' (Malawi Communication Regulatory Authority 2018); M Andrianaivo and K Kpodar, 'ICT, Financial Inclusion, and Growth: Evidence from African Countries' (International Monetary Fund Working Paper WP/11/73 2011) 7; Alexandre and Eisenhart (note 32 above) 301; Asian Development Bank, 'Accelerating Financial Inclusion in South-East Asia with Digital Finance' (Oliver Wyman 2017).
63 Alexandre and Eisenhart (note 32 above) 288; Winn and De Koker (note 62 above) 159.
64 See previous paragraph.
65 Beck, Demirgüç-Kunt and Levine (note 1 above) 32; Zins and Weill (note 1 above) 49.
66 Winn and L De Koker (note 62 above) 156.
67 Andrianaivo and Kpodar (note 62 above) 7.
68 Winn and L De Koker (note 62 above) 156: Banking services include deposits, withdrawals, account transfers, bill payments, and balance inquiries; Demirguc-Kunt et al. (note 62 above) 7 and 11.
69 Louw and Nieuwenhuizen (note 57 above) 1; Fanta et al. (note 39 above) 1.
70 V Bleyen and L Van Hove, 'Western European Newspapers and their Online Revenue Models: An Overview' (2007) 12(12) *First Monday* 1–13.
71 Louw and Nieuwenhuizen (note 57 above) 1.
72 Ibid, 4.
73 Ibid, 5.

74 A Futter and A Gillwald, 'Zero-rated Internet Services: What is to be Done?' (Broadband 4 Africa Policy Paper 1 September 2015) 6.
75 C Geerdts et al., 'Developing Smart Public Wi-Fi in South Africa' (Canadian International Development Research Centre 2016) 87.
76 Fanta et al. (note 39 above) 1.
77 C Louw, 'Towards a Smartphone Application User Security Competency Evolution Model' (Doctoral Thesis University of Johannesburg 2017); C Louw and B Von Solms, 'Smartphone Usage and Security Maturity: A South African Student Evaluation' *European Conference on Cyber Warfare and Security* 2018 268; Louw and Nieuwenhuizen (note 57 above) 5.
78 Louw and Nieuwenhuizen (note 57 above) 4.
79 Ibid, 7.
80 Louw (note 77 above) 147.
81 Financial Inclusion Policy (note 1 above) 93.
82 Louw and Nieuwenhuizen (note 57 above) 6.
83 Ibid.
84 T Laukkanen and M Pasanen, 'Mobile Banking Innovators and Early Adopters: How they Differ from Other Online Users' (2008) 13(2) *Journal of Financial Services Marketing* 86-94, 86; U Akturan and N Tezcan 'Mobile Banking Adoption of the Youth Market: Perceptions and intentions' (2012) 30(4) *Marketing Intelligence & Planning* 444-459, 444.
85 JM Chigada and B Hirschfelder 'Mobile Banking in South Africa: A Review and Directions for Future Research' 2017 *South African Journal of Information Management* 1-9, 3.
86 Ibid, 4; LT Khrais, 'Highlighting the Vulnerabilities of Online Banking System' (2015) 20(3) *Journal of Internet Banking & Commerce* 1; S Raitani and V Vyas, 'An Exploratory Study of Factors Influencing the e-Loyalty of Online Banking Consumers' (2014) 13(3) *Journal of Bank Management* 34-47, 34.
87 Ibid, 4.
88 LJ Couse and DW Chen, 'A Tablet Computer for Young Children? Exploring its Viability for Early Childhood Education' (2010) 43(1) *Journal of Research on Technology in Education* 75-98, 75; E Granado-Font et al., 'Effectiveness of a Smartphone Application and Wearable Device for Weight Loss in Overweight or Obese Primary Care Patients: Protocol for a Randomised Controlled Trial' (2015) 15(1) *BMC Public Health* 1.
89 Chigada and Hirschfelder (note 85 above) 4.
90 M Seidel and A Liebetrau, *Banking & innovation 2015: Ideen und Erfolgskonzepte von Experten für die Praxis*, Springer-Verlag in Chigada and Hirschfelder (note 85 above) 5.
91 G20 (note 11 above); OECD (note 11 above) 8; GPFI (note 13 above) 13.
92 Louis and Chartier (note 6 above) 182.
93 GPFI (note 13 above) 3.
94 AH Van de Ven, 'Central Problems in the Management of Innovations' (1986) 32(5) *Management Science* 590–607, 590; EM Rogers, *Diffusion of Innovations* 1st ed (2010).
95 Chigada and Hirschfelder (note 85 above) 6; E Korpelainen, 'Theories of ICT System Implementation and Adoption – A Critical Review' (Department of Industrial Engineering and Management Working Paper series 1 2011) 14–17.
96 Chigada and Hirschfelder ibid, 6.
97 P Luarm and H Lin, 2005, 'Towards an Understanding of the Behavioral Intention to Use Mobile Banking' (2005) 21(6) *Computers in Human Behaviour* 873-891, 873.
98 Chigada and Hirschfelder (note 85 above) 8.
99 Ibid, 8.
100 GPFI (note 13 above) 13.

101 Ibid.
102 Financial Inclusion Policy (note 1 above) 93.
103 GPFI (note 13 above) 13.

Bibliography

U Akturan & N Tezcan 'Mobile banking adoption of the youth market: Perceptions and intentions' (2012) 30(4) *Marketing Intelligence & Planning* 444.

C Alexandre & L C Eisenhart 'Mobile money as an engine of financial inclusion and lynchpin of financial integrity' (2013) 8 *Washington Journal of Law, Technology and Arts* 285.

M Andrianaivo & K Kpodar *ICT, Financial Inclusion, and Growth: Evidence from African Countries* (International Monetary Fund working paper WP/11/73, 2011).

Asian Development Bank *Accelerating Financial Inclusion in South-East Asia with Digital Finance* (Oliver Wyman, 2017).

T Beck, A Demirguc-Kunt & R Levine 'Finance, inequality, and the poor' (2007) 12(1) *Journal of Economic Growth* 27.

T Beck, R Levine & N Loayza 'Finance and the sources of growth' (2000) 58(1) *Journal of Financial Economics* 261.

V Bleyen & L Van Hove 'Western European newspapers and their online revenue models: An overview' (2007) 12(12) *First Monday* 1.

Centre for Financial Inclusion 'About' undated, available at https://www.centerforfinancialinclusion.org/, accessed on 14 July 2021.

J M Chigada & B Hirschfelder 'Mobile banking in South Africa: A review and directions for future research' (2017) *South African Journal of Information Management* 1.

H Chitimira 'Historical aspects of the statutory regulation of financial inclusion for the poor and low-income earners in South Africa' (2020) 16(5) *Acta Universitatis Danubius: Juridica* 269.

H Chitimira & M Ncube 'Legislative and other selected challenges affecting financial inclusion for the poor and low-income earners in South Africa' (2020) 64(3) *Journal of African Law* 337.

G Clarke, C Xu & H Zou 'Finance and inequality: What do the data tell us?' (2006) 72(3) *Southern Economic Journal* 578.

L J Couse & D W Chen 'A tablet computer for young children? Exploring its viability for early childhood education' (2010) 43(1) *Journal of Research on Technology in Education* 75.

I Currie & J De Wall *Bill of Rights Handbook* 6 ed (2017).

A Demirguc-Kunt *The Global Findex Database 2017: Measuring Financial Inclusion and the Fintech Revolution* (International Bank for Reconstruction and Development/The World Bank, 2018).

A Demirgüc,-Kunt & L Klapper *Financial Inclusion in Africa. An Overview* (Policy research working paper no. 6088 World Bank).

A Demirguc-Kunt, L Klapper & D Singer *Financial Inclusion and Inclusive Growth* (Policy research working paper 8040 World Bank).

Department of the Presidency Republic of South Africa *National Development Plan 2030 – Our Future – Make It Work* (National Planning Commission, 2012).

Department of Trade and Industry 'An inclusive financial sector for all' referred to as financial inclusion policy (2020), available at http://www.treasury.gov.za/comm_media

/press/2020/Financial%20Inclusion%20Policy%20-%20An%20Inclusive%20Financial %20Sector%20For%20All.pdf, accessed on 20 April 2021.

A B Fanta *The Role of Mobile Money in Financial Inclusion in the SADC Region – Evidence Using FinScope Surveys* (Finmark Trust Policy research paper no. 03/2016).

FinMark Trust 'FinScope SA 2018 fact sheet' undated, available at https://www.finmark.org .za/finscope-south-africa-consumer-2018-results-factsheet/, accessed on 10 June 2019.

Finmark Trust 'Finscope South Africa 2014' undated, available at http://www.finmark.org .za/wp-content/uploads/2016/08/FS-SA_2014-Brochure.pdf, accessed on 14 April 2020.

A Futter & A Gillwald *Zero-Rated Internet Services: What is to Be Done?* (Broadband 4 Africa policy paper 1, September 2015).

G20 'About the G20' undated, available at https://www.g20.org/, accessed on 23 July 2021.

C Geerdts *Developing Smart Public Wi-Fi in South Africa* (Canadian International Development Research Centre, 2016).

Genesis Analytics 'Fintech Scoping in South Africa' (Genesis Analytics, 2019).

Global Partnership for Financial Inclusion (GPFI) 'G20 high-level principles for digital financial inclusion' 2016, available at https://www.gpfi.org/publications/g20-high-level -principles-digital-financial-inclusion, accessed on 23 July 2021.

Global Partnership for Financial Inclusion (GPFI) 'Global standard-setting bodies financial inclusions: the evolving landscape' 2016, available at https://www.gpfi .org/sites/gpfi/files/documents/GPFI_WhitePaper_Mar2016.pdf, accessed on 20 April 2021.

A J Godwin & A D Schmulow 'The financial sector regulation bill in South Africa, second draft: Lessons from Australia' (2015) 132 *SALJ* 756.

E Granado-Font 'Effectiveness of a smartphone application and wearable device for weight loss in overweight or obese primary care patients: Protocol for a randomised controlled trial' (2015) 15(1) *BMC Public Health* 1.

A S Ikdal 'Improving financial inclusion in South Africa' 2017, available at https://www .bcg.com/publications/2017/globalization-improving-financial-inclusion-south-africa .aspx, accessed on 27 July 2021.

L Kambale 'Digital financial services – A case of Malawi' (Malawi Communication Regulatory Authority, 2018).

L T Khrais 'Highlighting the vulnerabilities of online banking system' (2015) 20(3) *Journal of Internet Banking & Commerce*.

L Klapper, M El-Zoghbi & J Hess 'Achieving the sustainable development goals: The role of financial inclusion' 2016 (Consultative Group to Assist the Poor and United Nations Secretary General's Special Advocate for Inclusive Finance for Development, 2016).

E Korpelainen *Theories of ICT System Implementation and Adoption – A Critical Review* (Department of Industrial Engineering and Management working paper series 1, 2011).

P Kostov, T Arun & S Annim 'Access to financial services – The case of the Mzansi account in South Africa' (2015) 5 *Review of Development Finance* 34.

T Laukkanen & M Pasanen 'Mobile banking innovators and early adopters: How they differ from other online users' (2008) 13(2) *Journal of Financial Services Marketing* 86.

L Louis & F Chartier 'Financial inclusion in South Africa: An integrated framework for financial inclusion of vulnerable communities in South Africa's regulatory system reform' (2017) 1(1) *Journal of Comparative Urban Law and Policy* 170.

C Louw *Towards a Smartphone Application User Security Competency Evolution Model* (doctoral thesis, University of Johannesburg, 2017).

C Louw & C Nieuwenhuizen 'Digitalisation strategies in a South African banking context: A consumer services analysis' (2020) 22(1) *South African Journal of Information Management* 1.

C Louw & B Von Solms 'Smartphone usage and security maturity: A South African student evaluation' *European Conference on Cyber Warfare and Security*, 2018 268.

P Luarm & H Lin 'Towards an understanding of the behavioral intention to use mobile banking' (2005) 21(6) *Computers in Human Behaviour* 873.

A M Matongela 'Understanding the state of financial inclusion in Namibia' (2014) 5(23) *Research Journal of Finance and Accounting* 171.

V Matsebula & D Yu 'An analysis of financial inclusion in South Africa' (2020) 12(1) *African Review of Economics and Finance* 171.

National Treasury 'A safer financial sector to serve South Africa better' (2011) 4, available at http://www.treasury.gov.za/twinpeaks/20131211%20%20Item%202%20A%20safer%20financial%20sector%20to%20serve%20South%20Africa%20better.pdf, accessed on 15 March 2017.

D Posel, A Oyenubi & U Kollamparambil 'Job loss and mental health during the COVID-19 lockdown: Evidence from South Africa' (2021) 16(3) *PLoS ONE.*

S Raitani & V Vyas 'An exploratory study of factors influencing the e-loyalty of online banking consumers' (2014) 13(3) *Journal of Bank Management* 34.

E M Rogers *Diffusion of Innovations* 1 ed (2010).

M Seidel & A Liebetrau *Banking & Innovation 2015: Ideen und Erfolgskonzepte von Experten für die Praxis*.

South African Government 'Let's grow South Africa together', available at https://www.gov.za/covid-19/about/about-alert-system, accessed on 17 August 2021.

The Organisation for Economic Co-operation and Development (OECD) 'About the OECD' (undated), available at https://www.oecd.org/g20/about/, accessed on 23 July 2021.

United Nations 'Sustainable development goals' (undated), available at https://www.un.org/sustainabledevelopment/sustainable-development-goals/, accessed on 16 July 2021.

A H Van de Ven 'Central problems in the management of innovations' (1986) 32(5) *Management Science* 590.

G Van Niekerk & C Van Heerden 'The importance of a legislative framework for co-operation and collaboration in the twin peaks model of financial regulation' (2020) 137(1) *SALJ* 108.

M G Van Niekerk & N H Phaladi 'Digital financial services: Prospects and challenges' (2021) 24 *PER/PELJ* 1.

J K Winn & L De Koker 'Introduction to mobile money in developing countries: Financial inclusion and financial integrity conference special issue' (2013) 8(3) *Washington Journal of Law, Technology and Arts* 155.

World Bank 'Achieving effective financial inclusion in South Africa: A payments perspective' (2018) 18, available at http://www.treasury.gov.za/publications/other/Achieving%20Effective%20Financial%20Inclusion%20in%20South%20Africa.pdf, accessed on 6 September 2020.

World Bank 'Financial inclusion: Overview' (undated), available at http://www.worldbank.org/en/topic/financialinclusion/overview, accessed on 22 April 2021.

A Zins & L Weill 'The determinants of financial inclusion in Africa' (2016) 6 *Review of Development Finance* 46.

10 "Economic inclusion" as a prerequisite and catalyst to "financial inclusion"? A case study of the economic exclusion of refugees in the Gauteng Township Economic Draft Bill

Tinashe Kondo and Yvette Basson

10.1 Introduction

Prior to the outbreak of Covid-19, township economies provided much-needed economic growth to township inhabitants.[1] The township economy is a lifeblood for many entrepreneurs in South Africa, foreign and local alike. It provides for those lacking capital, is plentiful for those with skills and drive and is an opportunity to build businesses and eke out a living. Considering that many persons do not have access to formal employment as a result of high unemployment rates in South Africa,[2] the importance of the township economy cannot be overstated.

To date, many foreign nationals have owned and continue to operate small businesses in townships, ranging from small grocery stores (spaza shops) to barbers. The first draft of the Gauteng Township Economic Draft Bill (the Bill) that was published for comment, however, seeks to change this position in the province. The Bill *inter alia* aims to provide for the promotion and development of the township economy.[3] This involves the provision of assistance for small and medium enterprises in navigating the plethora of laws, by-laws and regulations applicable to these businesses as well as the simplification of the business start-up process in the township. Laws to comply include the National Small Enterprise Act 1999,[4] the Compensation for Occupational Injuries and Diseases Act (COIDA), the Unemployment Insurance Act 63 of 2001 and the Income Tax Act 58 of 1962. The central aim of the Bill is therefore to foster the rights of self-determination and equality of persons living in townships in Gauteng.

The Bill was born out of the Gauteng Township Economic Revitalisation Strategy, which seeks to promote the significant participation and meaningful inclusion of township residents into the mainstream economy of Gauteng.[5] It has specifically been championed by the former Premier of Gauteng, David Makhura. He first announced the plans to introduce the Bill in 2019 at the State of the Province address.[6] After the address, the province moved speedily to provide a Draft Bill for public comment on 30 September 2020.[7] The most controversial aspects of the first draft Bill reserved certain economic activities for the sole and

DOI: 10.4324/9781003369400-10

exclusive use of South African citizens and permanent residents.[8] This excluded other classes of foreign nationals such as those with temporary residence visas (TRVs), refugees and asylum seekers.[9] This was done through chapter 3 of the first draft Bill, which provided for "economic activities reserved for citizens or persons with permanent residence status".

While, as discussed earlier, plans for the Bill were made in 2019,[10] the Bill was unduly fast-tracked[11] for publication in the middle of the global coronavirus (Covid-19) pandemic that has devasted communities across the globe (the Covid-19 pandemic began in South Africa in March 2020). It brings to the fore the question of whether the pandemic has accelerated existing tensions between locals and foreign nationals. Before the pandemic, the ill-treatment of foreign nationals in law and practice in South Africa was already rife.[12] Often, this was projected through recurrent incidences of xenophobic violence[13] and unjust laws that unduly impeded the rights of foreign nationals.[14]

A key motivator for this in the South African context has been the scarcity of resources. Citizens believe that foreign nationals are crowding meagre resources meant for locals. During the Covid-19 pandemic, the problem of scarcity of resources has only been exacerbated.[15] Social interventions by the government have focused primarily on citizens and permanent residents to ensure their sustainability.[16] However, this has disproportionately impacted on the socio-economic rights (SERs) of various classes of foreign nationals, especially refugees and asylum seekers.

Beyond this, the first draft Bill potentially had implications on the ability of foreign nationals to participate in the economy. The first draft Bill restricted equitable access to participate in the township economy. Accordingly, this chapter discusses whether economic exclusion would have jeopardised the project of meaningful financial inclusion. This is important in order to understand the consequences of such actions in future. In addition, the chapter considers the legality of such an approach. This is done by considering the constitutionality of the first draft Bill to the extent that it restricted certain classes of foreign nationals from participating in certain sectors of the township economy in Gauteng, with a particular focus on refugees. It further interrogates the impact of the Bill on the SERs of refugees, more specifically, their right to occupational choice. While other classes of foreign nationals are equally impacted by the Bill, this chapter limits itself to refugees because they are a class of persons particularly vulnerable to discrimination and historically the target of xenophobic violence. Their case generally calls for compassion as they often find themselves in desperate situations in which they have no control. This includes persecution, human rights violations and conflict. Further, discrimination in the host country on the basis of their origin can therefore not be condoned.

10.2 Reserved sectors in law

Previously, South Africa has not maintained reserved sectors. However, the government in the past has placed restrictions on certain sectors.[17] For example, foreign nationals wanting to participate in certain sectors such as mining have to comply with broad-based black economic empowerment (BBBEE) rules. The Broad-Based Socio-economic Empowerment Charter for the Mining and Minerals Industry 2018 (the Charter), for instance, provides that new mining rights can only be awarded to companies that have a 30% BEE shareholding.[18] The aim of this is to promote meaningful economic participation for historically disadvantaged persons and expand the social and economic well-being of South Africans.[19]

The BBBEE provisions in the mineral sector have already been challenged before in the case of *Piero Foresti, Laura de Carli and others v Republic of South Africa*.[20] In this case, foreign investors argued that certain provisions of the MPRDA effectively "extinguished" their mineral rights without providing adequate compensation. The foreign investors argued that the provisions violated certain provisions of the Italy–South Africa and Luxemburg–South Africa bilateral investment treaties (BITs).[21] While the matter was never finalised because of a consent order, the case raised important questions on the implication of certain legislation on foreign nationals and their businesses.

It is important, however, to note that the recent case *of Minerals Council of South Africa v Minister of Mineral Resources and Energy and Others*[22] provides more clarity on the matter. In this case, the court held that the Charter was not binding and was rather an instrument of policy.[23] It was observed that s 100(2) of the Mineral and Petroleum Resources Development Act (MPRDA) did not empower the minister to make law.[24] The court was of the view that such an interpretation was consistent with the objects of the MRPDA.[25] The court further noted that it was impermissible for the minister to attempt to derive his law-making powers directly from the Constitution of the Republic of South Africa, 1996.[26]

The above notwithstanding, within the context of international investment law, sector requirements are not new.[27] Some countries restrict the economic participation of foreign nationals in certain sectors of the economy. In others, local content policies (LCPs) can be placed on producers requiring them to source part of their inputs, labour or capital from the domestic economy.[28] This may typically also involve technology or skills transfer to allow space for locals to grow. As witnessed above, in the *Piero Foresti* case, LCPs can potentially violate a number of trade and investment instruments at bilateral and multilateral levels.

In international investment law, host states typically have the right to regulate.[29] This may include the imposition of reserved sectors to promote the welfare of citizens. For example, the Ghana Investment Promotion Centre Act[30] reserves eight sectors for locals. These include the following: petty trading or hawking; taxis and car hiring services with fleets of less than 25; salons and barber shops; scratch cards for the telecommunications sector; production of books and basic stationery; retailing of finished pharmaceutical products; production, supply and retail of bottled water; and pool betting and lotteries. China also prohibits foreign investment in certain industries such as news agencies.[31] This is despite China's general openness to investment by foreign nationals.

Closer to home, the neighbouring country of Zimbabwe also reserved sectors for locals over the years. The Third Schedule of the Indigenisation and Economic Empowerment (General) Regulations 2010 listed a number of restricted sectors such as agriculture, transportation, retail and wholesale trade, barbershops, hairdressing and beauty salons, employment agencies, valet services and fuel retailing. Only in exceptional circumstances would line ministries consider the approval of a foreign-owned business.

Further to the reservation of these sectors, the government also put in place quantitative restrictions. The Indigenisation and Economic Empowerment Act[32] required, at its inception, all businesses to have 51% ownership by Indigenous Zimbabweans.[33] This law has since been amended to only apply to the diamond and platinum sectors for enterprises valued at over US$500,000.[34] The conditions with respect to reserved sectors have also been eased. The number of reserved sectors has now been trimmed down to 12.[35] These are transportation – passenger buses, taxis and car hire services; retail and wholesale trade; barber shops, hairdressing and beauty salons; employment agencies; estate agencies; valet services; grain milling; bakeries; tobacco grading and packaging; advertising agencies; the provision of local arts and crafts and their marketing and distribution; and artisanal mining.

Foreign nationals seeking to establish a business in a reserved sector after 1 January 2018 can request permission from the relevant minister.[36] Such permission will only be granted in certain circumstances stated in the new section 3A.[37] In addition, while previously the reserved sectors were only for "Indigenous locals" as opposed to Zimbabwean citizens; under the Amended Act, any Zimbabwean citizen qualifies irrespective of race.[38]

Zimbabweans have received the laws on reserved sectors differently. Some have argued that they were being crowded out by some foreign nationals, mainly Nigerians and Chinese workers in certain markets. They were of the belief that they had to fully participate in the economic activities of their countries, especially in sectors that they could easily access with minimum skills and capital.[39] However, others believed that a law that discriminated against other fellow Africans was an unjust law that reeked of xenophobia.

The sentiments on both sides of the divide are no different to those currently being expressed in South Africa with regard to the Bill. While some believe that they are being crowded out by foreign nationals in the township economy, others believe that the reservation of sectors unfairly discriminates against foreign nationals. However, as mentioned previously, there is nothing in international investment law that prohibits a state from reserving certain business areas for locals. However, constitutional constraints may exist within domestic country contexts. Furthermore, there may be other considerations from international human rights law. The first draft Bill, in as far as it reserved certain sectors of the economy in Gauteng needs to be evaluated from the South African legal context to ascertain its constitutionality. This will be interrogated in the forthcoming sections.

10.3 The economic exclusion of refugees in the Bill

Section 7 of the Bill provides that certain economic activities are reserved for South African citizens and residents. Although the Bill does not expressly exclude any groups of persons from these activities, the application of the *expressio unius est exclusio alterius*[40] rule of legal interpretation results in the clear conclusion that the reservation of these activities for citizens and permanent residents effectively excludes all persons who are not one of these categories. Essentially, many categories of migrant worker are excluded from participating in these activities, specifically refugees and asylum seekers.

The Refugees Act[41] defines a refugee as "any person who has been granted asylum in terms of this Act"[42] and an asylum seeker is defined as "a person who is seeking recognition as a refugee in the Republic".[43] Neither refugees nor asylum seekers are granted permanent resident status or citizenship through the granting of asylum. However, the Refugees Act expressly provides that a refugee "enjoys full legal protection, which includes the rights set out in Chapter 2 of the Constitution".[44] This is an unequivocal statement that refugees are entitled to the enjoyment of all rights in the Bill of Rights, including the right to equality as set out in section 9 of the Constitution. In *Union of Refugee Women & Others v Director: Private Security Industry Regulatory Authority & Others*,[45] it was noted by the minority that:

> Refugees who have been granted asylum are a special category of foreign nationals. They are more closely allied to permanent residents than to those foreign nationals who have rights to remain in South Africa temporarily only. Permanent residents have a right to reside in South Africa and enjoy "all the rights, privileges, duties and obligations" of citizens save for those which a law or the Constitution explicitly ascribes to citizenship. Recognised refugees also have a right to remain in South Africa indefinitely in accordance with the provisions of the Refugees Act so their position is closer to that of permanent residents than it is to foreign nationals who have only a temporary right to be in South Africa or foreign nationals who have no right to be here at all. To understand the special position of refugees, it is important to understand how refugee status is conferred in our law, as well as South Africa's international obligations in respect of refugees.[46]

Having regard to this case, it follows that the full legal protection envisaged in the Refugees Act also extends to the right to choose a trade, occupation or profession as provided for in section 22 of the Constitution. This same protection is also afforded to asylum seekers in the Refugees Act, albeit indirectly. Since these persons may eventually be granted refugee status, the argument has been made by Human Rights Watch that an asylum seeker must be given the full protection of chapter 2 of the Constitution, as a refugee would be entitled.[47] In the next section, the considerations for the constitutionality of the exclusion of refugees from the Bill will be discussed.

10.4 Considerations for constitutionality

In dealing with the question of the constitutionality of this Bill, it is important to first consider the contents of the Constitution and its values. To begin, the

Constitution of South Africa[48] provides that South Africa is a democratic country that is built on, among other values, human dignity, the achievement of equality and the advancement of human rights and freedoms.[49] These values are further entrenched in other parts of the Constitution. Section 7 of the Constitution enshrines the rights of all people in the country and affirms the values of human dignity, equality and freedom. The state in s 7(2) is then called upon to respect, protect and promote the rights in the Bill of Rights.[50]

Section 9 of the Constitution has come to be known as the equality clause. Section 9(1) provides that "everyone" is equal before the law and has the right to equal protection and benefit of the law.[51] The purpose of section 9 is manifold. The legal system that existed in South Africa during apartheid was based on inequality and the deprivation of rights of groups of persons.[52] The systematic discrimination against these groups of persons has resulted in significant levels of inequality within South African society.[53]

Section 9 has therefore been included in the Constitution of South Africa to address the consequences of the discrimination experienced by marginalised groups in the past and allows for special measures to be taken to avoid the repetition of such discrimination today.[54] The provisions of the Bill thus must be measured against the standards set by section 9 in order to determine whether the restriction of certain economic activities to South Africans and permanent residents is in conflict with the right to equality.

10.4.1 Everyone has the right to equality

The extension of the right to equality to "everyone" has been considered in a number of Constitutional Court judgments. In *Khosa and Others v Minister of Social Development and Others*,[55] the Constitutional Court considered the meaning of the word "everyone" for the purposes of the right of access to social security.[56] The word "everyone" was considered in light of the founding values of the Constitution, specifically equality.[57] The Court found that the restriction of the word "everyone" to citizens did not comply with the guarantee of constitutional rights to "all people in our country" as per section 7(1) of the Bill of Rights.[58] Consequently, it was held that "everyone" refers to both permanent residents of South Africa as well as citizens.[59]

Considering that the right to equality is meant to be interpreted in a purposive and generous manner, it would not be overreaching to extend the protection afforded by section 9 to refugees in South Africa. A generous interpretation of the Constitution requires that rights be given as broad a meaning as is possible, considering the language used to describe them and the context in which they are used.[60] The approach of purposive interpretation provides that the purpose for which a right was included in the Bill of Rights determines the scope thereof.[61] In order to interpret the Constitution in context, tconstitutional rights cannot be interpreted in a vacuum; they must be interpreted in light of the founding values of the Constitution and in conjunction with each other.[62] Particularly when one considers the provisions of the Refugees Act that provides that refugees are entitled to the enjoyment of the rights in the Bill of Rights, the right to equality must thus be extended to include refugees.[63]

10.4.2 Test for unfair discrimination

The question of how to determine whether a person has been unfairly discriminated against was addressed by the Constitutional Court in 1997. In *Harksen v Lane*,[64] the Constitutional Court established a general test for determining whether unfair discrimination has taken place.[65] The test consists of a number of stages and each of these stages leads to a finding of whether a person's right to equality has been infringed or not.

The first stage of the test involves a determination as to whether differentiation between categories of people has taken place.[66] If this question is answered in the affirmative, the next stage of the test involves a dual investigation. The first aspect of this dual investigation is whether the proven differentiation amounts to discrimination and the next is whether this discrimination (if proven) is unfair.[67] The onus of proof falls upon the person alleging the existence of unfair discrimination to prove such discrimination as per the *Harksen* test. Provided that all three of the aforementioned questions are answered in the affirmative (in other words, differentiation has been proven; that differentiation amounts to discrimination; and that discrimination is considered unfair), the final stage of the test may be embarked upon.

The final stage of the test considers whether there is any justification for any of the types of treatment established in the first three steps.[68] In other words, the final stage determines whether the actor has any valid reason for differentiating between persons, discriminating against persons or unfairly discriminating against persons. In the following paragraphs, this test will be applied to section 7 of the Bill.

10.4.2.1 Differentiation

In order to prove that unfair discrimination has taken place, the first investigation is whether differentiation is present. Differentiation consists of the classification or categorisation of persons. Differentiation itself is not prohibited by law; however, the differentiation must be linked rationally to a justifiable purpose.

10.4.2.2 Discrimination

The enquiry as to whether differentiation amounts to unfair discrimination involves two separate questions: first, whether there is a rational connection between the differentiation and a legitimate government purpose and, if the answer to that question is no, discrimination has been established. The next question is then whether such discrimination is unfair.

10.4.2.3 Unfair discrimination

Discrimination on a number of grounds is considered automatically unfair. If the discrimination is not based on one of these listed grounds, then the person alleging unfair discrimination must prove that the discrimination is unfair. Grounds that render discrimination automatically unfair include race, gender, sex, pregnancy, marital status, ethnic or social origin, colour, sexual orientation, age, disability, religion, conscience, belief, culture, language and birth.[69] When automatically unfair discrimination has been proven *prima facie*, the onus of proof shifts from the alleger to the actor. When a person alleges that they have been discriminated against based on a listed ground, that discrimination is considered automatically unfair until the actor can prove that the alleged discrimination either did not occur or that it was based on something other than the complainant's alleged ground for considering the discrimination to be unfair.

10.5 Why the Bill could be deemed unconstitutional

Considering the framework and precedent laid out previously, it is plausible to argue that the Bill is unconstitutional. It can be established that the first draft Bill differentiates between categories of persons. In this regard, South African citizens and permanent residents are given certain privileges.[70] Such privileges are, however, not extended to anyone else not falling within the scope of this class. The question then becomes whether such alleged discrimination constitutes unfair discrimination.

The ostensible purpose for the differentiation put forward by the Bill is the promotion of employment and economic opportunities for persons in townships.[71] The Bill suggests that depriving certain persons of economic opportunities within townships would result in other persons taking advantage of those opportunities themselves. The aim of the first draft Bill is to some extent laudable as proactive measures to combat unemployment and inequality must be introduced.

It can be submitted, however, that the exclusion of refugees from certain economic activities is neither appropriate nor rational. There is no evidence to suggest that the reservation of economic activities for South African citizens or permanent residents will guarantee that these persons will take up these opportunities. Conversely, there may well be refugees in townships who are more able to take up these opportunities but will be prevented from doing so through the implementation of the Bill.

One must also consider that refugees are often part of the most vulnerable groups in society. Refugees are not in their home country, not able to continue in the careers they had established in those countries and they may also be deprived of their personal support systems. Refugees living in townships are arguably also experiencing high levels of poverty and are subjected to xenophobic sentiments in the communities they live in.[72] Further, deprivation of any rights and freedoms of refugees must be considered in view of these factors. The provincial legislature should not engage in any activity that could further reinforce notions of xenophobia, particularly considering that xenophobic attacks have taken place in South Africa in the recent past. For these reasons, it could be successfully argued that there is no clear rational purpose for the exclusion of refugees from the ambit of the Bill.

Furthermore, in the case of the Bill, the discrimination is based on the fact that refugees are not South African citizens or permanent residents. The discrimination is therefore based on ethnic origin, which is a listed ground in section 9(3) of the Constitution. This means that the discrimination is automatically unfair, and the provincial legislature must therefore provide proof that the discrimination is not unfair.

Moreover, the right to equality has to be interpreted in a spirit of inclusivity as discussed earlier. Thus, it may be argued that any person who has been granted protection by the state is entitled to the right to equality before the law on the same basis as a citizen or permanent resident.[73] The right to equality does not only encompass equality before the law but also the right to equal protection of the law and the prohibition of unfair discrimination. It is the latter of these concepts that may prove problematic for the Gauteng legislature in promulgating the Bill.

Beyond the arguments raised above, emanating from a reading of the equality clause as drawn from *Harksen v Lane*, further arguments could be raised to support this understanding. For instance, it can be noted that the township economy is vital to the economic wellness of South African citizens or foreign nationals who lack the necessary skills or education to participate in the broader formal part of the economy. This is largely attributable to the history of apartheid whose effects still permeate these neighbourhoods. This accords with the averment in *JR 1013 Investments CC and Others v Minister of Safety and Security and Others*.[74] Therefore, protecting economic opportunities for all who live and work in these areas is important. As noted in the Preamble of the Bill, the Constitution also "empowers the State to undertake legislative and other measures designed to promote the achievement of equality by protecting and advancing persons or categories of persons disadvantaged by unfair discrimination". Considering that one of the aims of the Bill is to advance persons who are disadvantaged by unfair discrimination, it is a particularly egregious instance of unfair discrimination to exclude a historically marginalised group from the ambit of the first draft Bill.

10.6 Arguments for the constitutionality of the Bill

Arguments for the constitutionality of the Bill can also be advanced. Section 3 of the first draft Bill provided that the object of the Bill is "to designate business activities within the township areas that are reserved for the exclusive and sole of citizens and persons who has permanent residency status in the Republic". This was further entrenched in section 7 of the first draft Bill, which outlined the economic sectors that would be gazetted as reserved in consultation with the ministers for trade and industry and labour and employment. This excludes various classes of foreign nationals who may enjoy the protection of the law. The relevant question is therefore whether there is relevance to citizenship or permanent residency as a requirement for this purpose.

While the Constitution uses broad wording such as "everyone" when it comes to the right to freedom of trade, occupation and profession, this right is only extended to citizens. Section 22 of the Constitution provides that: "[e]very citizen has the right to choose their trade, occupation or profession freely. The practice of a trade, occupation or profession may be regulated by law".[75] This is different to the framing considered in the Interim Constitution, which envisaged that "everyone shall have the right to freely engage in economic activity and to pursue a livelihood anywhere in the territory".[76] This framing was objected to during the Certification process[77] as it was envisaged that the right should be granted to everyone, irrespective of citizenship.

This was expressly rejected by the Constitutional Court in *Ex parte Chairperson of the Constitutional Assembly: In re Certification of the Amended Text of the Constitution of the Republic of South Africa, 1996*.[78] The court was of the view that the right to occupational choice as extended to citizens was not a universally acceptable fundamental right and the concept of extending this right to everyone was fundamentally flawed. It was accepted that there was nothing within international human rights instruments that prohibited state parties from imposing suitable conditions, which would not otherwise conflict with the instruments, limiting the rights of non-nationals in respect of freedom of occupational choice. It also held that neither the European Convention for the Protection of Human Rights and Fundamental Freedoms nor the International Covenant on Civil and Political Rights provided for such a right to occupational choice. This does not in any manner entail that the court did not consider the importance of this right in international law, but it entails that the court distinguished the nature and enforceability of this right as being materially different to that of other rights.

A number of countries framed this right in their constitutions in a similar manner. Examples of these countries include Germany and Japan. Judge Denny Davis points out that the framing of s 22 in South Africa's Final Constitution must therefore be read as corrective to the historical employment inequities created by apartheid.[79] This is as noted in *JR 1013 Investments CC and Others v Minister of Safety and Security and Others*,[80] South Africa has a history of repression in the choice of a trade, occupation or profession. This has resulted in the disadvantaging of millions of South Africans in terms of their ability to earn.

The above notwithstanding, judicial precedent over the years has developed the above position. In *Khosa and Others v Minister of Social Development and Others*,[81] the court declared that it is unconstitutional to exclude permanent residents in providing for rights.[82] Any reading of the term citizen in the Constitution or any other legislation conferring rights is implied to include "or permanent resident" except in the case of voting.[83] Rightfully, the first draft Bill made this inclusion to allow for this thinking.

The next question becomes whether a similar reading can be made for other classes of foreigners. To begin, we will first consider the case of refugees and asylum seekers. As denoted in the Preamble to the Refugees Act:

> [T]he Republic of South Africa has acceded to the 1951 Convention Relating to Status of Refugees, the 1967 Protocol Relating to the Status of Refugees and the 1969 Organisation of African Unity Convention Governing the Specific Aspects of Refugee Problems in Africa as well as other human rights instruments, and has in so doing, assumed certain obligations to receive and treat in its territory refugees in accordance with the standards and principles established in international law.[84]

This demands that South Africa act in accordance with this mandate. Article 17(1) of the Convention Relating to the Status of Refugees[85] provides in relation to wage-earning employment that "Contracting States shall accord to refugees lawfully staying in their territory the most favourable treatment accorded to nationals of a foreign country in the same circumstances, as regards the right to engage in wage-earning employment".

Importantly, Article 17(2) exempts refugees from restrictive measures placed on aliens or protections to the domestic labour market where they have completed three years residency in the country, have a spouse in the nationality of residency or if they have one or more children in the nationality of the country of residence. States also have to give treatment as favourable as possible with regard to the right to engage in commerce and industrial enterprise.[86] Therefore, it is possible for governments to restrict access to employment and establishment of businesses for refugees, but it will be good practice for the country to provide these opportunities to refugees because of the difficulties they face settling in a foreign country.

In South Africa, a number of restrictions have been placed on refugees. In *Union of Refugee Women & Others v Director: Private Security Industry Regulatory Authority & Others*,[87] the court dealt with the question of whether there was tension between the legal status afforded to refugees and the Private Security Industry Regulation Act,[88] which prohibited non-nationals who are not permanent residents from entering the security industry.[89] This was notwithstanding section 27(f) of the Refugees Act,[90] which provides that a refugee is entitled to full legal protection that includes the rights in the Bill of Rights, a South African identity document, and the right to seek employment.

In writing for the majority in the matter, Kondile AJ noted that this case had to be considered in the proper context. This was especially important in a country where xenophobia was causing increasing suffering.[91] It was important to note that the security industry was a particular environment with important implications for public safety and security. The non-employment of foreign nationals who are not permanent residents did not entail that they were less trustworthy, rather, it only signified there was a need for everyone to prove their trust.[92] This in reality was easier to prove in the case of citizens and permanent residents in terms of the Security Act.[93]

The differentiation of citizens and permanent residents was therefore considered by the majority in *Union of Refugee Women* to have a rational foundation and a legitimate government purpose.[94] While Article 17(1) of the United Nations Convention demanded that refugees be accorded the most favourable treatment afforded to a national of a foreign country in the same circumstances as regards the right to engage in wage-earning employment, it was found that the applicants could not be treated as permanent residents because they were not in the same position as they had not met the requirements for permanent residence.[95] Accordingly, the challenge for the constitutionality of the Security Provisions had to fail. The judgment is problematic in that it seems to contradict earlier cases such as *Khosa* and *Labi Ordam*, which initiated the move towards a more expansive interpretation of constitutional citizenship.

Having observed the findings in *Union of Refugee Women*, it can be argued that there was a legal basis for the exclusion of foreign nationals who are not permanent residents in the first draft Bill. This is clearly pointed out by the majority – refugees cannot be placed in the same position as permanent residents as they have not met the requirements for permanent residency. Furthermore, as noted by the minority, officials could use the powers of exemption granted to them in order to make certain exclusions.[96] In making such considerations, the nature of the activity had to be determined to consider fairness.

Another argument that could be supplied is that because of the low cost of setting up business enterprise in the township, this is an essential economic opportunity for foreign nationals, especially refugees who are fleeing unparalleled crises such as war and have no skills or qualifications to undertake employment in the formal sector. Accordingly, their situation is no different to that of citizens suffering from the legacy of apartheid and finding themselves in desperate situations.

The challenge to this has however been that foreign nationals engaged in the township economy have excelled in their respective trades.[97] This has drawn the ire of some locals who accuse them of stealing their opportunities and using anti-competitive business methods to drive them out of business. This is not necessarily true as the same opportunities available to locals to collaborate and use buying power and economies of scale to grow their businesses are the same being used by foreign shop owners. These are often Somalian, Pakistani, Bangladeshi and Indian nationals who are in the country as refugees. Importantly, however, some of these refugees are economic migrants. This is because of the blurred lines between the two concepts.

10.7 Economic inclusion as a precursor to financial inclusion

Up to this point, this chapter has considered the legality or illegality of excluding refugees from participating in the Gauteng economy. However, what is interesting to note is that the exclusion of refugees can have an impact on the financial inclusion of refugees. In order to get to an understanding of this, one has to understand what economic inclusion is and thereafter demonstrate the potential linkages between these two concepts. There is no common understanding of what is meant by economic inclusion. The United Nations Educational, Scientific and Cultural Organisation (UNESCO) defines economic inclusion as:

> Everyone – regardless of citizenship – has the right to work, and Governments are obliged to take progressive measures to safeguard this right. Non-citizens who are lawfully present in a State are entitled to treatment equal to that enjoyed by citizens in the realm of employment and work.[98]

This definition captures the fact that everyone in a particular country has a right to work regardless of their nationality. This is vital, especially in the South African context where there are sentiments in some quarters that foreigners should not have the right to work in South Africa as they take up opportunities meant for citizens.[99] The first draft Bill was among one of many measures being proposed to limit the economic participation of foreign nationals in the country. The Minister of Labour and Employment, Thulani Nxesi, for example, recently announced that his department was working with the International Labour Organisation to impose prohibitions or quotas in sectors such as ride-hailing services.[100]

The UNESCO definition, however, is very narrow. One view is that it does not capture the fact that economic inclusion goes beyond providing work opportunities in the economy, but it also speaks to other issues such as sharing in the gains of the economy, as opposed to mere participation. These structuralist perspectives opine that, if not managed properly, economic exclusion could lead to the perpetuation of poverty through employment.[101]

This notwithstanding, there is also a general understanding that there is a strong correlation between inequality and economic inclusion.[102] The idea behind this is that rising income inequality casts a shadow over the economy.[103] When people are excluded from the economy, this leads to income challenges that hamstring their well-being. The outcome of this is that wealth is then concentrated in the hands of the few. It is estimated that 85 of the richest people in the world control the same amount of wealth as half the global population.[104]

Other commentators have also linked economic inclusion to economic education and cultural inclusion. Robles argues that economic education is a tool that can be utilised to bolster the financial capabilities of a family.[105] Furthermore, there are those that come from families with generational information on managing finances that improves their chances in the economy. The understanding is, therefore, that without economic education or cultural influence, economic inclusion will remain a persistent problem of our time.

The State of Economic Inclusion Report 2021 notes that there is an expectation to strengthen economic inclusion to curb the persistence of poverty among the poor.[106] The Report further observes that:

> While transformative economic growth will be the ultimate driver of poverty reduction, it is not automatically inclusive and does not always penetrate the poorest households. In strengthening economic inclusion for the poorest, it is important to recognize "poverty traps" and to realize that unleashing the productive potential of people living in poverty involves the removal of multiple constraints through a multidimensional response.[107]

At the centre of such responses should be programmes advancing livelihoods and jobs. This is consistent with the approach suggested in the Sustainable Development Goals (SDGs). SGD 1 speaks to the eradication of poverty everywhere in all its forms.[108]

Another view is that it does not speak to matters such as market participation. Market-led approaches are of the view that economic inclusion is linked to greater market participation. This approach advocates that:

> Addressing poverty and economic exclusion involves reducing the barriers to participation by enhancing labour market flexibility and bridging market failures that limit access to resources and employment opportunities among the poor and unemployed. An emphasis on "inclusive markets", "financial inclusion" and "inclusive growth" seeks to address economic exclusion by connecting the poor more directly into the global economy.[109]

Therefore, it can be said financial inclusion is linked to better economic inclusion. For instance, a financial inclusion strategy to use alternative financial providers and extend banking services to unbanked neighbourhoods could be seen as a measure to include more people in the economy. In the same vein, it can also be averred that economic inclusion is also a precursor to financial inclusion. This is because if people are excluded from participating in the economy, especially the informal economy in the case of unskilled workers, they will have no means for taking care of themselves. Offering them access to banking services would not make much of a difference as they lack income.

When one considers the case of refugees in Gauteng, many of them are engaged in the informal economy. This makes it difficult for refugees in Gauteng to participate in the economy if they are restricted from participating in the township economy. For many refugees, starting a business in the township poses as the only option to irk a living in South Africa. Many of these refugees in their home countries were not involved in business enterprises. A study found that:

> On average, South Africans have been in business for longer than refugees with 19% of South Africa and only 2% of refugee businesses established before 2000. In total, 61% of refugee businesses and 44% of South African businesses were established after 2010. Only 9% of South Africans and 18% of refugees were operating informal businesses before migrating. This does not suggest a competitive advantage conferred by prior experience. Over 80% of the refugee entrepreneurs were not operating an informal sector business prior to migrating to South Africa. The stereotypical idea that refugees somehow have "business in their blood" is therefore not supported by the evidence of this survey.[110]

It is clear from the study above that the opportunities available to refugees drive them into the informal sector. If they are restricted from taking part in this economic activity, many of them will have no access to income. As a result, even if they are given access to banking products, these products will be of little value to them. Therefore, financial inclusion has taken place in the context of economic inclusion.

10.8 A final position on the Bill

Given the fact that both arguments for constitutionality and unconstitutionality have been presented, the authors are of the view that, by and large, the first draft Bill was unconstitutional. This was because of the fact that it sought to limit the rights of foreign nationals such as refugees and asylum seekers from practising their trade. The basis for this argument is that the courts have recognised the importance of providing economic opportunities for refugees and asylum seekers who have no other means of support (this is because some refugees are supported by the United Nations Refugee Agency (UNHCR)).

It was held by the Supreme Court of Appeal in *Minister of Home Affairs and Others v Watchenuka and Others*[111] that a general prohibition on employment for asylum seekers would inevitably harm asylum seekers that had no other means of supporting themselves.[112] The court went further to underscore that a prohibition of employment under these circumstances constituted a material invasion of the right to dignity that could not be justified in terms of the limitations clause.[113]

Moreover, the principles articulated in *Watchenuka* were also extended to apply to self-employment in the case of *Somali Association of South Africa and Others v Limpopo Department of Economic Development Environment and Tourism and Others.*[114] The court noted that it was to be expected that, in a number of instances, a three-year stay could be expected from persons awaiting refugee status in South Africa.[115] It was noted that a key challenge, however, was the fact that South Africa, unlike other countries, did not provide financial assistance to asylum seekers and refugees.[116]

The court highlighted the fact that the state's argument that asylum seekers had to be tracked in order to prevent extending benefits to non-genuine asylum seekers could not be accepted as it would ultimately lead to their destitution.[117] Such an attitude by the law and policymakers was seen to be contrary to the values and ethos of the constitution.[118] The court asserted that while the authorities had to deal with an ever-expanding number of asylum applications, they could not be distracted from their constitutional and international obligations by regulating in a manner that diminished the value and dignity of asylum seekers.[119]

Furthermore, such actions could also have the impact of unwittingly fuelling xenophobia.[120] The court concluded that the actions taken by the authorities in relation to the licensing of spaza shops and tuckshops were thus a deliberate attempt to force asylum seekers to leave the country.[121] The court, therefore, declared that asylum seekers and refugees were entitled to apply for business and trading licenses in terms of the relevant municipal by-laws.[122]

Against this backdrop, it is evident that the restrictions imposed in the first draft Bill constituted a material violation of the right to dignity of asylum seekers and refugees in the Gauteng province. The first draft Bill ran contrary to the values of the constitution and the country's international obligations. This thinking has been supported by the Helen Suzman Foundation.[123] The Helen Suzman Foundation noted that the differentiation contained in the first draft Bill constituted discrimination in a manner that had the potential to impair human dignity.[124] Such discrimination had to be deemed to be unfair.

Accordingly, by the time of the publication of this chapter, the first draft Bill had been amended following public debate.[125] A key change in the revised Bill is the removal of the chapter titled "Economic Activities Reserved for Citizens or Persons with Permanent Residency Status" whose provisions have been the subject matter of this paper. The International Commission for Jurists noted that the removal of these discriminatory provisions was welcome as the potential exclusion of certain classes of non-citizens was in violation of the prohibition on discrimination against non-citizens that was binding on the South African government. These obligations emanated from both the constitution and international human rights law.[126]

Speaking in relation to this, the Africa Director for the International Commission for Jurists, Kaajal Ramjathan-Keogh, noted that:

> Both domestic and international human rights law are clear that all people living in South Africa have a right to work in South Africa, irrespective of their citizenship or documentary status … The ICJ hopes that provincial governments and legislatures throughout the country take heed of the legal advice received by the Gauteng government and desist from any further attempts to legislate the xenophobic exclusion of non-citizens.[127]

Rightfully, the ICJ notes the importance of averting any such future regulation. It brings to the fore an important challenge of regulating xenophobia. It is disheartening that such a piece of legislation could be crafted in democratic South Africa where human rights are of the utmost importance. Nomzamo Zondo, Executive Director at the Socio-Economic Rights Institute of South Africa (SERI) noted that:

> While we recognise that the Gauteng government took legal advice on these matters which led to this change in the Bill, it is still concerning that those tasked with the initial drafting of the Bill appeared to have instructions to make unlawful provision for the discriminatory exclusion of non-citizens from work opportunities. Government can and should boost township economies without discriminating against non-citizens.[128]

Accordingly, going into the future, it is particularly important that the government and all relevant institutions understand the importance of making laws that are consistent with South Africa's domestic and international obligations. This is important because if decisions such as these, where refugees and migrants are economically excluded, financial inclusion for these classes of non-citizens will remain elusive. Economic inclusion not only has importance for the financial inclusion of these classes of persons, but it also has vital implications for other important human rights such as the right to dignity and the right to work.

10.9 Conclusion

The overall impression one got from the first draft Bill was that the Gauteng provincial legislature sought to address the high levels of unemployment and inequality in townships but was somewhat unsure of how this could be done in practice. The first draft Bill aimed to exclude a significant number of non-citizens from a substantial number of economic activities. Such an approach, however, was fraught with many challenges. This was particularly because it went against South Africa's domestic and international obligations. It is therefore laudable that the Gauteng legislators considered legal advice and removed the problematic provisions. However, what was particularly more important for the purpose of this chapter was to demonstrate how such unconstitutional provisions could have an effect on financial inclusion. It was shown that there is a connection between economic exclusion and financial inclusion. It is argued in the chapter that economic exclusion has the ability to limit financial inclusion. If people are excluded from participating in the economy, it makes no sense that they should be included in financial inclusion measures. This is because such individuals lack the opportunity to work and subsequently the opportunity to utilise banking products effectively.

Notes

1 See JA Wiid & MC Cant, 'The Future Growth Potential of Township SMMEs: An African Perspective' (2021) 18 *Journal of Contemporary Management* 513.
2 According to StatsSA, South Africa's unemployment rate increased to 34.4% in the second quarter of 2021. See R Maluleke, 'Quarterly Labour Force Survey' (2021) http://www.statssa.gov.za/publications/P0211/Presentation%20QLFS%20Q2_2021.pdf, accessed on 14 December 2021.
3 The Gauteng township economy is large and is valued at approximately R20 billion per annum. The industry and business potential in townships are, therefore, an important tool in empowering persons living in townships economically and addressing the lingering social inequalities and unemployment endemic in certain township societies.
4 Act 102 of 1996.
5 See the Gauteng Province, 'Gauteng Township Economy Revitalisation Strategy 2014–2019' 2014 *Gauteng Province Economic Development* 2.
6 See Gauteng Legislature, 'State of the Province Address by Premier David Makhura' (Gauteng Legislature 2019) https://www.gpl.gov.za/state-of-the-province-address-2019/, accessed on 14 December 2021.
7 See The Province of Gauteng, 'Provincial Notice 467 of 2020' (The Province of Gauteng 2020) https://archive.opengazettes.org.za/archive/ZA-GT/2020/provincial-gazette-ZA-GT-vol-26-no-182-dated-2020-09-30.pdf, accessed on14 November 2021.
8 Gauteng Township Economic Development First Draft Bill, section 7(2).
9 The second category of foreign nationals that would be affected by the first draft Bill were those that have temporary stay through the issue of various temporary resident visas. Many of these visas establish the right to work or study, but not to establish an enterprise. A business permit may, however, be issued to a foreigner intending to establish or invest in a business in South Africa. Once the foreign national has

invested the requisite capital contribution, currently set at a minimum of R5 million, then they may be awarded a business permit that also entitles them to work. Thus, if a business owner is in possession of such a visa, they can ply their trade anywhere in the country. The Immigration Act 13 of 2002 places no limitations on them in this regard. It would therefore be unlawful for the Bill to prohibit them from doing so. Those with existing permits already doing business in the township will then be allowed to continue business until the expiry of their permits if they do not qualify for permanent residency. The Bill cannot be implemented with retrospective effect and disenfranchise those already operating in the region. The estimation however is potentially that the class of those with business permits and operating in the township is limited because of the size of the capital contribution required.

10 See Businesstech, 'Gauteng's Plan to Restrict Jobs for Foreign Workers – What You Need to Know' (Businesstech 2020) https://businesstech.co.za/news/business/436219/gautengs-plans-to-restrict-jobs-for-foreign-workers-what-you-need-to-know/, accessed on 12 October 2020.

11 Section 7(2) of the Bill provides that "[t]he business activities that are designated in column 3 of Table A of Schedule 2 are, in a designated township, exclusively and solely reserved for ownership and operation by a citizen of, or a person who has permanent residency status in, the Republic". This is an example of how the Bill has not been constructed properly since Schedule 2 contains no such list, but rather contains the list of existing laws that are amended by the Bill. The list of activities that are reserved for South African citizens and permanent residents can instead be found in Schedule 1, although even then it is not clear which activities are reserved for South African citizens and residents. The column in Schedule 1 that is meant to indicate that an activity is reserved is entirely blank. Interpretation of this table is thus difficult, since it does not expressly indicate which activities are reserved and which are not. Notwithstanding this ambiguity and vagueness, it appears from Schedule 1 that the list of reserved economic activities is extremely extensive, and includes the growing of crops, the farming of animals, the extraction of gas, mining and manufacturing of food items.

12 See Canada: Immigration and Refugee Board of Canada, South Africa: Treatment by society and authorities of black Africans of foreign origin who are citizens or permanent residents; state protection' (IRBC 2018) https://www.refworld.org/docid/5b3c95ce4.html, accessed 14 December 2021.

13 See C Steenkamp, 'Xenophobia in South Africa: What Does it Say About Trust? (2009) 98 *The Round Table* 439, 447.

14 For example, certain foreign workers are excluded from the scope of unemployment insurance in South Africa as well as not being covered for occupational injuries that occur in the course of their work in South Africa. This is particularly clear under the Unemployment Insurance Act 63 of 2001. According to section 3(1)(d) of this Act, "persons who enter the country for the purpose of carrying out a contract of service, apprenticeship or learnership, are not covered by the Act, if there is a legal or a contractual requirement (agreement or undertaking) that such a person must leave the country, or that such a person be repatriated, upon termination of the contract". See Miller, Bosman & Le Roux Attorneys, 'Migrant workers – are there any social insurance for them in the employment sphere?' (2019) https://www.mblh.co.za/NewsResources/NewsArticle.aspx?ArticleID=2787, accessed on 11 December 2021.

15 W Buckwalter & A Peterson, 'Public Attitudes Towards Allocating Scarce Resources in the Covid-19 Pandemic' (2020) 15 *PLoS ONE* 1–20.

16 See, for example, the case of *Scalabrini Centre of Cape Town and Another v Minister of Social Development and Others* where the court had to deal with the exclusion of asylum seekers and social permit holders from receiving social assistance in terms of

the distress grant for those affected by Covid-19. It was found that such an exclusion was unconstitutional and impermissible.

17 For example, in the banking sector, foreign banks are affected by restrictions such as the minimum initial amount of deposits they are allowed to accept. See K Mlambo & M Ncube, 'Competition and Efficiency in the Banking Sector in South Africa (2011) 23 *African Development Review* 7.

18 See s 2.1.3.2 of the Broad-Based Socio-economic Empowerment Charter for the Mining and Minerals Industry 2018.

19 See s 1(c) Broad-Based Socio-economic Empowerment Charter for the Mining and Minerals Industry 2018.

20 *Piero Foresti, Laura de Carli and others v Republic of South Africa* ICSID Case No. ARB(AF)/07/1.

21 *Piero Foresti, Laura de Carli and others v Republic of South Africa*, para 1.

22 (20341/19) [2021] ZAGPPHC 623 (21 September 2021).

23 *Minerals Council of South Africa v Minister of Mineral Resources and Energy and Others*, para 59.

24 *Minerals Council of South Africa v Minister of Mineral Resources and Energy and Others, para 59.*

25 *Minerals Council of South Africa v Minister of Mineral Resources and Energy and Others, para 59.*

26 Minerals Council of South Africa v Minister of Mineral Resources and Energy and Others, para 59.

27 See, for example, OECD, 'Investment for African Development: Making it Happen' 2005 *OECD Investment Committee* 1, 53.

28 I Ramdoo, 'Local Content, Trade and Investment: Is There Policy Space Left for Linkages Development in Resource-Rich Countries' 2016 *European Centre for Developing Centre Management No. 205* 1.

29 MA Gwynn, 'Balancing the State's Right to Regulate with Foreign Investment Protection: A Perspective Considering Investment Disputes in the South American Region' (2018) 6 *Groningen Journal of International Law* 111.

30 865 of 2013.

31 Cuninghame et al., 'Global Foreign Investment Control Regimes – Changes in Light of Covid-19' (2020) https://www.ashurst.com/en/news-and-insights/legal-updates/global-foreign-investment-control-regimes---changes-in-light-of-covid-19/, accessed on 10 October 2020.

32 Chapter 14:33.

33 See s 3(1)(a) of the Indigenisation and Economic Empowerment Act (before its amendment).

34 The Act was amended through the Finance Act 1 of 2018 which was published in the Zimbabwean Government Gazette Extraordinary published on the 14th of March 2018.

35 See First Schedule of the Indigenisation and Economic Empowerment Act.

36 See s 3A(10) of the Indigenisation and Economic Empowerment Act.

37 Exceptional circumstances include, but are not limited to, the significant and sustainable creation of employment in Zimbabwe, the transfer of skills and technology for the benefit of the people of Zimbabwe, the creation of sustainable value chains and other prescribed socially and economically viable objectives.

38 Those companies operating in reserved sectors before 1 January 2018 could continue to operate in these sectors provided that they registered themselves.

39 The Herald, 'Foreigners not allowed to Operate in Reserved Sectors' (2021) https://www.herald.co.zw/foreigners-not-allowed-to-operate-in-reserved-sectors/, accessed on 16 December 2021.

40 This *Latin maxim* translated means the expression of one subject, object or idea is the exclusion of other subjects, objects or ideas. It is a vital rule in the construction of statutes. See C Williams, 'Expressio Unius Est Exclusio Alterious' (1931) 4 *Marquette Law Review* 191.
41 130 of 1998.
42 See s 1 of the Refugees Act.
43 See s 1 of the Refugees Act
44 See s 27(b) of the Refugees Act.
45 2007 (4) SA 395 (CC) (12 December 2006).
46 *Union of Refugee Women & Others v Director: Private Security Industry Regulatory Authority & Others*, para 99.
47 Human Rights Watch, 'Appendix A: South Africa's Obligation Under International and Domestic Law' (1998) https://www.hrw.org/legacy/reports98/sareport/App1a.htm, accessed on 13 December 2021.
48 Constitution of the Republic of South Africa, 1996.
49 See s (1)(a) of the Constitution of South Africa.
50 See s 7(2) of the Constitution of South Africa.
51 See s 9(1) of the Constitution of South Africa.
52 See A Smith, 'Equality Constitutional Adjudication in South Africa' (2014) 14 *African Human Rights Law Journal* 609 610.
53 See J Seekings and N Nattrass *Class, Race, and inequality in South Africa* (2005) 3.
54 CRM Dlamini, 'Equality or Justice? Section 9 of the Constitution Revisited – Part II' (2002) 27 *Journal of Juridical Science* 16.
55 BCLR 569 (CC) (4 March 2004).
56 See *Khosa and Others v Minister of Social Development and Others* para's 38, 42, 45, 46 and 47.
57 *Khosa and Others v Minister of Social Development and Others*, para's 38, 40, 42 and 44.
58 *Khosa and Others v Minister of Social Development and Others*, para 85.
59 *Khosa and Others v Minister of Social Development and Others,* para 89.
60 *S v Zuma* 1995 (2) SA 642 (CC), para 14. See also *S v Mhlungu* 1995 (3) SA 391 (CC), para 8.
61 I Currie & J De *Waal, Bill of Rights Handbook* 6ed (2013) 137.
62 *Matatiele Municipality v President of the Republic of South Africa* 2007 (6) SA 477 (CC), para 36.
63 See s 1 of the Refugees Act.
64 [1997] ZACC 12.
65 See *Harksen v Lane*, para's 42 and 43.
66 See *Harksen v Lane*, para 42.
67 See *Harksen v Lane*, para 42.
68 See *Harksen v Lane*, para 44.
69 See s 9(3) of the Constitution of South Africa.
70 See s 7(2) of the First Draft Gauteng Township Economic Development Bill.
71 See s 3 of the First Draft Gauteng Township Economic Development Bill.
72 See S Masuku, 'How South Africa is Denying Refugees their Rights: What Needs to Change' (2020) https://theconversation.com/how-south-africa-is-denying-refugees-their-rights-what-needs-to-change-135692, accessed on 13 December 2021.
73 Of course, this does raise many practical questions such as whether the state is able to afford granting rights with economic implications to non-residents.
74 [1996] ZACC 7.
75 See s 22 of the Constitution of South Africa.
76 See s 26 of the Constitution of South Africa.
77 After the Interim Constitution was drafted. A final text had to be produced which required the Certification of the Constitutional Court to ensure that the text had satis-

fied the principles set in Schedule 4 of the Interim Constitution. See Constitutional Court of South Africa, 'The Certification Process' https://www.concourt.org.za/index.php/constitution/the-certification-process, accessed on 12 October 2020.

78 1997 (2) SA 97 (CC), 1997 (1) BCLR 1 (CC)

79 D Davis, 'Freedom of Trade, Occupation and Profession' https://constitutionallawofsouthafrica.co.za/wp-content/uploads/2018/10/Chap54.pdf, accessed on 15 December 2021.

80 1997 (7) BCLR 950.

81 CCT 13/03, CCT 12/03) [2004] ZACC 11; 2004 (6) SA 505 (CC); 2004 (6) BCLR 569 (CC) (4 March 2004).

82 *Khosa and Others v Minister of Social Development and Others*, para 87.

83 *Khosa and Others v Minister of Social Development and Others, para* 88.

84 See the Preamble of the Refugees Act.

85 Adopted on 28 July 1951 by the United Nations Conference of Plenipotentiaries on the Status of Refugees and Stateless Persons convened under General Assembly resolution 429(V) of 14 December 1950.

86 See Article 18 of the Convention Relating to the Status of Refugees.

87 CCT 39/06) [2006] ZACC 23; 2007 (4) BCLR 339 (CC); (2007) 28 ILJ 537 (CC); 2007 (4) SA 395 (CC) (12 December 2006).

88 Act 56 of 2001.

89 *Union of Refugee Women & Others v Director: Private Security Industry Regulatory Authority & Others*, para 1.

90 Act 130 of 1998.

91 *Union of Refugee Women & Others v Director: Private Security Industry Regulatory Authority & Others*, para 38.

92 *Union of Refugee Women & Others v Director: Private Security Industry Regulatory Authority & Others*, para 38.

93 *Union of Refugee Women & Others v Director: Private Security Industry Regulatory Authority & Others*, para 38.

94 *Union of Refugee Women & Others v Director: Private Security Industry Regulatory Authority & Others*, paras 74 and 118.

95 *Union of Refugee Women & Others v Director: Private Security Industry Regulatory Authority & Others*, para 65.

96 *Union of Refugee Women & Others v Director: Private Security Industry Regulatory Authority & Others*, para 126.

97 See Liedeman et al., 'Why are Foreign-run Spaza Shops More Successful? The Rapidly Changing Spaza Sector in South Africa' (2013) https://www.econ3x3.org/article/why-are-foreign-run-spaza-shops-more-successful-rapidly-changing-spaza-sector-south-africa, accessed on 13 December 2013 & B Lamb, LN Kunene & NF Dyili 'Lessons from Foreign Owned Spaza Shops in South African Townships' (2019) 8 *Journal of Reviews on Global Economics* 1351.

98 United Nations Educational, Scientific and Cultural Organisation, 'Economic Inclusion' http://www.unesco.org/new/en/social-and-human-sciences/themes/urban-development/migrants-inclusion-in-cities/good-practices/economic-inclusion/, accessed on 17 August 2021.

99 See R Chaskalson, 'Do Immigrants Steal Jobs in South Africa? What Does the Data Tell Us' (2017) https://www.groundup.org.za/article/do-immigrants-steal-jobs-south-africa-what-data-tell-us/, accessed on 18 September 2021.

100 Businesstech, 'Government wants to block foreigners from taking certain jobs in South Africa – including Uber drivers' (2021) https://businesstech.co.za/news/business/501217/government-wants-to-block-foreigners-from-taking-certain-jobs-in-south-africa-including-uber-drivers/, accessed on 17 August 2021.

101 K Meagher, L Mann & M Bolt, 'Introduction: Global Economic Inclusion and African Workers' 2016 (52) *The Journal of Development Studies* 471.

102 Trade and Industrial Policy Strategies, 'Inequality and Economic Inclusion' (2020) https://www.tips.org.za/research-archive/inequality-and-economic-inclusion, accessed on 16 August 2021.
103 C Lagarde, 'Economic Inclusion and Financial Integrity' (Lagarde 2014) https://www.elibrary.imf.org/view/books/076/22782-9781513513751-en/ch01.xml, accessed on 16 August 2021.
104 Lagarde 2014 (note 103 above).
105 B Robles 'Economic Inclusion and Financial Education in Culturally Diverse Communities: Leveraging Cultural Capital and Whole-Family Learning' (2014) 141 *New Directions for Adult and Continuing Education* 59 – 60.
106 Andrew et al., 'The State of Economic Inclusion Report 2021: The Potential to Scale' (Andrew et al. 2021) https://openknowledge.worldbank.org/bitstream/handle/10986/34917/9781464815980.pdf?sequence=24&isAllowed=y, accessed on 20 August 2021 17.
107 B Robles, 'Economic Inclusion and Financial Education in Culturally Diverse Communities: Leveraging Cultural Capital and Whole-Family Learning' (2014) 141 *New Directions for Adult and Continuing Education* 59–60.
Andrew et al., 2021 (note 106 above).
108 United Nations Department of Social and Economic Affairs, 'The 17 Goals' https://sdgs.un.org/goals, accessed on 17 August 2021.
109 K Meagher, L Mann L & M Bolt, 'Introduction: Global Economic Inclusion and African Workers' 2016(52) *The Journal of Development Studies* 471.
110 Crush et al., 'Comparing Refugees and South Africans in the Urban Informal Sector' 2017 *SAMP Migration Policy Series* No 78 2.
111 (010/2003) [2003] ZASCA 142; [2004] 1 All SA 21 (SCA) (28 November 2003).
112 *Minister of Home Affairs and Others v Watchenuka and Others*, para 33.
113 *Minister of Home Affairs and Others v Watchenuka and Others*, para 33.
114 (48/2014) [2014] ZASCA 143; 2015 (1) SA 151 (SCA); [2014] 4 All SA 600 (SCA) (26 September 2014)
115 *Somali Association of South Africa and Others v Limpopo Department of Economic Development Environment and Tourism and Others*, para 44.
116 *Somali Association of South Africa and Others v Limpopo Department of Economic Development Environment and Tourism and Others*, para 44.
117 *Somali Association of South Africa and Others v Limpopo Department of Economic Development Environment and Tourism and Others*, para 44.
118 *Somali Association of South Africa and Others v Limpopo Department of Economic Development Environment and Tourism and Others*, para 44.
119 *Somali Association of South Africa and Others v Limpopo Department of Economic Development Environment and Tourism and Others*, para 44.
120 *Somali Association of South Africa and Others v Limpopo Department of Economic Development Environment and Tourism and Others*, para 44.
121 *Somali Association of South Africa and Others v Limpopo Department of Economic Development Environment and Tourism and Others*, para 44.
122 *Somali Association of South Africa and Others v Limpopo Department of Economic Development Environment and Tourism and Others*, para 46.
123 See Hellen Suzman Foundation, 'Submission on the Gauteng Township Economic Development Draft Bill, 2020' (HSF 2020) https://hsf.org.za/publications/submissions/hsf-submission-on-gauteng-township-economic-development-draft-bill-2020.pdf, accessed on 14 December 2021.
124 HSF 2020 (note 123 above).
125 See the Province of Gauteng Provincial Gazette, 17 June 2021.
126 International Commission of Jurists, 'South Africa: Scrapping of Discriminatory Provisions Against Non-Citizens in Gauteng Bill a Welcome Step Forward' (ICJ 2021)

https://www.icj.org/south-africa-scrapping-of-discriminatory-provisions-against-non-citizens-in-gauteng-bill-a-welcome-step-forward/, accessed on 14 December 2021.

127 ICJ 2021 (note 126 above).

128 ICJ 2021 (note 126 above).

Bibliography

C Andrew, A de Montesquiou, IA Sánchez, PV Dutta, S Samaranayake, J Heisey, T Clay & S Chaudhary 'The state of economic inclusion report 2021: The potential to scale' (2021), available at https://openknowledge.worldbank.org/bitstream/handle/10986/34917/9781464815980.pdf?sequence=24&isAllowed=y, accessed on 20 August 2021.

Broad-Based Socio-economic Empowerment Charter for the Mining and Minerals Industry 2018.

W Buckwalter & A Peterson 'Public attitudes towards allocating scarce resources in the Covid-19 pandemic' (2020) 15 *PLoS ONE* 1.

Businesstech 'Gauteng's plan to restrict jobs for foreign workers – What you need to know' (2020), available at https://businesstech.co.za/news/business/436219/gautengs-plans-to-restrict-jobs-for-foreign-workers-what-you-need-to-know/, accessed on 12 October 2020.

Businesstech 'Government wants to block foreigners from taking certain jobs in South Africa – Including Uber drivers' (2021), available at https://businesstech.co.za/news/business/501217/government-wants-to-block-foreigners-from-taking-certain-jobs-in-south-africa-including-uber-drivers/, accessed on 17 August 2021.

R Chaskalson 'Do immigrants steal jobs in South Africa? What does the data tell us' (2017), available at https://www.groundup.org.za/article/do-immigrants-steal-jobs-south-africa-what-data-tell-us/, accessed on 18 September 2021.

Constitution of the Republic of South Africa, 1996.

Constitutional Court of South Africa 'The certification process' available at https://www.concourt.org.za/index.php/constitution/the-certification-process, accessed on 12 October 2020.

Convention Relating to the Status of Refugees Adopted on 28 July 1951 by the United Nations Conference of Plenipotentiaries on the Status of Refugees and Stateless Persons convened under General Assembly resolution 429(V) of 14 December 1950.

Cuninghame 'Global foreign investment control regimes – Changes in light of Covid-19' (2020), available at https://www.ashurst.com/en/news-and-insights/legal-updates/global-foreign-investment-control-regimes---changes-in-light-of-covid-19/, accessed on 10 October 2020.

I Currie & J De Waal *Bill of Rights Handbook* 6 ed.

CRM Dlamini 'Equality or justice? Section 9 of the constitution revisited – Part II' (2002) 27 *Journal of Juridical Science* 14 at 40.

European Convention for the Protection of Human Rights and Fundamental Freedoms.

Ex parte Chairperson of the Constitutional Assembly: In Re Certification of the Amended Text of the Constitution of the Republic of South Africa, 1996 1997 (2) SA 97 (CC), 1997 (1) BCLR 1 (CC).

Finance Act 1 of 2018.

Gauteng Legislature 'State of the province address by Premier David Makhura' (2019), available at https://www.gpl.gov.za/state-of-the-province-address-2019/, accessed on 14 December 2021.

Gauteng Province 'Gauteng township economy revitalisation strategy 2014–2019' (2014) *Gauteng Province Economic Development* 1 at 35.

J Goldstein & M Peters 'Nativism or economic threat: Attitudes towards foreigners during the great recession' (2014) 40 *International Interactions* 376 at 401.

MA Gwynn 'Balancing the state's right to regulate with foreign investment protection: A perspective considering investment disputes in the South American region' (2018) 6 *Groningen Journal of International Law* 110 at 127.

Harksen v Lane [1997] ZACC.

Hellen Suzman Foundation 'Submission on the Gauteng township economic development draft bill, 2020' (2020), available at https://hsf.org.za/publications/submissions/hsf-submission-on-gauteng-township-economic-development-draft-bill-2020.pdf, accessed on 14 December 2021.

Human Rights Watch 'Appendix A: South Africa's obligation under international and domestic law' (1998), available at https://www.hrw.org/legacy/reports98/sareport/App1a.htm, accessed on 13 December 2021.

Immigration Act 13 of 2002.

Indigenisation and Economic Empowerment Act Chapter 14:33.

Indigenisation and Economic Empowerment (General) Regulations 2010.

International Commission of Jurists 'South Africa: Scrapping of discriminatory provisions against non-citizens in Gauteng bill a welcome step forward' (2021), available at https://www.icj.org/south-africa-scrapping-of-discriminatory-provisions-against-non-citizens-in-gauteng-bill-a-welcome-step-forward/, accessed on 14 December 2021.

International Covenant on Civil and Political Rights.

Investment Promotion Centre Act 865 of 2013.

JR 1013 Investments CC and Others v Minister of Safety and Security and Others [1996] ZACC.

Khosa and Others v Minister of Social Development and Others BCLR 569 (CC).

C Lagarde 'Economic inclusion and financial integrity' (2014), available at https://www.elibrary.imf.org/view/books/076/22782-9781513513751-en/ch01.xml, accessed on 16 August 2021.

B Lamb, LN Kunene & NF Dyili 'Lessons from foreign owned spaza shops in South African townships' (2019) 8 *Journal of Reviews on Global Economics* 1351 at 1362.

Liedeman 'Why are foreign-run spaza shops more successful? The rapidly changing spaza sector in South Africa' (2013), available at https://www.econ3x3.org/article/why-are-foreign-run-spaza-shops-more-successful-rapidly-changing-spaza-sector-south-africa, accessed on 13 December 2013.

R Maluleke 'Quarterly labour force survey' (2021), available at http://www.statssa.gov.za/publications/P0211/Presentation%20QLFS%20Q2_2021.pdf, accessed on 14 December 2021.

S Masuku 'How South Africa is denying refugees their rights: What needs to change' (2020), available at https://theconversation.com/how-south-africa-is-denying-refugees-their-rights-what-needs-to-change-135692, accessed on 13 December 2021.

Matatiele Municipality v President of the Republic of South Africa 2007 (6) SA 477 (CC).

K Meagher, L Mann & M Bolt 'Introduction: Global economic inclusion and African workers' (2016) 52 *The Journal of Development Studies* 471 at 482.

B Miller & Le Roux Attorneys 'Migrant workers – Are there any social insurance for them in the employment sphere?' (2019), available at https://www.mblh.co.za/NewsResources/NewsArticle.aspx?ArticleID=2787, accessed on 11 December 2021.

Minerals Council of South Africa v Minister of Mineral Resources and Energy and Others (20341/19) [2021] ZAGPPHC 623 (21 September 2021).

Mineral and Petroleum Resources Development Act 28 of 2002.

K Mlambo & M Ncube 'Competition and efficiency in the banking sector in South Africa' (2011) 23 *African Development Review* 4 at 15.

OECD 'Investment for African development: Making it happen' (2005) OECD Investment Committee 1 at 53.

Piero Foresti, Laura de Carli and others v. Republic of South Africa ICSID Case No. ARB(AF)/07/1.

Private Security Industry Regulation Act 56 of 2001.

Province of Gauteng Provincial Gazette, 17 June 2021 of 1998.

I Ramdoo 'Local content, trade and investment: Is there policy space left for linkages development in resource-rich countries' 2016 *European Centre for Developing Centre Management* No. 205 1 at 58.

Refugees Act 130 of 1998.

B Robles 'Economic inclusion and financial education in culturally diverse communities: Leveraging cultural capital and whole-family learning' (2014) 141 *New Directions for Adult and Continuing Education* 57 at 66.

J Seekings & N Nattrass *Class, Race, and inequality in South Africa.*

A Smith 'Equality constitutional adjudication in South Africa' (2014) 14 *African Human Rights Law Journal* 609 at 632.

State of Economic Inclusion Report 2021.

C Steenkamp 'Xenophobia in South Africa: What does it say about trust? (2009) 98 *The Round Table* 439 at 447.

S v Mhlungu 1995 (3) SA 391 (CC).

S v Zuma 1995 (2) SA 642 (CC).

The Herald 'Foreigners not allowed to operate in reserved sectors' (2021), available at https://www.herald.co.zw/foreigners-not-allowed-to-operate-in-reserved-sectors/, accessed on 16 December 2021.

The Province of Gauteng 'Provincial notice 467 of 2020' (2020), available at https://archive.opengazettes.org.za/archive/ZA-GT/2020/provincial-gazette-ZA-GT-vol-26-no-182-dated-2020-09-30.pdf, accessed on 14 November 2021.

Trade and Industrial Policy Strategies 'Inequality and economic inclusion' (2020), available at https://www.tips.org.za/research-archive/inequality-and-economic-inclusion, accessed on 16 August 2021.

Union of Refugee Women & Others v Director: Private Security Industry Regulatory Authority & Others 2007 (4) SA 395 (CC).

United Nations Department of Social and Economic Affairs 'The 17 goals', available at https://sdgs.un.org/goals, accessed on 17 August 2021.

United Nations Educational, Scientific and Cultural Organisation 'Economic inclusion', available at http://www.unesco.org/new/en/social-and-human-sciences/themes/urban-development/migrants-inclusion-in-cities/good-practices/economic-inclusion/, accessed on 17 August 2021.

JA Wiid & MC Cant 'The future growth potential of township SMMEs: An Africa perspective' (2021) 18 *Journal of Contemporary Management* 508 at 530.

C Williams 'Expressio Unius Est Exclusio Alterious' (1931) 4 *Marquette Law Review* 191 at 196.

11 The provision and administration of the Covid-19 social relief distress grant to promote financial inclusion for the poor and unemployed persons in South Africa

Howard Chitimira and Phemelo T. Magau

11.1 Introductory remarks

Financial inclusion of the poor and unemployed persons has become increasingly important for stability and growth in the financial sector in South Africa. The concept of financial inclusion can be defined as the development and provision of access to financial products and services offered by the government, financial institutions and other relevant stakeholders to all financial consumers, including the poor and unemployed persons in an affordable and useful manner.[1] Notably, in order to achieve financial inclusion, the government, financial institutions and all other relevant stakeholders must have the ability to create an environment that is suitable for economic investment to take place to improve access to financial services and products by financial consumers.[2] In addition to this, the attainment of financial inclusion for the poor and unemployed persons in South Africa depends on such financial consumers having access to financial institutions and the services offered by financial institutions without too many difficulties.[3] To this end, the promotion of financial inclusion is significant for curbing financial exclusion of the poor and unemployed persons in South Africa, especially during the ongoing coronavirus (Covid-19) pandemic. Financial exclusion takes place when the government, financial institutions and other relevant stakeholders fail to ensure that there is access and the use of reasonably cheap and suitable financial services within the formal financial system in a particular country by financial consumers, including the poor and unemployed persons.[4] Consequently, combatting financial exclusion during the ongoing Covid-19 pandemic is important owing to the fact that the promotion of financial inclusion is vital for building a viable economy and financial market that can be accessed by everyone, including the poor and unemployed persons in South Africa.

The arrival of the Covid-19 pandemic has caused serious disorders, not only to the health system but also to the economy, livelihood, service delivery, financial sector and how life used to be in general.[5] Most companies were forced to shut down their businesses, thus resulting in the retrenchment of many people leading

DOI: 10.4324/9781003369400-11

to acute economic austerity.[6] Before all these disruptions caused by the Covid-19 pandemic, South Africa had been battling with addressing challenges such as the financial exclusion of the poor and low-income earners, the prolonged economic recession, high levels of poverty and unemployment.[7] In an effort to provide financial assistance to unemployed people during the lockdown,[8] the government introduced the Covid-19 Social Relief Distress (SRD) grant. The SRD grant, also known as the special R350 Covid-19 grant, is one of the relief measures the South African government has put in place and extended several times to try to sustain the poor and unemployed persons most affected by the pandemic. However, the administration of this grant has not been without challenges, thus thwarting the objective of the grant and resulting in some poor and unemployed persons being excluded from accessing the grant on time or at all.

This chapter examines the process of providing and administering the SRD grant to promote the financial inclusion of poor and unemployed persons in South Africa. Particular attention is made to the purpose of the SRD grant and the requirements to access and apply for the same by poor and unemployed persons in South Africa. The role of selected key role-players involved in the provision and administration of the SRD grant is also discussed. Such role-players include the South African Social Security Agency (SASSA), the South African Post Office (SAPO) and the Department of Social Development (DSD). The role played by these institutions is discussed to investigate whether they have adopted and put adequate measures in place to promote financial inclusion of the poor and unemployed in the provision and administration of the SRD grant. This chapter also explores the possible advantages and disadvantages of the SRD grant. It is argued that the effective provision and administration of the SRD grant could have led to the promotion of financial inclusion for the poor and unemployed persons in South Africa.

11.2 The purpose of the Covid-19 SRD grant and the promotion of financial inclusion of the poor and unemployed persons during the Covid-19 pandemic in South Africa

The term social relief of distress grant is not comprehensively defined under the Social Assistance Act 13 of 2004, nonetheless, it refers to a social relief granted to a person who qualifies for such a relief as may be prescribed by the Minister of Social Development.[9] The Covid-19 SRD grant was introduced in terms of the Regulations made under the Disaster Management Act 57 of 2002 in the year 2020 as one of the measures to combat the socio-economic effects of the Covid-19 pandemic on the poor and unemployed persons in South Africa.[10] This is owing to the fact that the provision of social relief of distress is one of the social grants that are available to qualifying persons under the Social Assistance Act, which has been amended by the Social Assistance Amendment Act 16 of 2020.[11] This social relief of distress was introduced as a temporary provision of assistance intended for persons who are in dire material need to an extent that they are unable to meet their basic needs or those of their families.[12] The special R350 Covid-19 grant was first paid out to recipients in May 2020 for a period of six months and thereafter it has been extended by three-month intervals until April 2021.[13] The grant was reinstated in August 2021 and it is expected to be provided until the end of March 2022.[14] The reinstatement in the provision of the grant was necessitated by the ongoing socio-economic pressures suffered by the poor and unemployed persons in South Africa due to the lockdown.[15] Moreover, most businesses are still struggling to recover from the impact of the lockdown restrictions, thus causing many families to suffer as a result of the employment market's gradual recovery.[16] According to President Ramaphosa, the special R350 Covid-19 grant has proven to be an effective and efficient short-term measure aimed at reducing the impact on the livelihoods of poor and unemployed South Africans.[17] In January 2021, SASSA reported that it had processed more than 9.6 million applications and that more than R16 billion had been paid in the SRD grant to over 6.5 million recipients per month since May 2020 when the payments of the grant commenced.[18] The authors argue that given the economic effects of the Covid-19 pandemic in South Africa, the provision of the SRD grant should be seen as an opportunity the South African government took to reintegrate the poor and unemployed persons into the formal financial sector.[19] Amidst the pandemic, the poor and unemployed persons could participate in formal economic activities of the country. Thus, the financial inclusion of poor and unemployed persons was not entirely on hold since some of them could still receive the SRD grant.

11.3 Application process and access requirements for the Covid-19 SRD grant

11.3.1 The application process for the SRD grant

The application process for the SRD grant is done electronically by the applicants themselves or through the assistance of SASSA staff and appointed volunteers for those who experience difficulties applying electronically.[20] Paper-based applications are not accepted for the SRD grant.[21] The applicants can apply through various electronic platforms such as WhatsApp, email, USSD number and SASSA website or by way of calling the call centre.[22] There are no payable application fees for the SRD grant.[23] The approach of having the applications done online electronically is a commendable move, especially owing to the fact that when the applications were first done, there were serious restrictions imposed relating to travelling and physical distancing in order to prevent the spread of the virus. While having the applications done online was commendable in the circumstances, it also had a major disadvantage of excluding persons without access to the internet or necessary devices,, a point that will be discussed further in this chapter.

11.3.2 Access requirements for the SRD grant

Although the SRD grant was established to help the poor and unemployed persons to survive during the severe economic effects of the Covid-19 pandemic, not every poor or unemployed person is eligible to benefit from this grant since certain requirements must be complied with. The eligibility of the SRD grant, in particular, is not quite comprehensive and fully detailed in terms of the Social Assistance Act.[24] This is owing to the fact that the Social Assistance Act only mentions that the Minister of Social Development may provide social relief of distress to a person who qualifies for such relief as may be prescribed.[25] However, in terms of the regulations made under the Social Assistance Act[26] and guidelines available from SASSA,[27] the SRD grant is aimed at benefitting South African citizens, permanent residents, refugees and holders of special permits from Lesotho, Angola and Zimbabwe as well as asylum-seekers who are above the age of 18, unemployed and not receiving any income.[28] In addition to this, the applicant must meet one or more of the following criteria: the applicant is awaiting payment of an approved social grant[29] or the applicant has been found medically unfit to undertake remunerative work for a period of less than six months.[30] The applicant could also be someone coming from a family where the main source of income is deceased and an application is made within three months of the date of death.[31] The applicant could also come from a family where the breadwinner of that person's family has been admitted to an institution funded by the state (such institutions include prison, psychiatric hospital, state home for older persons, a treatment centre for substance abuse or child and youth care centre).[32] Moreover, the applicant should not receive maintenance from a parent, child or spouse obliged in law to pay maintenance, and proof is furnished that efforts made to obtain maintenance have been unsuccessful.[33] Furthermore, the applicant should not be a person receiving assistance from any other organisation.[34] The applicant could be a person who has been affected by the Covid-19 disaster.[35] Lastly, the applicant can be someone whose refusal of the application for social relief of distress will cause undue hardships.

11.4 Selected role-players in the administration of the Covid-19 SRD grant and promotion of financial inclusion for the poor and unemployed persons in South Africa

11.4.1 The role of SASSA

SASSA was established under the South African Social Security Agency Act.[36] The objectives of SASSA include acting as the sole agent that has to ensure the efficient and effective management, administration and payment of social assistance and security as well as rendering services relating to such payments.[37] SASSA has several legislative functions accorded to it which include administering social assistance in terms of the relevant applicable laws that regulate the provision of social grants in South Africa including the SRD grant.[38] SASSA is responsible for collecting, collating and administering information that is necessary for the payment of social security and social assistance to the beneficiaries through proper reconciliation and management of payment of transfer funds.[39] Moreover, SASSA has to establish a compliance and fraud mechanism to ensure that the integrity of the social security system is maintained in rendering its services.[40] To realise its objectives, SASSA may enter into an agreement with anyone to ensure effective payments to beneficiaries.[41] The agreement must include provisions relating to the effective, efficient and economical use of funds designated for payment to beneficiaries of social security.[42] The agreement should also include provisions dealing with the promotion and protection of the human dignity of applicants and beneficiaries of social security.[43] In entering into an agreement with another person, SASSA must ensure the protection of confidential information held by it to promote honest, impartial, fair and equitable service delivery.[44] The agreement must also include provisions relating to mechanisms to regulate community participation and consultation as well as financial penalties for non-compliance with the provisions of the agreement.[45] Although SASSA is empowered to administer and provide social grants, including the SRD grant, and do everything necessary to achieve this objective, the agency is not empowered to promote financial inclusion of the beneficiaries who are mostly poor and unemployed in South Africa. In this regard, SASSA has not put any measures in place to promote financial inclusion in carrying out its statutory functions and objectives of ensuring the efficient and effective management, administration and payment of social assistance and security as well as rendering services relating to such payments.[46] For instance, having the applications completed online has had a major disadvantage of excluding persons without access to the internet or the necessary devices. After applying successfully despite the aforementioned challenge, most poor and unemployed persons have to travel a long distance, especially those living in informal settlements and remote areas, to join long queues at SAPO branches to access the grant. SASSA should have considered other means of conducting applications for the grant such as having paper-based applications, especially where the lockdown restrictions have been eased to allow travel and movement of people.

11.4.2 The role of the SAPO

The SAPO is a postal public company established in terms of the Post Office Act[47] and given continued existence by the South African Post Office SOC Ltd Act.[48] As the name suggests, the SAPO is mainly responsible for ensuring the universal and affordable provision of postal services in the interest of the economic growth and development of the country.[49] It is also supposed to be innovative in the provision of postal services that are responsive to the needs of the users and the consumers.[50] The SAPO has to ensure universal access to postal services by providing an acceptable level of effective, reliable and regular postal services to all areas, including rural areas and small towns where post offices are not sustainable.[51] In addition to this, the SAPO has to ensure that there is equity in respect of the distribution of services, mainly within the areas of historically disadvantaged communities, including rural areas.[52] Other duties of the SAPO include ensuring that the needs of disabled persons are addressed in the provision of postal services and safeguarding the development of human resources and capacity within the postal industry.[53] The SAPO must act in the best interest of postal users and other clients by maintaining an effective and efficient system of collecting, sorting and delivering mail nationwide.[54] It must actively provide and develop a citizens' post office that contributes to the community and rural development and education to ensure compliance with international commitments relevant to the postal industry.[55]

Additionally, the SAPO has powers to, *inter alia*, purchase or acquire immovable property and dispose of such property and erect any buildings or facilities that can be used for its benefit as a public company. The SAPO was contracted by SASSA to assist in the provision and administration of the SRD grant mainly through making payments available to the recipients.[56] Evidently, the provisions that must be adhered to when entering into an agreement of this nature have not been followed by the SAPO.[57] From the SAPO's functions and powers above, it is not very clear how the SAPO is empowered to administer and provide the SRD from a legislative point of view. However, the decision to have the SAPO administer and provide the SRD is a strategic one given that the SAPO distributes postal services all over the country and it has been contracted by SASSA as a payment channel in the past.[58] It is also not very clear how the SAPO is statutorily promoting financial inclusion since its primary function is to provide postal services and not administer or provide the SRD grant. Moreover, despite the powers accorded to it to acquire facilities pertinent to assisting it to carry out its functions, most of the infrastructure of the SAPO is not in good condition, which has resulted in delays in the delivery of postal services to the communities. The SAPO has not been doing well in terms of providing and administering the SRD grant. This has been evident from the long, winding queues that poor and unemployed persons, the recipients of the SRD grant, had to endure since the commencement of payment of this grant in 2020.[59] SAPO has also experienced technical glitches that caused delays in the provision of the SRD grant.[60] One of the efforts that the SAPO has made in trying to resolve the complaints about the long queues is to work with supermarkets such as Boxer and Pick ‘n Pay to allow beneficiaries to withdraw their special R350 grants from these supermarkets.[61] Although this effort is commendable, it is submitted that SAPO should consider putting more measures in place to promote financial inclusion of the poor and unemployed persons in its role of administering the payments of the SRD grant to such consumers by entering into effective partnerships with more retailers and banks to enhance access to the SRD grant.

11.4.3 The role of the DSD

The DSD is a national department with provincial offices across the nine provinces in the country. The DSD derives its primary mandate from the Constitution.[62] The Constitution provides for the right of access to appropriate social assistance to those unable to support themselves and their dependents.[63] Moreover, the Constitution identifies welfare services, population development and disaster management as functional areas of concurrent national and provincial legislative competence.[64] The DSD further derives its legislative mandate from various pieces of legislation including, among others, the SASSA Act and the Social Assistance Act.

Accordingly, the DSD's primary core functions that are derived from its legislative mandate include the management and oversight role over social security, incorporating social assistance and social insurance policies.[65] The aim of this managerial and oversight role of the DSD is aimed at preventing and alleviating poverty resulting from factors such as loss of income owing to unemployment, disability and developmental social welfare services. Social welfare services that are developed by the DSD are designed to provide support to reduce poverty, vulnerability and the impact of disasters such as the Covid-19 pandemic. The SRD grant is not a sustainable development programme, it is only a temporary arrangement meant to provide relief for the poor and unemployed persons to mitigate against the impact of the Covid-19 pandemic on such persons. The DSD is not expressly empowered by any legislation to promote financial inclusion through its managerial and oversight role over social assistance and security initiatives. Nonetheless, given its legislative mandate and oversight role, it is submitted that this department is one of the channels that the government should utilise to promote financial inclusion of the poor and unemployed persons in South Africa. This should be done to achieve the goal of attaining 90% financial inclusion of all members of the society by 2030 as envisaged in the National Development Plan (NDP) 2030.[66] The provision and administration of the SRD grant should have been used as an opportunity to ensure that the poor and unemployed are not financially excluded, especially amidst the ongoing Covid-19 pandemic. During the period from 1 May 2020 until 30 April 2021, there were 45,141 outstanding payments for applications that have been approved but not paid due to the fact that the recipients could not be traced or they had changed their personal details.[67] Moreover, a total of 571,724 SRD grants had been approved but remained uncollected from the SAPO.[68] All unpaid grants were forfeited to the state on 31 August 2021. The authors argue that the DSD should have adopted adequate measures to trace the applicants of unpaid grants to ensure that the applicants received the money.[69] Nonetheless, the DSD as the government department with the role of managing and overseeing the administration and provision of the SRD grant in South Africa has also failed to adopt adequate measures to promote financial inclusion of the poor and unemployed persons.

11.5 Advantages of the Covid-19 SRD Grant and the financial inclusion of the poor and unemployed persons in South Africa

11.5.1 Poverty alleviation

Like most other social grants available in South Africa,[70] the special R350 Covid-19 grant is important for poverty alleviation. This follows the fact that poverty remains one of the huge challenges affecting the full realisation of financial inclusion in South Africa.[71] The SRD grant is in line with the South African government's blueprint for creating socio-economic change, the NDP, which has a focus on poverty and inequality reduction.[72] As part of the core elements of the NDP, South Africa should endeavour to reduce poverty through the promotion of financial inclusion, particularly among poor and unemployed persons.[73] Without the expansion of government grants, poverty would have worsened over time as opposed to improving.[74] Therefore, the expansion of the SRD grant should be celebrated as a positive step in the right direction towards poverty alleviation that the government initiated right at the centre of a global pandemic in order to offer a small cushion to poor and unemployed persons against the adverse economic impact of the pandemic. Moreover, the expansion of the SRD grant should also be seen as a commendable effort of eradicating poverty and promoting financial inclusion as envisaged in the NDP.[75]

11.5.2 A short-term solution to ease the impact of Covid-19 on the poor and unemployed persons in South Africa

Unemployment also remains one of the major challenges affecting the full realisation of financial inclusion for the poor in South Africa.[76] According to Statistics South Africa, the unemployment rate increased from 30.8% in the third quarter to 32.5% in the fourth quarter of 2020 in South Africa.[77] Without the expansion of government grants, not only poverty would have worsened but the impact of unemployment would have also been much more aggravated due to the Covid-19 pandemic.[78] In this regard, the expansion of the SRD grant should once more be seen as an advantage that has eased the severity of the impact of Covid-19 on the poor and unemployed persons in South Africa. This is despite the expansion of the SRD grant only being a temporary relief that is not sustainable in the long run. Moreover, the expansion of the SRD grant should be welcomed as a positive effort by the government to promote financial inclusion through developing a socio-economic relief measure in response to an unprecedented pandemic. After all, financial inclusion is about the development of financial products and services offered by the government, financial institutions and other relevant stakeholders to all financial consumers, including the poor and unemployed persons in an affordable and useful manner.[79] The SRD was one such financial service that has proven to be useful to those who have managed to access it during the pandemic. This is despite the shortcomings that came to the fore as this grant was provided and administered to the poor and unemployed persons. Such shortcomings are discussed below as the disadvantages related to the provision and administration of the SRD grant for the poor and unemployed persons in South Africa.

11.6 Disadvantages of the Covid-19 SRD grant and the financial inclusion of the poor and unemployed persons in South Africa

Central to the concept of financial inclusion are three elements that include accessibility, usability and availability of financial products and services offered by the government, financial institutions and other stakeholders to financial consumers.[80] The provision and administration of the SRD grant have been marred by numerous challenges that are bordering on financial exclusion in that some poor and unemployed persons could not access the SRD grant for their use on time due to delays and the poor provision and administration of the grant. These disadvantages in the provision and the administration of the SRD grant are discussed below in light of the need for promoting the financial inclusion of poor and unemployed persons in South Africa.

11.6.1 The SRD grant cannot be received simultaneously with any other social grant

The SRD grant cannot be received simultaneously with any other social grant.[81] Any person who, for some reason, may receive both the SRD grant and another social grant simultaneously has to repay the SRD grant received. The recovery of the SRD grant received at the same time as any other social grant is made from the social grant payment, including an arrears payment.[82] However, in an instance where a recipient of a social grant received the SRD as a result of a disaster, the amount will not be recovered.[83] The practicality of this is not quite clear. Although the requirement that the SRD grant cannot be received by a person who receives both social grant and the SRD at the same time holds merit, it is a disadvantage to most poor and unemployed persons. This follows the fact that poverty and unemployment remain serious challenges affecting the social and economic welfare of many households in South Africa.[84] Furthermore, the SRD grant is intended for persons in such dire material need that they are unable to meet their or their families' most basic needs. Thus, precluding poor and unemployed persons from receiving the SRD grant with any other grant is not ideal for the promotion of financial inclusion and reintegrating such persons within the formal economic activities of the country.

11.6.2 Delays caused by the use of the SAPO as a payment channel

The SRD grant can be accessed in two ways, first, through bank accounts in the recipient's name, and second, through the SAPO for the recipients who do not have bank accounts. Most poor and unemployed persons find it difficult to afford bank accounts and keep up with the transaction costs and other related bank charges to keep those bank accounts active.[85] In 2017, Statistics South Africa reported that about 30.4 million South Africans were living in poverty and unable to maintain bank accounts.[86] Consumers who cannot afford to sustain bank accounts remain excluded from accessing financial services and products on time, this has also proven to be the case with the provision of the SRD grant.[87] Most poor and unemployed persons in South Africa utilise cash in their daily transactions owing to the fact that they cannot afford high banking fees.[88] The use of cash by the poor and unemployed persons, as opposed to transacting digitally, does not necessarily amount to financial exclusion.[89] However, the problem lies with the fact that it has been difficult for the poor and unemployed persons to access the SRD grant in the form of cash from the SAPO. The SAPO, which has been contracted by SASSA and the DSD to pay the SRD grant in cash to the recipients, has not been making the payments available to the recipients effectively. This is evident from the snaking queues outside post offices on a daily basis where poor and unemployed persons found themselves stranded since the start of the payments of the SRD grant.[90] The delays in paying the monies on time to the recipients were caused by a lack of proper communication from SASSA to the recipients and the poor technological infrastructure of the SAPO, which is not adequate to deal with large crowds.[91]

11.6.3 The exclusive electronic application process and the lack of access to a reliable and affordable internet connection by the poor and unemployed persons in informal settlements and rural areas

The application process for the SRD grant is done exclusively electronically or online. There are no paper-based applications that have been considered for the SRD grant since its inception in 2020. The communication from SASSA to the applicants on the status of their applications has also been done primarily online and through electronic platforms. This has resulted in most applicants for the grant not being able to receive communication effectively and on time. The reality may be that most, but not all, poor and unemployed persons including those living in informal settlements and rural areas, have smartphones that can access the internet, which they can use to apply electronically and receive communication from SASSA. However, poor connectivity in rural areas and informal settlements made it difficult for the applicants to easily apply and receive feedback on the status of their applications without personally going into the branches of the SAPO to check the payments of their grants. Accordingly, the role of internet connectivity in the challenges of financial inclusion remains huge and impacts the effective promotion of financial inclusion to the poor and unemployed persons without access to reliable and affordable internet connectivity in South Africa.

In an effort to try to deal with the challenge that was faced by the SAPO in terms of overwhelming numbers of recipients queuing daily at their branches, SASSA sought to partner with banks to allow some recipients to switch to receiving their SRD grants into their bank accounts. This approach is a commendable effort on the part of SASSA and the banking sector in trying to promote financial inclusion to ensure that people with bank accounts get to receive their grants in their personal bank accounts. Nonetheless, the South African banking sector has undergone drastic changes and developments in recent years.[92] Most changes included those relating to the offering of new products and services as well as engaging the poor, low-income earners and the previously unbanked market.[93] The new changes included technology-related developments and changes in the manner banking services and products were offered by banks and other financial institutions to financial consumers. Such developments and convenient changes included the use of websites and mobile banking apps, which makes banking easier, especially for the poor and low-income earners living in informal settlements and rural areas who cannot always afford to travel to access banking services from branches. The issue of access to these initiatives is quite important, especially for poor and unemployed persons who applied for the SRD grant to utilise technology-related services offered by their banks in accessing grant monies and transacting conveniently. Although these commendable developments and measures may be undertaken, if they do not reach the intended target audience, financial inclusion will remain a pipe dream. Consequently, missing out on the golden opportunity to increase financial inclusion through the use of innovative technology to curb the financial exclusion of low-income earners in South Africa.[94] For some poor and unemployed persons, banking services offered on websites and banking apps are beyond their reach, especially for those residing in informal settlements and rural areas with poor internet connectivity. In this regard, the issue of financial inclusion may not necessarily be an issue of financial institutions per se, but the government and its inability to adequately deal with the issue. The services and products that are offered by financial institutions should be brought closer to those in remote areas and informal settlements so that they do not have to travel to urban areas to access these services and standing in long queues at the SAPO branches waiting to receive their grant monies.

11.6.4 The provision of the SRD grant and its strain on the country's public finances

The expansion of social grants has had a mildly favourable and short-term impact on poverty in South Africa.[95] Similarly, the provision of the SRD grant, although it was administered in the face of a pandemic that has affected the livelihood of many South Africans, this grant has managed to mildly reduce the socio-economic impact of the pandemic on the poor and unemployed persons. Notwithstanding its positive impact on poverty, this grant has also put the country's public finances under strain.[96] Consequently, the SRD grant cannot be provided and administered indefinitely despite the advantages it has yielded, especially in helping to mitigate the impact of the Covid-19 pandemic on the most vulnerable persons.[97] More than 4% of the GDP is spent on social welfare in South Africa and the fiscal sustainability of this expenditure, going forward, is not quite clear.[98] In this regard, it is submitted that to avoid putting the public finances under extreme constraint, proper budgeting should be done by the relevant government departments and SASSA to make funding available for SRD grants aimed at providing relief in the event of any disasters that might occur in the future.

11.7 Concluding remarks

From the discussion above, it is clear that the SRD grant should be celebrated as a positive step in the right direction towards poverty alleviation which the government initiated amidst the ongoing global pandemic. The SRD grant was aimed at offering a small cushion to the poor and unemployed persons against the adverse economic impact of the pandemic. Moreover, the expansion of the SRD grant should be welcomed as a positive effort by the government to promote financial inclusion of the poor and unemployed persons in South Africa. In a country ravaged by poverty, unemployment and financial exclusion, the South African government should be applauded for its response of developing a socio-economic relief measure for the poor and unemployed persons in an unprecedented pandemic.

Notwithstanding the above, it was noted that there were delays[99] experienced in paying the monies on time to the recipients which were, *inter alia*, caused by the lack of proper communication from SASSA to the recipients and the poor infrastructure of the SAPO that is not sufficient to deal with large crowds. It was submitted that the SAPO, SASSA and the DSD as the role-players who were mainly involved in the provision and administration of the SRD grant have not adopted adequate measures in promoting financial inclusion of the poor and unemployed persons through the process of administering and providing the SRD grant.

It was also noted that although the requirement that the SRD grant cannot be received by a person who receives both social grant and the SRD at the same time holds merit, it remains a disadvantage to most poor and unemployed persons. This follows the fact that poverty and unemployment remain serious challenges affecting the social and economic welfare of many households in South Africa.

Furthermore, it was also noted that internet connectivity plays a major role in financial inclusion and impacts the effective promotion of financial inclusion to the poor and unemployed persons without access to reliable and affordable internet connectivity in South Africa. This follows the fact that the applications for the SRD grant were only conducted online or electronically, thus affecting those without the necessary electronic devices and an internet connection to apply for the grant. To this end, it is argued that the government should view access to financial services as an important service to the general population. In this regard, the government should invest in infrastructural development by expediting the solution to challenges relating to the spectrum. This should be done by reduction of data costs, which is a long-standing challenge that has long been the subject of debate in South Africa. Moreover, the government together with mobile phone companies or internet service providers should act with speed in erecting network towers in the informal settlements and rural areas across South Africa. Putting up more network towers will help financial consumers residing in informal settlements and rural areas to stay connected and transact remotely. The need to streamline access to financial services through the use of technology has become more urgent now than ever. The urgency is necessitated by the Covid-19 pandemic that has affected all aspects of life, including the economy and service delivery.

Lastly, it was noted that the administration and provision of the SRD grant have put the country's public finances under strain,[100] resulting in the SRD grant not being provided and administered indefinitely. In this regard, it is submitted that to avoid putting the public finances under extreme constraint and a huge deficit, proper budgeting should be done by the relevant government departments. Moreover, SASSA should make funding available for SRD grants aimed at providing relief in the event of any disasters that might occur in the future.

Notes

1 M Sharma *Dynamics of Indian Banking Views and Vistas* (2008) 100; H Chitimira and M Ncube 'The Role of Regulatory Bodies and Other Role-Players in the Promotion of Financial Inclusion in South Africa' (2020) 16(1) *Acta Universitatis Danubius Juridica* 24 at 25; S Mago and S Chitokwindo 'The Impact of Mobile Banking on Financial Inclusion in Zimbabwe: A Case for Masvingo Province' (2014) *Mediterranean Journal of Social Sciences* 221 at 222; E Barruetabeña 'Impact of New Technologies on Financial Inclusion' (2020) *Economic Bulletin, Banco de España Article* 1 at 2; PK Ozili 'Optimal Financial Inclusion' (2020) *International Finance Review* 1 at 3–4. It is important to note that there is no universally accepted definition of financial inclusion. However, for the purposes of this chapter, this definition suffices.

2 Kessler K et al., 'Improving Financial Inclusion in South Africa' (2017) https://www.bcg.com/en-za/publications/2017/globalization-improving-financial-inclusion-south-africa, accessed on 15 July 2021 at 5.

3 JI Mohammed, L Mensah and A Gyeke-Dako 'Financial Inclusion and Poverty Reduction in Sub- Saharan Africa' 2017 *The African Finance Journal* 1 at 2; HT Williams 'Role of Financial Inclusion in Economic Growth and Poverty Reduction in a Developing Economy' (2017) *International Journal of Research in Economics and Social Sciences* 265 at 266.

4 Mohammed, Mensah and Gyeke-Dako 2017 (n 3) 2; L Louis and F Chartier 'Financial inclusion in South Africa: An Integrated Framework For Financial Inclusion of Vulnerable Communities In South Africa's Regulatory System Reform' (2017) 1 *Journal of Comparative Urban Law and Policy* 170 173; Chitimira and Ncube (n 1) 25, 26; B Ngwenya, T Pelser and T Chivaura 'Perceptions of Post-multicurrency Regime Financial Inclusion Confidence Challenges in Zimbabwe' 2018 *South African Journal of Economic and Management Sciences* 1 at 3.

5 See related comments by F Hamadziripi and H Chitimira 'The Socio-Economic Effects of the COVID-19 National Lockdown on South Africa and its Response to the COVID-19 Pandemic' (2021) 17/1 *Acta Universitatis Danubius Juridica* 24; see more related comments by C De Villiers, D Cerbone and W Van Zijl 'The South African Government's Response to COVID-19' (2020) *Journal of Public Budgeting, Accounting & Financial Management* 797, 799; see also M Buheji et al. 'The Extent of Covid-19 Pandemic Socio-Economic Impact on Global Poverty. A Global Integrative Multidisciplinary Review' (2020) *American Journal of Economics* 213, 215; also see P Ozili 'COVID-19 in Africa: Socio-Economic Impact, Policy Response and Opportunities' (2020) *International Journal of Sociology and Social Policy* 1, 9.

6 See related comments by C Dandara, K Dzobo and S Chirikure 'COVID-19 Pandemic and Africa: From the Situation in Zimbabwe to a Case for Precision Herbal Medicine' (2020) *OMICS-A Journal of Integrative Biology* 1 1-5; also see more related comments by FC Mukumbang, AN Ambe and BO Adebiyi 'Unspoken Inequality: How COVID-19 has Exacerbated Existing Vulnerabilities of Asylum-Seekers, Refugees and Undocumented Migrants in South Africa' (2020) *International Journal for Equity in Health* 1, 2.

7 RA Ssebagala 'Relieving Consumer Over indebtedness in South Africa: Policy Reviews and Recommendations' (2017) *Journal of Financial Counseling and Planning* 235 237; also see S Granlund and T Hochfeld 'That Child Support Grant Gives Me Powers' – Exploring Social and Relational Aspects of Cash Transfers in South Africa in Times of Livelihood Change' (2020) *The Journal of Development Studies* 1230, 1232; see also Hamadziripi and Chitimira (n 5) 26.

8 The first lockdown commenced on 26 March 2020 in South Africa and has since been readjusted to different alert levels to minimise the economic impact. The Covid-19 induced lockdowns have had a negative effect on the economy, and as a result, most poor and unemployed people were also affected. See Hamadziripi and Chitimira (n

5) 30; also see N Spaull, and S Van der Berg 'Counting the Cost: COVID-19 School Closures in South Africa and its Impact on Children' (2020) *South African Journal of Childhood Education* 1–13.

9 See ss 2 and 13 of the Social Assistance Act 13 of 2004 as amended by the Social Assistance Amendment Act 16 of 2020; also see section 27 of the Constitution of the Republic of South Africa, 1996; see further MP Olivier and ER Kalula 'Scope and Coverage' in MP Olivier, N Smit and ER Kalula (eds) *Social Security: A Legal Analysis* (2003) 143. See also G Nkosi 'An Analysis of the South African Social Assistance System as it Applies to Children in Rural Communities: A Perspective from the Grootboom Case' (2011) *SAPL* 81, 84.

10 See s 27(2) of the Disaster Management Act 57 of 2002; see related comments by H Chitimira and O Animashaun 'The Adequacy of Nigeria, South Africa and Other Sub-Saharan Countries' Response to the COVID-19 Pandemic and Unemployment' (2021) *Acta Universitatis Danubius Juridica* 36, 38. See related comments by PA Igwe 'Coronavirus with Looming Global Health and Economic Doom' (2020) *African Development Journal of Research Methodology* 1, 2.

11 See ss 2 and 13 of the Social Assistance Act as amended by the Social Assistance Amendment Act.

12 See Regulation 4(10) of the GN No. R480 in Government Gazette 43528 of 29 April 2020 as amended (Measures to prevent and combat the spread of COVID-19).

13 See Government Gazette No. 43182, Government Notice No. R. 430 of 30 March 2020 as amended by Government Notices No. R. 455 of 07 April 2020, No. R. 517 of 09 May 2020, No. R. 727 of 02 July 2020, No. R. 853 of 6 August 2020, No. R. 1063 of 07 October 2020 and No. 131 of 02 November 2020.

14 See Government Gazette 44938, GN. R. 647 of 03 August 2021. Despite the third extension and reinstatement of the SRD grant, there are numerous calls from civil society and civic organisations for the provision of the grant to be made a permanent measure to help the poor and unemployed persons in South Africa.

15 According to Hamadziripi and Chitimira, the Covid-19-induced lockdown restrictions have slowed economic growth in South Africa. The authors also argue that the lockdown has resulted in the highest level of unemployment in South Africa since 2008. See Hamadziripi and Chitimira (n 5) 28–31. See also National Treasury Republic of South Africa 'Special Adjustment Budget Guidelines 2020' (2020) www.treasury.gov.za, accessed on 14 July 2021 at 17.

16 Parliament of the Republic of South Africa 'State of the Nation Address by President Cyril Ramaphosa 11 February 2021' (February 2021) https://www.parliament.gov.za/state-nation-address-president-cyril-ramaphosa-11-february-2021, accessed on 24 February 2021.

17 Ibid; also see related comments by Chitimira and Animashaun (n 10) 49; also see related comments by W Naudé and M Cameron 'Failing to Pull Together: South Africa's Troubled Response to COVID-19' (2020) *Institute of Labor Economics Discussion Paper IZADP* No. 13649. http://ftp.iza.org/dp13649.pdf last accessed 14 June 2021.

18 SASSA 'Special R350 COVID-19 Grant Extension' (2021) https://www.sassa.gov.za/newsroom/articles/Pages/Special_350_Covid-19_Grant_Extension.aspx, accessed on 21 February 2021.

19 See Hamadziripi and Chitimira (n 5) 28. See also National Treasury of the Republic of South Africa (n 15) 1. See also H Chitimira and P Magau 'Synoptical Analysis of Debt Relief Intervention Measures for Low Income Earners under the National Credit Amendment Act 7 of 2019' (2021) 10 *Interdisciplinary Journal of Economics and Business Law* 284 at 286, 287, where the authors argue that it is important to reintegrate low-income earners into the formal South African economic activities despite the contemporary challenges posed by the Covid-19 pandemic, which have somewhat led to poor gross domestic productions (GDPs) and economic inequalities.

20 SASSA (n 18); also see related comments by G Nkosi 'Traditional and Contemporary Social Assistance Measures in South Africa: A Historical Perspective' (2013) *Southern African Public Law* 308, 324. The introduction of the online application for the SRD grant is an innovative measure that had to be introduced due to the challenges posed by the Covid-19 pandemic such as social distancing measures and lockdown restrictions.

21 See related comments by Nkosi (n 20) 322. Historically, the application process for all types of grants and social assistance aid was paper based.

22 Parliament of the Republic of South Africa (n 16). The policy responses which were adopted by the government such as lockdowns, restrictions on movements of people and social distancing, among others, have necessitated the need to swiftly adopt electronic measures of doing things including applying for the SRD grant. In this regard, see related comments by Chitimira and Animashaun (n 10) 37.

23 SASSA (n 18); see related comments by N De Villier 'Social Grants and the Promotion of Administrative Justice Act' (2002) *South African Journal on Human Rights* 320, 322. The absence of application fees for the SRD grant (as is the case with other social grants) is a commendable stride to ensure seamless access to the grants. This follows that most of the beneficiaries of the social grants (including the SRD grant) form part of society's poorest people.

24 See s 5 of the Social Assistance Act dealing with the eligibility for social assistance. Also see related comments by De Villier (n 23) who outlines how the administration of the social grants offers a panoply of the experiences of the ordinary people who depend on it.

25 See s 13 read with s 5 of the Social Assistance Act; also see related comments by Nkosi (n 20) 308; see further Nkosi (n 9) 83.

26 See s 32 of the Social Assistance Act; also see Reg 9 of GN R511 in G. 39978 of 6 May 2016.

27 SASSA (n 18). The recent extension of the SRD grant which is expected to end in March 2022 has been expanded to include non-South African citizens as well to benefit from the grant.

28 See ss 5(1)(a) and (b) and 32 of the Social Assistance Act; also see Reg 9 of GN R511 in G. 39978 of 6 May 2016.

29 This relates to grants in terms of ss 6–7 of the Social Assistance Act. These grants include the child support grant in terms of s 6, care dependency grant in terms of s 7, foster child grant in terms of s 8, disability grant in terms of s 9, older persons grant in terms of s 10, war veterans' grant in terms of s 11 and grant in aid in terms of s 12.

30 See G Kelly 'Regulating access to the disability grant in South Africa, 1990–2013' (2013) *Centre for Social Science Research* 38, 39. In the past, there have been challenges regarding the medical assessments relating to disability grants in South Africa, which led to serious delays in the provision and administration of disability grants. Nonetheless, there has been an increased oversight of medical officers and SASSA administrative staff to address this issue. It is not clear if measures have been put in place to deal with challenges related to medical assessments for the provision and administration of the SRD grant. However, it is hoped that with lessons learned through the administration and provision of the disability grant, the process will be improved and made more seamless for SRD grant applicants who are medically unfit to undertake remunerative work for a period of fewer than six months.

31 See s 32 of the Social Assistance Act read with Reg 9 of GN R511 in G. 39978 of 6 May 2016.

32 See SASSA (n 18).

33 Ibid.

34 Ibid.

35 In terms of s 23(6) of the Disaster Management Act, a "disaster is a national disaster if it affects more than one province, or a single province which is unable to do deal with it effectively".

36 South African Social Security Agency Act 9 of 2004 (SASSA Act), see s 2(1); also see related comments by NT Vally 'Insecurity in South African Social Security: An Examination of Social Grant Deductions, Cancellations and Waiting' (2016) *Journal of Southern African Studies* 965 at 977.

37 See ss 3(a)–(c) of the SASSA Act; also see Vally (n 36) 978.

38 See s 27(1) of the Constitution; also see s 4(1)(a) of the SASSA Act; also see Chapter 3 of the Social Assistance Act 13 of 2004 as amended by the Social Assistance Amendment Act 16 of 2020.

39 S 4(1)(b) of the SASSA Act; see related comments by Wright G et al. 'Social Assistance and Dignity: South African Women's Experiences of the Child Support Grant' (2015) *Development Southern Africa* 443, 446.

40 S 4(1)(c) and (d) of the SASSA Act; see related comments by C Fombad 'An Overview of the Constitutional Framework of the Right to Social Security with Special Reference to South Africa' (2013) *African Journal of International and Comparative Law* 1, 27.

41 S 4(2)(a) and (b) of the SASSA Act; also see related comments by Vally (n 36) 978.

42 S 4(3)(a) of the SASSA Act; also see related comments by Vally (n 36) 978

43 S 4(3)(b) of the SASSA Act; also see s 27(1) of the Constitution; see further related comments by Fombad (n 40) 27.

44 See ss 4(2)(a), 4(3)(c) and (d) read with s 16 of the SASSA Act; see related comments by Vally (n 36) 979.

45 See ss 4 (3)(e) and (f) of the SASSA Act; see related comments by Vally (n 36) 970.

46 See ss 3(a)-(b) of the SASSA Act; also see See s 27(1) of the Constitution; also see related comments by Nkosi (n 20) 308.

47 See s 3 of the Post and Telecommunications-related Matters Act (previously Post Office Act) 44 of 1958 as amended.

48 See s 3 of the South African Post Office SOC Ltd Act 22 of 2011 (SAPO Act).

49 See s 4(1)(a) and (b) of the SAPO Act; see related comments by Williams (n 3) 271.

50 See s 4(1)(c) and (d) of the SAPO Act; see related comments by BZ Chummun 'An Analysis of the Development Influences of the Low-income Cover Market-end in South Africa' (2017) *African Journal of Science, Technology, Innovation and Development* 795, 798.

51 See s 4(1)€ of the SAPO Act; most financial consumers in rural areas are struggling to gain access to basic financial services and products. See related comments by M Rouse and G Verhoef 'Mobile Banking in Sub-Saharan Africa: Setting the Way Towards Financial Development' (2017) *Munich Personal Research Papers No 78006* https://mpra.ub.uni-muenchen.de/78006/1/MPRA_paper_78006.pdf, accessed 28 July 2021.

52 See s 4(1)(f) of the SAPO Act; see related comments by B Myers, J Louw and N Fakier 'Alcohol and Drug Abuse: Removing Structural Barriers to Treatment for Historically Disadvantaged Communities in Cape Town' (2008) *International Journal of Social Welfare* 156 157. Notably, most Black communities were previously precluded from receiving state-funded services (including postal services) during the apartheid government in South Africa.

53 See s 4(1)(g)–(h) of the SAPO Act; see related comments by T Hongchintakul and BH Kleiner 'Discrimination and Harassment in the United States Postal Service' (2001) *International Journal of Sociology and Social Policy* 184 at 188.

54 See s 4(1)(i)–(j) of the SAPO Act; see related comments by A Águila-Obra, A Padilla-Meléndez and RM Al-dweeri 'The Influence of Electronic Service Quality on Loyalty in Postal Services: The Mediating Role of Satisfaction' (2013) *Total Quality Management & Business Excellence* 1111 at 1112.

55 See s 4(1)(k)–(l) of the SAPO Act; see related comments by FT Chan et al. 'An AHP Approach in Benchmarking Logistics Performance of the Postal Industry' (2006) *Benchmarking: An International Journal* 636 at 637.

56 See s 4(2)(a) and (b) of the SASSA Act that empowers SASSA to enter into an agreement with anyone to ensure effective payments to beneficiaries. Also see related comments by Vally (n 36) 978.

57 See s 4(3)(a)–(f) of the SASSA Act for the provisions which must be included in any agreement that SASSA concludes with anyone in terms of s 4(2)(a) of the SASSA Act.

58 See related comments by South African Government 'Post Office Gazetted as the Preferred Payment Channel for all Social Grants' (2018) available at https://www.gov.za/speeches/post-office-gazetted-preferred-payment-channel-all-social-grants-26-jun-2018-0000, accessed on 01 November 2021.

59 Human L et al. 'Long queues at Post Offices as Activists Picket for Covid-19 Grant Extension' (2021) https://www.dailymaverick.co.za/article/2021-05-02-long-queues-at-post-offices-as-activists-picket-for-covid-19-grant-extension/, accessed 01 November 2021.

60 Shoba S 'The Post Office's Financial Troubles May Jeopardise Social Grant Payments' (2020) https://www.dailymaverick.co.za/article/2020-10-12-the-post-offices-financial-troubles-may-jeopardise-social-grant-payments/, accessed on 01 November 2021.

61 South African Government 'Post Office on Collection of R350 by SRD Recipients' (2021) https://www.gov.za/speeches/post-office-collection-r350-srd-recipients-26-oct-2021-0000, accessed on 1 November 2021.

62 See section 27 of the Constitution; also see related comments by Nkosi (n 20) 324; also see related comments by Fombad (n 40) 27.

63 See s 27(1) of the Constitution; also see related comments by Nkosi (n 20) 308.

64 See s 27(1) read with schedule 4 of the Constitution; also see related comments by Nkosi (n 20) 308.

65 Department of Social Development 'Legislative Mandate' available at https://www.dsd.gov.za/index.php/about/legislative-mandate, accessed on 01 March 2020.

66 TA Manuel 'National Development Plan Vision 2030' *National Planning Committee* (11 November 2011) https://www.gov.za/sites/default/files/gcis_document/201409/devplan2.pdf, accessed on 12 February 2021 at 129.

67 South African Government 'Minister Lindiwe Zulu: Re-introduction of special COVID-19 SRD Grant' (2021) available at https://www.gov.za/speeches/minister-lindiwe-zulu-re-introduction-special-covid-19-srd-grant-4-aug-2021-0000, accessed on 1 November 2021.

68 Ibid.

69 Ibid.

70 See s 4 of the Social Assistance Act as amended by the Social Assistance Amendment Act 16 of 2020 for the different types of social grants available in South Africa.

71 H Chitimira and M Ncube 'Legislative and Other Selected Challenges Affecting Financial Inclusion for the Poor and Low-Income Earners in South Africa' (2020) *Journal of African Law* 337 at 341.

72 See related comments by Chitimira and Ncube (n 71) 342.

73 See Manuel (n 66); also see Chitimira and Ncube (n 71) at 342.

74 See I Woolard and M Leibbrandt 'The Evolution and Impact of Unconditional Cash Transfers in South Africa' 2010 *Southern Africa Labour and Development Research Unit Working Paper No. 51, University of Cape Town* 18.

75 See H Chitimira and M Ncube 'Overview Legislative Flaws Hampering the Promotion of Financial Inclusion for the Poor and Low-Income Earners in South Africa' (2021) 10(1) *Interdisciplinary Journal of Economics and Business Law* 67 at 82.

76 See Chitimira and Ncube (n 71) 341.

77 Statistics South Africa 'More People Participate in the South African Labour Market in the 4th Quarter of 2020' (2020) available at http://www.statssa.gov.za/?p=14031, accessed on 2 March 2020.
78 See related comments by Woolard and Leibbrandt (n 74) 18.
79 Sharma (n 1) 100; see Chitimira and Ncube (n 1) 25; Mago and Chitokwindo (n 1) 222; Barruetabeña (n 1) 1, 2; Ozili (n 1) 3, 4.
80 M Sarma and J Pais 'Financial Inclusion and Development' (2011) 23/5 *Journal of International Development* 613 at 613–625.
81 See section 32 of the Social Assistance Act; also see Reg 9(3) of GN R511 in G. 39978 of 6 May 2016.
82 See section 32 of the Social Assistance Act; also see Reg 9(4) of GN R511 in G. 39978 of 6 May 2016.
83 See section 32 of the Social Assistance Act; also see Reg 9(5) of GN R511 in G. 39978 of 6 May 2016.
84 T Meiring, C Kannemeyer and E Optimeter 'The Gap between Rich and Poor: South African Society's Biggest Divide Depends on Where You Think You Fit in' (2018) *South African Labour and Development Research Unit Working Paper Series Number 20 Version 1* 1 at 15.
85 Chitimira and Ncube (n 71) 342.
86 Statistics South Africa 'Poverty Trends in South Africa: An Examination of Absolute Poverty Between 2006 and 2015' (2017) http://www.statssa.gov.za/?p=10341, accessed on 23 February 2021 at 14.
87 See related comments by J Goldberg 'Products and policies to promote saving in developing countries' (2014) *IZA World of Labor* 1.
88 Kessler et al. (n 2) 3.
89 Ozili (n 1) 329.
90 Times Live 'Post Offices "Overwhelmed" with Covid-19 Grant Recipients' (2020) available at https://www.timeslive.co.za/news/south-africa/2020-11-06-post-offices-overwhelmed-with-covid-19-grant-recipients/, accessed on 1 March 2021.
91 See related comments by B Larkin *Signal and Noise: Media, Infrastructure, and Urban Culture in Nigeria* (2008); also see B Larkin 'The Politics and Poetics of Infrastructure' (2013) *Annual Review of Anthropology* 327 330; see also A Von Schnitzler 'Citizenship Prepaid: Water, Calculability, and Techno-Politics in South Africa' (2008) *Journal of Southern African Studies* 899, 908.
92 R Sharrock *The Law of Banking and Payment in South Africa* (2016) 63. See also H Chitimira and PT Magau 'A Legal Analysis of the Use of Innovative Technology in the Promotion of Financial Inclusion for Low-Income Earners in South Africa' (2021) 24 *PER/PELJ* 1 at 6.
93 Ibid.
94 VA Lawack 'Mobile Money, Financial Inclusion and Financial Integrity: The South African Case' (2013) *Washington Journal of Law, Technology and Arts* 318 at 345. See also Chitimira and Magau (n 93) 6.
95 See Woolard and Leibbrandt (n 74) 18; also see M Chibba and JM Luiz 'Poverty, Inequality and Unemployment in South Africa: Context, Issues and the Way Forward' (2011) 30(3) *A Journal of Applied Economics and Policy* 309.
96 The Presidency of the Republic of South Africa 'Statement by President Cyril Ramaphosa on Progress in the National Effort to Contain the COVID-19 Pandemic' (2021) available at http://www.thepresidency.gov.za/speeches/statement-president-cyril-ramaphosa-progress-national-effort-contain-covid-19-pandemic-0, accessed on 28 February 2021.
97 Ibid.
98 J Fedderke 'Social Welfare: Social Stasis' 2009 *Focus* 1 at 16.
99 See para 11.6.2 of this chapter.
100 The Presidency of the Republic of South Africa (n 96).

Bibiliography

A Águila-Obra, A Padilla-Meléndez & R M Al-dweeri 'The influence of electronic service quality on loyalty in postal services: The mediating role of satisfaction' (2013) *Total Quality Management & Business Excellence* 1111 at 1123.

E Barruetabeña 'Impact of new technologies on financial inclusion' (2020) *Economic Bulletin, Banco de España* 1 at 14.

M Buheji, K da Costa Cunha, G Beka, B Mavric, Y L De Souza, S S da Costa Silva, M Hanafi & T C Yein 'The extent of Covid-19 pandemic socio-economic impact on global poverty: A global integrative multidisciplinary review' (2020) *American Journal of Economics* 213 at 224.

F T Chan, H K Chan, H C Lau & R W Ip 'An AHP approach in benchmarking logistics performance of the postal industry' (2006) *Benchmarking: An International Journal* 636 at 661.

M Chibba & J M Luiz 'Poverty, inequality and unemployment in South Africa: Context, issues and the way forward' (2011) 30(3) *A Journal of Applied Economics and Policy* 307 at 315.

H Chitimira & M Ncube 'Legislative and other selected challenges affecting financial inclusion for the poor and low-income earners in South Africa' (2020) *Journal of African Law* 337 at 355.

H Chitimira & M Ncube 'Overview legislative flaws hampering the promotion of financial inclusion for the poor and low-income earners in South Africa' (2021) 10(1) *Interdisciplinary Journal of Economics and Business Law* 67 at 87.

H Chitimira & M Ncube 'The role of regulatory bodies and other role-players in the promotion of financial inclusion in South Africa' (2020) *Acta Universitatis Danubius Juridica* 24 at 37.

H Chitimira & O Animashaun 'The adequacy of Nigeria, South Africa and other Sub-Saharan countries' response to the COVID-19 pandemic and unemployment' (2021) *Acta Universitatis Danubius Juridica* 36 at 55

H Chitimira & P Magau 'Synoptical analysis of debt relief intervention measures for low-income earners under the National Credit Amendment Act 7 of 2019' (2021) 10 *Interdisciplinary Journal of Economics and Business Law* 284 at 304.

H Chitimira & P T Magau 'A legal analysis of the use of innovative technology in the promotion of financial inclusion for low-income earners in South Africa' (2021) 24 *PER/PELJ* 1 at 27.

B Z Chummun 'An analysis of the development influences of the low-income cover market-end in South Africa' (2017) *African Journal of Science, Technology, Innovation and Development* 795 at 802.

Constitution of the Republic of South Africa, 1996.

C Dandara, K Dzobo & S Chirikure 'COVID-19 pandemic and Africa: From the situation in Zimbabwe to a case for precision herbal medicine' (2020) *OMICS: A Journal of Integrative Biology* 1 at 5.

N De Villier 'Social grants and the promotion of administrative justice act' (2002) *South African Journal on Human Rights* 320 at 349.

C De Villiers, D Cerbone & W Van Zijl 'The South African Government's response to COVID-19' (2020) *Journal of Public Budgeting, Accounting & Financial Management* 797 at 811.

Department of Social Development 'Legislative mandate', available at https://www.dsd.gov.za/index.php/about/legislative-mandate, accessed on 1 March 2020.

Disaster Management Act 57 of 2002.

J Fedderke 'Social welfare: Social stasis' (2009) *Focus* 1 at 25.

C Fombad 'An overview of the constitutional framework of the right to social security with special reference to South Africa' (2013) *African Journal of International and Comparative Law* 1 at 31.

J Goldberg 'Products and policies to promote saving in developing countries' (2014) *IZA World of Labor.*

S Granlund & T Hochfeld 'That child support grant gives me powers'–Exploring social and relational aspects of cash transfers in South Africa in times of livelihood change' (2020) *The Journal of Development Studies* 1230 at 1244.

F Hamadziripi & H Chitimira 'The socio-economic effects of the COVID-19 national lockdown on South Africa and its response to the COVID-19 pandemic' (2021) 17(1) *Acta Universitatis Danubius Juridica* 24 at 42.

T Hongchintakul & B H Kleiner 'Discrimination and harassment in the United States postal service' (2001) *International Journal of Sociology and Social Policy* 184 at 191.

L Human 'Long queues at post offices as activists picket for Covid-19 grant extension', available at https://www.dailymaverick.co.za/article/2021-05-02-long-queues-at-post-offices-as-activists-picket-for-covid-19-grant-extension/, accessed on 1 November 2021.

P A Igwe 'Coronavirus with looming global health and economic doom' (2020) *African Development Journal of Research Methodology* 1 at 6.

G Kelly 'Regulating access to the disability grant in South Africa, 1990–2013' (2013) *Centre for Social Science Research* 1 at 55.

K Kessler 'Improving financial inclusion in South Africa' (2017), available at https://www.bcg.com/en-za/publications/2017/globalization-improving-financial-inclusion-south-africa, accessed on 15 July 2021.

B Larkin *Signal and Noise: Media, Infrastructure, and Urban Culture in Nigeria* (2008).

B Larkin 'The politics and poetics of infrastructure' (2013) *Annual Review of Anthropology* 327 at 343.

V A Lawack 'Mobile money, financial inclusion and financial integrity: The South African case' (2013) *Washington Journal Law, Technology & Arts* 317 at 346.

L Louis & F Chartier 'Financial inclusion in South Africa: An integrated framework for financial inclusion of vulnerable communities in South Africa's regulatory system reform' (2017) *Journal of Comparative Urban Law and Policy* 170 at 196.

S Mago & S Chitokwindo 'The impact of mobile banking on financial inclusion in Zimbabwe: A case for Masvingo province' (2014) *Mediterranean Journal of Social Sciences* 221 at 230.

T A Manuel 'National development plan vision 2030' *National Planning Committee* (11 November 2011), available at https://www.gov.za/sites/default/files/gcis_document/201409/devplan2.pdf, accessed on 12 February 2021.

T Meiring, C Kannemeyer & E Optimeter 'The gap between rich and poor: South African society's biggest divide depends on where you think you fit in' (2018) *South African Labour and Development Research Unit Working Paper Series Number 20 Version 1.*

J I Mohammed, L Mensah & A Gyeke-Dako 'Financial inclusion and poverty reduction in Sub-Saharan Africa' (2017) *African Finance Journal* 1 at 22.

F C Mukumbang, A N Ambe & B O Adebiyi 'Unspoken inequality: How COVID-19 has exacerbated existing vulnerabilities of asylum-seekers, refugees and undocumented migrants in South Africa' (2020) *International Journal for Equity in Health* 1 at 7.

B Myers, J Louw & N Fakier 'Alcohol and drug abuse: Removing structural barriers to treatment for historically disadvantaged communities in Cape Town' (2008) *International Journal of Social Welfare* 156 at 165.

National Treasury Republic of South Africa 'Special adjustment budget guidelines 2020' (2020), available at www.treasury.gov.za, accessed on 14 July 2021.

W Naudé & M Cameron 'Failing to pull together: South Africa's troubled response to COVID-19' (2020) *Institute of Labor Economics Discussion Paper IZADP No. 13649*,available at http://ftp.iza.org/dp13649.pdf, accessed on 14 June 2021.

B Ngwenya, T Pelser & T Chivaura 'Perceptions of post-multicurrency regime financial inclusion confidence challenges in Zimbabwe' (2018) *South African Journal of Economic and Management Sciences* 1 at 15.

G Nkosi 'An analysis of the South African social assistance system as it applies to children in rural communities: A perspective from the grootboom case' (2011) *South African Public Law* 81 at 96.

G Nkosi 'Traditional and contemporary social assistance measures in South Africa: A historical perspective' (2013) *Southern African Public Law* 308 at 328.

M P Olivier & E R Kalula 'Scope and coverage' in M P Olivier, N Smit & E R Kalula (eds) *Social Security: A Legal Analysis* (2003).

P Ozili 'COVID-19 in Africa: Socio-economic impact, policy response and opportunities' (2020) *International Journal of Sociology and Social Policy* 1 at 24.

P K Ozili 'Optimal financial inclusion' (2020) *International Finance Review* 1 at 18.

Parliament of the Republic of South Africa 'State of the nation address by President Cyril Ramaphosa 11 February 2021', available at https://www.parliament.gov.za/state-nation-address-president-cyril-ramaphosa-11-february-2021, accessed on 24 February 2021.

Post and Telecommunications-related Matters Act 44 of 1958.

Presidency of the Republic of South Africa 'Statement by President Cyril Ramaphosa on progress in the national effort to contain the COVID-19 pandemic' (2021), available at http://www.thepresidency.gov.za/speeches/statement-president-cyril-ramaphosa-progress-national-effort-contain-covid-19-pandemic-0, accessed on 28 February 2021.

M Rouse & G Verhoef 'Mobile banking in Sub-Saharan Africa: Setting the way towards financial development' (2017) *Munich Personal Research Papers No. 78006*, available at https://mpra.ub.uni-muenchen.de/78006/ 1/MPRA_paper_78006.pdf, accessed on 28 July 2021.

M Sarma & J Pais 'Financial inclusion and development' (2011) 23(5) *Journal of International Development* 613 at 625.

SASSA 'Special R350 COVID-19 grant extension', available at https://www.sassa.gov.za/newsroom/articles/Pages/Special_350_Covid-19_Grant_Extension.aspx, accessed on 21 February 2021.

M Sharma *Dynamics of Indian Banking: Views and Vistas* (2008).

R Sharrock *The Law of Banking and Payment in South Africa* (2016).

S Shoba 'The post office's financial troubles may jeopardise social grant payments', available at https://www.dailymaverick.co.za/article/2020-10-12-the-post-offices-financial-troubles-may-jeopardise-social-grant-payments/, accessed on 1 November 2021.

Social Assistance Act 13 of 2004.

Social Assistance Amendment Act 16 of 2020.

South African Post Office SOC Ltd Act 22 of 2011.

South African Social Security Agency Act 9 of 2004.

South African Government 'Minister Lindiwe Zulu: Re-introduction of special COVID-19 SRD grant', available at https://www.gov.za/speeches/minister-lindiwe-zulu-re-introduction-special-covid-19-srd-grant-4-aug-2021-0000, accessed on 1 November 2021.

South African Government 'Post office on collection of R350 by SRD recipients', available athttps://www.gov.za/speeches/post-office-collection-r350-srd-recipients-26-oct-2021-0000, accessed on 1 November 2021.

South African Government 'Post office gazetted as the preferred payment channel for all social grants', available at https://www.gov.za/speeches/post-office-gazetted-preferred-payment-channel-all-social-grants-26-jun-2018-0000, accessed on 1 November 2021.

N Spaull & S Van der Berg 'Counting the cost: COVID-19 school closures in South Africa and its impact on children' (2020) *South African Journal of Childhood Education* 1 at 13.

R A Ssebagala 'Relieving consumer over-indebtedness in South Africa: Policy reviews and recommendations' (2017) *Journal of Financial Counseling and Planning* 235 at 246.

Statistics South Africa 'More people participate in the South African labour market in the 4th quarter of 2020' (2020), available at http://www.statssa.gov.za/?p=14031, accessed on 2 March 2020.

Statistics South Africa 'Poverty trends in South Africa: An examination of absolute poverty between 2006 and 2015' (2017), available at http://www.statssa.gov.za/?p=10341, accessed on 23 February 2021.

Times Live 'Post offices "overwhelmed" with Covid-19 grant recipients', available at https://www.timeslive.co.za/news/south-africa/2020-11-06-post-offices-overwhelmed-with-covid-19-grant-recipients/, accessed on 1 March 2021.

N T Vally 'Insecurity in South African social security: An examination of social grant deductions, cancellations, and waiting' (2016) *Journal of Southern African Studies* 965 at 982.

G Verhoef 'Savings and survival in a modern African economy: Informal savings organisations and poor people in South Africa' (2001) *Historia* 519 at 542.

A Von Schnitzler 'Citizenship prepaid: Water, calculability, and techno-politics in South Africa' (2008) *Journal of Southern African Studies* 899 at 917.

H T Williams 'Role of financial inclusion in economic growth and poverty reduction in a developing economy' (2017) *International Journal of Research in Economics and Social Sciences* 265 at 271

I Woolard & M Leibbrandt *The Evolution and Impact of Unconditional Cash Transfers in South Africa* (Southern Africa Labour and Development Research Unit working paper no. 51, University of Cape Town, 2010).

G Wright 'Social assistance and dignity: South African women's experiences of the child support grant' (2015) *Development Southern Africa* 443 at 457.

12 Financial inclusion and youth empowerment in Botswana, Namibia, South Africa and Zimbabwe

Eukeria Wealth, Tendai D. Svotwa and Charles Makanyeza

12.1 Introduction

Financial inclusion remains one of the priority areas on the sustainable economic development agenda of many developing nations. Financial inclusion (FI) deals with the quality and availability of financial products on offer as well as equality of opportunities to access these financial services at a reasonable cost and sustainable basis.[1] It has been identified as an important tool not only to curtail the global financial crisis effects but to the realisation of the United Nations' Sustainable Development Goals (SDGs).[2] It has been associated with high economic growth and poverty reduction,[3] a macro-economic fundamental that most African states are battling with. The literature concedes the undeniable benefits of financial inclusion for socio-economic development. These include improved financial attitude and financial behaviour, which translates to the increased usage of financial products and a stable financial system.[4] Despite the optimism regarding the effects of FI on socio-economic development, it has remained very low in Southern African Development Community (SADC) countries.[5]

These low levels of FI largely arise from vulnerable population groups such as the youth. The youth's access to saving and credit facilities is often hindered by banking regulations, the financial behaviour of this clientele, the perception of their creditworthiness and limited products that meet their financial needs.[6] Youth is usually referred to as the period of transition from childhood to adulthood. Its definition in terms of age has always been an area of controversy. The European Union define them as those aged between 15 and 24, while Africa delimits the age range to 15–35 years.[7] The latter age range is adopted in this chapter. Reports have revealed that one billion young people in low-income countries are navigating their transition into adulthood.[8] The bulging of youth in any jurisdiction can present either an opportunity or a threat to stability and economic growth.[9] It has been reported that youth are not only the fast-growing component of the Sub-Saharan African (SSA) population but are usually economically vulnerable as well.[10] With the tripling figures of graduate students in countries such as Botswana, Namibia, South Africa and Zimbabwe every year, youth become vulnerable to financial

DOI: 10.4324/9781003369400-12

inequalities because of high unemployment as they contribute 60% of unemployment.[11] Youth tend to be at a disadvantage as their unemployment levels are estimated to be three times more than that of adults, with rural youth more vulnerable.[12] This exacerbates their plight as their road to financial autonomy is protracted in the face of global economic uncertainties.[13] This scourge is unfortunate for a population group that has high financial needs and aspirations such as school fees, tertiary tuition, securing a job, marriage prospects and so on. Continued financial exclusion of youth promotes marginalisation and abject poverty.[14]

In Africa, there is limited knowledge of the extent of financial inclusion (formal and informal) and the extent to which vulnerable groups such as the youth, children and women are excluded from formal financial systems.[15] This chapter responds to the need to identify barriers to youth financial inclusion to inform policy. The aim of this chapter is therefore to add to the literature regarding the nexus between financial inclusion and youth empowerment in SADC. The concept of youth empowerment is an essential subject for research and practice,[16] as scholars argue that the theoretical and empirical dimensions of empowerment for adults are covered in the existing literature while the concept of youth empowerment remains fuzzy.[17] Youth empowerment is therefore vital for the emancipation and granting of autonomy in terms of financial decisions to the highly active segment of the economy that has remained marginalised in Botswana, Namibia, South Africa and Zimbabwe. This chapter explores the financial inclusion of youth, discusses the challenges that young people in the four countries face in terms of financial inclusion and finally presents the attendant relationship between youth financial inclusion and empowerment.

12.2 Overview of the financial inclusion of the youth

Financial inclusion has been widely discussed in the context of mobile money,[18] gender[19] and trade.[20] This chapter adds to the existing literature on the financial inclusion of youth. Because of the elusivity of this population group, its position between childhood and adulthood has often left the group's unique needs neglected with much focus on the two ends of the spectrum.[21] SSA has the youngest population yet their access to financial services is lower than those of adults.[22] Young people are often victims of social and income inequality, yet these inequalities are believed to be reduced by financial inclusion, particularly in high-fragility countries than in low-fragility countries.[23] Fragility has to do with the weak capacity to provide conditions necessary for human and economic development, and Africa accommodates the largest number of fragile nations where access to economic opportunities is designed in favour of rich societies while poor and marginalised segments of the community are neglected, thus widening income inequalities.[24] Highly fragile countries are associated with high poverty and inequality arising from financially excluded population groups and communities. Financial exclusion often leads to financial fragility, a concept that has to do with a poor capacity to deal with financial shocks. These groups include women, youth, informal labourers, rural inhabitants and the disabled and have been further disadvantaged by the unbearable socio-economic effects of global shocks such as Covid-19. Covid-19 impacts negatively on low-income earners, thus affecting the realisation of development goals that are centred on poverty in Zimbabwe and South Africa.[25] According to Global Findex data, 83% of youth in developed countries are formally banked compared with 38% of youth in developing countries. This translates to an estimated 700 million unbanked youth in developing countries. Poor access to financial services coupled with limited financial literacy poses a significant risk to the economic future and financial stability of youth.[26] Yet sufficient levels of financial inclusion of youth have a positive impact on youth productivity and socio-economic development.

Financial inclusion is not limited to gaining access to financial products, but also includes the quality of the products, the purpose they serve, the timing of the products and where and when they can be accessed with minimum restrictions. The ability for young people to open a formal account with any financial institution and receive, send or save money with ease is crucial. This improves their livelihoods and enables them to finance their education or entrepreneurial activities as well as gain access to credit facilities that demand deposits and bank statements. Young people normally lack collateral and documentation to borrow compared with adults. Yet their access to credit drives the economy by their participation in key investment decisions such as insurance, acquisition of assets or starting a family. Several financial houses such as traditional banks and microfinance companies have been shunning banking the youth based on a number of reasons, including perception and risk profile.

It matters whether the financial products are available to marginalised groups, such as low-income earners who are young. Creating opportunities for all population groups to enjoy socio-economic well-being in terms of financial inclusion is envisaged to improve youth empowerment and development in line with SDGs 1–7. Yet empowering the youth in SSA is lagging, as a large portion remains unbanked, reportedly 74%.[27] This is because the unique financial needs and inequalities of youth are often overlooked. The majority of the countries including those in Botswana, Namibia, South Africa and Zimbabwe are short of policies that promote financial knowledge and access to financial products for the youth. The following is a comparison of the financial inclusion levels of youth compared with adults.[28]

Table 12.1 shows that compared with adults, youths are generally lagging in terms of traditional financial systems, and equally the same with adults in mobile money and digital transactions. Overall, SSA is performing lower in all financial products than in the world at large. This is confirmed by the report that 80% of the population is not using formal banking systems relative to digital systems. What is of concern is that Africa has the youngest and largest population where 90% of the population is below 30 years. This is an age group that is hyperactive, and whose energy needs to be harnessed and channelled towards economic development.

Table 12.1 Financial inclusion statistics

Details	*Category*	*World (%)*	*SSA (%)*
Account at a financial institution	Youth	40	24
	Adults	63	33
Saved at a financial institution	Youth	15	10
	Adults	26	13
Borrowed from a financial institution	Youth	6	5
	Adults	14	8
Mobile money account ownership	Youth	15	25
	Adults	13	24
Made or received digital payments in 2017	Youth	33	33
	Adults	36	33

This status *quo* is unfortunate when financial inclusion is the pathway to youth economic and social empowerment. Youth financial inclusion is a necessary tool to enable them to realise their financial, economic and social goals. Youth financial inclusion entails making available financial products that are tailor-made for their unique needs. Youth are a specialised category of customers and granting them access to products such as bank accounts, credit facilities, low interest rates and so on provides them with access to economic opportunities that are normally in limited supply to them. Failure to devise strategies and tools that help them engage in productive activities will result in possible civil unrest as they engage in social ills such as drugs, theft, violence and prostitution.

12.3 Financial challenges faced by youth in Botswana, Namibia, South Africa and Zimbabwe

Compared to other developing continents, Africa has the youngest population with SSA leading with a more than 75% of the population comprised of youths.[29] These young people tend to be disadvantaged more than adults in countries with high unemployment, poverty and inequality rates such as Botswana, Namibia, South Africa and Zimbabwe. The youth unemployment rate in these countries is twice that of adults (12.8% vs 6.5%), with South Africa at 50%, while Botswana had 33% and Namibia stood at +30%.[30] Zimbabwe is leading with a 94% unemployment rate.[31] These statistics confirm that most young people in Botswana, Namibia, South Africa and Zimbabwe are excluded from economic and social spaces, which include income-generating activities and financial products.

Although the barriers to financial inclusion vary from one country to the next, there are some overlaps and similarities. These might be divided into supply side or demand-side factors. The supply side barriers comprise those that result from the providers of financial products, for example, unavailability of financial products, documentation requirements or unsuitable products. The demand-side factors arise from the consumer side, and these include religion, culture, perception and financial knowledge.[32] Unstable sources of income, low income, irregular cashflows, financial illiteracy, psychological factors and geographic distances are among the issues that hinder young people from having formal financial services. While on the supply side, formalities and documentation requirements, for instance, pay slips, high transaction costs, negative stereotypes that they are ineligible and are high risk and age restrictions, for example, in some countries the minimum age for a bank account is 16 years, limit youth from accessing formal financial services.

High transaction costs are experienced in these nations, for example, Zimbabwean banks charge exorbitant transaction costs, which are compounded by the 2% intermediated money transfer (IMT) tax on every transaction. A survey also reported that steep transaction fees and costs to access financial products hinder most people from participating in the formal financial system.[33] The borrowing and saving abilities of the youth are also limited. In the four countries, even if one wanted to open a savings account, no interest accrues to the account as most banks are now dependent on customer deposits for their survival. This also acts as a disincentive for the youth to open or maintain formal bank accounts because if one deposits US$1000 today, in no time the money will have been eroded by monthly charges and inflation. The accounts are also expected to have a minimum bank balance at any time, these and other reasons preclude youth from using formal financial services and opting for informal banking services such as pillow banking. Youth who are enterprising also face high borrowing costs to finance their business ventures as there are no preferential rates for them. The lack of specialised financial products that address the specific needs of young people as they transition from childhood to adulthood and from school to the labour market derail youth financial inclusion. Lack of awareness, misdirected policies and regulations and limited banking infrastructure in remote areas forbid the youth from much-needed financial services.[34]

Financial exclusion of vulnerable groups is more rampant in youth and poor segments of the population and even higher in post-conflict economies[35] such as Zimbabwe, which has had decades of political conflict, and South Africa, which has had apartheid and episodes of xenophobia. These economic and political landscapes have exposed the youth to protracted social and economic turmoil. In the case of Namibia, other limitations to youth financial inclusion are that the underbanked population of vulnerable groups is highly dispersed, making it difficult and costly to mobilise resources and infrastructure for these groups.[36] In Botswana, youth unemployment is more than double that of adults[37] and extracurricular activities are said to be in short supply because of limited finances, thus exposing youth to unhealthy mindsets and immoral activities that shorten their lifespan.[38]

Youth are the rapidly growing part of the SSA population, yet many are not saving and are economically vulnerable. In some instances, parents preclude their children from joining the financial systems for fear of being victims of illicit transactions and cyber-attacks. Youth are also a hard-to-reach population group through mainstream channels due to the glaring disparities that arise from age, gender and the rural-urban divide. Gender plays a role as females have restricted access compared with males, for instance, in remote communities where one has to travel a long distance to access formal financial services.[39] Youth are also limited in terms of age, as most SSA countries prohibit the opening of a bank account for ages below 18 years.[40] Collectively, low levels of financial literacy remain a major constraint to youth accessing mainstream financial services.[41]

12.4 Regulatory support of financial inclusion for the youth in Botswana, Namibia, South Africa and Zimbabwe

Apart from supply and demand-driven factors, support pillars such as the regulatory framework and other policies have limited the requisite support for youth financial inclusion. For example, all four countries have introduced national initiatives aimed at promoting financial inclusion. For example, Zimbabwe has the Financial Inclusion Strategy (launched in March 2016), and Namibia has the Financial Literacy Initiative spearheaded by the Ministry of Finance, as well as the Namibian Financial Sector Strategy 2011–2021 initiated by the Bank of Namibia, but none of these are specifically targeted at the youth. Even Zimbabwe's Indigenization and Economic Empowerment Act did not yield significant results for the youth.[42] Governments have gone as far as putting pieces of legislation in place. Namibia enacted the National Youth Service Act in 2005, South Africa enacted a National Youth Act in 2008 and Zimbabwe recently promulgated its National Youth Act in 2019, while Botswana relies on a national youth policy alone. The idea of these government policies and laws is good, however, most of them have overlooked the role of financial inclusion.

Prior research has revealed deficiencies in the existing regulatory frameworks for financial inclusion in SADC countries.[43] Fragmented policy and legislation and lack of customer protection leaving youth vulnerable to unscrupulous adults are some of the major weaknesses. Other barriers to effective financial inclusion of youth include gender inequality, unemployment, irregular income flows and poor infrastructure.[44]

Botswana's financial services sector is regulated by two authorities, the Bank of Botswana (BoB) and the Non-Bank Financial Institutions Regulatory Authority (NBFIRA), which is responsible for overseeing pension funds, microfinance and credit institutions.[45] Although not specific to youth, the financial inclusion initiatives and policies have yielded fruits in Botswana as evidenced by a decline in the financially excluded population from 96% to 49%.[46]

The Central Bank of Namibia, which was established through the promulgation of the Bank of Namibia Act 15 of 1997, regulates the operations of the banking sector, while non-banking financial institutions are regulated by the Namibia Financial Institutions Supervisory Authority (NAMFISA), established through the Namibia Financial Institutions Supervisory Authority Act 3 of 2001.[47] Namibia also introduced the New Equitable Economic Empowerment Framework (NEEEF) of 2008, which was meant to increase the levels of financial participation and inclusion for disadvantaged citizens.[48] Namibia has also shown commitment to improve its financial inclusion by introducing the Namibian Financial Sector Strategy (NFSS), 2011–2021, and the Financial Literacy Strategy (2012), which was targeted at vulnerable groups such as women and youth. All these efforts prove vital to the cause; however, the youth remain financially excluded because of a lack of appropriate financial products that suit the specific needs of the youth and outstanding fundamentals such as lack of collateral demanded by banks in advancing credit and an inability to provide documentation.[49]

South Africa enacted the Black Economic Empowerment Act 2003 to address some economic imbalances, as well as the National Credit Act (NCA) in 2005 and Consumer Protection Act (CPA) in 2008 to promote financial literacy and consumer protection.[50] However, all these laws do not specifically target the youth and their unique needs. Furthermore, South Africa's National Youth Economic Empowerment Strategy and Implementation Framework (2009–2019) failed to explicitly address financial inclusion drivers. Despite these legislative and policy tools, more than 30 million South Africans are financially excluded because of challenges such as financial illiteracy and lack of the required documentation to open a bank account such as national identity cards, which are more common among the youth than other cohorts.[51]

The Zimbabwean financial services sector is mainly governed by the Reserve Bank as per the Reserve Bank of Zimbabwe Act (1999) and the Banking Act [Chapter 24:20] 9 of 1999.[52] Enthusiastic about promoting financial inclusion, Zimbabwe introduced a National Financial Inclusion Strategy (NFIS) (2016–2020) in 2016 in order to bring the unbanked into the system. Recently, the government introduced the Banking (Money Transmission, Mobile Banking and Mobile Money Interoperability) Regulations of 2020 (Banking Regulations, 2020).[53] The Government of Zimbabwe also enacted the Indigenisation and Economic Empowerment Act 2007 in a bid to improve the participation and inclusion of marginalised citizens. Despite all these efforts, the Zimbabwean youth remain the most vulnerable, unemployed, financially excluded and misunderstood cohort.[54] Efforts and initiatives by SADC countries have produced less satisfactory results, and more action needs to be taken to introduce youth-centric policies and implement the existing laws and policies in order to achieve the intended outcome.

While the traditional banking system is slowly becoming redundant, it remains relevant for services such as credit facilities and security that are currently not offered by digital financial systems in most parts of the world. Nonetheless, digital financial services are expected to revolutionise the financial system and offer more opportunities to young people through low transaction costs.[55] Digital financial products are becoming popular among the youth probably because of the less stringent requirements to own an account, but digitalisation also comes with its costs such as the costs of owning a smart mobile device, which is often unreachable to young people. Apart from that, Zimbabwe also practises rationing of financial services, for example, in terms of imposed withdrawal limits. Individuals are only allowed to withdraw a maximum of US$500 per day, there are mobile money transfer daily limits and a restricted number of mobile money accounts per person. The imposition of the 2% IMT on all financial transactions stifles economic activities such as entrepreneurship since most young people dominate the informal sector and find employment in the gig economy (self-employment).[56] It becomes difficult to equitably allocate resources to productive sectors of the economy and achieve youth empowerment in an economy with limited access to formal financial services and products. The youth are reservoirs of energy, yet are excluded from financial tools that can empower them to increase productivity and ultimately economic growth.

12.5 The role of financial inclusion in empowering youth

Extant literature shows that SADC has low levels of youth financial inclusion. There is a general consensus that negative stereotypes, financial illiteracy, psychological factors, gender, legal restrictions, rural-urban divide, stringent requirements, high transaction costs, income levels and a lack of customised financial products are among the reasons for youth financial exclusion. Of these, the lack of income remains predominant due to the high unemployment rates common in Botswana, Namibia, South Africa and Zimbabwe. It is believed that economies with high unemployment rates have the highest financial exclusion rates that decelerate economic growth and development.[57] Financial inclusion increases access to formal credit facilities. Access to credit facilities means youth can engage in productive activities such as entrepreneurship. This will increase their income levels and thus increase their participation in local, regional and national debates. This process can be defined as empowerment as it grants youth an opportunity to exercise control within the economic, social and political spheres of life.[58] This also enables youth to shape their own future, which is often predetermined by adults and a few elites that control economic resources. Financial inclusion also promotes savings that help youth to invest in their education and business ventures as well as acquire properties. Academic advancement, property ownership and business investments increase individual awareness and their power to take responsibility for their lives, family and the community. It improves self-confidence, assertiveness and proactiveness in shaping one's own fate and improves their socio-economic environment. This is called empowerment.

Youth financial exclusion dampens youth empowerment efforts and widens income and social inequality gaps. Therefore, financial inclusion should be pursued with energy if the four countries are to realise inclusive sustainable development. While youth are viewed as the backbone of national development, they remain the most exploited by impervious systems. Economic and financial policies need to be aligned with the unique needs of this specialised group. Youth is described as the age of discontent, militancy and rebellion, and if their behaviour is not checked and their potential unnurtured, it could result in an unhealthy society. The need to empower youth has birthed initiatives such as youth empowerment programmes (YEPs), which are mainly the brainchild of non-governmental organisations. Some banks have joined the band, and Zimbabwe's CBZ runs a YEP created to finance youth projects. These organisations have recognised the importance of youth financial inclusion. By expanding their choices and liberties, they gain autonomy over critical decisions, narrowing the degree of inequality with adults and preparing them for their future.[59] Without empowerment, youth cannot even react to the rampant economic and social injustices that they face daily. Financial exclusion breeds counterproductivity, hence the need for inclusivity to empower youth to reach their potential and actualise their dreams.

There is overwhelming evidence that financial inclusion is associated with increased socio-economic development.[60] It has been statistically proven that there is a positive correlation between credit facilities and the use of formal financial services as these induce innovation and entrepreneurship.[61] Thus, it suffices to say that increasing access to financial services boosts confidence, innovation and creativity in youth. Developing financial tools and strategies promotes youth livelihoods and mental development. Financial inclusion does not only encompass access to financial products, hence the need to ensure quality financial tools and actual usage of these services.[62] Because of conflicting demands for money in youth, cultivating a savings behaviour in them yields positive socio-economic effects and eliminates social alienation.[63] Once the youth are financially independent in terms of access to financial products and spending, saving and borrowing plans, they are empowered and capacitated to survive this volatile, uncertain, complex and ambiguous (VUCA) environment and are ready for the future. This means youth can now freely participate in the political, economic and social development of their respective economies. The literature affirms that increased financial inclusion reduces the unemployment rate in developing economies.[64] The attendant relationship between financial inclusion and youth empowerment is thus positive.

12.6 Conclusion

Youth are among the demographics that are often overlooked in terms of access to economic opportunities and financial inclusion. This chapter established the nexus between youth financial inclusion and empowerment. The chapter shows that youth financial inclusion has a positive relationship with youth empowerment. Despite this positive association, financial ecosystems targeted at the youth are still lacking in Botswana, Namibia, South Africa and Zimbabwe as many have limited access to mainstream financial streams. Negative stereotypes, financial illiteracy, psychological factors, gender, legal restrictions, rural-urban divide, stringent requirements, high transaction costs, income levels and a lack of financial products that are pro-youth are the key barriers to youth financial inclusion. Apart from supply side and demand-side barriers, there is a lack of supporting platforms such as regulation and policy in Botswana, Namibia, South Africa and Zimbabwe. National financial inclusion strategies have limited scope on financial inclusion strategies targeted at the youth. While there is an undeniable need for the youth to be financially educated through financial literacy programmes, it is only one piece of the financial inclusion puzzle. The youth have unique financial needs that require specialised redress. Young people are a specialised category of customers with unique needs that require tailor-made measures that will address their financial needs and impact generations. Stakeholders call for policies formulated to address the financial exclusion of vulnerable groups such as youth since it threatens national development.[65] Investing in youth empowerment through financial inclusion is key for economic development and social rest. Young people need to be equipped with appropriate financial tools for them to exercise independent financial decision-making that propels them towards an easy transition to adulthood and the labour market. Financial inclusion will obviate them from financial dependency.

Regulatory authorities such as central banks and governments should devise policies and measures that support financial solutions targeted at young people by establishing youth financial houses or banking institutions that offer, for instance, less stringent requirements such as documentation and collateral, offer low to zero interest rates and low transaction costs. With the perpetual increase in technology and the fourth industrialisation, digital financial service providers should also create financial products that are accessible to young people at affordable transaction costs. This will afford them independence in making financial plans with regard to generating income and spending and saving money. Financial service providers should provide financial products that can be accessed by the youth, especially in rural areas, based on a know-your-customer basis. However, a collective effort by various stakeholders is required since some of the suggested specialised financial products might be costly to the financial providers.

The chapter recommends that Botswana, Namibia, South Africa and Zimbabwe should consider coming up with youth-oriented financial models, youth-friendly borrowing facilities, gender-responsive financial models and financial ecosystems specially designed for the youth. For example, financial products that exempt the youth from other prerequisites such as a regular income. The financial products should be designed bearing in mind that the youth are not a homogenous group and require specialised products depending on their particular circumstances.[66] There is a need for national youth programmes, initiatives and strategies that help youth transition from childhood to adulthood with some sense of financial autonomy. Creating an inclusive and enabling environment for youth financial inclusion will promote youth productivity and ultimately economic growth and development. The legislative pieces should also be explicitly crafted to address the needs of this unique cohort.

Research on the *nexus* between financial inclusion and youth empowerment is still nascent, especially in Botswana, Namibia, South Africa and Zimbabwe. This chapter is one of the very few studies that consider the link between financial inclusion and youth empowerment. It is based on a review of the literature, and there is a need for empirical evidence of the connection between financial inclusion and youth empowerment. Considering that the young population is the fastest growing in Africa, and youth financial exclusion is a prevalent phenomenon in Botswana, Namibia, South Africa and Zimbabwe, policies and strategies that empower them financially are imperative. Given the heterogeneity of economic fundamentals in each of these countries (Botswana, Namibia, South Africa and Zimbabwe), further research could explore the barriers to youth financial inclusion through those lenses.

Notes

1 A Grohmann et al. 'Does Financial Literacy Improve Financial Inclusion? Cross Country Evidence' (2018) 111 *World Development* 84–96.
2 Ibid.
3 P Mader 'Contesting Financial Inclusion' (2018) 49(2) *Development and Change* 461–483.
4 MK Refera et al. 'Financial Literacy for Developing Countries in Africa: A Review of Concept, Significance and Research Opportunities' (2016) 8(1) *Journal of African Studies and Development* 1–12.
5 SADC 'Financial Inclusion Strategy 2016-2021' (2016) 7; T Chinoda and F Kwenda 'Do Mobile Phones, Economic Growth, Bank Competition and Stability Matter for Financial Inclusion in Africa?' (2019) 7(1) *Cogent Economics & Finance* 1–20.
6 D Filmer and L Fox 'Youth Employment in Sub-Saharan Africa' (2014) *World Bank Publications* 1–249.
7 N Garg and S Singh 'Financial Literacy Among Youth' (2018) 45(1) *International Journal of Social Economics* 173–186.
8 J Anderson et al. 'The Role of Financial Services in Youth Education and Employment' (2019) *CGAP Working Paper* 1–26.
9 S Gukurume 'Navigating Precarious Livelihoods: Youth in the SME Sector in Zimbabwe' in Ayele S, Glover D & Oosterom M (eds) *IDS Bulletin Transforming Development Knowledge* (2018) 89-105; D Filmer and L Fox (2014) World Bank Publications 1–249.
10 D Filmer and L Fox (2014) *World Bank Publications* 1–249.
11 M Ncube 'Inclusive Growth in Africa' in Monga C & JY Lin (eds) *The Oxford Handbook of Africa and Economics: Volume 1 Context and Concepts*' (2015) 154.
12 J Anderson et al. (2019) *CGAP Working Paper* 1–26.
13 F Angulo-Ruiz and A Pergelova 'An Empowerment Model of Youth Financial Behavior' (2015) 49(3) *Journal of Consumer Affairs* 550–575.
14 A Babajić et al. 'Identification of Barriers to Financial Inclusion Among Youth' (2018) 11(7) *International Business Research* 120–129.
15 L Klapper and D Singer 'The Role of Informal Financial Services in Africa' (2015) *Journal of African Economies* i12–i31.
16 NA Peterson et al. 'Measuring Youth Empowerment: Validation of A Socio-Political Control Scale for Youth in an Urban Community Context' (2011) 39(5) *Journal of Community Psychology* 592–605.
17 S T Russell et al. 'Youth Empowerment and High School Gay-Straight Alliances' (2009) 38(7) *Journal of Youth & Adolescence* 891–903.
18 G Okello et al. 'Mobile Money and Financial Inclusion in Sub-Saharan Africa: The Moderating Role of Social Networks' (2018) 19(3) *Journal of African Business* 361–384.
19 JO Abebe et al. 'Background Paper: Driving Gender-Responsive Financial Inclusion Models in Africa' (2017) *United Nations Women* 1–41.
20 T Chinoda 'The Nexus Between Financial Inclusion, Trade and Economic Growth in Africa?' (2020) 12(3) *Transnational Corporations Review* 266–275.
21 JJ Baker 'Beyond Problem Solving Development Initiatives for Youth in Botswana: A Youth Development Approach for Risk Reduction' (2008) Masters of Development thesis, University of the Witwatersrand, 9–121.
22 PO Asuming et al. 'Financial Inclusion in Sub-Saharan Africa: Recent Trends and Determinants' (2019) 20(1) *Journal of African Business* 112–134.
23 JH Kim 'A Study on the Effect of Financial Inclusion on the Relationship Between Income Inequality and Economic Growth' (2016) 52(2) *Emerging Markets, Finance & Trade* 498–512.
24 B Fowowe and EO Folarin 'The Effects of Fragility and Financial Inequalities on Inclusive Growth in African Countries' (2019) 23(3) *Review of Development Economics* 1141–1176.

25 D Mhlanga and T Moloi 'COVID-19, and Sustainable Development Goals: A Comparative Analysis of Zimbabwe and South Africa' (2021) 18(1) *African Renaissance* 247–269.
26 A Babajić et al. (2018) 11(7) *International Business Research* 120–129.
27 A Gasparri and L Munoz 'Inclusive Finance and Rural Youth' (2019) *IFAD Research Series 51* 1–23 www.ifad.org/ruraldevelopmentreport, accessed on 18 June 2021.
28 J Anderson et al. (2019) *CGAP Working Paper* 1–26.
29 The African Capacity Building Foundation 'Youth unemployment in Africa: Capacity Building and Innovative Strategies' (2017) *Occasional Paper No. 30* 1–68.
30 Ibid.
31 S Gukurume in Ayele S, Glover D & Oosterom M (eds) *IDS Bulletin Transforming Development Knowledge* (2018) 89–105.
32 S Shankar 'Financial Inclusion in India: Do Microfinance Institutions Address Access Barriers?' (2013) 2(1) *ACRN Journal of Entrepreneurship Perspectives* 60–74.
33 Namibia Statistics Agency 'Namibia Financial Inclusion Survey (NFIS) 2017' (2017) 1-96 https://d3rp5jatom3eyn.cloudfront.net/cms/assets/documents/NFIS_2017_Report.pdf, accessed on 10 June 2021.
34 A Rani and P Roy 'Youth in Agriculture: Role of Government Initiatives' (2017) *Journal of Agricultural Extension Management* 167–175.
35 Africa Centre for Economic Transformation 'Promoting Women and Youth Financial Inclusion for Entrepreneurship and Job Creation: Comparative Study of Selected Sub-Saharan African Countries' (2019) *Synthesis Report* 1–48.
36 H Mannan et al. 'Core Concepts of Human Rights and Inclusion of Vulnerable Groups in the Disability and Rehabilitation Policies of Malawi, Namibia, Sudan, and South Africa' (2012) 23(2) *Journal of Disability Policy Studies* 67–81.
37 L Sechele 'Unemployed Youth and Self-Employment in Botswana' (2016) 19 *Mosenodi Journal* 31–44.
38 JJ Baker (2008) Masters of Development thesis, University of the Witwatersrand, 9–121.
39 Alliance for Financial Inclusion 'Integrating Youth into A National Financial Inclusion Strategy' (2020) *Guideline Note No.38* 1–32.
40 D Filmer and L Fox (2014) *World Bank Publications* 1–249.
41 N Garg and S Singh (2018) 45(1) *International Journal of Social Economics* 173–186.
42 P Hlungwani et al. 'Mainstreaming Youth Policy in Zimbabwe – What Role for Rural Youth?' (2021) 7(1) *Cogent Social Sciences* 1–19.
43 SADC 'Financial Inclusion Strategy 2016-2021' (2016) 1–63.
44 J Sykes, S Elder, Y Gurbuzer and M Principi 'Exploring the Linkages Between Youth Financial Inclusion and Job Creation Evidence from the ILO School-To-Work Transition Surveys' (2016) *Work4Youth Publication Series No. 42* 1–55; F Barugahara 'Financial Inclusion in Zimbabwe: Determinants, Challenges and Opportunities' (2021) 12(3) *International Journal of Financial Research* 261–270.
45 Ministry of Finance & Economic Development 'Botswana Demand, Supply, Policy and Regulation' (2015) *Diagnostic Final Report* 1–131.
46 K Molefhi 'Financial Inclusion and its Impact on Employment Creation in Botswana' (2019) *Botswana Institute for Development Policy Analysis Working Paper 60* 1–18.
47 E Haiyambo 'An Impact Assessment of the Regulation of Microfinance Institutions in Namibia' (PhD thesis, Stellenbosch University, 2016) 44–74.
48 Government of The Republic of Namibia 'New Equitable Economic Empowerment Framework' (2008) 10 https://www.ecb.org.na/images/docs/Investor_Portal/NEEEF.pdf, accessed on 10 February 2021.
49 AM Matongela 'Understanding the State of Financial Inclusion in Namibia' (2014) 5(12) *Computer Engineering and Intelligent Systems* 71–75.

50 H Chitimira and M Ncube 'Legislative and Other Selected Challenges Affecting Financial Inclusion for the Poor and Low-Income Earners in South Africa' (2020) 64(3) *Journal of Africa Law* 337–355.
51 Ibid.
52 F Barugahara (2021) 12(3) *International Journal of Financial Research* 261–270.
53 C Dzingirai et al. 'Drivers of Platform Level Interoperability: Evidence from Zimbabwean Mobile Money Operators' (2021) *International Conference in Accounting and Business* 595–624.
54 S Gukurume in Ayele S, Glover D & Oosterom M (eds) *IDS Bulletin Transforming Development Knowledge* (2018) 89–105.
55 Africa Centre for Economic Transformation (2019) *Synthesis Report* 1–48.
56 S Gukurume in Ayele S, Glover D & Oosterom M (eds) *IDS Bulletin Transforming Development Knowledge* (2018) 89–105; J Anderson et al. (2019) *CGAP Working Paper* 1–26.
57 S Chivasa and P Simbanegavi 'Financial Inclusion in Zimbabwe Post Hyper Inflationary Period: Barriers and Effects on Societal Livelihoods, A Qualitative Approach: A Case of Matebeleland North' (2016) 18(1) *Journal of Sustainable Development in Africa* 53–72.
58 LB Jennings et al. 'Toward a Critical Social Theory of Youth Empowerment' (2006) 14 *Journal of Community Practice* 31–55.
59 D Mwesigwa and BC Mubangizi 'Contributions of the Youth Livelihood Programme (YLP) to Youth Empowerment in Hoima District, Uganda' (2019) 11(1) *International Journal of Business and Management Studies* 54–73
60 D Avom, C Bangake and H Ndoya 'Does Bank Concentration Stem from Financial Inclusion in Africa?' (2021) *Applied Economics* 1–18.
61 LL Gakpa 'Financial Inclusion and Entrepreneurship in Sub-Saharan African Countries: Cross-Country Evidence from the Finscope and Finances Surveys' (2020) *AERC Africa Paper* 1–20.
62 A Gasparri and L Munoz (2019) *IFAD Research Series 51* 1–23 www.ifad.org/ruraldevelopmentreport, accessed on 18 June 2021
63 L Zou et al. 'Facilitators and Obstacles in Youth Saving: Perspectives from Ghana and Kenya' (2015) 2(2) *Global Social Welfare* 65–74.
64 EB Mehry et al. 'The Impact of Financial Inclusion on Unemployment Rate in Developing Countries' (2021) 11(1) *International Journal of Economics and Financial Issues* 79–93.
65 PO Asuming et al. (2019) 20(1) *Journal of African Business* 112–134.
66 Alliance for Financial Inclusion (2020) *Guideline Note No. 38* 1–32.

Bibliography

J O Abebe, L Maina, J Ondiek & C Ogolla 'Background paper driving gender-responsive financial inclusion models in Africa' (2017) *United Nations Women* 1 at 41.

Africa Centre for Economic Transformation 'Promoting Women and Youth Financial Inclusion for Entrepreneurship and Job Creation: Comparative Study of Selected Sub-Saharan African Countries' (2019) *Synthesis Report* 1 at 48.

Alliance for Financial Inclusion 'Integrating youth into a national financial inclusion strategy' (2020) *Guideline Note No. 38* 1 at 32.

J Anderson, D Hopkins & M Valenzuela *The Role of Financial Services in Youth Education and Employment* (CGAP working paper, 2019) 1 at 26.

F Angulo-Ruiz & A Pergelova 'An empowerment model of youth financial behavior' (2015) 49(3) *Journal of Consumer Affairs* 550 at 575.

P O Asuming, L G Osei-Agyei & J I Mohammed 'Financial inclusion In Sub-Saharan Africa: Recent trends and determinants' (2019) 20(1) *Journal of African Business* 112 at 134.

D Avom, C Bangake & H Ndoya 'Does bank concentration stem from financial inclusion in Africa?' (2021) *Applied Economics* 1 at 18.

A Babajić, J Okičić & M K Jukan 'Identification of barriers to financial inclusion among youth' (2018) 11(7) *International Business Research* 120 at 129.

J J Baker 'Beyond problem solving development initiatives for youth in Botswana: A youth development approach for risk reduction' (Masters of Development thesis, University of the Witwatersrand, 2008).

F Barugahara 'Financial inclusion in Zimbabwe: Determinants, challenges and opportunities' (2021) 12(3) *International Journal of Financial Research* 261 at 270.

T Chinoda 'The nexus between financial inclusion, trade and economic growth in Africa?' (2020) 12(3) *Transnational Corporations Review* 266 at 275.

T Chinoda & F Kwenda 'Do mobile phones, economic growth, bank competition and stability matter for financial inclusion in Africa?' (2019) 7(1) *Cogent Economics & Finance* 1 at 20.

S Chivasa & P Simbanegavi 'Financial inclusion in Zimbabwe post hyper inflationary period: Barriers and effects on societal livelihoods, a qualitative approach: A case of Matebeleland North' (2016) 18(1) *Journal of Sustainable Development in Africa* 53 at 72.

C Dzingirai, E Mashiri & C Makanyeza 'Drivers of platform level interoperability: Evidence from Zimbabwean mobile money operators' (2021) *International Conference in Accounting and Business* 595 at 624.

D Filmer & L Fox 'Youth employment in Sub-Saharan Africa' (2014) *World Bank Publications* 1 at 249.

B Fowowe & E O Folarin 'The effects of fragility and financial inequalities on inclusive growth in African countries' (2019) 23(3) *Review of Development Economics* 1141 at 1176.

L L Gakpa 'Financial inclusion and entrepreneurship in Sub-Saharan African countries: Cross-country evidence from the finscope and finances surveys' (2020) *AERC Africa Paper* 1 at 20.

A Gand & L Munoz 'Inclusive finance and rural youth' (IFAD research series 51, 2019), available at www.ifad.org/ruraldevelopmentreport, accessed on 18 June 2021.

N Garg & S Singh 'Financial literacy among youth' (2018) 45(1) *International Journal of Social Economics* 173 at 186.

A Gasparri & L Munoz 'Inclusive finance and rural youth' (IFAD research series 51, 2019), available at www.ifad.org/ruraldevelopmentreport, accessed on 18 June 2021.

Government of The Republic of Namibia 'New equitable economic empowerment framework' (2008), available at https://www.ecb.org.na/images/docs/Investor_Portal/NEEEF.pdf, accessed on 10 February 2021.

A Grohmann, T Klühs & L Menkhoff 'Does financial literacy improve financial inclusion? Cross country evidence' (2018) 111 *World Development* 84 at 96.

S Gukurume '# ThisFlag and# this gown cyber protests in Zimbabwe: Reclaiming political space' (2017) 38(2) *African Journalism Studies* 49 at 70.

S Gukurume 'Navigating precarious livelihoods: Youth in the SME sector in Zimbabwe' in S Ayele, D Glover & M Oosterom (eds) *IDS Bulletin Transforming Development Knowledge* (2018) 89 at 105.

E Haiyambo *An Impact Assessment of the Regulation of Microfinance Institutions in Namibia* (PhD thesis, Stellenbosch University, 2016).

P Hlungwani, S Masuku & M Magidi 'Mainstreaming youth policy in Zimbabwe – What role for rural youth?' (2021) 7(1) *Cogent Social Sciences* 1 at 19.

L B Jennings, D M Parra-Medina, D K Hilfinger-Messias & K McLoughlin 'Toward a critical social theory of youth empowerment' (2006) 14 *Journal of Community Practice* 31 at 55.

J H Kim 'A study on the effect of financial inclusion on the relationship between income inequality and economic growth' (2016) 52(2) *Emerging Markets, Finance & Trade* 498 at 512.

L Klapper & D Singer 'The role of informal financial services in Africa' (2015) *Journal of African Economies* i12 at i31.

P Mader 'Contesting financial inclusion' (2018) 49(2) *Development and Change* 461 at 483.

H Mannan, J McVeigh, M Amin, M MacLachlan, L Swartz, A Munthali & G Van Rooy 'Core concepts of human rights and inclusion of vulnerable groups in the disability and rehabilitation policies of Malawi, Namibia, Sudan, and South Africa' (2012) 23(2) *Journal of Disability Policy Studies* 67 at 81.

A M Matongela 'Understanding the state of financial inclusion in Namibia' (2014) 5(12) *Computer Engineering and Intelligent Systems* 71 at 75.

E B Mehry, S Ashraf & E Marwa 'The impact of financial inclusion on unemployment rate in developing countries' (2021) 11(1) *International Journal of Economics and Financial Issues* 79 at 93.

D Mhlanga & T Moloi 'COVID-19, and sustainable development goals: A comparative analysis of Zimbabwe and South Africa' (2021) 18(1) *African Renaissance* 247 at 269.

Ministry of Finance & Economic Development 'Botswana demand, supply, policy and regulation' (Diagnostic Final Report 1-131, 2015).

K Molefhi *Financial Inclusion and its Impact on Employment Creation in Botswana* (Botswana Institute for Development Policy Analysis working paper 60, 2019) 1 at 18.

D Mwesigwa & B C Mubangizi 'Contributions of the youth livelihood programme (YLP) to youth empowerment in Hoima district, Uganda' (2019) 11(1) *International Journal of Business and Management Studies* 54 at 73.

Namibia Statistics Agency 'Namibia financial inclusion survey (NFIS) 2017' (2017), available at https://d3rp5jatom3eyn.cloudfront.net/cms/assets/documents/NFIS_2017_Report.pdf, accessed on 10 June 2021.

M Ncube 'Inclusive growth in Africa' in C Monga & J Y Lin (eds) *The Oxford Handbook of Africa and Economics: Volume 1 Context and Concepts* (2015) 154.

G Okello Candiya Bongomin, J M Ntayi, J C Munene & C A Malinga 'Mobile money and financial inclusion in Sub-Saharan Africa: The moderating role of social networks' (2018) 19(3) *Journal of African Business* 361 at 384.

E Olaniyi 'The effects of economic and financial development on financial inclusion in Africa' (2015) *Review of Economic and Development Studies* 17 at 25.

N A Peterson, C H Peterson, L Agre, B D Christens & C M Morton 'Measuring youth empowerment: Validation of a socio-political control scale for youth in an urban community context' (2011) 39(5) *Journal of Community Psychology* 592 at 605.

A Rani & P Roy 'Youth in agriculture: Role of government initiatives' (2017) *Journal of Agricultural Extension Management* 167 at 175.

M K Refera, N K Dhaliwal & J Kaur 'Financial literacy for developing countries in Africa: A review of concept, significance and research opportunities' (2016) 8(1) *Journal of African Studies and Development* 1 at 12.

S T Russell, A Muraco, A Subramaniam & C Laub 'Youth empowerment and high school gay-straight alliances' (2009) 38(7) *Journal of Youth & Adolescence* 891 at 903.

SADC 'Financial inclusion strategy 2016–2021' (2016).

L Sechele 'Unemployed youth and self-employment in Botswana' (2016) 19 *Mosenodi Journal* 31 at 44.

S Shankar 'Financial inclusion in India: Do microfinance institutions address access barriers?' (2013) 2(1) *ACRN Journal of Entrepreneurship Perspectives* 60 at 74.

J Sykes, S Elder, Y Gurbuzer & M Principi 'Exploring the linkages between youth financial inclusion and job creation evidence from the ILO school-to-work transition surveys' (2016) *Work4Youth Publication Series No. 42* 1 at 55.

The African Capacity Building Foundation 'Youth unemployment in Africa: Capacity building and innovative strategies' (2017) *Occasional Paper No. 30* 1 at 68.

L Zou, S M Tlapek, G Njenga, E Appiah, D Opai-Tetteh & M S Sherraden 'Facilitators and obstacles in youth saving: Perspectives from Ghana and Kenya' (2015) 2(2) *Global Social Welfare* 65 at 74.

13 An analysis of the policy and regulatory framework for financial inclusion in Zimbabwe

Friedrich Hamadziripi and Vimbai Jana

13.1 Introduction

Financial inclusion refers to the ability of individuals, especially poor, marginalised and disadvantaged people, to access formal financial services such as payments, savings, credit and insurance services on reasonable terms.[1] In this chapter, the terms "poor, marginalised and disadvantaged people" refer to financial consumers who struggle to access and benefit from several financial products and services mainly due to a lack of financial resources. Examples of financial consumers that can be described as "poor, marginalised and disadvantaged" include low-income earners, women, asylum seekers and small business owners. Conversely, financial exclusion is the voluntary or involuntary inability of individuals to access formal financial products and services that enable them to conduct financial transactions, keep savings, access credit and insurance products in a sustainable manner.[2] Accordingly, in Zimbabwe's context, financial inclusion could be understood to mean the ability of a majority of the population to access and utilise financial products and services offered to the public by financial institutions in the formal sector. In this regard, financial inclusion entails the ability to access the said products and services on reasonable terms that are sustainable and not exploitative to the majority of the population.

One way of promoting financial inclusion in Zimbabwe is by enacting legislation that enhances access to formal financial products and services by marginalised groups such as low-income earners, women, asylum seekers and small business owners.[3] Zimbabwe is a developing country with 70% of its population residing in rural areas.[4] Furthermore, only 28% of Zimbabwe's population have accounts with formal financial institutions such as banks and insurance companies.[5] In light of this, it can be submitted that the majority of Zimbabwe's population is financially excluded. Some of the challenges that lead to financial exclusion in Zimbabwe include the lack of proper identification documents required when opening bank accounts, poverty, unstable income patterns and a lack of financial education.[6] These challenges could be addressed by developing specific policies and enacting legislation that encourages financially excluded people to access formal financial services in Zimbabwe. At present, several statutes attempt to promote financial inclusion in Zimbabwe. However, these pieces of legislation do not specifically deal with

DOI: 10.4324/9781003369400-13

financial inclusion in great detail. Thus, Zimbabwe does not currently have legislation that is specifically dedicated to addressing or promoting financial inclusion.[7]

Accordingly, the government of Zimbabwe, through the Reserve Bank of Zimbabwe (RBZ) introduced the 2016–2020 National Financial Inclusion Strategy (NFIS) in 2016.[8] The NFIS was a roadmap of actions agreed upon and defined at the national and subnational levels, which various stakeholders were to follow to achieve set financial inclusion objectives.[9] In other words, the NFIS was a comprehensive public document that presented a strategy developed at the national level to systematically accelerate the level of financial inclusion in Zimbabwe.[10] The period 2016 to 2020 was envisaged by the NFIS to promote financial inclusion efforts in Zimbabwe has now passed. Therefore, it is pertinent to analyse the statutory and policy efforts that have been made thus far to achieve the objectives set out in the NFIS.

13.2 The NFIS as a guide to policy development and legislative enactments

Financial inclusion is a means through which Zimbabwe could improve its economic growth. However, in order to achieve the desired level of financial inclusion, which realises considerable economic growth, the majority of the population of Zimbabwe needs to be financially educated. In this regard, financial education is the process of becoming knowledgeable and skilled in prudent money management practices such as spending, saving, borrowing and investing one's earnings.[11] Financial education empowers an individual with the knowledge to make decisions in a proactive manner after assessing the available financial products and services to achieve a particular financial goal. Consequently, it became necessary for the government of Zimbabwe to develop a comprehensive national strategy to achieve financial inclusion. Accordingly, the NFIS sought to identify barriers that inhibit some financial consumers from accessing relevant financial services and products.[12] Through the NFIS, the government of Zimbabwe also identified opportunities that it could utilise to create an environment that supports financial inclusion for the majority of its population, especially those dwelling in rural areas.[13] For instance, the NFIS identified financial innovations in service provision to the people of Zimbabwe and proposed legislative changes to enable or facilitate financial innovations.[14]

The success of the NFIS hinged on the presence of an enabling or supporting legislative framework that guides and regulates role-players involved in the implementation of the NFIS.[15] The 2016–2020 NFIS identified four broad thematic areas by which Zimbabwe could promote financial inclusion.[16] These thematic areas are financial capability and financial consumer protection, financial innovation, financial infrastructure and microfinance.[17] Together, these identified thematic areas will ostensibly assist in promoting the achievement of financial inclusion for the majority of the population in Zimbabwe.

13.3 Thematic areas on the promotion of financial inclusion in Zimbabwe

13.3.1 Financial capability and consumer protection

Financial capability or financial literacy refers to the knowledge and skills that are required by a person in order to understand their financial circumstances.[18] Therefore, financial literacy initiatives could assist in promoting financial inclusion in Zimbabwe by empowering financial consumers to make wise borrowing, saving and investing decisions.[19] A financially literate person is better positioned to make informed financial decisions. Consequently, financially literate people plan how to spend their money, which could lead to better chances for them to become financially included.[20] Recognising that financial literacy and consumer protection are pivotal in promoting financial inclusion in Zimbabwe, the RBZ issued the Financial Consumer Protection Framework (FCPF) in June 2017.[21] The purpose of the FCPF is to ensure the protection of financial consumers' rights.[22] The FCPF also seeks to promote transparency in the provision of relevant financial services and products by banks and other financial institutions to the public.[23] In this regard, the FCPF was established to promote the fair treatment of financial consumers by financial institutions.[24] Consequently, the FCPF has to provide effective ways of dispute resolution for financial consumers in the event of any disagreements with financial institutions in Zimbabwe.[25] The FCPF further intends to enable the development and implementation of financial literacy programmes that target financially excluded groups such as youths and women.[26]

Furthermore, Empower Bank was established to promote financial literacy by educating youths to open bank accounts to better manage and save their money.[27] Empower Bank is a microfinance institution that was established by the government of Zimbabwe in 2018.[28] Empower Bank seeks to assist in curbing financial exclusion through the provision of microfinance.[29] In this regard, Empower Bank has a specific focus on serving the poor and marginalised financial consumers.[30] Another objective of Empower Bank is to ensure that the youths in Zimbabwe are assisted to access formal financial products.[31] In this regard, Empower Bank is regulated by the RBZ as a deposit-taking institution.[32]

In addition, Empower Bank assists the poor and marginalised people in Zimbabwe when seeking microfinance assistance. This way, Empower Bank protects vulnerable and financially illiterate people against unscrupulous financial institutions.[33] Moreover, Empower Bank promotes financial inclusion by advancing financial loans to the youth and poor people without imposing strict and arbitrary requirements for collateral security.[34] Empower Bank also promotes financial inclusion for the poor in Zimbabwe by providing loans at relatively low interest rates.[35]

Additionally, the Registrar of microfinance banks (the Registrar) in Zimbabwe is responsible for determining or establishing the minimum capitalisation requirements and liquidity thresholds for banks.[36] Consumer protection is an integral component of meaningful financial inclusion initiatives. The Registrar protects financial consumers in Zimbabwe from abuse by disreputable banking institutions by imposing minimum capitalisation requirements and liquidity thresholds for banks. This is important because some banks may operate without the capacity to honour depositors' requests to withdraw their money on demand. When financial consumers fail to access their money on demand, they may not trust banking institutions.[37] Ultimately this may lead to voluntary financial exclusion. In this regard, the Registrar plays a pivotal role in protecting depositors' money by establishing the minimum capitalisation requirements and liquidity thresholds for banks.

Another way by which the Registrar protects financial consumers in Zimbabwe is by supervising the activities of microfinance banks.[38] This is important since most poor people and low-income earners have limited knowledge of the available financial products or services. Through the Registrar, microfinance institutions in Zimbabwe are obliged to provide fair products and services to their clients.[39] Additionally, poor and marginalised groups often fall into unfair loan repayment terms because of ignorance, desperation and lack of bargaining latitude against financial institutions.[40] Consequently, in the absence of regulation and supervision of microfinance activities by the Registrar, some financially illiterate people may be taken advantage of by unscrupulous microfinance institutions.

Moreover, the Banking Act[41] was amended through the Banking Amendment Act of 2015 to enhance financial consumer protection in Zimbabwe. Accordingly, the Banking Act mandates that all banks should disclose to their customers the terms and conditions under which the bank accepts deposits and provides loans.[42] However, more should be done by banks to promote financial inclusion to accommodate poor and financially excluded people. Apart from mere disclosure of their terms and conditions to the customer, banks could be mandated by the legislature in Zimbabwe to provide special concessionary lending rates to the poor.[43] In this regard, concessionary borrowing terms refer to the securing of credit on more favourable repayment conditions than which the borrower could ordinarily secure on the open marketplace.[44]

Concessionary borrowing terms could therefore benefit the poor and financially excluded people by encouraging them to save money rather than merely utilising bank services to perform day-to-day financial transactions. Thus, as a consumer protection measure, concessionary terms could also provide for debt restructuring options where consumers struggle to abide by the contractual obligations due to financial strain.[45] In this regard, the authors suggest that statutory amendments could be made to the Banking Act to allow for formal debt rehabilitation intervention processes to be pursued before a customer could be penalised for defaulting on their contractual obligations. A formal debt rehabilitation intervention process therefore could promote the financial inclusion of poor consumers who may genuinely face financial challenges to maintain their contractual obligations with financial institutions.

13.3.2 Financial innovation

Digital financial inclusion is a sub-category of financial inclusion and it refers to the ability of the majority of people to access formal financial services through electronic means.[46] Therefore, digital financial inclusion involves digital technologies and the widespread use of mobile phones to serve the financially excluded population with formal financial services in a sustainable and affordable manner.[47] Financial innovation and technological advancements have enabled more financial and banking institutions to use digital platforms such as internet banking and mobile money to promote financial inclusion in Zimbabwe.[48] Through innovative digital financial services, more Zimbabweans have been able to access affordable financial services such as mobile money.[49] While banks and financial institutions have harnessed technological innovations to offer digital financial services, most of these services are only accessible to clients with active bank accounts. Therefore, the poor or marginalised groups in Zimbabwe who cannot open bank accounts due to a lack of relevant identity documents are excluded from these digital financial services.[50] Nonetheless, mobile network operators (MNOs)[51] have also harnessed technological innovation to provide electronic payment platforms such as mobile money facilities. These electronic payment platforms such as Ecocash, One Wallet and TeleCash enable their subscribers to pay bills and save money without the need for a bank account.[52] At present, MNOs namely Econet, Telecel and Netone, which provide mobile money services in Zimbabwe, are regulated by the Postal and Telecommunications Act.[53] However, the Postal and Telecommunications Act does not regulate digital financial services such as mobile money. The RBZ is the default regulator of the financial services including mobile money by virtue of its obligation to oversee the payments system in Zimbabwe.[54] However, the RBZ does not regulate MNOs. Currently, there is no law in Zimbabwe that adequately regulates the provision of digital financial services by MNOs. Thus, this vacuum in the regulation of digital financial services by MNOs could result in inadequate protection of financial consumers when mobile money users seek recourse in the event of a dispute.[55]

The introduction of mobile money services by MNOs in Zimbabwe has reduced the number of people who are financially excluded.[56] By leveraging high mobile telephone subscribers, mobile money platforms have promoted financial inclusion in Zimbabwe.[57] However, the ability to conduct financial transactions is only a single element of financial inclusion. Full financial inclusion encompasses access to various other financial services such as credit, savings and insurance.[58] Attaining full financial inclusion is gradual and partial achievements in attaining financial inclusion should not be misunderstood as attaining total financial inclusion.[59]

Consequently, there is a need for the introduction of other financial services by financial institutions that could be implemented through digital financial services such as mobile money in Zimbabwe.[60] Additionally, there are currently no specific laws in Zimbabwe to regulate digital financial innovations such as mobile money apart from guidelines that are issued by the RBZ in terms of the Banking Act.[61] It is pertinent that the legislature enacts legislation to regulate mobile money in a manner that appropriately balances the need to promote financial innovation and the provision of non-exploitative financial products to the poor.[62]

13.3.3 Financial infrastructure

Financial infrastructure refers to the systems and electronic platforms through which the participants in Zimbabwe's economic activities or, in simple terms, role-players such as the government, financial institutions and people negotiate and conduct financial transactions.[63] Failure to access formal financial products and services due to poor infrastructure networks by financial services providers such as banks could increase financial exclusion in Zimbabwe.[64] The poor financial infrastructure in Zimbabwe has impeded the provision of financial services and products, thereby negatively affecting national financial inclusion efforts. The National Payment Systems Act[65] was enacted to regulate and supervise systems that pertain to the settlement of customer obligations and the clearing of payments between banking institutions in Zimbabwe.[66] In this regard, the RBZ is empowered by the NPS Act to regulate mobile money service providers since they provide a financial service to the public.[67] Accordingly, the NPS Act facilitates the settlement of client transactions between banking institutions. For instance, automated teller machines (ATMs) increase access to financial services by allowing clients of all banks to use shared infrastructure and conduct interbank transactions as mandated by the NPS Act. Thus, the NPS Act assists in national financial inclusion efforts by promoting the use of shared infrastructure by financial institutions, which positively impacts the ability of the public to carry out their transactions.

Furthermore, the Government of Zimbabwe, through the RBZ, designated Zimswitch Technologies Private Limited Company (Zimswitch) to be the only electronic funds switching and clearinghouse in Zimbabwe.[68] This designation was made in terms of the NPS Act.[69] Zimswitch was established in 1994 as a privately owned company that originally focused on facilitating the connectivity of ATMs and point-of-sale (POS) machines between different banking institutions.[70] However, over the years, Zimswitch has since expanded its scope of operations to incorporate the provision of mobile phone transactions as part of its services.[71]

The services that are provided by Zimswitch are essential to the promotion of financial inclusion since it connects the majority of banks, financial institutions and retail companies in Zimbabwe through its electronic system.[72] Increased usage of Zimswitch services by more banks could lead to low transaction or processing costs. Lower transaction costs in turn could encourage financial inclusion because financial consumers usually avoid banks for fear of exorbitant bank charges. The designation of Zimswitch as the only clearing house for Zimbabwe could be attributed to the government's desire to create an interoperable clearing system for payments in order to lower transaction costs which assists to improve financial inclusion.

Additionally, the RBZ also manages and supervises its payments settlement system called the Zimbabwe Electronic Transfer and Settlement System (ZETSS) or Real-Time Gross Settlement System (RTGS).[73] The ZETSS/RTGS was launched as part of efforts to curb financial exclusion arising out of a hyperinflationary economy in Zimbabwe at the time.[74] As highlighted previously, voluntary financial exclusion also exists when financial consumers exclude themselves from some financial services to avoid financial losses that could be incurred due to market or government failure.[75] In this regard, the ZETSS/RTGS is a government initiative that seeks to promote financial inclusion by reducing the liquidity challenges of processing high-value payments due to a hyperinflationary economy in Zimbabwe.[76]

In 2017, the RBZ noted that the ZETSS/RTGS constituted the largest proportion of payment settlement methods used in Zimbabwe.[77] Therefore, the ZETSS/RTGS payment method helped curb voluntary financial exclusion of financial consumers who may have feared that they could fail to access their money from banks given the volatile nature of Zimbabwe's economy. In this regard, the ZETSS/RTGS functions as an electronic interbank payment settlement system that allows banks to transfer funds to other banks through the use of settlement accounts maintained by the RBZ.[78] The ZETSS/RTGS is designed to handle payments of high values. The RBZ is therefore responsible for supervising the infrastructure as well as setting the rules that regulate participation in the ZETSS/RTGS by all financial institutions in Zimbabwe.[79]

Accordingly, the Zimswitch and ZETSS/RTGS payment settlement systems are notable financial inclusion efforts that enable financial consumers in Zimbabwe to transact at low costs. However, while the ZETSS/RTGS payment settlement systems are valuable, they merely partially solve the problem of financial exclusion because for one to enjoy these services, a bank account is needed. This is a huge drawback to financial inclusion efforts since a significant proportion of Zimbabwe's population is unbanked. Most financial consumers lack the relevant documents to open a bank account and cannot afford the high maintenance costs.

13.3.4 Microfinance

Women comprise a significant proportion of Zimbabwe's population.[80] However, a large number of women in Zimbabwe are financially excluded due to a myriad of factors, which include stringent bank account opening requirements, prohibitive costs of accessing and maintaining bank accounts, discriminatory religious beliefs and low incomes.[81] It is important to note that there is a positive relationship between access to financial products and services by women and increased economic growth in Zimbabwe.[82] This is because women generally invest their money in the education, health care and welfare of their children and families.[83] Through these socio-economic investments, women's economic activities contribute to the long-term development of the economy.[84] In order to realise the potential of economic growth that lies in the financial inclusion of women, the government of Zimbabwe has undertaken several initiatives to ensure that women are not financially excluded.

In this regard, the Zimbabwe Women's Bank was established by the Ministry of Women's Affairs, Gender and Community Development in 2017 in terms of the Microfinance Act.[85] The Women's Bank commenced its operations in June 2018 to target women as its core client base. However, the Women's Bank does not exclusively serve female clients only. It is a microfinance institution that caters for all poor and low-income earners in Zimbabwe.[86] Nevertheless, the Women's Bank is different from other microfinance institutions in that it also acts as a deposit-taking institution. Accordingly, as the deposits received by the Women's Bank increase, it is in turn able to offer more loans to other applicants thereby growing its client base.[87] In this way, the Women's Bank is able to expand its reach to women in a sustainable manner and promote financial exclusion among women in Zimbabwe.

The establishment of the Women's Bank is integral for the advancement of financial inclusion as women face several challenges to obtain loans because of a lack of acceptable collateral security like immovable property.[88] Traditional property rights in Zimbabwe disadvantage women from advancing security for loans on their behalf.[89] Traditional property rights are usually vested in men, especially in the rural areas of Zimbabwe.[90] Accordingly, women often lack collateral security since immovable property is usually owned by men.[91] Collateral security is a prerequisite for most financial institutions when applying for credit. However, most marginalised and poor people do not have any form of collateral security against which they may secure loans from financial institutions. To curb financial exclusion that arises from lack of collateral security, the government of Zimbabwe through the RBZ is working towards establishing a security assets register. The envisaged security assets register will further financial inclusion efforts by the government of Zimbabwe by allowing the poor, low-income earners and small business owners to secure credit by using their movable assets as a form of collateral security against loans.[92]

Furthermore, the government of Zimbabwe has made efforts to ensure the financial inclusion of women by re-establishing the credit guarantee scheme in 2017.[93] The credit guarantee scheme allows marginalised groups in Zimbabwe, especially women, to access loans provided by the government without providing collateral security in the form of immovable property.[94] If successfully implemented, the credit guarantee scheme could curb financial exclusion resulting from a lack of acceptable security.[95] Accordingly, with greater financial inclusivity being targeted within the above-mentioned population groups, there could be increased access to financial services that promote economic growth and curb poverty in Zimbabwe.[96]

13.4 Selected legislation affecting financial inclusion in Zimbabwe

The success of the NFIS relied on the availability of legislation that promotes its aims and objectives. Accordingly, laws that promote financial inclusion in Zimbabwe should address the four thematic areas identified in the NFIS.[97] For instance, legislation such as the BUP Act that promotes the use of formal financial institutions should also address the thematic areas of financial inclusion presented in the NFIS. The four thematic areas discussed earlier also depend on a vibrant and efficient banking system. This is because banking is an integral element of financial inclusion that enables individuals to access several other financial services and products such as insurance and investment.[98] However, the use of financial institutions and banks depends on whether financial consumers trust the integrity of the banking system.[99] In the absence of public trust in financial institutions to safeguard depositors' money, financial consumers will avoid the services and products offered by banking institutions which leads to voluntary financial exclusion.[100] In this regard, a few selected pieces of legislation affecting financial inclusion in Zimbabwe are discussed below.

13.4.1 Bank Use Promotion Act

The Bank Use Promotion Act[101] was enacted to curb the informal financial market that grew because of hyperinflation in Zimbabwe. With the advent of hyperinflation in early 2000, the public avoided and limited the use of banks due to mistrust and fear over the safety of their money.[102] Through the BUP Act, the government of Zimbabwe sought to promote financial inclusion by ensuring that all business entities and entrepreneurs open business accounts and bank the proceeds of their business activities regularly and consistently.[103] However, it is argued that the BUP Act is disconnected from the real conditions under which most small and medium enterprises operate in Zimbabwe. Businesses and private individuals are hesitant to deposit their monies in banks mainly due to arbitrary withdrawal limits. Furthermore, the high interest rates and bank charges also discourage small business owners from using banks.[104] Accordingly, despite the efforts to encourage financial inclusion through the BUP Act, the use of banks by the majority of Zimbabweans remains low.[105] This low uptake of banking services could also be attributed to hyperinflation and inconsistent monetary policies which at one time resulted in many losing all their banked money.[106] This eroded public confidence in formal financial institutions.

Consequently, the majority of Zimbabweans avoided using banks and resorted to cash transactions.[107] Additionally, due to past experiences of losing their banked money, many financial consumers in Zimbabwe, especially informal traders, remain sceptical of opening and using bank accounts.[108] This could be because most informal traders run small businesses that are sources of their day-to-day survival and do not make significant profit margins that they cannot risk.[109] As a result, small business owners in Zimbabwe avoid using banks and as such, they cannot access other bank services that they could utilise to grow their businesses.

To a greater extent, the BUP Act's objective of promoting the use of banks in Zimbabwe[110] has not been achieved as small traders and the poor and marginalised have not changed their negative perception towards banking. Unfortunately, small traders and individuals in Zimbabwe continue to prefer to keep their money outside banks.[111] In this regard, the BUP Act could be amended to incentivise individuals to bank their money and allow them to open and maintain basic accounts that do not incur bank charges up to a certain account balance after which the bank can impose reasonable bank charges. In this way, the BUP Act could promote the financial inclusion of risk-averse small traders and individuals by using banking institutions in Zimbabwe.

13.4.2 Microfinance Act

The Microfinance Act was enacted in 2013 by the Zimbabwean legislature in response to the difficulties that small traders encountered in obtaining official banking services and products. Accordingly, the Microfinance Act sought to promote the financial inclusion of marginalised informal traders in accessing banking services.[112] Microfinance refers to the provision of financial products and services to persons surviving near the poverty datum line in Zimbabwe.[113] Microfinancing is primarily a government-driven initiative as banks view it as a threat to their profitability due to the low interest rates involved.[114] Formal financial institutions usually fail to cater for small traders' needs on the premise that they are unprofitable and of high risk to their business.[115]

According to the NFIS, microfinance is an important enabler of financial inclusion in Zimbabwe[116] because it assists the poor to access affordable loans that could be used to start income-generating projects.[117] As highlighted previously, most poor people struggle to access certain financial products and services due to their low and seasonal/irregular incomes.[118] Most banks in Zimbabwe require a constant source of income before one can open an account with them.

Furthermore, as a part of legislative efforts to protect depositors' money, the Microfinance Act prohibits any person from conducting a deposit-taking microfinance business without obtaining a valid licence from the RBZ.[119] This measure prevents unscrupulous persons from exploiting and defrauding financially illiterate people. Furthermore, this statutory measure is important because most marginalised persons may not understand whether or not a financial institution complies with its statutory obligations. In addition, an ordinary customer might not know whether a financial institution is required to have certain capitalisation thresholds to prevent the loss of depositors' funds. Consequently, the Microfinance Act promotes financial inclusion by encouraging responsible lending practices for the poor in Zimbabwe.

13.5 Concluding remarks

From the previous discussion, Zimbabwe has made notable efforts to promote financial inclusion among financially excluded groups of people such as the youth, women, the unbanked, low-income earners and the poor.[120] Legislative intervention to protect the marginalised and poor financial consumers in Zimbabwe has been done through statutes such as the Microfinance Act and the NPS Act.[121] However, more could still be done to promote financial inclusion in Zimbabwe. To that end, a few recommendations are proffered. First, it is recommended that the government of Zimbabwe introduces more financial literacy initiatives, especially for low-income earners, women and youths to make better financial decisions. This could promote financial inclusion in Zimbabwe as financial consumers become exposed to several products and services including savings and investment. Furthermore, it is important that the poor and marginalised are educated, particularly on unfair lending practices. This is because some unscrupulous money lenders impose unduly burdensome loan repayment terms. Second, it is further recommended that Zimbabwe's legislature enact legislation that adequately regulates digital financial services such as mobile money to balance the need to promote financial innovation and the provision of non-exploitative financial products to the poor. Third, it is also recommended that mobile money transactions be used in high-value transactions since the use of ZETSS/RTGS requires an active bank account.

Notes

1 A Singh 'Exploring Demand-Side Barriers to Credit Uptake and Financial Inclusion' (2021) 48(6) *International Journal of Social Economics* 898, 899; H Chitimira and M Ncube 'Legislative and Other Selected Challenges Affecting Financial Inclusion for the Poor and Low-Income Earners in South Africa' (2020) 64(3) *Journal of African Law* 337, 338; PK Ozili 'Social Inclusion and Financial Inclusion: International Evidence' (2020) 19(2) *International Journal of Development Issues* 169–171; PL Makoni 'From Financial Exclusion to Financial Inclusion through Microfinance: The Case of Rural Zimbabwe' (2014) 11(4) *Corporate Ownership & Control* 447, 448; SL Schwarcz and TL Leonhardt 'Scoping and Defining Financial Inclusion, Access to Credit, and Sustainable Finance' (2021) 84(1) *Law & Contemporary Problems* 1, 4; United Nations Conference on Trade and Development (UNCTAD) 'Financial Inclusion For Development: Better Access To Financial Services For Women, the Poor, And Migrant Work Report' (UNCTAD 2021) 7.

2 Makoni (note 1 above) 448; World Bank 'Global Financial Development Report: Financial Inclusion' (World Bank 2014) 16.

3 Schwarcz and Leonhardt (note 1 above) 1.

4 A Maune, E Matanda and J Mundonde 'Does Financial Inclusion Cause Economic Growth in Zimbabwe? An Empirical Investigation' (2020) 16(1) *Acta Universitatis Danubius Œconomica* 195–199; see related comments by S Chivasa and P Simbanegavi 'Financial Inclusion in Zimbabwe Post Hyper Inflationary Period: Barriers and Effects on Societal Livelihoods, A Qualitative Approach: A Case of Matebeleland North' (2016) 18(1) *Journal of Sustainable Development in Africa* 53–58.

5 Only 28% of the population in Zimbabwe have accounts with formal financial institutions. See United Nations Capital Development Fund (UNCDF) 'MAP Zimbabwe Financial Inclusion Refresh Report' (UNCDF 2020) 10; Chivasa and Simbanegavi (note 4 above) 57; Maune, Matanda and Mundonde (note 4 above) 199.

6 Chivasa and Simbanegavi (note 4 above) 64.

7 H Chitimira and E Torerai 'The Nexus between Mobile Money Regulation, Innovative Technology and the Promotion of Financial Inclusion in Zimbabwe' (2021) 24 *Potchefstroom Electronic Law Journal* 1 12.

8 The National Financial Inclusion Strategy was officially launched on 11 March 2016 by the Minister of Finance and Economic Development. See G Ngoma 'Financial Inclusion and its Determinants in Zimbabwe' (2019) 5(3) *International Journal for Innovative Research in Multidisciplinary Field* 78; see also related discussion by P Mader 'Contesting Financial Inclusion' (2018) 49(2) *Development & Change* 461–464.

9 World Bank 'Developing and Operationalizing a National Financial Inclusion Strategy Report' (World Bank 2018) 4.

10 S Abel, L Mutandwa and P Le Roux 'A Review of Determinants of Financial Inclusion' (2018) 8(3) *International Journal of Economics and Financial Issues* 1 1; World Bank 2018 (note 9 above) 4.

11 WG Bonga and N Mlambo 'Banks and Financial Literacy Enhancement in Zimbabwe' (2016) 7 (2) *IOSR Journal of Economics and Finance* 69 and 71.
12 World Bank 2018 (note 9 above) 1.
13 World Bank 2018 (note 9 above) 1.
14 Chitimira and Torerai (note 7 above) 12.
15 Reserve Bank of Zimbabwe (RBZ) 'Zimbabwe National Financial Inclusion Journey Report 2016–2020' (RBZ 2021) 22.
16 Maune, Matanda and Mundonde (note 4 above) 198; Reserve Bank of Zimbabwe (RBZ) 'RBZ Governor's Mid-Term Policy Statement' (RBZ 2016) 51; RBZ 2021 (note 15 above) 2.
17 Maune, Matanda and Mundonde (note 4 above) 198.
18 Chitimira and Ncube (note 1 above) 342; HM Treasury 'Financial Capability: The Government's Long-Term Approach' HM Treasury Report (2007) https://dera.ioe.ac.uk/7551/1/fincap_150107.pdf, accessed on 6 August 2021.
19 A Grohmann, and L Menkhoff 'Financial Literacy Promotes Financial Inclusion in Both Poor and Rich Countries' (2017) 7(41) *DIW Economic Bulletin* 399, 403 and 405; RBZ 2021 (note 15 above) 32.
20 HM Treasury 'Financial Capability: The Government's Long-Term Approach' HM Treasury Report (2007) https://dera.ioe.ac.uk/7551/1/fincap_150107.pdf, accessed on 6 August 2021.
21 Reserve Bank of Zimbabwe (RBZ) 'Financial Consumer Protection Framework 1-2017/BSD' (RBZ 2017) 4.
22 RBZ 2017 (note 21 above) 4; see related discussion by JD Conroy, JC Parreñas and W Manupipatpong *Promoting Financial Inclusion through Innovative Policies* (Asian Development Bank Institute 2009) 42.
23 RBZ 2021 (note 15 above) 18; see related discussion by Conroy, Parreñas and Manupipatpong (note 22 above) 42.
24 RBZ 2021 (note 15 above) 18; see related discussion by Conroy, Parreñas and Manupipatpong (note 22 above) 42.
25 RBZ 2021 (note 15 above) 18.
26 RBZ 2021 (note 15 above) 11.
27 See related discussion in RBZ 2021 (note 15 above) 24.
28 B Nyagadza 'Conceptual Model for Financial Inclusion Development through Agency Banking in Competitive Markets' (2019) 49(2) *Africanus* 1, 11.
29 Nyagadza (note 28 above) 11.
30 Ibid.
31 Nyagadza (note 28 above) 11; M Oosterom and S Gukurume 'Managing the Born-Free Generation: Zimbabwe's Strategies for Dealing with the Youth' (2019) 2 CMI Working Paper 2, 8 and 17.
32 See ss 4 and 36 of the Microfinance Act [Chapter 24:29] 3 of 2013 as amended (Microfinance Act).
33 Ibid.
34 Oosterom and Gukurume (note 31 above) 17.
35 Oosterom and Gukurume (note 31 above) 17.
36 See s 4 of the Microfinance Act.
37 B Ngwenya, T Pelser and T Chivaura 'Perceptions of Post-Multicurrency Regime Financial Inclusion Confidence Challenges in Zimbabwe' (2018) 21(1) *South African Journal of Economic and Management Sciences* 1, 4; K Bannigol and SG Hundekar 'Strategic Role of Governments in Financial Inclusion: A Worldwide Diagnosis' (2018) 9(11) *CLEAR International Journal of Research in Commerce & Management* 12 13; M Simatele and E Mbedzi 'Consumer Payment Choices, Costs, and Risks: Evidence from Zimbabwe' (2021) 9(1) *Cogent Economics & Finance* 1, 6.

38 See s 4 of the Microfinance Act; see related comments by L Mbira and J Tapera 'Key Success Drivers for Microfinance Institutions in Zimbabwe: Developing Core Competences for Financial Inclusion' (2016) 7(3) *International Journal of Business and Social Science* 128, 129.
39 See ss 4 and 6(3) of the Microfinance Act.
40 S Mishi and F Kapingura 'Women's Access to Microfinance and Poverty Alleviation in Zimbabwe: Case Study of Chinhoyi Town' (2012) 6(29) *African Journal of Business Management* 8667–8669.
41 See s 28D of the Banking Act [Chapter 24:20] Act 9 of 1999 as amended.
42 See s 18 of the Banking Amendment Act 12 of 2015.
43 See related discussion by Mbira and Tapera (note 38 above) 132.
44 K Sierra-Escalante, A Karlin, ML Lauridsen 'Blended Concessional Finance: Governance Matters for Impact' International Finance Corporation EM Compass Note No. 66 March 2019 2; L Hlanze, Z Stephenson, A Deuchert *Promoting Women's Financial Inclusion: A Toolkit* (United Kingdom Department for International Development 2012) 70.
45 Hlanze, Stephenson and Deuchert (note 44 above) 70.
46 DW Arner, RP Buckley, DA Zetzsche and R Veidt 'Sustainability, FinTech and Financial Inclusion' (2020) 21(1) *European Business Organization Law Review* 7, 9.
47 Arner, Buckley, Zetzsche and Robin (note 46 above) 10.
48 A Demirgüç-Kunt and L Klapper 'Financial Inclusion in Africa: A Snapshot' in T Triki and I Faye (eds) *Financial Inclusion in Africa* (African Development Bank 2013) 44; see related discussion by Conroy, Parreñas and Manupipatpong (note 22 above) 20; Financial Sector Deepening Africa (FSDA) 'Zimbabwe Fintech Ecosystem Study Report' (FSDA 2020) 7; L De Koker and N Jentzsch 'Financial Inclusion and Financial Integrity: Aligned Incentives?' (2013) 44(C) *World Development* 267, 268.
49 JDG Nhavira 'Whither Financial Inclusion: A Holistic Approach' (2015) 6(1) *Journal of Strategic Studies* 79, 83; see related discussion by De Koker and Jentzsch (note 48 above) 268; G Robb, I Tausha and T Vilakazi 'Competition and Regulation in Zimbabwe's Emerging Mobile Payments Markets' in J Klaaren, S Roberts and I Valodia (eds) *Competition Law and Economic Regulation: Addressing Market Power in Southern Africa* (Wits University Press 2017) 215.
50 A Bara 'Mobile Money for Financial Inclusion: Policy and Regulatory Perspective in Zimbabwe' (2013) 5(5) *African Journal of Science, Technology, Innovation and Development* 345, 346; E Dumbu 'Banking the Unbanked: Perceptions of the International Cross Border Women Entrepreneurs in Beitbridge, Zimbabwe' (2018) 18(1) *London Journal of Research in Management and Business* 23–25.
51 These mobile money transfer platforms are Ecocash, One Wallet and TeleCash which are owned by Econet, Netone and Telecel respectively. See also Chivasa and Simbanegavi (note 4 above) 60.
52 Bara (note 50 above) 346.
53 See s 31 of the Telecommunications Act [Chapter 12:05] 4 of 2000 (as amended); also see Robb, Tausha and Vilakazi (note 49 above) 216.
54 See s 6(1)(e) of the Reserve Bank of Zimbabwe Act [Chapter 22:15] 5 of 1999 (as amended) (RBZ Act); Robb, Tausha and Vilakazi (note 49 above) 217 and 219.
55 World Bank 'Zimbabwe Diagnostic Review of Consumer Protection and Financial Literacy Report: Key Findings and Recommendations' (World Bank 2015) 13.
56 Ibid; see related discussion by Arner, Buckley, Zetzsche and Robin (note 46 above) 10.
57 Ibid.
58 See related comments by Chivasa and Simbanegavi (note 4 above) 60.
59 De Koker and Jentzsch (note 48 above) 268; Grohmann and Menkhoff (note 19 above) 401; T Arun and R Kamath 'Financial Inclusion: Policies and Practices' (2015) 27(4) *IIMB Management Review* 267, 270, 271.

60 Robb, Tausha and Vilakazi (note 49 above) 216; Bara (note 50 above) 346.

61 Bara (note 50 above) 349.

62 Chivasa and Simbanegavi (note 4 above) 61.

63 B Bossone, S Mahajan and F Zahir 'Financial Infrastructure, Group Interests, and Capital Accumulation: Theory, Evidence, and Policy' (2003) IMF Working Paper No. 03/24 3.

64 RBZ 2021 (note 15 above) 11; N Marime and L Chakazamba 'Urban Financial Exclusion in Zimbabwe: An Exploratory Study' (2016) 7(7) *Research Journal of Finance and Accounting* 1, 2.

65 See s 7 of the National Payment Systems Act [Chapter 24:23] 21 of 2001 as amended (NPS Act).

66 Se s 7 and 10 of the NPS Act. According to the NPS Act, the term 'financial institution' means a banking institution that is duly registered in terms of the Banking Act [Chapter 24:20] 9 of 1999 as amended as well as any other institution which lawfully engages in banking activities identified in the Banking Act [Chapter 24:20] 9 of 1999.

67 Bara (note 50 above) 347.

68 See s 3 of the NPS Act; Statutory Instrument 80 of 2020: Banking (Money Transmission, Mobile Banking and Mobile Money Interoperability) Regulations. Switching is understood as the facilitation of an electronic retail payment settlement system between banking institutions.

69 See s 3 of the NPS Act.

70 FinMark Trust 'Mapping the Retail Payment Services Landscape Zimbabwe Report 2012' (FinMark Trust 2012) 15.

71 Robb, Tausha and Vilakazi (note 49 above) 219; FinMark Trust (note 70 above) 15.

72 Robb, Tausha and Vilakazi (note 49 above) 219; FinMark Trust (note 70 above) 14, 15.

73 Simatele and Mbedzi (note 37 above) 6; FinMark Trust (note 70 above) 14.

74 Ibid.

75 See note 2 which references a discussion on the types of financial exclusion, including voluntary financial exclusion. Also see Bannigol and Hundekar (note 37 above) 13; Ngwenya, Pelser and Chivaura (note 37 above) 4.

76 Simatele and Mbedzi (note 37 above) 6; FinMark Trust (note 70 above) 14.

77 Reserve Bank of Zimbabwe (RBZ) 'Monetary Policy Statement' (RBZ 2018) 9.

78 Simatele and Mbedzi (note 37 above) 6; FinMark Trust (note 70 above) 14.

79 Simatele and Mbedzi (note 37 above) 6; FinMark Trust (note 70 above) 15.

80 Approximately 52% of the population in Zimbabwe are women. See NB Mazonde and T Carmichael 'The Influence of Culture on Female Entrepreneurs in Zimbabwe' (2016) 8(1) *Southern African Journal of Entrepreneurship and Small Business Management* 1, 2; Nyagadza (note 28 above) 11; RBZ 2021 (note 15 above) 27.

81 Chivasa and Simbanegavi (note 4 above) 59; RBZ 2021 (note 15 above) 11 and 27.

82 A Demirgüç-Kunt, L Klapper and D Singer 'Financial Inclusion and Legal Discrimination Against Women: Evidence from Developing Countries' World Bank Policy Research Working Paper 6416 2–3; S Hendriks 'The Role of Financial Inclusion in Driving Women's Economic Empowerment' (2019) 29(8) *Development in Practice* 1029 1030; C Pazarbasioglu 'Women and Finance: Unlocking New Sources of Economic Growth' Voices: Perspectives on development, World Bank Blogs World Bank (2017) https://blogs.worldbank.org/voices/women-and-finance-unlocking-new-sources-economic-growth?__cf_chl_jschl_tk__=pmd_d0f2275cbdbb1cefe29da6aeaa1f3bbb75259aae-1628282409-0-gqNtZGzNAiKjcnBszQu6, accessed on 6 August 2021; see also Reserve Bank of Zimbabwe (RBZ) 'Women Financial Inclusion' (2019) https://www.rbz.co.zw/documents/bank_sup/financial-inclusion-women.pdf, accessed on 7 July 2021.

83 Hendriks (note 82 above) 1030 and 1034; Pazarbasioglu (note 82 above).

84 Hendriks (note 82 above) 1030 and 1034; Pazarbasioglu (note 82 above).

85 The Zimbabwe Women's Microfinance Bank was registered as a private company on 10 January 2017, with company registration number 134/2017 under the name of Zimbabwe Women's Bank (Private) Limited (Women's Bank).
86 See RBZ (Women Financial Inclusion) (note 82 above).
87 Alliance for Financial Inclusion 'Gender, Women's Economic Empowerment and Financial Inclusion in Zimbabwe' Alliance for Financial Inclusion (2018) https://www.afi-global.org/wp-content/uploads/2019/10/AFI_BTG_Zim_CS19_AW_digital.pdf, accessed on 7 July 2021.
88 RBZ 2021 (note 15 above) 28; Makoni (note 1 above) 451; see related discussion by Demirgüç-Kunt, Klapper and Singer (note 82 above) 7.
89 Makoni (note 1 above) 451; see related discussion by Demirgüç-Kunt, Klapper and Singer (note 82 above) 7.
90 Ibid.
91 Makoni (note 1 above) 451; see related discussion by Demirgüç-Kunt, Klapper and Singer (note 82 above) 7.
92 RBZ 2021 (note 15 above) 18.
93 Established in terms of s 20 of the Public Debt Management Act [Chapter 22:21] 7 of 2014; RBZ 2021 (note 15 above) 20.
94 RBZ 2021 (note 15 above) 20.
95 Ibid.
96 RBZ 2021 (note 15 above) 20. See related discussion on the relationship between financial inclusion and economic growth by De Koker and Jentzsch (note 48 above) 267.
97 RBZ 2021 (note 15 above) 17.
98 P Nandru, A Byram and S Rentala 'Determinants of Financial Inclusion: Evidence from Account Ownership and Use of Banking Services' (2016) 4(2) *International Journal of Entrepreneurship and Development Studies* 141, 142.
99 CJ Cowton 'Integrity, Responsibility and Affinity: Three Aspects of Ethics in Banking' (2002) 11(4) *Business Ethics: A European Review* 393 394, 395.
100 Cowton (note 99 above) 394, 395.
101 See s 10 of the Bank Use Promotion Act [Chapter 24:24] 2 of 2004 as amended (BUP Act).
102 See ss 5, 10, 11, 12 and 17 of the BUP Act; RBZ 2021 (note 15 above) 58.
103 See s 11 of the BUP Act.
104 Ngwenya, Pelser and Chivaura (note 37 above) 2.
105 Nhavira (note 49 above) 82; see related discussion by Ngwenya, Pelser and Chivaura (note 37 above) 4.
106 Nhavira (note 49 above) 82; see related discussion by Ngwenya, Pelser and Chivaura (note 37 above) 4; Ngwenya, Pelser and Chivaura (note 37 above) 4.
107 Nhavira (note 49 above) 82; see also Ngwenya, Pelser and Chivaura (note 37 above) 1.
108 Nhavira (note 49 above) 82; see also Ngwenya, Pelser and Chivaura (note 37 above) 1.
109 S Khavul 'Microfinance: Creating Opportunities for the Poor?' (2010) 24(3) *Academy of Management Perspectives* 58 61.
110 See ss 10 and 11 of the BUP Act.
111 Nhavira (note 49 above) 82; see also Ngwenya, Pelser and Chivaura (note 37 above) 1.
112 See ss 7, 8 and 10 of the Microfinance Act.
113 J Ghosh 'Microfinance and the Challenge of Financial Inclusion for Development' (2013) 37(6) *Cambridge Journal of Economics* 1203, 1217, 1218; Nhavira (note 49 above) 80.
114 Ghosh (note 113 above) 1217, 1218; Nhavira (note 49 above) 80; L Bangoura 'Microfinance as an Approach to Development in Low Income Countries' (2012) 35(4) *The Bangladesh Development Studies* 87, 91, 92.
115 According to Zimbabwe National Statistics Agency 'Poverty Datum Lines – May 2021' (2021) https://www.zimstat.co.zw/wp-content/uploads/publications/Income/Prices/2021/PDL/PDL_05_2021.pdf, accessed on 20 July 2021, the poverty datum

line was approximately 5770.64 Zimbabwean dollars or US$18 for May 2021. The poverty datum line is a calculation employed to measure standards of living and is used as an estimate of the income needed by a person to attain a defined minimum level of health and feeding. See also E Batson 'The Poverty Datum Line in Cape Town in 1938-39 and in 1949' (1950) 46(7) *South African Journal of Science* 212; Ghosh (note 113 above) 1217.

116 RBZ 2021 (note 15 above) 20.

117 G20 Financial Inclusion Experts Group, 'Innovative Financial Inclusion' (2010) Access through Innovation Sub-Group of the G20 Financial Inclusion Experts Group Report 6.

118 M Otero 'Bringing Development Back into Microfinance' (1999) 1(1) *Journal of Microfinance* 8 8; Khavul (note 109 above) 58; N Hermes and R Lensink 'Microfinance: Its Impact, Outreach and Sustainability' (2011) 39(6) *World Development* 875.

119 See s 7 of the Microfinance Act.

120 RBZ 2021 (note 15 above) 20.

121 Ghosh (note 113 above) 1215.

Bibliography

S Abel, L Mutandwa & P Le Roux 'A review of determinants of financial inclusion' (2018) 8(3) *International Journal of Economics and Financial Issues* 1 at 8.

Alliance for Financial Inclusion 'Gender, women's economic empowerment and financial inclusion in Zimbabwe' (2018), available at https://www.afi-global.org/wp-content/uploads/2019/10/AFI_BTG_Zim_CS19_AW_digital.pdf, accessed on 7 July 2021.

D W Arner, R P Buckley, D A Zetzsche & R Veidt 'Sustainability, FinTech and financial inclusion' (2020) 21(1) *European Business Organization Law Review* 7 at 35.

T Arun & R Kamath 'Financial inclusion: Policies and practices' (2015) 27(4) *IIMB Management Review* 267 at 287.

L Bangoura 'Microfinance as an approach to development in low-income countries' (2012) 35(4) *The Bangladesh Development Studies* 87 at 111.

Banking Act [Chapter 24:20] 9 of 1999.

Banking Amendment Act 12 of 2015.

Bank Use Promotion Act [Chapter 24:24] 2 of 2004.

K Bannigol & S G Hundekar 'Strategic role of governments in financial inclusion: A worldwide diagnosis' (2018) 9(11) *CLEAR International Journal of Research in Commerce & Management* 12 at 16.

A Bara 'Mobile money for financial inclusion: Policy and regulatory perspective in Zimbabwe' (2013) 5(5) *African Journal of Science, Technology, Innovation and Development* 345 at 354.

E Batson 'The poverty datum line in Cape Town in 1938–39 and in 1949' (1950) 46(7) *South African Journal of Science* 212 at 216.

W G Bonga & N Mlambo 'Banks and financial literacy enhancement in Zimbabwe' (2016) 7 (2) *IOSR Journal of Economics and Finance* 69 at 74.

B Bossone, S Mahajan & F Zahir *Financial Infrastructure, Group Interests, and Capital Accumulation: Theory, Evidence, and Policy* (IMF working paper no. 03/24, 2003) 1 at 34.

H Chitimira & M Ncube 'Legislative and other selected challenges affecting financial inclusion for the poor and low-income earners in South Africa' (2020) 64 *Journal of African Law* 337 at 355.

S Chivasa & P Simbanegavi 'Financial inclusion in Zimbabwe post hyper inflationary period: Barriers and effects on societal livelihoods, a qualitative approach: A case of Matebeleland North' (2016) 18(1) *Journal of Sustainable Development in Africa* 53 at 72.

J D Conroy, J C Parreñas & W Manupipatpong *Promoting Financial Inclusion Through Innovative Policies* (Asian Development Bank Institute, 2009).

C J Cowton 'Integrity, responsibility and affinity: Three aspects of ethics in banking' (2002) 11(4) *Business Ethics: A European Review* 393 at 400.

L De Koker & N Jentzsch 'Financial inclusion and financial integrity: Aligned incentives?' (2013) 44 *World Development* 267 at 280.

A Demirgüç-Kunt & L Klapper 'Financial inclusion in Africa: A snapshot' in T Triki & I Faye (eds) *Financial Inclusion in Africa* (African Development Bank, 2013).

A Demirgüç-Kunt, L Klapper & D Singer *Financial Inclusion and Legal Discrimination Against Women: Evidence from Developing Countries* (World Bank Policy research working paper 6416) 1 at 45.

E Dumbu 'Banking the unbanked: Perceptions of the international cross border women entrepreneurs in Beitbridge, Zimbabwe' (2018) 18(1) *London Journal of Research in Management and Business* 23 at 32.

Financial Sector Deepening Africa (FSDA) 'Zimbabwe Fintech ecosystem study report' (FSDA 2020) 1 at 45.

FinMark Trust 'Mapping the retail payment services landscape Zimbabwe report 2012' (FinMark Trust 2012) 1 at 65.

J Ghosh 'Microfinance and the challenge of financial inclusion for development' (2013) 37(6) *Cambridge Journal of Economics* 1203 at 1219.

A Grohmann & L Menkhoff 'Financial literacy promotes financial inclusion in both poor and rich countries' (2017) 7(41) *DIW Economic Bulletin* 399 at 407.

G20 Financial Inclusion Experts Group 'Innovative financial inclusion' (2010) Access through Innovation Sub-Group of the G20 Financial Inclusion Experts Group Report 1-25.

S Hendriks 'The role of financial inclusion in driving women's economic empowerment' (2019) 29(8) *Development in Practice* 1029 at 1038.

N Hermes & R Lensink 'Microfinance: Its impact, outreach, and sustainability' (2011) 39(6) *World Development* 875 at 881.

L Hlanze, Z Stephenson & A Deuchert *Promoting Women's Financial Inclusion: A Toolkit* (Department for International Development, 2012) 70.

HM Treasury 'Financial capability: The government's long-term approach' *HM Treasury Report* (2007), available at https://dera.ioe.ac.uk/7551/1/fincap_150107.pdf, accessed on 6 August 2021.

S Khavul 'Microfinance: Creating opportunities for the poor?' (2010) 24(3) *Academy of Management Perspectives* 58 at 72.

P Mader 'Contesting financial inclusion' (2018) 49(2) *Development & Change* 461 at 483.

P L Makoni 'From financial exclusion to financial inclusion through microfinance: The case of rural Zimbabwe' (2014) 11(4) *Corporate Ownership & Control* 447 at 455.

N Marime & L Chakazamba 'Urban financial exclusion in Zimbabwe: An exploratory study' (2016) 7(7) *Research Journal of Finance and Accounting* 1 at 6.

A Maune, E Matanda & J Mundonde 'Does financial inclusion cause economic growth in Zimbabwe? An empirical investigation' (2020) 16(1) *Acta Universitatis Danubius Œconomica* 195 at 215.

N B Mazonde & T Carmichael 'The influence of culture on female entrepreneurs in Zimbabwe' (2016) 8(1) *Southern African Journal of Entrepreneurship and Small Business Management* 1 at 10.

L Mbira & J Tapera 'Key success drivers for microfinance institutions in Zimbabwe: Developing core competencies for financial inclusion' (2016) 7(3) *International Journal of Business and Social Science* 128 at 136.

Microfinance Act [Chapter 24:29] 3 of 2013.

S Mishi & F Kapingura 'Women's access to microfinance and poverty alleviation in Zimbabwe: Case study of Chinhoyi town' (2012) 6(29) *African Journal of Business Management* 8667 at 8676.

Moneylending and Rates of Interest Act [Chapter 14:14] 9 of 1930.

P Nandru, A Byram & S Rentala 'Determinants of financial inclusion: Evidence from account ownership and use of banking services' (2016) 4(2) *International Journal of Entrepreneurship and Development Studies* 141 at 155.

National Payment Systems Act [Chapter 24:23] 21 of 2001.

G Ngoma 'Financial inclusion and its determinants in Zimbabwe' (2019) 5(3) *International Journal for Innovative Research in Multidisciplinary Field* 78 at 87.

B Ngwenya, T Pelser & T Chivaura 'Perceptions of post-multicurrency regime financial inclusion confidence challenges in Zimbabwe' (2018) 21(1) *South African Journal of Economic and Management Sciences* 1 at 15.

J D G Nhavira 'Whither financial inclusion: A holistic approach' (2015) 6(1) *Journal of Strategic Studies* 79 at 91.

B Nyagadza 'Conceptual model for financial inclusion development through agency banking in competitive markets' (2019) 49(2) *Africanus* 1 at 22.

M Oosterom & S Gukurume *Managing the Born-Free Generation: Zimbabwe's Strategies for Dealing with the Youth* (2 CMI working paper 2, 2019) 1 at 26.

M Otero 'Bringing development back into microfinance' (1999) 1(1) *Journal of Microfinance* 8 at 19.

P K Ozili 'Social inclusion and financial inclusion: International evidence' (2020) 19(2) *International Journal of Development Issues* 169 at 186.

C Pazarbasioglu 'Women and finance: Unlocking new sources of economic growth' voices: Perspectives on development, World Bank Blogs World Bank' (2017), available at https://blogs.worldbank.org/voices/women-and-finance-unlocking-new-sources-economic-growth?__cf_chl_jschl_tk__=pmd_d0f2275cbdbb1cefe29da6aeaa1f3bbb75259aae-1628282409-0-gqNtZGzNAiKjcnBszQu6, accessed on 6 August 2021.

Public Debt Management Act [Chapter 22:21] 7 of 2014.

Reserve Bank of Zimbabwe (RBZ) 'Financial consumer protection framework 1–2017/BSD' (RBZ 2017) 1–37.

Reserve Bank of Zimbabwe (RBZ) 'Monetary policy statement' (RBZ 2018).

Reserve Bank of Zimbabwe (RBZ) 'RBZ governor's mid-term policy statement' (RBZ 2016) 1 at 56.

Reserve Bank of Zimbabwe (RBZ) 'Women financial inclusion' (2019), available at https://www.rbz.co.zw/documents/bank_sup/financial-inclusion-women.pdf, accessed on 7 July 2021.

Reserve Bank of Zimbabwe (RBZ) 'Zimbabwe national financial inclusion journey report 2016–2020' (RBZ 2021) 1 at 49.

G Robb, I Tausha & T Vilakazi 'Competition and regulation in Zimbabwe's emerging mobile payments markets' in J Klaaren, S Roberts & I Valodia (eds) *Competition*

Law and Economic Regulation: Addressing Market Power in Southern Africa (Wits University Press, 2017).

S L Schwarcz & T L Leonhardt 'Scoping and defining financial inclusion, access to credit, and sustainable finance' (2021) 84(1) *Law & Contemporary Problems* 1 at 15.

K Sierra-Escalante, A Karlin & M L Lauridsen 'Blended concessional finance: Governance matters for impact' International Finance Corporation EM Compass Note No. 66 March 2019 1 at 8.

M Simatele & E Mbedzi 'Consumer payment choices, costs, and risks: Evidence from Zimbabwe' (2021) 9(1) *Cogent Economics & Finance* 1 at 23.

A Singh 'Exploring demand-side barriers to credit uptake and financial inclusion' (2021) 48(6) *International Journal of Social Economics* 898 at 913.

Statutory Instrument 80 of 2020: Banking (Money Transmission, Mobile Banking and Mobile Money Interoperability) Regulation.

United Nations Capital Development Fund (UNCDF) 'MAP Zimbabwe financial inclusion refresh report' (UNCDF 2020) 10 at 100.

United Nations Conference on Trade and Development (UNCTAD) 'Financial inclusion for development: Better access to financial services for women, the poor, and migrant work report' (UNCTAD 2021) 1 at 45.

World Bank *Developing and Operationalizing a National Financial Inclusion Strategy Report 2018* (World Bank, 2018) 1 at 55.

World Bank *Global Financial Development Report: Financial Inclusion* (World Bank, 2014) 1 at 203.

World Bank *Zimbabwe Diagnostic Review of Consumer Protection and Financial Literacy Report: Key Findings and Recommendations* (World Bank, 2015) 1 at 58.

Zimbabwe National Statistics Agency 'Poverty datum lines - May 2021' (2021), available at https://www.zimstat.co.zw/wp-content/uploads/publications/Income/Prices/2021/PDL/PDL_05_2021.pdf, accessed on 20 July 2021.

14 Climate change and financial inclusion in Namibia

A contemporary legal perspective

Tapiwa V. Warikandwa, Eugene L. Libebe, Elize Shakalela, Lineekela Usebiu and Marvin R. Awarab

14.1 Introduction

Globally, an estimated 230 million people are adversely impacted by natural disasters brought on by climate change.[1] Developmentally underdeveloped nations, which have little potential for adaptation, are particularly threatened by droughts, flooding, pollution and other meteorological catastrophes. The poor and marginalised in those nations are most at risk because of the effects of climate change, which raises the cost of food, increases the risk of waterborne illness and extreme weather (especially in places with poor infrastructure and sanitation) and restricts farmers' ability to establish and maintain sustainable livelihoods. Extreme weather-related income shocks are difficult for the underprivileged to handle. This chapter will discuss the significance of financial inclusion in mitigating the effects of climate change in Namibia. It will place emphasis on the fact that as the effects of climate change become more severe, it is vital to assist the poor in adapting to these problems and empowering them to lessen their environmental impact. The chapter will explore ways in which financial services and products may address the threats that climate change poses to the poor in Namibia.

14.2 Climate change in Namibia

Namibia is placed 107th out of 182 nations on an index that considers both a nation's sensitivity to climate change (Namibia is ranked 122nd) and its readiness to adapt (Namibia is ranked 104th); Norway is at the top of the list and Chad is at the bottom.[2] Namibians are particularly vulnerable due to the semi-arid climate and heavy reliance on agriculture for rural livelihoods, as well as the fact that Namibia faces many of the same problems as other nations in the Global South. As humans and elephants fight for water and predators take more cattle, rates of human-wildlife conflict may also increase. Many of these weaknesses were exposed by the recent multi-year drought, and climate change estimates foretell an increase in the frequency of droughts in the future.

On the southwest coast of Africa, Namibia is a huge, sparsely populated nation with little yearly rainfall, even in a good year. The majority of the nation (85%) is classified as arid or semi-arid.[3] The spectacular Namib Desert, which stretches

DOI: 10.4324/9781003369400-14

down the continent's southern coast, the enormous Central Plateau and the semi-arid Kalahari savannah are all part of the rough scenery. The Kavango region in the north along the border with Angola offers a relatively small sliver of fertile soil and greenery, ideal for agriculture but also a vital, rare resource that needs careful management and conservation.[4] It receives an average rainfall of 550 mm to 600 mm per year in the Kavango East and Kavango West regions.[5]

This delicate balance is threatened by climate change. According to experts, Namibia's mean annual temperature will rise by 2.7°C during the next two decades, while yearly precipitation will drop by 7%.[6] According to climate predictions for Namibia, annual temperatures are quite likely to keep rising faster than they already are over the course of the next century, maybe by as much as 4°C.[7] Thus, the temperature projections for Namibia are worse than the global average. For mean annual precipitation, there is an indication that projections of a potential decline of 14% over the next century are much less certain.[8] Due to the altered rain patterns, this would result in longer and more frequent droughts, more heat waves and even more flooding. The Namibian government, civic society and the international community are attempting to lessen the effects on the environment and public health.

With one year of drought conditions reported in the 1980s, three in the 1990s, two in the 2000s and three in the 2010s, the frequency of droughts already looks to be rising.[9] The most recent of these occurred as a result of the nearly disastrous 2018–2019 rains, which caused severe drought conditions throughout most of Namibia (measured as a combination of rainfall, vegetation condition, surface temperature and soil moisture).[10] A third of Namibians, on average, experienced food shortages; between October 2018 and June 2019, 90,000 animals perished and the City of Windhoek announced a water crisis.[11] Although the frequency of droughts appears to be rising, Namibia's mean annual rainfall between 1901 and 2020 shows no noticeable trend.

Leading the charge is Namibia's foremost conservation NGO, the Namibia Nature Foundation (NNF), which encourages sustainable development and the preservation of natural resources by utilising a comprehensive, knowledge-sharing approach to enhance agricultural practices. The NNF and farmers collaborated with USAID's Resilient Waters Program, run by Chemonics, in late 2019, to explore solutions that increase crop output and yields while also strengthening farmers' resistance to future climate shocks. NNF created a programme to increase Kavango farmers' ability to use conservation agriculture in their lands. The programme evaluates local conditions and identifies ways that make use of the resources at hand using a systems approach. In order to achieve the Resilient Water Program's goal of creating more water-secure communities and ecosystems, a systems approach is essential. Government priorities, sustainable livelihoods, biodiversity and ecosystem health are dynamically linked by water policies and practices. As a result, strategies for managing water and conservation must be equally thorough and provide adaptive feedback to changing circumstances.

Farmers frequently congregate in public areas to fortify their relationships and talk about insightful observations on the weather, the market and support through government extension services – they exchange questions and ideas. Lead farmers receive continuing advice on communication strategies, training methods, pest control, post-harvest loss management training and efficient conservation agriculture implementation. Thanks to the dedication of the NNF and lead farmers, more farmers are implementing conservation agriculture, also known as CA, on their fields in the Kavango region.

Through the adoption and successful implementation of appropriate and effective climate change adaptation and mitigation measures in accordance with Namibia's National Development Goals and Vision 2030, Namibia has significantly reduced the vulnerability of its population and sectors to predicted climate change impacts.[12] Due to the fact that more than half of Namibia's population depends on natural resources and the environment for both food and income, the country is extremely vulnerable to the detrimental effects of climate change. The expected effects on Namibia's natural and human environments are probably severe.[13] Namibia must explore adaptation and mitigation strategies applicable to various sectors, the local situation and the goals outlined in Vision 2030 in order to appropriately confront climate change as a challenge and respond in a timely, effective and appropriate manner.[14]

A number of challenges pertaining to climate change are worth discussing in the context of Namibia. It is therefore imperative to discuss key aspects of Namibia's Climate Change Policy. Namibia's climate change policy acts as a legal framework for developing and implementing a strategy and action plan to address the challenges of climate change, even though Namibia has made significant progress towards achieving its national development goals despite the anticipated impacts of climate change.[15] Numerous sectors in Namibia will be impacted by the complicated effects of climate change. The effects of climate change will also vary significantly across the nation. Tackling Climate Change is a fundamental objective set out in the United Nations' Sustainable Development Goal 13.[16] All 16 of the other goals of the 2030 Agenda for Sustainable Development[17] are inextricably tied to it. The Paris Agreement was ratified by nations in order to combat climate change and keep the increase in global temperature to well below 2°C.

14.3 Sustainable water supply and/or access

Namibia's most valuable natural resource is water. It is projected that Namibia will soon experience total water scarcity.[18] Water availability is anticipated to be impacted by climate change effects such as greater rainfall unpredictability, rising temperatures, protracted and more severe droughts and increased evapotranspiration.[19] Climate change response methods should include water harvesting and capture during the rainy season as well as more effective water use by sectors, homes and individuals in order to ensure sustainable long-term access to water.[20] To encourage greater output per unit of water consumed, integrated water resources management is more crucial than ever.

14.4 The availability of sustainable resources and food

Climate change is expected to have a significant impact on Namibia's rainfall variability, shorten the rainy season, boost temperatures, enhance the capacity for evapo-transpiration and heighten sea level rises.[21] Predicted increases in aridity and droughts will have an impact on ecosystems, water supplies, forests, fisheries and agricultural production. The growing season, food availability and supply will all be impacted by these effects. Namibia's natural resource base and food security will suffer as a result of climate change.[22] The poor and vulnerable, in particular women and children, will be negatively impacted. The National Climate Change Policy places great significance on addressing climate change challenges that affect Namibia's sustainable resource base and food security.[23]

14.5 Human well-being and health

Sustainable development depends on encouraging well-being at all ages and ensuring healthy lives.[24] Covid-19, which has caused billions of people's lives to be turned upside down while spreading human agony around the world, has caused a global health crisis unlike any other.[25] As such, it is important for the Government of Namibia to:

> Ensure a healthy, food-secure, and breastfeeding nation, in which all preventable infectious and parasitic diseases are securely under control, and in which people enjoy a high standard of living, with access to high-quality education, health care, and other essential services, in an environment of sustainable population growth and development.[26]

Sustainable Development Goal 3 calls for nations' instant action towards ensuring "healthy lives and promoting the well-being for all at all ages".[27]

A further indication of the significance the Government of Namibia places on the health and well-being of Namibians is the inclusion of health-related concerns.[28] Climate change may make people more susceptible to some vector-borne illnesses like malaria as well as diseases like cholera that are transmitted by contaminated water, food or personal contact.[29] Additionally, the anticipated drop in drinking water supply and quality will have an impact on health. Poor sanitary conditions due to predicted floods in some areas, as well as malnutrition due to reduced crop yields and reduced livestock productivity, will increase illness and child mortality.[30] Therefore, health and well-being are an important sector that the national climate change policy addresses.

14.6 Fisheries and marine resources

Fishing and fish processing are significant contributors to the national economy.[31] Hake, horse mackerel, rock lobster and crab make up the majority of the catch.[32] Potential changes to the west coast ocean circulation pose a threat to Namibia's marine fishery.[33] The cool Benguela Current's nutrient-rich upwellings are essential to the fisheries. Any change in the upwelling's frequency, timing or distribution will have an impact on production and a big impact on the economy as a whole.[34] Over the northern Benguela area off the coast of Namibia, the sea surface temperature has already risen.[35] The recent decline in fish stocks may be caused by a number of environmental variables, including the warming trend.[36] Fishery and marine resource issues must consequently be included in the national policy.

The One Ocean Hub project, which aims to safeguard the environment for sustainable development and address problems related to the depletion of marine resources as a result of climate change, includes Namibia as a participant.[37] The role that the blue economy may play in promoting environmental protection, the protection of the rights of marginalised groups of people like the Topnaar and the small-scale fishers in the nation is being highlighted in this respect.[38] All of these marginalised groups could experience the severe consequences of climate change insofar as it results in the depletion of marine resources. The likelihood of hunger and poverty for these socially and economically disadvantaged people will limit their capacity to exercise their human rights.[39]

Furthermore, it is possible that the negative consequences of climate change on the marine ecosystem will also have a negative impact on the cultural rights and/or heritage[40] of Namibia's minority coastal populations. Therefore, it is important to protect fisheries and marine resources in light of climate change and its possibly negative consequences. Small-scale commercial and subsistence fishing in inland and coastal areas of least-developed countries is an essential source of income, livelihood and food security for hundreds of millions of people worldwide.[41] Coastal or inland fisheries are vital to Namibia's economy.[42] A significant number of people relying on subsistence fishing in Namibia's fishing industry are small-scale aquaculture (including mariculture) producers and artisanal fishermen.[43] Small-scale fisheries and mariculture face considerable problems due to climate change, which is also expected to have a substantial influence on the livelihoods of those who depend on these industries.[44] The distribution and quantity of marine resources are already being impacted by changes in ocean temperature and chemistry.[45] A considerable rise in the frequency and/or intensity of extreme weather events like storms and floods are also predicted by recent climate projections.

Since small-scale fisheries include many interactions with delicate and complex ecosystems[46] that are frequently already impacted by other stressors like overfishing or pollution, it is still unclear how much climate change will affect fisheries in the future in Namibia. International collaboration, especially through the One Ocean Hub project and the Benguela Current Commission, should therefore focus on assessing and managing risks to improve resilience and reduce poverty, inequality and food insecurity through the blue economy agenda. Solutions must be obtained to avert risks and economic shocks that could potentially be induced by climate change in Namibia.

14.7 Infrastructure

The infrastructure in Namibia, such as homes, buildings, roads, trains, dams, water pipelines, energy transmission, communication, sewerage and drainage systems, is likely to be impacted by the predicted effects of climate change.[47] The only deep-water port in Namibia, Walvis Bay, as well as the Lüderitz diamond and fishing harbour, may be submerged by rising sea levels.[48] Roads in Namibia's densely populated, flood-prone north central and north east regions frequently flood, destroying homes and businesses and limiting access to homesteads and facilities.[49] Infrastructure is more severely affected by climate change in areas with poorly planned and constructed towns and houses.[50] Despite being difficult to predict, the financial cost of climate change's effects on infrastructure damage, insurance claims and repairs and reconstructions is likely to be quite substantial. Therefore, a major issue that is included in the national climate change policy is infrastructure.[51]

14.8 Sustainable development and low-carbon energy

The SADC region has been suffering from a lack of power capacity since 2007, which raises the possibility of an impending energy crisis in southern Africa.[52] The energy crisis not only makes the enormous task of regional electrification more difficult, but it also has cross-sector effects because energy and economic development are intimately interwoven.[53] It is of the utmost importance to adapt to the effects of climate change on the energy industry given the impending, pervasive threat of such a crisis. Energy sector adaptation should ideally occur on both the supply and demand sides.

Through the use of renewable and energy-efficient production technologies, energy production adaptation strives to reduce reliance on non-renewable, unstable and ecologically hazardous resources and promote long-term energy security.[54] Energy demand adaptation, on the other hand, focuses on reducing energy consumption through the use of energy-efficient and renewable energy technology and equipment. Namibia's development route (low carbon versus high carbon) and climate change mitigation contribution will be greatly influenced by the energy policy it chooses. The National Climate Change Policy explores low-carbon development and sustainable energy.

14.9 Sustainable and equitable use of natural resources

The effective management of natural resources for the benefit of the entire human community is sustainable resource use. The basic goal of sustainable development is to meet the requirements of the present generation without jeopardising those of the future. The policy firmly backs the equitable and sustainable use of natural resources as called for by existing development, legal and policy tools, as well as the improvement of the enabling environment as needed. In recognition of Namibia's reliance on natural resources, this is done. Namibia passed the Nature

Conservation Act in 1996,[55] granting local communities that organised management entities known as conservancies authority over wildlife and tourism. This action enabled communities to profit from wildlife on shared land by collaborating with private businesses to develop a tourism industry.

14.10 Development based on human rights[56] and cultural heritage[57]

All people's fundamental rights are recognised and upheld by the Namibia Climate Policy, which also recognises that marginalised persons and groups – such as women, children and rural poor people in general – will be most negatively impacted by climate change.[58] Thus, the policy encourages the implementation of human rights-based development while pursuing initiatives to address climate change, always in accordance with national and international law.[59]

Additionally, coastal areas are under a great deal of stress as a result of the effects of climate change, pollution, real estate development and population growth.[60] They serve as excellent cultural crossroads and incubators for the emergence of new ocean-related values, beliefs and lifestyles. As a result, the 100-year coastal severe event is expected to affect all of the coastal historic sites in Sub-Saharan African nations,[61] including Namibia. Beach restocking, erecting groins and constructing breakwaters can all be utilised to protect coasts where it is technically and economically feasible to do so.[62] The natural biological and morphological equilibrium of the heritage site is known to be disturbed by "hard" conservation techniques; thus, they must take future sea level rise into account.[63]

Utilising hybrid defences that combine natural infrastructure, like rock sills combined with saltmarshes, seagrasses or restored mangroves, may be more advantageous.[64] Enhancing local and Indigenous governance, monitoring and evaluation as well as more broad land management practices like enlarged buffer zones can all help conserve heritage sites.[65] How Namibia addresses climate change is important for its cultural heritage. If greenhouse gas emissions are reduced from a high to a moderate pathway as part of climate change mitigation, the number of extremely vulnerable heritage sites can be reduced.[66]

14.11 Policy formulation

The Namibian government has developed a wide range of legal and policy instruments with regard to climate change. These include, among others, the National Drought Policy and Strategy,[67] the National Land Policy,[68] the Agriculture Policy,[69] a policy on desertification,[70] the Namibian Poverty Reduction Strategy and Action Plan[71] and the National Policy and Strategy for Malaria Control.[72] The majority of these sector-specific policies were created without giving climate change enough thought because it was not regarded at the time as a serious threat. But given that it is now recognised that some of these sectors will be impacted by climate change, this should be considered. For instance, the agriculture industry is likely to be badly impacted by climate change, thus the agriculture policy must take climate change into account in order to mitigate the effects of the shift. While some sector policies may address aspects of climate change, it is necessary to pinpoint climate change challenges that are shared by all sector policies to increase synergies, enable cost effectiveness and prevent effort duplication. In order to address climate change, new policies might also need to be created. The National Climate Change Policy must also provide periodic policy reviews.

14.11.1 The National Policy for Disaster Risk Management in Namibia

The National Policy for Disaster Risk Management in Namibia[73] acknowledges that various types, degrees of severity and sizes of disasters can occur in Namibia and are brought on by a variety of causes. Disasters cause environmental deterioration, the destruction of infrastructure and habitats, the extinction of wildlife and the loss of human lives.[74] The livelihoods of people, particularly the rural poor, are also in danger because of the growing vulnerability brought on by shifting socio-economic, technological and demographic trends. Climate variability, environmental degradation, haphazard construction in high-risk areas and other anticipated effects of climate change are factors that raise vulnerability to disasters.[75]

By enhancing national capacity to lower risk and increase community resilience to climate change, this National Policy for Disaster Risk Management helps to achieve sustainable development goals in line with Vision 2030.[76] The National Policy for Disaster Risk Management seeks to achieve this goal by minimising the harm that hazards of natural, technological and ecological origin do to people, property and the environment. The following are the key objectives of the policy:

- Advocate an approach to disaster risk management that focuses on reducing risks, especially to populations who are most vulnerable due to poverty and a general lack of resources.
- Advocate for shared awareness and responsibility to reduce disaster risk in homes, communities, places of work and in society generally.
- Give effect to the application of cooperative governance on issues concerning disaster and disaster risk management among the levels of government and allocate responsibilities in this regard to relevant stakeholders.
- Facilitate involvement of the private sector, non-government organisations, communities and volunteers in disaster risk management.
- Facilitate partnerships between the state and the private sector, non-government organisations and communities.[77]

The National Climate Change Policy in Namibia is highly relevant to the implementation of Namibia's National Policy for Disaster Risk Management since estimates of the impacts of climate change include a rise in climate-related disasters such as floods, cyclones and drought.

14.11.2 Namibia's White Paper on Energy

The White Paper on Energy[78] acknowledges Namibia's potential for renewable energy in the form of its abundant solar and wind resources, hydropower and substantial gas deposits. The White Paper outlines a comprehensive energy strategy that will guarantee that the energy needs of the economy's productive sectors are addressed while also paying attention to previously underserved groups, such as low-income urban and rural households.[79] The White Paper specifically encourages rural electrification and access to other commercial fuels. It is clear that the government's emphasis on promoting the use of renewable energy through the creation of an appropriate institutional and planning framework, the development of human resources, increased public awareness and appropriate financing systems all have a strong connection to energy-related climate change issues.[80]

The National Climate Change Policy will address low carbon development and sustainable energy concerns in part thanks to the White Paper on Energy in Namibia, which is highly relevant and important. How energy is connected to climate change adaptation and mitigation can be seen in the White Paper's focus on energy efficiency, environmental impact assessments for large development projects, including energy-related projects, private sector investment in renewable energy and rural electrification, rural water supply and solar water heating. The implementation of energy and climate change policies will encourage interactions between them.

14.11.3 Namibia's Vision 2030

Namibia's Vision 2030,[81] introduced by its founding president Dr Sam Nujoma in June 2004, offers potential long-term policy scenarios on the country's future course of growth at various points in time until the target year of 2030. Access to clean water, as well as productive, healthy and biodiverse natural wetlands, are long-term objectives of Vision 2030.

Through accomplishments that result from the adoption and successful implementation of appropriate and effective climate change adaptation and mitigation measures, the climate change policy will contribute to the realisation of Vision 2030 goals. In particular, it is expected that climate change adaptation will mitigate effects that might otherwise impede efforts to reduce poverty and raise people's standards of living and health. Therefore, the climate change strategy will aid in the realisation of Vision 2030 and subsequent development.

14.11.4 National development plans

Medium-term national development plans have a five-year lifespan. The Transitional National Development Plan and the NDP4 were the first two five-year plans, and NDP5 builds on those accomplishments. It also acknowledges the difficulties encountered in carrying out the earlier plans. The frameworks for global, continental, regional and national development have been used to inform the current plan. These include the Harambee Prosperity Plan, the African Union Agenda 2063, SADC, the Regional Integrated Strategic Plan, the Global Sustainable Development Goals and the SWAPO Party Manifesto.

NDP5 is infused with the idea of sustainable development. In order to ensure that future generations can prosper, the plan frames the attainment of progress within this framework. The NDP5 has four key goals, namely:

- Achieve inclusive, sustainable and equitable economic growth
- Build capable and healthy human resources
- Ensure sustainable environment and enhance resilience
- Promote good governance through effective institution.[82]

Namibia is endowed with an abundance of natural resources, including animals, fishing, forests and minerals, as well as a good solar and wind regime. Moreover, 30% of the workforce in the nation is employed by industries with a focus on natural resources, which are among the major contributors to GDP.[83] Sustainable management and exploitation of natural resources as well as environmental sustainability are Namibia's environmental goals.

14.12 An outline of the relevant legal framework

Due to the interconnectedness of climate change, it is essential that all industries assess its effects and develop policies for adaptation and mitigation. The important current policy frameworks that support the National Climate Change Policy are discussed in the next section.

14.12.1 The Namibian Constitution of 1990

The Namibian Constitution emphasises the importance of formulating and putting into practice policies to preserve ecosystems, ecological processes and biological variety for the benefit of current and future generations. The state's ability to carry out its constitutional commitments may be compromised by the expected negative effects of climate change. The state has developed and will continue to develop preventative and adaptive efforts to address environmental and climate change challenges and problems through its different government agencies and departments and in full partnership with the non-governmental and private sectors.

The Constitution of the Republic of Namibia is the supreme law of the land.[84] The Constitution, which serves as the cornerstone for all laws and policies, includes a number of significant environmental provisions that are crucial to the sustainable exploitation of natural resources.[85] It is essential that the Ombudsman fulfil their duties in relation to environmental preservation. Insofar as it pertains to the actions of the legislature and administration, the Ombudsman essentially acts as the Constitution's custodian and protector.[86] The Ombudsman's environmental responsibilities are particularly crucial in light of the following aspects: 1) overutilisation of living natural resources; 2) irrational exploitation of non-renewable resources; 3) degradation and destruction of ecosystems; 4) failure to protect the beauty and character of Namibia; and 4) failure to take appropriate action to call for the remediation, correction and reversal of activities related to the above through means that are fair, proper and effective.[87]

14.12.2 The Pollution Control and Waste Management Bill

Namibia offers a wide range of sectoral regulations regarding ozone-depleting substances and their effects on climate change. If properly applied, these rules can promote sustainable growth in a variety of resource- or environment-based industries. The Pollution Control and Waste Management Bill is one legal document that is significant in relation to climate change. The proposed legislation aims to: 1) promote sustainable development; 2) provide for the establishment of a pollution control and waste management unit; 3) prevent and regulate the discharge of pollutants to the air, water and land; 4) make provision for the establishment of an appropriate framework for integrated pollution prevention and control; 5) regulate noise, dust and odour pollution; 6) establish a system of waste planning and management; and 7) enable Namibia to comply with its obligations under international law in this regard.

14.12.3 Environmental Management Act

Namibia's environmental regulatory framework is provided by the Environmental Management Act (EMA).[88] The Act lays out environmental management concepts that are pertinent to climate change. The key objectives of the EMA are as follows:

- To conduct environmental assessments of all projects that may affect the environment or the use of natural resources
- To promote sustainable development in everything that affects the environment
- To adopt the best possible methods for reducing waste or pollution at its source
- To promote the reduction, reuse and recycling of waste
- To take precautions to prevent environmental damage.

14.13 Policy recognition of regional and international protocols and conventions

The Namibia Climate Change Policy acknowledges that the effects of climate change are multi-sectoral and that they transcend national borders. Despite the absence of a SADC-specific climate change policy or strategy, Namibia's National Climate Change Policy recognises the necessity for regional cooperation in the development and implementation of climate change adaptation and mitigation interventions.

As a result, Namibia's national climate change policy must be in line with pertinent African Union policies, which are also in line with SADC policies that have climate change-related components. They are the Lusaka Agreement – SADC,[89] the SADC Regional Water Policy and Regional Strategy,[90] New Partnership for Africa's Development,[91] the SADC Protocol for Fisheries,[92] the SADC Regional Agriculture Policy,[93] the SADC Protocol on Forestry[94] and the SADC Regional Biodiversity Strategy,[95] among others.

14.14 Sustainable Development Goals

Namibia is a party to the United Nations' Sustainable Development Goals (SDGs).[96] The goals include the following: eliminate poverty, erase hunger, establish good health and well-being, provide quality education, enforce gender equality, improve clean water and sanitation, grow affordable and clean energy, create decent work and economic growth, increase industry, innovation and infrastructure, reduce inequality, mobilise sustainable cities and communities, influence responsible consumption and production, organise climate action, develop life below water, advance life on land, guarantee peace, justice and strong institutions and build partnerships for the goals.[97]

Everywhere, climate change poses the single greatest threat to sustainable development,[98] and its extensive, unprecedented effects disproportionately affect the most vulnerable and underprivileged people. In order to successfully achieve the SDGs, immediate action is needed to stop climate change and address its effects. Together, the Paris Agreement,[99] the 2030 Agenda for Sustainable Development and the Sendai Framework for Disaster Risk Reduction[100] serve as the cornerstone for resilient, sustainable development in the face of climate change. The accomplishment of all three agendas depends on achieving the main objective of the Paris Agreement, which is to keep the average global temperature rise well below 2°C degrees and as near as possible to 1.5°C above pre-industrial levels. Since then, the average global temperature has risen by about one degree, highlighting the need for immediate action if we are to stay as close to 1.5°C as possible.

The Paris Agreement expands on the United Nations Framework Convention on Climate Change[101] by uniting all countries in a common effort to reduce greenhouse gas emissions quickly and improve their capacity to build resilience and adapt to climate change, including by ensuring that developing countries receive adequate support. The world has entered a new era in our collective efforts on combating climate change, focusing on urgently increasing ambition and implementation, at all levels of government, business and civil society, with the early entry into force of the Paris Agreement and successful operationalisation through the achievement of the Katowice Climate Package.

14.15 Financial inclusion and climate change

There are two ways in which financial services and climate change are related. First is the notion of using financial services to increase resilience to climate change-related shocks.[102] The lack of resources to support the poor in coping with the threats to their health and way of life posed by climate change is one of the factors that puts them in the greatest danger. Giving the poor access to formal financial services like insurance, savings or loans might help them manage their spending when faced with unforeseen setbacks. Second is the use of financial services as a tool for expanding the availability, affordability and adoption of greener technology that lessens its impact on climate change.[103] Financial services with a focus on the poor may make it possible for them to invest in green initiatives at reasonable costs, reducing environmental harm.

14.15.1 Using financial services to increase resilience against climate change

The poor can cope with unforeseen obstacles by having better access to official financial services, whether they are weather-related (such as drought or floods), hazards to their health and well-being or other unexpected difficulties. More investigation is required to learn how to: (1) create financial products and services that effectively address the needs of farmers and other groups whose livelihoods are being disrupted by climate change; (2) make these products more affordable for the poor; and (3) boost the use of these products and services. Increasing access to different insurance options helps shield the underprivileged from a range of climate-related dangers, such as ongoing droughts, increasing water levels, the spread of disease and an increase in pests that threaten crops and transmit disease.

14.16 Lessons for Namibia from selected African countries

In terms of financial inclusion and climate change, Namibia can take a lot of lessons from a few African countries. Some significant instances of the use of financial services to address the effects of climate change are mentioned in the following sections.

14.16.1 Ghana

Weather index insurance, which bases rewards on an easily observable variable like rainfall, is a cutting-edge financial product made to make insurance available to underprivileged smallholder farmers.[104] When farmers receive subsidised insurance, the security motivates them to undertake investments that raise farm productivity.[105] In some circumstances, using insurance products as a financial tool to help growth may be preferable to using cash or credit.[106] For example, research in northern Ghana discovered that offering insurance against changes in rainfall encouraged farmers to make bigger investments and riskier production decisions than just giving them cash.[107] Smallholder farmers are particularly aware of the risk associated with their investments and will take action to reduce risk in the lack of suitable insurance solutions, which may also reduce profitability.

Investments can be facilitated by providing capital, whether in the form of credit or cash, but such investments may increase risk (since they are not guaranteed to pay off). Additionally, they are unable to provide the same level of assurance against weather-related risk as insurance. The lack of demand has impeded the development of commercial markets for weather index insurance, indicating that it is doubtful that insurance will find a solution that is competitively priced.[108] However, the study conducted in Ghana raises the possibility that insurance could be a useful instrument for governments looking to promote profitable investments in agriculture. Another financial instrument that the underprivileged can use to budget their spending and make it easier to invest in climate-resilient technologies is savings.[109] Additionally, institutional savings accounts offer a better way to hold cash than informal savings in livestock or other products that can be adversely impacted by climate change.

The Mumuadu Rural Bank in Ghana provided randomly chosen farmers with a loan that included crop price insurance.[110] The loan specifically stated that the bank pledged to erase 50% of the loan and interest payments if crop prices at harvest fell below a certain threshold.[111] Farmers who received the loan and the crop price insurance spent much more on inputs (mostly fertiliser) than farmers who did not. However, the insurance component did not seem to affect farmers' other types of investments, and a separate study done in Malawi revealed that bundling insurance with a credit product intended to boost technology adoption decreased demand for the product.[112]

14.16.2 Malawi

People can save more money by allocating cash for particular expenditures via commitment devices or labelling (in which a client labels money as they set them aside for a specific reason). Additionally, these technologies can assist users in allocating funds to agriculture, the sector most at risk from the consequences of climate change. Farmers in Malawi, for instance, raised their investment in agricultural inputs by 13% and improved productivity by 21% after being offered savings accounts with a commitment feature.[113] According to a thorough study, smallholder farmers' resistance to climate-related shocks can be increased by using climate-resistant inputs like hybrid seeds. According to this research, farmers can invest in technologies that boost crop yields and productivity by expanding their access to credit.[114] These technologies include better seeds, irrigation, fertiliser and insecticides.

14.16.3 Kenya

The adoption of rainwater harvesting tanks surged in Kenya, according to researchers, as a result of asset-collateralised loans.[115] This enabled dairy farmers to have more reliable and convenient access to water, which in turn raised output. Furthermore, loan products' impact can be increased by timed delivery and repayment to coincide with farmers' planting and harvest seasons. Farmers' investment in agricultural inputs can be increased by giving them the option to postpone loan repayments until after the harvest and by assisting them in saving money between harvest and planting. In Mali, giving farmers a cutting-edge loan product customised for their seasonal cash flow resulted in a marked increase in farm investments and spending (fertiliser, insecticides and herbicides).[116] Further, in Kenya, it was discovered that giving farmers the choice to purchase fertiliser when they got their harvest money increased fertiliser usage by 14% (on a base of 23 percentage points).[117] Increasing loan availability during the lean season can also aid farming households in more effectively allocating labour, enhancing both production and well-being.[118]

14.16.4 Zambia

Farming households in Zambia that had access to loans that were made available at the beginning of the lean season and were to be returned after harvest produced, on average, 5.6% more than comparable households.[119] Additionally, they had a nearly 40% lower chance of being without food during the lean season.[120] Customers who experience natural catastrophes or other unforeseen situations can benefit from credit packages that offer flexible repayment plans. The outcomes of research examining this strategy are conflicting, despite the fact that bundling credit products with insurance may also aid clients who face risk due to climate change.[121]

14.16.5 Finance and environmentally friendly technologies

Financial services are a tool for expanding access to, affordability of and adoption of cleaner technology that lessens the impact of climate change.[122] Financial services can stimulate the adoption of improved environmental practices that reduce contributions to climate change and may potentially improve welfare at the individual level.[123] They can also enable the poor to make reasonable investments in alternative, cleaner technology. There may be a market for these innovative solutions, but more study is needed to determine how to design and market goods that promote the adoption of cleaner technologies and better environmental practices.

One way in which financial products can help boost the use of improved environmental practices is through payments for ecosystem services, wherein compensation is given to people or businesses to carry out ecologically protective services. According to research conducted in Uganda, encouraging landowners to leave trees alone slowed the rate at which villages' tree cover was being lost.[124] The programme dramatically reduced deforestation in the targeted villages and prevented the release of carbon dioxide in an efficient and affordable manner.

There is evidence that farmers may be persuaded to invest in environmentally friendly practices with the correct incentives, but there is still room for creativity in terms of how to include these incentives into the current financial goods and services.[125] For instance, "green loans" give customers access to finance they may use to purchase ecologically friendly goods like solar technology, better-insulated homes and organic seeds and fertilisers.[126] However, because these loans are relatively new, they must undergo a thorough analysis to determine whether they can promote the adoption of eco-friendly behaviours and lessen the carbon footprint of the populace.

Microgrids powered by solar energy are an illustration of a clean energy technology that can be integrated with financial services in ways that may be advantageous to customers, service providers and the environment.[127] These networks, which are designed to be affordable for customers, may make underprivileged communities more resilient to power outages during severe weather, while simultaneously lowering carbon emissions because they use fewer fossil fuels.[128] Customers may have access to green technology like these solar microgrids and other alternative power sources through pay-as-you-go (PAYGO) services.[129]

To purchase electricity from an off-grid solar panel, a customer can take out a small loan, which can then be repaid in manageable instalments through a mobile money account.[130] The devices can be turned off as a reminder if customers forget to make a payment. These platforms are less hazardous for providers because they can discontinue the service if they do not get payment, making them more convenient for users who can buy as much electricity as they require. Observational study indicates that when this technology is offered, South African customers take advantage of the flexibility that prepaid power meters offer.[131] According to preliminary findings from an interpretative phenomenological analysis study carried out in Kenya, distributing PAYGO solar lamps to Nairobi shops may have reduced kerosene consumption.[132]

14.17 Green financing that is inclusive and supports the most vulnerable people's resilience: Developments from the Alliance for Financial Inclusion

Lessons can be drawn by Namibia from the webinar on inclusive green finance (IGF), which was put on by Insurance Finance Network Luxembourg (InFiNe.lu) and the Alliance for Financial Inclusion (AFI) to examine the relationship between climate change and financial inclusion, concentrated on the connections between climate change and environmental degradation, vulnerable populations, social injustice and tensions and financial stability.[133] A large group of Luxembourg stakeholders gathered to talk with AFI about how financial inclusion policies and regulations created and put in place in developing and emerging markets are facilitating mitigation and strengthening resilience to adverse effects of climate change.[134] The occasion provided by the event allowed AFI and its partners in Luxembourg to highlight their continuing partnerships and explore potential future options for collaboration with InFiNe.lu, its members and the larger community of Luxembourg stakeholders engaged in policymaking.[135]

Luxembourg stakeholders' policymaking process is plausible as climate action and sustainability are key objectives that should be integrated into all countries' initiatives and strategic operations. Although all countries, industries and demographic groupings are impacted by climate change, not all of them are in the same way.[136] Numerous variables affect the severity of the effects, the degree of sensitivity and the capacity to recover from climatic shocks.[137] The poorest and most vulnerable are primarily impacted by these changes, much like with Covid-19. One of the best methods for increasing both individual and societal resistance to the effects of climate change is financial inclusion.[138] Additionally, there is growing support from donors for inclusive green finance. The focus of all financial inclusion activities is on micro, small and medium-sized firms (MSMEs), women and young people.[139]

While describing how the use of DFS might provide adaptation solutions for climate change, AFI emphasised the necessity to ensure the spread and utilisation of savings, credit and insurance, money transfers and humanitarian help after abrupt and harsh weather events. Although the cost of these technologies may deter the poor and MSMEs from employing them, financial inclusion can also boost access to green technologies that combat climate change.

Central banks and regulators have been putting various schemes into place to improve financial inclusion and involve the poor in the shift to a low-carbon economy.[140] FinTech's role in all of this is critical because it is a key vehicle for promoting green financing.[141] The 4Ps of inclusive green finance, which stand for provision, promotion, protection and prevention and represent the current state of IGF policy practices globally, should also be highlighted.[142] The AFI network provides information on current IGF policy trends as well as specific examples of actions taken by central banks and financial regulators.[143]

Financial authorities now have easy access to the full spectrum of measures they may use to promote inclusive green financing thanks to the 4P framework.[144] Bangko Sentral ng Pilipinas (BSP) pushed commercial banks to recognise the potential of green financing, while Bangladesh Bank set a regulatory aim of 5% for the annual disbursement of green finance in 2014.[145] BSP has attempted to narrow knowledge gaps on green lending and investment for commercial banks and other financial institutions through capacity-building efforts.

The Central Bank of Armenia designed and oversees a system of agricultural climate insurance.[146] The development of the farm insurance industry is the responsibility of a public-private partnership known as the Agricultural Insurers' National Agency.[147] The programme pays insurance premiums, and the subsidy amount for 2020 varies per product and ranges from 50% to 60%.[148] It thus becomes evident that SDGs cannot be achieved without inclusive green finance, a developing policy field that has been pioneered by AFI member institutions on how adopting policies, legislation and national initiatives can reduce or raise resilience to climate change.

The European Green Deal is starting to influence a variety of projects, including inclusive green funding.[149] As a significant hub for sustainable finance, Luxembourg is paving the way. The German Federal Ministry for the Environment, Nature Conservation and Nuclear Safety, which was founded by a German Bundestag Act,[150] supports the International Climate Initiative (IKI). The IGF workstream of the AFI is a component of the IKI.[151]

14.18 Recommendations and the way forward for Namibia

Regarding financial inclusion as a measure for reducing the effects of climate change, the following suggestions are made:

a) Further product development in Namibia could lead to product delivery experiments and improved acceptance of financial services as powerful tools for boosting financial inclusion and climate change resilience and adaptation. To encourage financial inclusion and lessen the effects of climate change, a range of incentives could be employed, such as tax exemptions for banks that provide services to low-income households or new bankers.
b) In Namibia, banks should be evaluated publicly on how successfully they provide accessible credit and fundamental banking services to low-income consumers.
c) Namibia needs branching legislation requiring banks to open rural branches before additional urban ones, as well as incentives to foster an atmosphere that is conducive to the adoption of cutting-edge technological solutions.
d) Banks and funders in Namibia ought to promote knowledge sharing and management. By considering all facets of a market system and removing obstacles to financial inclusion by incentivising market actors to fill in for absent or underdeveloped functions in the market through rules or financial incentives, these initiatives should support systemic approaches to financial inclusion. The creation and expansion of innovative financial services is one of many entry points (such as government-to-people payment schemes, laws requiring "no frills" bank accounts and programmes to support value chain finance through value chain re-structuring) for achieving universal financial inclusion and its associated development and resilience goals.
e) Public-private partnerships (PPPs) are a creative method to get the private sector involved in boosting financial inclusion and mitigating the effects of climate change in Namibia. Due to their asset-backed character and emphasis on shared risks, Namibian financial arrangements are an ideal fit for PPPs. Since multi-stakeholder partnerships can bring together participants from many industries and work as an effective instrument for coordinating action at different scales, this is particularly significant in the context of resilience.
f) Namibia must accurately calculate the benefits to its resilience from investments in expanding financial inclusion and related climate change adaptation measures. The benefits and co-benefits should be more extensive and go beyond simple financial measurements to include the economy, society and the environment.[152]
g) The Development Bank of Namibia must create a division dedicated to integrating climate action throughout the entire organisation. All of its assets need to begin receiving a climate risk assessment. The chance to guarantee that climate risks are better understood and managed and, thus, strengthen the argument for upfront investments in resilience, would be provided by pushing for climate-related financial disclosure among partner organisations

and businesses. To encourage learning and product innovation in Namibia's micro- and meso-level finance sectors, emphasis should be focused not only on usage and adequacy assessments but also on traditional financial inclusion indicators (such as account ownership).

14.19 Conclusion

A key element of mitigating climate change is financial inclusion, particularly for Namibia's poor and marginalised communities. In order to do this, and as is emphasised in this chapter, the early stages of enhancing financial inclusion for climate resilience and adaptation depend greatly on access to financial services. As a result, a long-term vision of the Namibian financial services industry is required. This vision should be based on self-sustaining models, as shown, among other things, by the examples of Ghana, Kenya and Malawi that are provided in this chapter. Therefore, increasing financial inclusion in Namibia should not be seen as a philanthropic endeavour but rather as a profitable endeavour in order to mitigate the effects of climate change. For instance, the best model for establishing larger and more dependable commercially oriented funding streams in Namibia to lessen the effects of climate change should be microfinance.

It is important to advance climate risk disclosure while also assisting Namibia in developing its resilience finance. Namibian finance has a significant stake in better understanding how to evaluate risks for physical assets given the asset-based nature of transactions and underlying concepts surrounding avoidance of uncertainty. Therefore, Namibia finance would be in a good position to lead the way in promoting the disclosure of climate risk. Recent years have seen this propelled by programmes like the Climate Risk Disclosure Project and the Task Force on Climate-related Financial Disclosures. Initiatives to support financial services should be combined with interventions to enhance financial literacy, planning abilities, risk awareness, anticipation and preventative capacities in order to strengthen resilience more thoroughly. To involve the poorest and most vulnerable, graduation packages that include financial services, training and assistance, life skills coaching and subsidies for productive assets are necessary. Initiatives to increase financial inclusion for low-income households should include components that attempt to change attitudes and behaviours.

Notes

1 Berlemann, M, and Steinhardt, MF (2017) "Climate Change, Natural Disasters, and Migration - a Survey of the Empirical Evidence, CESifo Economic Studies", vol. 63(4), 353–385, https://doi.org/10.1093/cesifo/ifx019.

2 Namibia's 2010 National Policy on Climate Change available at https://www.adaptation-undp.org/sites/default/files/downloads/namibia_nationalclimatechangepolicyfornamib.pdf, accessed 30 June 2022.

3 Ibid.

4 Ibid.
5 Ibid.
6 Thomson, G.C. "Climate Change in Namibia Part 2: Current and Projected Changes" Namibia Chamber of Environment 29 October 2021.
7 Namibia's 2010 National Policy on Climate Change supra.
8 Ibid.
9 Ibid.
10 Ibid.
11 Ibid.
12 See Namibia's 2010 National Policy on Climate Change available at https://www.adaptation-undp.org/sites/default/files/downloads/namibia_nationalclimatechangepolicyfornamib.pdf, accessed 30 June 2022. See also Ruppel, OC (2011) "Foundations, sources and implications of National Environmental Law" in Ruppel, OC and Ruppel-Schlichting (eds) Environmental Law and Policy in Namibia (Hanns Seidel Foundation, Namibia) 79; and Mapaure, I (2011) "Climate Change in Namibia: Projected Trends and Effects" in Ruppel, OC and Ruppel-Schlichting (eds) Environmental Law and Policy in Namibia (Hanns Seidel Foundation, Namibia) 291.
13 See the Dirkx, E, Hager, C, Tadross, M, Bethune, S and Curtis, B "Climate Change Vulnerability & Adaptation Assessment Namibia", Desert Foundation of Namibia & Climate Analysis Group for the Ministry of Environment and Tourism, Final Report of March 2008. See also Thomson, G.C "Climate Change in Namibia Part 2: Current and Projected Changes" 29 October 2021.
14 See Namibia's 2013–2020 National Climate Change Strategy and Action Plan available at https://www.meft.gov.na/files/files/National%20Climate%20Change%20Strategy%20&%20Action%20Plan%202013%20-%202020.pdf, accessed 30 June 2022.
15 See Namibia's First Adaptation Communication titled "Republic of Namibia First Adaptation Communication: Namibia's Climate Change Adaptation Communication to the UNFCCC" available at https://unfccc.int/sites/default/files/resource/namibia-adaptation-communication-to-the-unfccc.pdf, accessed 23 June 2022.
16 In order to address climate change and its effects, Goal 13 asks for immediate action. SDG 13 calls for nations to take urgent action to combat climate change and its impacts.
17 The Sustainable Development Goals (SDGs), sometimes referred to as the Global Goals, were enacted by the United Nations in 2015 as a global call to action to eradicate poverty, safeguard the environment and guarantee that by the year 2030, peace and prosperity will be experienced by everyone. The 17 SDGs are as follows: SDG 1 (No poverty); SDG 2 (Zero hunger); SDG 3 (Good health and well-being); SDG 4 (Quality Education); SDG 5 (Gender Equality); SDG 6 (Clean Water and Sanitation); SDG 7 (Affordable and Clean Energy); SDG 8 (Decent Work Agenda); SDG 9 (Industry, Innovation and Infrastructure; SDG 10 (Reduced Inequalities); SDG 11 (Sustainable cities and communities); SDG 12 (Responsible consumption and production; SDG 13 (Climate Change); SDG 14 (Life below Water); SDG 15 (Life on Land); SDG 16 (Peace, justice and strong Institutions); and SDG 17 (Partnerships for the goals).
18 Thomson, supra.
19 Namibia's 2010 National Policy on Climate Change, supra.
20 United Nations Climate Change "Rainwater Harvesting System to Reduce Climate Change Vulnerability - Indonesia" available at https://unfccc.int/climate-action/momentum-for-change/activity-database/rainwater-harvesting-system-to-reduce-climate-change-vulnerability, accessed 21 June 2022.
21 See the Climate Risk Profile: Namibia (2021): The World Bank Group available at https://climateknowledgeportal.worldbank.org/sites/default/files/2021-08/15931-WB_Namibia%20Country%20Profile-WEB.pdf

22 Reid, H, Sahlen, L, Stage, J and Macgregor, J (2008) "Climate Change Impacts on Namibia's Natural Resources and Economy" *Climate Policy*, vol. 8(5), 452–466.

23 Namibia's 2010 National Policy on Climate Change, supra.

24 Howden-Chapman, P, Siri, J, Chisholm, E, Chapman, R, Doll, CNH, and Capon, A (2017) "SDG3: Ensure Healthy lives and Promote well-being for all at all ages" available https://council.science/wp-content/uploads/2017/03/SDGs-interactions-3-healthy-lives.pdf, accessed 22 June 2022.

25 Marenga, R and Amupanda, JS (2021) "The Coronavirus and Social Justice in Namibia" *South African Journal of Political Studies*, vol. 48(2), 206–225.

26 See the Government of Namibia "Namibia Vision 2030" Policy Framework for Long-Term National Development (Summary), Office of the President, 2004.

27 Previously, Namibia's commitment to the health and well-being of its citizens was evidenced by the Millennium Declaration, which obliged Namibia to achieve the eight Millennium Development Goals, including the elimination of child mortality (MDG4), enhancement of maternal health (MDG5) and combating HIV/AIDS, malaria, and other diseases (MDG6).

28 See the World Health Organisation (2019) "Country Cooperation Strategy III 2018-2022: Accelerating Progress Towards Universal Health Coverage" available at https://www.afro.who.int/sites/default/files/2019-12/CCS%20Namibia%20-%2007%20August%202019.pdf, accessed 25 June 2022. See also The Namibian Ministry of Health and Social Services (MoHSS), National Health Policy Framework 2010-2020 (2010); Zere E, Oluwole D, Kirigia JM, Mwikisa CN, Mbeeli T. Inequities in skilled attendance at birth in Namibia: a decomposition analysis. BMC Pregnancy Childbirth, (2011) 11:34; and Uwamahoro T. Bringing Primary Health Care to Remote Populations through Public-Private Partnerships: the SHOPS Mister Sister Experience. USAID (2013).

29 Namibia's 2010 National Policy on Climate Change, supra.

30 Namibia's 2010 National Policy on Climate Change, supra.

31 Moyo, T "Fishing Industry Resurgence 2022" The Namibian, 28 April 2022.

32 Food and Agriculture Organisation (n.d.) "Fishery and Aquaculture Country Profiles: Namibia" available at https://www.fao.org/fishery/en/facp/nam?lang=en, accessed 21 June 2022.

33 Iitembu, JA, Erasmus, VN, Uanivi, U, Nakwaya, D, Horeb, RR and Nangolo, E (2021) "The hits and misses of Namibia's attempt to implement the Ecosystem Approach to Fisheries (EAF) Management" *Ecosystem Health and Sustainability*, vol. 7(1), 1–12.

34 Hutchings, L et al (2009) "The Benguela Current: An ecosystem of four components" Progress in Oceanography, vol. 83(1-4), 15–32.

35 Amapindi, H (2022) "Climate change in Namibia" available https://www.benguelacc.org/climate-change-in-namibia/, accessed 21 June 2022.

36 See Namibia Chamber of Environment (2021) "Why the Namibian moratorium on sardine fishing must continue" Conservation Namibia, 15 November 2021. See also Byers, BA (1997) "Environmental threats and opportunities in Namibia: A comprehensive assessment" Research Discussion Paper No. 21, Directorate of Environmental Affairs, Ministry of Environment and Tourism, Windhoek, Namibia.

37 One Ocean Hub "Namibia" available at https://oneoceanhub.org/where-we-work/namibia/, accessed 22 August 2022. See also Khan, U (2022) "Exploring the 'Blue Carbon' Potential in Namibia" available at https://oneoceanhub.org/exploring-the-blue-carbon-potential-in-namibia/, accessed 22 June 2022.

38 Remmert, D (2018) "Towards a Blue Economy: Harnessing Namibia's Coastal Resources Sustainability" available at https://ippr.org.na/wp-content/uploads/2019/02/BlueEconomy_WEB-1.pdf, accessed 23 June 2022. See also Ministry of Fisheries and Marine Resources (2022) "Namibia Sustainable Blue Economy Policy 2022-

2031" available at file:///C:/Users/twarikandwa/Downloads/Draft%20Blue%20Economy%20Policy.pdf, accessed 10 August 2022.
39 Human Rights Watch (2020) "Breaking the Poverty Trap: Why Poverty and Inequality are Human Rights Issues" 14 October 2020, available at https://www.hrw.org/news/2020/10/14/breaking-poverty-trap, accessed 10 June 2022.
40 Massey, JM (2020) "Climate Change, Culture and Cultural Rights" Memo/Expanded Outline prepared by Justine Marrion Massey with contributions from Spring 2020 United Nations Practicum Students, University of California Davis School of Law, 15 May 2020 available at https://www.ohchr.org/sites/default/files/Documents/Issues/CulturalRights/Call_ClimateChange/JMassey.pdf, accessed 10 May 2022.
41 Arthur, RI, Skerritt, DJ, Schuhbauer, A, Ebrahim, N, Friend, RM, and Sumaila, UR (2021) "Small-scale fisheries and local food systems: Transformations, threats and opportunities" *Fish and Fisheries*, vol. 23(1), 109–124.
42 Ministry of Fisheries and Marine Resources Strategic Plan – 2017/18-2021/22, p. 7.
43 Benguela Current Commission (2022) "Launch of Namibia's National Programme on Small-Scale Fisheries (NPOA-SSF) and acceleration of IYAFA-2022 (8–10 June 2022), Swakopmund, Namibia" 7 July 2022 available at https://www.benguelacc.org/launch-of-namibias-national-programme-on-small-scale-fisheries-npoa-ssf-and-celebration-of-iyafa-2022-8-10-june-2022-swakopmund-namibia/, accessed 8 July 2022.
44 Abu Samah, A, Shaffril, HAM, Hamzah, A, and Abu Samah, B (2019) "Factors Affecting Small-Scale Fishermen's Adaptation Toward the Impacts of Climate Change: Reflections from Malaysian Fishers" *SAGE Open*, 9(3). https://doi.org/10.1177/2158244019864204.
45 Griffins, R and Howard, J (eds) (2012) Oceans and Marine Resources in a Changing Climate: A technical input to the 2013 National Climate Assessment (Washington, DC: Island Press) 58.
46 Frawely, TH, Finkbeiner, EM, and Crowder, LB (2019) "Environmental and institutional degradation in the globalized economy: Lessons from small-scale fisheries in the Gulf of California" *Ecology and Society*, vol. 24(1), available at https://www.jstor.org/stable/26796922, accessed 20 June 2022. See also Westlund, L and Zelasney, J (eds) *Securing sustainable small-scale fisheries: Sharing good practices from around the world* Food and Agriculture Organisation of the United Nations Fisheries and Aquaculture Technical Paper 644.
47 Namibia's 2010 National Policy on Climate Change, supra. See also Dirkx et al supra.
48 Sparks, DL (1984) "Namibia's Coastal and Marine Development Potential" *African Affairs*, vol. 83(333), 477–496. See also Ministry of Fisheries and Marine Resources, Current Status Report: Knowledge Baseline for Namibia's Central Marine Plan available https://mfmr.gov.na/documents/411764/430830/National+Overview+for+Marine+Spatial+Planning+and+Knowledge+Baseline+for+Namibia+-+reduced.pdf/a0a419aa-ebe8-1966-0a78-dd772861ad5b, accessed 23 June 2022.
49 Namibia's 2010 National Policy on Climate Change, supra.
50 Namibia's 2010 National Policy on Climate Change, supra.
51 Namibia's 2010 National Policy on Climate Change, supra.
52 Sanzila, G (2022) "Namibian MPs call for collaboration to avert energy crisis in SADC, 11/07/2022" available at https://www.parliament.na/namibian-mps-call-for-collaboration-to-avert-energy-crisis-in-sadc-11-07-2022/, accessed 7 August 2022. See also SADC "SADC Regional Infrastructure Development" Short Term Action Plan Assessment 2019 available at https://www.sadc.int/sites/default/files/2021-07/SADC_Regional_Infrastruture_Development.pdf, accessed 2 June 2022; and Mureverwi, B (n.d.) "Energy Situation in Southern Africa" available at https://www.tralac.org/discussions/article/8474-energy-situation-in-southern-africa.html, accessed 3 June 2022.

53 Mukumbira, G (2020) "Can Green Hydrogen be the Future Fuel?" available at https://www.sasscal.org/can-green-hydrogen-be-the-future-fuel/, accessed 22 June 2022. See also The Economist Namibia (2020) "SADC Creates Centre for Renewable Energy to Stimulate Rural Electrification" 26 February 2020.

54 Wang, F et al. (2021) "Technologies and perspectives for achieving carbon neutrality" The Innovation, vol. 2(4) https://doi.org/10.1016/j.xinn.2021.100180.

55 Nature Conservation Amendment Act, 1996 (Act No. 5 of 1996). See also the Nature Conservation Ordinance of 1975.

56 See Chapter III of the Constitution of the Republic of Namibia, 21 March 1990.

57 See the National Heritage Act, 2004 (Act 27 of 2004).

58 Namibia's 2010 National Policy on Climate Change, supra.

59 Namibia's 2010 National Policy on Climate Change, supra.

60 USAID (2009) "Adapting to Coastal Climate Change: A Guidebook for Development Planners" available at https://www.crc.uri.edu/download/CoastalAdaptationGuide.pdf, accessed 1 June 2022.

61 Vousdoukas, MI, Clarke, J, Ranasinghe, R et al. (2022) "African heritage sites threatened as sea-level rise accelerates" *Nature Climate Change*, vol. 12, 256–262.

62 Pranzini E, Anfuso G, Cinelli I, Piccardi M, Vitale G (2018) "Shore Protection Structures Increase and Evolution on the Northern Tuscany Coast (Italy): Influence of Tourism Industry" *Water*, vol. 10(11), 1647. https://doi.org/10.3390/w10111647

63 Vousdoukas et al., supra at 256.

64 Waryszak, P, Gavoille, A, Whitt, AA, Kelvin, J and Macreadie, PI, (2021) "Combining gray and green infrastructure to improve coastal resilience: lessons learnt from hybrid flood defenses", *Coastal Engineering Journal*, vol. 63(3), 335–350, DOI: 10.1080/21664250.2021.1920278.

65 Brondízio, ES, Aumeeruddy-Thomas, Y, Bates, P, Carino, J, Fernández-Llamazares, A, Farhan Ferrari, M Galvin, K, Reyes-García, V, McElwee, P, Molnár, Z, Samakov, A, Shrestha, UB (2021) "Locally Based, Regionally Manifested, and Globally Relevant: Indigenous and Local Knowledge, Values, and Practices for Nature" *Annual Review of Environment and Resources*, vol 46(1), 481–509.

66 Dunne, D and Chandrasekhar, A (2022) "Loss and Damage: What happens when Climate Change destroys lives and cultures?" PreventionWeb 28 September 2022.

67 National Drought Policy and Strategy, 1997.

68 National Land Policy, 1998.

69 Agriculture Policy, 2015.

70 Policy on desertification, 2014–2024.

71 See the Blue Print on Wealth Redistribution and Poverty Eradication, 2016.

72 National Malaria Programme Strategic Plan 2015–2020.

73 National Policy for Disaster Risk Management, 2011.

74 United Nations (2019) "UN Report: Nature's Dangerous Decline 'unnprecedented'; Species Extinction 'Accelerating'" available at https://www.un.org/sustainabledevelopment/blog/2019/05/nature-decline-unprecedented-report/, accessed 19 June 2022.

75 Chapagain, D, Bharati, L. & Borgemeister, C (2022) "Declining vulnerability but rising impacts: the trends of climatic disasters in Nepal" *Regional Environmental Change* vol. 22, 55, https://doi.org/10.1007/s10113-022-01903-5.

76 National Policy for Disaster Risk Management, supra.

77 National Policy for Disaster Risk Management.

78 Namibia's White Paper on Energy, 1998.

79 Namibia's White Paper on Energy, 1998.

80 Namibia's White Paper on Energy, 1998.

81 Namibia's Vision 2030 available at https://www.npc.gov.na/national-plans/vision-2030/, accessed 1 June 2022.

82 NDP5 available at https://www.npc.gov.na/national-plans/national-plans-ndp-5/, accessed 1 June 2022.

83 Namibia's 2010 National Policy on Climate Change, supra.
84 See article 1(6).
85 Article 95(l) stipulates that the state shall actively promote and maintain the welfare of the people by adopting policies that are aimed at the "maintenance of ecosystems, essential ecological processes and biological diversity of Namibia".
86 In terms of Article 91(c) of the Namibian Constitution, the Ombudsman has a duty to "investigate complaints concerning the over-utilization of living natural resources, the irrational exploitation of non-renewable resources, the degradation and destruction of ecosystems and failure to protect the beauty and character of Namibia".
87 See also section 3(1)(b) of the Ombudsman Act, 1990 (No. 7 of 1990).
88 Environmental Management Act, Act No. 7 of 2007.
89 Lusaka Agreement, 2008.
90 SADC Regional Water Policy and Regional Strategy, 2006.
91 New Partnership for Africa's Development, 2001.
92 SADC Protocol for Fisheries, 2006.
93 SADC Regional Agriculture Policy, 2013.
94 SADC Protocol on Forestry, 2002.
95 SADC Regional Biodiversity Strategy, 2008.
96 See Namibia's Second Voluntary National Review Report on the Implementation of the Sustainable Development Goals Towards Agenda 2030 available at https://sustainabledevelopment.un.org/content/documents/279462021_VNR_Report_Namibia.pdf, accessed 12 June 2022.
97 See the United Nations Sustainable Development Goals available at https://unfoundation.org/what-we-do/issues/sustainable-development-goals/?gclid=EAIaIQobChMI58jN77D8-gIVkt1RCh0iLAajEAAYASAAEgIlq_D_BwE, accessed 12 June 2022.
98 Kyte, R (2014) "Climate Change is a challenge for sustainable development" World Bank, 15 January 2014. See also The Intergovernmental Panel on Climate Change (IPCC) (2022) "Climate change: A threat to human wellbeing and health of the planet. Taking action now can secure our future" IPCC Reports 28 February 2022.
99 Paris Agreement, 4 November 2016.
100 Sendai Framework for Disaster Risk Reduction 2015-2030.
101 The majority of SADC members, including Namibia, are paying more attention to climate change. Three conventions were created at the 1992 United Nations Conference on Environment and Development (UNCED), often known as the Rio or Earth Summit. These are the United Nations Convention on Biological Diversity (UNCBD), the United Nations Convention to Combat Desertification (UNCCCD) and the United Nations Framework Convention on Climate Change (UNFCCC) (CBD). The UNFCCC allows for the introduction of Protocols to the Convention. The first is the Kyoto Protocol, which came into force on 16 February 2005. Namibia, like all other SADC nations, has ratified and signed the Kyoto Protocol as well as the UNFCCC. Namibia is not subject to particular GHG emission targets because it is a non-Annex I Party to the Protocol, but a variety of international projects are being carried out with the help of donors and other parties to aid in the UNFCCC's operationalisation.
102 Sirtaine, S and Mckay, C (2022) "In an Era of Urgent Climate Risk, Does Financial Inclusion Matter?" available at https://www.cgap.org/blog/era-urgent-climate-risk-does-financial-inclusion-matter, accessed 23 June 2022.
103 Park, H, Kim, JD, (2020) "Transition towards green banking: role of financial regulators and financial institutions", Asian Journal for Sustainability and Social Responsibility, vol. 5, 5.
104 Shumba, DS (2022) "Bundling Weather Index Insurance with Microfinance: Trekking the Long Road between Expectations and Reality – A Study on Sub-Saharan Africa"

In Ribeiro-Barros, AI, Tevera, DS, Goulao, LF and Tivana, LD (Eds.), *Food Systems Resilience*. IntechOpen. https://doi.org/10.5772/intechopen.101742.

105 Hazell, P, Sberro-Kessler, R and Varangis, P (2017) "When and How Should Agricultural Insurance be subsidized: Issues and Good Practices" World Bank Group available at https://openknowledge.worldbank.org/bitstream/handle/10986/31438/117363.pdf?sequence=4, accessed 3 June 2022.

106 MAPFRE Economics (2020), "Financial inclusion in insurance" Madrid, MAPFRE Economics available at https://www.mapfre.com/media/economic-research/2020/mapfre-economics-inclusion-financiera-11-06-2020-ENU.pdf, accessed 3 June 2022.

107 Karlan, D, Osei, R, Osei-Akoto, I and Udry, C (2014) "Agriculture Decisions after relaxing Credit and Risk Constraints" *The Quarterly Journal of Economics*, vol. 129(2), 597–652.

108 Carter, M, De Janvry, A, Sadoulet, E, and Sarris, A (2014) "Index-based weather insurance for developing countries: A review of evidence and a set of propositions for up-scaling" available at https://ferdi.fr/dl/df-kLB5hYBaUiR2Vysm2cH5DfCP/ferdi-p111-index-based-weather-insurance-for-developing-countries-a-review.pdf, accessed 4 June 2022.

109 Karlan et al supra, 597.

110 Karlan, D, Kutsoati, ED, McMillan, M and Udry. C, (2011) "Crop Price Indemnified Loans for Farmers: A Pilot Experiment in Rural Ghana" *The Journal of Risk and Insurance*, vol. 78(1), 37–55.

111 Ibid.

112 Yang, D and Gine, X (2005-2006) "Insurance, Credit and Technology adoption in Malawi" available at https://www.povertyactionlab.org/evaluation/insurance-credit-and-technology-adoption-malawi, accessed 11 June 2022.

113 Ibid.

114 Ibid.

115 Aroka, N (2010) "Rainwater Harvesting in Rural Kenya: Reliability in a Variable and Changing Climate" available at https://www.diva-portal.org/smash/get/diva2:354235/FULLTEXT02.pdf, accessed 11 June 2022.

116 World Bank (2022) "Creating Markets for Smallholder Farmers in Mali" available at https://www.worldbank.org/en/results/2022/05/17/afw-creating-markets-for-smallholder-farmers-in-mali, accessed 15 June 2022.

117 Duflo, E, Kremer, M, and Robinson, J (2011) "Nudging Farmers to Use Fertilizer: Theory and Experimental Evidence from Kenya" *The American Economic Review*, vol. 101(6), 2350–2390.

118 Fink, G, Jack, K and Masiye, F (2016) "The Impact of Seasonal Food and Cash Loans on Small-scale Farmers in Zambia" available at https://www.atai-research.org/wp-content/uploads/2016/07/Food-Constraints-Policy-Brief_final.pdf, accessed 15 June 2022.

119 Ibid.

120 Ibid.

121 Jain, DK, Chida, A, Pathak, RD et al. (2022) "Climate risk insurance in Pacific Small Island Developing States: possibilities, challenges and vulnerabilities- a comprehensive review" *Mitigation and Adaptation Strategies for Global Change*, vol. 27, 26.

122 Park (2020) supra, p. 5.

123 Organisation for Economic Co-operation and Development (2021) "Climate Change and the Long Term Fiscal Sustainability" available at https://www.oecd.org/gov/budgeting/scoping-paper-on-fiscal-sustainability-and-climate-change.pdf, accessed 13 June 2022.

124 Gaworecki, M (2017) "Randomised controlled trial in Uganda finds that paying people not to cut down trees works" MONGABAY 27 July 2017.

125 Pineiro, V, Arias, J and Dearlove, H (2021) "How to encourage farmers to adopt sustainable agriculture" available at https://www.ifpri.org/blog/how-encourage-farmers-adopt-sustainable-agriculture, accessed 14 June 2022.
126 Mhlanga, D (2022) "The role of financial inclusion and FinTech In addressing climate-related challenges in the industry 4.0: Lessons for sustainable development goals" available at https://www.frontiersin.org/articles/10.3389/fclim.2022.949178/full, accessed 30 September 2022.
127 Hirsch, A Parag, Y and Guerrero, J (2018) "Microgrids: A review of technologies, key drivers, and outstanding issues" *Renewable and Sustainable Energy Reviews*, vol. 90, 402–411.
128 Jessel S, Sawyer S, Hernández D, (2019) "Energy, Poverty, and Health in Climate Change: A Comprehensive Review of an Emerging Literature" *Front Public Health*, vol. 12(7), 357. See also Davis, M and Clemmer, S (2014) "Power Failure: How Climate Change puts our Electricity at Risk – and What we can do" available at https://www.ucsusa.org/sites/default/files/2019-10/Power-Failure-How-Climate-Change-Puts-Our-Electricity-at-Risk-and-What-We-Can-Do.pdf, accessed 12 June 2022.
129 Ockwell, D, Atela, J, Mbeva, K, Chengo, V, Byrne, R, Durrant, R, Kasprowicz, V, Ely, A (2019) "Can Pay-As-You-Go, Digitally Enabled Business Models Support Sustainability Transformations in Developing Countries? Outstanding Questions and a Theoretical Basis for Future Research" *Sustainability*, vol. 11(7), 2105.
130 Energy Sector Management Assistance Program (2020) "Funding the Sun: New Paradigms for Financing Off-Grid Solar Companies" Washington, DC: World Bank.
131 Jack, K and Smith, G (2015) "Pay as You Go: Prepaid Metering and Electricity Expenditures in South Africa" *American Economic Review: Papers & Proceedings*, vol. 105(5), 237–241.
132 Shupler, M, O'Keefe, M, Puzzolo, E et al (2021) "Pay-as-you-go liquified petroleum gas supports sustainable clean cooking in Kenya informal urban settlement during COVID-19 lockdown" Applied Energy 292, 116769.
133 InFiNe.lu (2021) "Webinar Inclusive Green Finance: Challenges and Opportunities" available at https://www.infine.lu/webinar-inclusive-green-finance-challenges-and-opportunities/, accessed 12 June 2022.
134 Ibid.
135 See the Luxembourg Sustainable Finance Strategy available at https://lsfi.lu/wp-content/uploads/2021/02/Luxembourg-Sustainable-Finance-Strategy_EN.pdf, accessed 10 August 2022.
136 Islam, SN and Winkel, J (2017) "Climate Change and Social Inequality" Department of Economic & Social Affairs Working Paper No. 152, October 2017.
137 Thomas, K, Hardy, RD, Lazrus, H, Mendez, M, Orlove, B, Rivera-Collazo, I, Roberts, JT, Rockman, M, Warner, BP, and Winthrop, R, (2019) "Explaining differential vulnerability to climate change: A social science review", *Wiley Interdisciplinary Review on Climate Change*, vol. 10(2), e565. doi: 10.1002/wcc.565.
138 He, C, Qiu, W and Yu, J (2022) "Climate Change Adaptation: A Study of Digital Financial Inclusion and Consumption among Rural Residents in China" available at https://www.frontiersin.org/articles/10.3389/fenvs.2022.889869/full, accessed 20 June 2022.
139 Lakuma, C.P., Marty, R. & Muhumuza, F (2019) "Financial inclusion and micro, small, and medium enterprises (MSMEs) growth in Uganda", *Journal of Innovation Entrepreneurship*, vol. 8, 15. https://doi.org/10.1186/s13731-019-0110-2. See Madan, N (2020) "A Review of Access to Finance by Micro, Small and Medium Enterprises and Digital Financial Services in Selected Asia-Pacific Least Developed Countries" Working Paper Series, Macroeconomic Policy and Financing for Development Division WP/20/03 April 2020.

140 Demekas, DG, & Grippa, P (2021) "Financial Regulation, Climate Change, and the Transition to a Low-Carbon Economy: A Survey of the Issues", IMF Working Papers, 2021(296), A001.
141 Muganyi, T, Yan, L and Sun, H (2021) "Green finance, fintech and environmental protection: Evidence from China" Environmental Science Ecotechnology, vol. 7, 100107.
142 Volz, U, Knaack, P, Nyman, J, Ramos, L, and Moling, J (2020) "Inclusive Green Finance: From Concept to Practice" Kuala Lumpur and London: Alliance for Financial Inclusion and SOAS, University of London.
143 AFI (2021) "Policy and Regulatory Reforms in the AFI Network 2021" available at https://www.afi-global.org/wp-content/uploads/2022/06/2021_Policy-Change-report.pdf, accessed 17 June 2022.
144 Prochaska, K (2019) "The 4P Framework of Inclusive Green Finance – Policy responses to climate change" AFI 18 June 2019.
145 Azad, MAK, Islam, MA, Sobhani, FA, Hassan, MS, Masukujjaman, M, (2022) "Revisiting the Current Status of Green Finance and Sustainable Finance Disbursement: A Policy Insights" *Sustainability*, vol. 14(14), 8911.
146 AFI (2020) "Climate Risk Insurance for the Agriculture Sector in Armenia" available at https://www.afi-global.org/wp-content/uploads/2020/12/AFI_IGF_armenia_CS_AW_digital.pdf, accessed 17 June 2022.
147 Ibid.
148 Ibid.
149 Grimm, S, Helwig, N, Reiners, W and Siddi, M (2021) "Leadership and Partnerships for the European Green Deal: EU Relations with (Re)Emerging Economies", *L'Europe en Formation*, vol. 393, 40–63. https://doi.org/10.3917/eufor.393.0040
150 Federal Nature Conservation Act, 2009.
151 AFI (2020) "AFI launches second edition of IGF policy landscape survey" available at https://www.afi-global.org/newsroom/news/afi-launches-second-edition-of-igf-policy-landscape-survey/, accessed 20 June 2022.
152 For instance, the Climate Finance Tracking Working Group, which includes the Islamic Development Bank, and the International Development Finance Club (IDFC) Climate Finance Working Group reached an agreement on a set of Common Principles for Climate Change Adaptation Finance Tracking in 2015. This was a voluntary joint initiative. A report on the lessons learned from the preceding three years of implementation was jointly released by the Working Groups at COP24 in 2018, and it highlighted the need to establish new methods for defining and documenting the impact of adaptation programmes.

Bibliography

A Abu Samah, H A M Shaffril, A Hamzah & B Abu Samah 'Factors affecting small-scale fishermen's adaptation toward the impacts of climate change: Reflections from Malaysian fishers' (2019) 9(3) *SAGE Open*. https://doi.org/10.1177/2158244019864204.

AFI 'AFI launches second edition of IGF policy landscape survey' (2020), available at https://www.afi-global.org/newsroom/news/afi-launches-second-edition-of-igf-policy-landscape-survey/, accessed on 20 June 2022.

AFI 'Climate risk insurance for the agriculture sector in Armenia' (2020), available at https://www.afi-global.org/wp-content/uploads/2020/12/AFI_IGF_armenia_CS_AW_digital.pdf, accessed on 17 June 2022.

AFI 'Policy and regulatory reforms in the AFI network 2021' (2021), available at https://www.afi-global.org/wp-content/uploads/2022/06/2021_Policy-Change-report.pdf, accessed on 17 June 2022.

Agriculture Policy, 2015.

H Amapindi 'Climate change in Namibia' (2022), available at https://www.benguelacc.org/climate-change-in-namibia/, accessed on 21 June 2022.

N Aroka 'Rainwater harvesting in rural Kenya: Reliability in a variable and changing climate' (2010), available at https://www.diva-portal.org/smash/get/diva2:354235/FULLTEXT02.pdf, accessed on 11 June 2022.

R I Arthur, D J Skerritt, A Schuhbauer, N Ebrahim, R M Friend & U R Sumaila 'Small-scale fisheries and local food systems: Transformations, threats and opportunities' (2021) 23(1) *Fish and Fisheries* 109 at 124.

M A K Azad, M A Islam, F A Sobhani, M S Hassan & M Masukujjaman 'Revisiting the current status of green finance and sustainable finance disbursement: A policy insights' (2022) 14(14) *Sustainability* 8911.

Benguela Current Commission 'Launch of Namibia's national programme on small-scale fisheries (NPOA-SSF) and acceleration of IYAFA-2022 (8–10 June 2022), Swakopmund, Namibia' (7 July 2022), available at https://www.benguelacc.org/launch-of-namibias-national-programme-on-small-scale-fisheries-npoa-ssf-and-celebration-of-iyafa-2022-8-10-june-2022-swakopmund-namibia/, accessed on 8 July 2022.

M Berlemann & M F Steinhardt 'Climate change, natural disasters, and migration - A survey of the empirical evidence' (2017) 63(4) *CESifo Economic Studies* 353 at 385. https://doi.org/10.1093/cesifo/ifx019.

Blue Print on Wealth Redistribution and Poverty Eradication, 2016.

E S Brondízio, Y Aumeeruddy-Thomas, P Bates, J Carino, A Fernández-Llamazares, M Farhan Ferrari, K Galvin, V Reyes-García, P McElwee, Z Molnár, A Samakov & U B Shrestha 'Locally based, regionally manifested, and globally relevant: Indigenous and local knowledge, values, and practices for nature' (2021) 46(1) *Annual Review of Environment and Resources* 481 at 509.

B A Byers 'Environmental threats and opportunities in Namibia: A comprehensive assessment' Research Discussion Paper No. 21, Directorate of Environmental Affairs, Ministry of Environment and Tourism, Windhoek, Namibia.

M Carter, A De Janvry, E Sadoulet & A Sarris 'Index-based weather insurance for developing countries: A review of evidence and a set of propositions for up-scaling' (2014), available at https://ferdi.fr/dl/df-kLB5hYBaUiR2Vysm2cH5DfCP/ferdi-p111-index-based-weather-insurance-for-developing-countries-a-review.pdf, accessed on 4 June 2022.

D Chapagain, L Bharati & C Borgemeister 'Declining vulnerability but rising impacts: The trends of climatic disasters in Nepal' (2022) 22 *Regional Environmental Change* 55. https://doi.org/10.1007/s10113-022-01903-5.

Climate Risk Profile: Namibia 'The World Bank Group' (2021), available at https://climateknowledgeportal.worldbank.org/sites/default/files/2021-08/15931-WB_Namibia%20Country%20Profile-WEB.pdf.

Constitution of the Republic of Namibia, 21 March 1990.

M Davis & S Clemmer 'Power failure: How climate change puts our electricity at risk – And what we can do' (2014), available at https://www.ucsusa.org/sites/default/files/2019-10/Power-Failure-How-Climate-Change-Puts-Our-Electricity-at-Risk-and-What-We-Can-Do.pdf, accessed on 12 June 2022.

D G Demekas & P Grippa 'Financial regulation, climate change, and the transition to a low-carbon economy: A survey of the issues' (IMF working papers, 2021(296), A001).

E Dirkx, C Hager, M Tadross, S Bethune & B Curtis 'Climate change vulnerability & adaptation assessment Namibia', Desert Foundation of Namibia & Climate Analysis Group for the Ministry of Environment and Tourism, Final Report of March 2008.

E Duflo, M Kremer & J Robinson 'Nudging farmers to use fertilizer: Theory and experimental evidence from Kenya' (2011) 101(6) *The American Economic Review* 2350 at 2390.

D Dunne & A Chandrasekhar 'Loss and damage: What happens when climate change destroys lives and cultures?' *PreventionWeb*, 28 September 2022.

Energy Sector Management Assistance Program *Funding the Sun: New Paradigms for Financing Off-Grid Solar Companies* (Washington, DC: World Bank, 2020).

Environmental Management Act, Act No. 7 of 2007.

Federal Nature Conservation Act, 2009.

G Fink, K Jack & F Masiye 'The impact of seasonal food and cash loans on small-scale farmers in Zambia' (2016), available at https://www.atai-research.org/wp-content/uploads/2016/07/Food-Constraints-Policy-Brief_final.pdf, accessed on 15 June 2022.

Food and Agriculture Organisation 'Fishery and aquaculture country profiles: Namibia' (n.d.), available at https://www.fao.org/fishery/en/facp/nam?lang=en, accessed on 21 June 2022.

T H Frawely, E M Finkbeiner & L B Crowder 'Environmental and institutional degradation in the globalized economy: Lessons from small-scale fisheries in the Gulf of California' (2019) 24(1) *Ecology and Society*, available at https://www.jstor.org/stable/26796922, accessed on 20 June 2022.

M Gaworecki 'Randomised controlled trial in Uganda finds that paying people not to cut down trees works' *MONGABAY* 27 July 2017.

Government of Namibia 'Namibia vision 2030' Policy Framework for Long-Term National Development (Summary), Office of the President, 2004.

R Griffins & J Howard (eds) *Oceans and Marine Resources in a Changing Climate: A Technical Input to the 2013 National Climate Assessment* (Washington, DC: Island Press, 2012).

S Grimm, N Helwig, W Reiners & M Siddi 'Leadership and partnerships for the European green deal: EU relations with (re)emerging economies' (2021) 393 *L'Europe en Formation* 40 at 63. https://doi.org/10.3917/eufor.393.0040.

P Hazell, R Sberro-Kessler & P Varangis 'When and how should agricultural insurance be subsidized: Issues and good practices' World Bank Group (2017), available at https://openknowledge.worldbank.org/bitstream/handle/10986/31438/117363.pdf?sequence=4, accessed on 3 June 2022.

C He, W Qiu & J Yu 'Climate change adaptation: A study of digital financial inclusion and consumption among rural residents in China' (2022), available at https://www.frontiersin.org/articles/10.3389/fenvs.2022.889869/full, accessed on 20 June 2022.

A Hirsch, Y Parag & J Guerrero 'Microgrids: A review of technologies, key drivers, and outstanding issues' (2018) 90 *Renewable and Sustainable Energy Reviews* 402 at 411.

P Howden-Chapman, J Siri, E Chisholm, R Chapman, C N H Doll & A Capon 'SDG3: Ensure healthy lives and promote well-being for all at all ages' (2017), available at https://council.science/wp-content/uploads/2017/03/SDGs-interactions-3-healthy-lives.pdf, accessed on 22 June 2022.

Human Rights Watch 'Breaking the poverty trap: Why poverty and inequality are human rights issues' (14 October 2020), available at https://www.hrw.org/news/2020/10/14/breaking-poverty-trap, accessed on 10 June 2022.

L Hutchings, C D Van der Lingen, L J Shannon, R J Crawford, H M Verheye, C H Bartholomae, A K Van der Plas, D Louw, A Kreiner, M Ostrowski & Q Fidel 'The Benguela Current: An ecosystem of four components' (2009) 83(1–4) *Progress in Oceanography* 15 at 32.

J A Iitembu, V N Erasmus, U Uanivi, D Nakwaya, R R Horeb & E Nangolo 'The hits and misses of Namibia's attempt to implement the Ecosystem Approach to Fisheries (EAF) management' (2021) 7(1) *Ecosystem Health and Sustainability* 1 at 12.

InFiNe.lu 'Webinar inclusive green finance: Challenges and opportunities' (2021), available at https://www.infine.lu/webinar-inclusive-green-finance-challenges-and-opportunities/, accessed on 12 June 2022.

Intergovernmental Panel on Climate Change (IPCC) 'Climate change: A threat to human wellbeing and health of the planet. Taking action now can secure our future' *IPCC Reports* (28 February 2022).

S N Islam & J Winkel 'Climate change and social inequality' (Department of Economic & Social Affairs working paper no. 152, October 2017).

K Jack & G Smith 'Pay as You Go: Prepaid Metering and Electricity Expenditures in South Africa' (2015) 105(5) *American Economic Review: Papers & Proceedings* 237 at 241.

D K Jain, A Chida & R D Pathak 'Climate risk insurance in pacific small island developing states: Possibilities, challenges and vulnerabilities - A comprehensive review' (2022) 27 *Mitigation and Adaptation Strategies for Global Change* 26.

S Jessel, S Sawyer & D Hernández 'Energy, poverty, and health in climate change: A comprehensive review of an emerging literature' (2019) 12(7) *Front Public Health* 357.

D Karlan, E D Kutsoati, M McMillan & C Udry 'Crop price indemnified loans for farmers: A pilot experiment in rural Ghana' (2011) 78(1) *The Journal of Risk and Insurance* 37 at 55.

D Karlan, R Osei, I Osei-Akoto & C Udry 'Agriculture decisions after relaxing credit and risk constraints' (2014) 129(2) *The Quarterly Journal of Economics* 597 at 652.

Kyoto Protocol, 16 February 2005.

R Kyte 'Climate change is a challenge for sustainable development' World Bank, 15 January 2014.

C P Lakuma, R Marty & F Muhumuza 'Financial inclusion and micro, small, and medium enterprises (MSMEs) growth in Uganda' (2019) 8 *Journal of Innovation Entrepreneurship* 15. https://doi.org/10.1186/s13731-019-0110-2.

Lusaka Agreement, 2008.

Luxembourg Sustainable Finance Strategy, available at https://lsfi.lu/wp-content/uploads/2021/02/Luxembourg-Sustainable-Finance-Strategy_EN.pdf, accessed on 10 August 2022.

N Madan 'A review of access to finance by micro, small and medium enterprises and digital financial services in selected Asia-Pacific least developed countries' Working Paper Series, Macroeconomic Policy and Financing for Development Division WP/20/03, April 2020.

I Mapaure 'Climate change in Namibia: Projected trends and effects' in O C Ruppel & Ruppel-Schlichting (eds) *Environmental Law and Policy in Namibia* (Hanns Seidel Foundation, Namibia, 2011).

MAPFRE Economics 'Financial inclusion in insurance' *Madrid, MAPFRE Economics* (2020), available at https://www.mapfre.com/media/economic-research/2020/mapfre-economics-inclusion-financiera-11-06-2020-ENU.pdf, accessed on 3 June 2022.

R Marenga & J S Amupanda 'The coronavirus and social justice in Namibia' (2021) 48(2) *South African Journal of Political Studies* 206 at 225.

J M Massey 'Climate change, culture and cultural rights' memo/expanded outline prepared by Justine Marrion Massey with contributions from Spring 2020 United Nations Practicum Students, University of California Davis School of Law, 15 May

2020' (2020), available at https://www.ohchr.org/sites/default/files/Documents/Issues/CulturalRights/Call_ClimateChange/JMassey.pdf, accessed on 10 May 2022.

D Mhlanga 'The role of financial inclusion and FinTech in addressing climate-related challenges in the industry 4.0: Lessons for sustainable development goals' (2022), available at https://www.frontiersin.org/articles/10.3389/fclim.2022.949178/full, accessed on 30 September 2022.

Ministry of Fisheries and Marine Resources'Current status report: Knowledge baseline for Namibia's central marine plan', available at https://mfmr.gov.na/documents/411764/430830/National+Overview+for+Marine+Spatial+Planning+and+Knowledge+Baseline+for+Namibia+-+reduced.pdf/a0a419aa-ebe8-1966-0a78-dd772861ad5b, accessed on 23 June 2022.

Ministry of Fisheries and Marine Resources 'Namibia sustainable blue economy policy 2022–2031' (2022), available at https://mfmr.gov.na/documents/411764/2631681/Draft+Namibia+Sustainable+Blue+Economy+Policy.pdf/b4b334bd-b3e7-4e8b-442f-cbbc6fac34e2, accessed on 10 August 2022.

Ministry of Fisheries and Marine Resources Strategic Plan – 2017/18-2021/2, p. 7.

T Moyo 'Fishing industry resurgence 2022' *The Namibian*, 28 April 2022.

T Muganyi, L Yan & H Sun 'Green finance, fintech and environmental protection: Evidence from China' (2021) 7 *Environmental Science Ecotechnology* 100107.

G Mukumbira 'Can green hydrogen be the future fuel?' (2020), available at https://www.sasscal.org/can-green-hydrogen-be-the-future-fuel/, accessed on 22 June 2022.

B Mureverwi 'Energy situation in Southern Africa' (n.d.), available at https://www.tralac.org/discussions/article/8474-energy-situation-in-southern-africa.html, accessed on 3 June 2022.

Namibia Chamber of Environment 'Why the Namibian moratorium on sardine fishing must continue' *Conservation Namibia*, 15 November 2021.

Namibia Ministry of Health and Social Services (MoHSS) 'National health policy framework 2010–2020' (2010).

Namibia's 2010 'National policy on climate change', available at https://www.adaptation-undp.org/sites/default/files/downloads/namibia_nationalclimatechangepolicyfornamib.pdf, accessed on 30 June 2022.

Namibia's 2013–2020 'National climate change strategy and action plan', available at https://www.meft.gov.na/files/files/National%20Climate%20Change%20Strategy%20&%20Action%20Plan%202013%20-%202020.pdf, accessed on 30 June 2022.

Namibia's First Adaptation Communication titled 'Republic of Namibia first adaptation communication: Namibia's climate change adaptation communication to the UNFCCC', available at https://unfccc.int/sites/default/files/resource/namibia-adaptation-communication-to-the-unfccc.pdf, accessed on 23 June 2022.

Namibia's Second Voluntary National Review Report on the Implementation of the Sustainable Development Goals Towards Agenda 2030, available at https://sustainabledevelopment.un.org/content/documents/279462021_VNR_Report_Namibia.pdf, accessed on 12 June 2022.

Namibia's Vision 2030, available at https://www.npc.gov.na/national-plans/vision-2030/, accessed on 1 June 2022.

Namibia's White Paper on Energy, 1998.

National Drought Policy and Strategy, 1997.

National Heritage Act, 2004 (Act 27 of 2004).

National Land Policy, 1998.

National Malaria Programme Strategic Plan 2015–2020.

National Policy for Disaster Risk Management, 2011.

Nature Conservation Amendment Act, 1996 (Act No. 5 of 1996).
Nature Conservation Ordinance of 1975.
NDP5, available at https://www.npc.gov.na/national-plans/national-plans-ndp-5/, accessed on 1 June 2022.
New Partnership for Africa's Development, 2001.
D Ockwell, J Atela, K Mbeva, V Chengo, R Byrne, R Durrant, V Kasprowicz & A Ely 'Can pay-as-you-go, digitally enabled business models support sustainability transformations in developing countries? Outstanding questions and a theoretical basis for future research' (2019) 11(7) *Sustainability* 2105.
Ombudsman Act, 1990 (No. 7 of 1990).
One Ocean Hub 'Namibia' available at https://oneoceanhub.org/where-we-work/namibia/, accessed on 22 August 2022. See also U Khan 'Exploring the 'Blue Carbon' potential in Namibia' (2022), available at https://oneoceanhub.org/exploring-the-blue-carbon-potential-in-namibia/, accessed on 22 June 2022.
Organisation for Economic Co-operation and Development 'Climate change and the long term fiscal sustainability' (2021), available at https://www.oecd.org/gov/budgeting/scoping-paper-on-fiscal-sustainability-and-climate-change.pdf, accessed on 13 June 2022.
Paris Agreement, 4 November 2016.
H Park & J D Kim 'Transition towards green banking: Role of financial regulators and financial institutions' (2020) 5 *Asian Journal for Sustainability and Social Responsibility* 5.
V Pineiro, J Arias & H Dearlove 'How to encourage farmers to adopt sustainable agriculture' (2021), available at https://www.ifpri.org/blog/how-encourage-farmers-adopt-sustainable-agriculture, accessed on 14 June 2022.
Policy on desertification, 2014–2024.
E Pranzini, G Anfuso, I Cinelli, M Piccardi & G Vitale 'Shore protection structures increase and evolution on the Northern Tuscany Coast (Italy): Influence of tourism industry' (2018) 10(11) *Water* 1647. https://doi.org/10.3390/w10111647.
K Prochaska 'The 4P framework of inclusive green finance – Policy responses to climate change' *AFI*, 18 June 2019.
H Reid, L Sahlen, J Stage & J Macgregor 'Climate change impacts on Namibia's natural resources and economy' (2008) 8(5) *Climate Policy* 452 at 466.
D Remmert 'Towards a blue economy: Harnessing Namibia's coastal resources sustainability' (2018), available at https://ippr.org.na/wp-content/uploads/2019/02/BlueEconomy_WEB-1.pdf, accessed on 23 June 2022.
O C Ruppel 'Foundations, sources and implications of national environmental law' in O C Ruppel & Ruppel-Schlichting (eds) *Environmental Law and Policy in Namibia* (Hanns Seidel Foundation, Namibia, 2011).
SADC 'SADC regional infrastructure development' Short Term Action Plan Assessment 2019, available at https://www.sadc.int/sites/default/files/2021-07/SADC_Regional_Infrastruture_Development.pdf, accessed on 2 June 2022.
SADC Protocol for Fisheries, 2006.
SADC Protocol on Forestry, 2002.
SADC Regional Agriculture Policy, 2013.
SADC Regional Biodiversity Strategy, 2008.
SADC Regional Water Policy and Regional Strategy, 2006.
G Sanzila 'Namibian MPs call for collaboration to avert energy crisis in SADC, 11/07/2022' (2022), available at https://www.parliament.na/namibian-mps-call-for-collaboration-to-avert-energy-crisis-in-sadc-11-07-2022/, accessed on 7 August 2022.
Sendai Framework for Disaster Risk Reduction 2015–2030.

D S Shumba 'Bundling weather index insurance with microfinance: Trekking the long road between expectations and reality – A study on Sub-Saharan Africa' in A I Ribeiro-Barros, D S Tevera, L F Goulao & L D Tivana (eds) *Food Systems Resilience*. IntechOpen (2022). https://doi.org/10.5772/intechopen.101742.

M Shupler, M O'Keefe & E Puzzolo 'Pay-as-you-go liquified petroleum gas supports sustainable clean cooking in Kenya informal urban settlement during COVID-19 lockdown' (2021) 292 *Applied Energy* 116769.

S Sirtaine & C Mckay 'In an era of urgent climate risk, does financial inclusion matter?' (2022), available at https://www.cgap.org/blog/era-urgent-climate-risk-does-financial-inclusion-matter, accessed 23 June 2022.

D L Sparks 'Namibia's coastal and marine development potential' (1984) 83(333) *African Affairs* 477 at 496.

The Economist Namibia 'SADC creates centre for renewable energy to stimulate rural electrification' 26 February 2020.

K Thomas, R D Hardy, H Lazrus, M Mendez, B Orlove, I Rivera-Collazo, J T Roberts, M Rockman, B P Warner & R Winthrop 'Explaining differential vulnerability to climate change: A social science review' (2019) 10(2) *Wiley Interdisciplinary Review on Climate Change* e565. https://doi.org/10.1002/wcc.565.

G C Thomson 'Climate change in Namibia part 2: Current and projected changes' 29 October 2021.

United Nations 'UN report: Nature's dangerous decline 'unnprecedented'; species extinction 'accelerating'' (2019), available at https://www.un.org/sustainabledevelopment/blog/2019/05/nature-decline-unprecedented-report/, accessed on 19 June 2022.

United Nations Climate Change 'Rainwater harvesting system to reduce climate change vulnerability – Indonesia', available at https://unfccc.int/climate-action/momentum-for-change/activity-database/rainwater-harvesting-system-to-reduce-climate-change-vulnerability, accessed on 21 June 2022.

United Nations Sustainable Development Goals, available at https://unfoundation.org/what-we-do/issues/sustainable-development-goals/?gclid=EAIaIQobChMI58jN77D8-gIVkt1RCh0iLAajEAAYASAAEgIlq_D_BwE, accessed on 12 June 2022.

USAID 'Adapting to coastal climate change: A guidebook for development planners' (2009), available at https://www.crc.uri.edu/download/CoastalAdaptationGuide.pdf, accessed on 1 June 2022.

T Uwamahoro. *Bringing Primary Health Care to Remote Populations through Public-Private Partnerships: The SHOPS Mister Sister Experience*. USAID (2013).

U Volz, P Knaack, J Nyman, L Ramos & J Moling *Inclusive Green Finance: From Concept to Practice*. Kuala Lumpur and London: Alliance for Financial Inclusion and SOAS, University of London (2020).

M I Vousdoukas, J Clarke & R Ranasinghe 'African heritage sites threatened as sea-level rise accelerates' (2022) 12 *Nature Climate Change* 256 at 262.

F Wang 'Technologies and perspectives for achieving carbon neutrality' (2021) 2(4) *The Innovation*. https://doi.org/10.1016/j.xinn.2021.100180.

P Waryszak, A Gavoille, A A Whitt, J Kelvin & P I Macreadie 'Combining gray and green infrastructure to improve coastal resilience: Lessons learnt from hybrid flood defenses' (2021) 63(3) *Coastal Engineering Journal* 335 at 350. https://doi.org/10.1080/21664250.2021.1920278.

L Westlund & J Zelasney (eds) 'Securing sustainable small-scale fisheries: Sharing good practices from around the world' Food and Agriculture Organisation of the United Nations Fisheries and Aquaculture Technical Paper 644.

World Bank 'Creating markets for smallholder farmers in Mali' (2022), available at https://www.worldbank.org/en/results/2022/05/17/afw-creating-markets-for-smallholder-farmers-in-mali, accessed on 15 June 2022.

World Health Organisation 'Country cooperation strategy III 2018–2022: Accelerating progress towards universal health coverage' (2019), available at https://www.afro.who.int/sites/default/files/2019-12/CCS%20Namibia%20-%2007%20August%202019.pdf, accessed on 25 June 2022.

D Yang & X Gine (2005–2006) 'Insurance, credit and technology adoption in Malawi', available at https://www.povertyactionlab.org/evaluation/insurance-credit-and-technology-adoption-malawi, accessed on 11 June 2022.

E Zere, D Oluwole, J M Kirigia, C N Mwikisa & T Mbeeli 'Inequities in skilled attendance at birth in Namibia: A decomposition analysis' (2011) 11 *BMC Pregnancy Childbirth* 34.

15 Exploring the legal protection of bank depositors as an instrument for promoting financial inclusion in Zimbabwe

Ashley B. Nyaude

15.1 Introduction

The importance of banks in the financial system has been emphasised over the course of many financial crises across the globe.[1] The crises also focus attention on the plight of bank depositors, who have deposited their money in banks that subsequently failed. While one small isolated bank failure may not have a systemic effect on a financial system, it is commonplace that the arrival of financial conglomeration has created a landscape of complex and contagious interconnectedness that transcends domestic borders.[2] The result is that a threatening bank failure may trigger a "bank run"[3] with seismic spill-over effects that can erode financial system stability on domestic and global levels.[4]

Over the years, many countries have attempted to avoid crises and maintain bank depositor confidence by applying implicit deposit protection arrangements that arise when the public, including depositors and other creditors, expect full protection in the event of a bank failure. These measures involve reimbursing depositors with funds obtained from taxpayers' money.[5] The need for a more structured approach to deposit protection in order to maintain public confidence was recognised by the United States in the wake of the Great Depression (1929–1933) when it pioneered an explicit deposit insurance scheme (EDIS or DIS) as the preferred framework to deal with depositor protection during a bank failure.[6] Many other countries subsequently followed suit and this number increased exponentially in recent years because an EDIS reduces uncertainty and risk for depositors and can be helpful in reducing expectations on the part of the public of government support in the event of a bank failure.[7]

A DIS is established by a government to protect all depositors against the loss of their insured deposits in the event of failure of member institutions licensed to operate banking or finance business.[8] As an integral component of an effective financial safety net, deposit insurance aims at reducing the risk of system failure and preventing bank runs, hence stabilising the financial system during financial turbulences.[9] Depositors will know when, how much and how their deposits are protected in the event of a bank failure. A DIS contributes to financial stability and prevents bank runs if depositors have confidence that they will have access to their funds quickly when a bank fails.[10]

DOI: 10.4324/9781003369400-15

Financial inclusion is very broadly defined as "the provision of access to financial services for all".[11] Financial inclusion, also defined as the accessibility of deposit and credit services for the integration of households, corporates and financial intermediaries, can enhance financial stability by increasing customers' access to the formal financial system, which will increase the aggregate saving.[12] For central banks, financial inclusion matters on the macroeconomic level by the way of poverty reduction and long-term economic growth, allowing the poor to invest in physical assets and education, reducing income inequality and contributing to economic growth.[13] An increased financial inclusion also gives a stable deposit-funding basis for depositors, especially when they are backed by an effective deposit insurance.[14]

Deposit insurance plays a key role in the promotion of financial inclusion as it contributes to financial stability and promotes competition in the financial sector, which can lead to a reduction in poverty. Potential depositors may have greater trust in banks if they believe their savings are insured and this may lead more individuals to open bank accounts. Deposit insurance also can promote confidence in financial institutions and thus potentially promote savings among the poor.

Zimbabwe is a developing country with a fragile economy[15] that, like most other countries, has to deal with many challenges, including failing banks. Zimbabwe has had a significant number of bank failures since its independence in 1980.[16] As a result, Zimbabwe has operated an EDIS since 1 July 2003 to protect all depositors, whether individuals or businesses, against loss of part of or all of their eligible deposits in the event of failure of a contributory institution.[17] The DIS in Zimbabwe is administered by the Deposit Protection Corporation (DPC). The DPC is an independent statutory body established by the government of Zimbabwe in terms of the DPC Act (Chapter 24:29) to administer the DIS in Zimbabwe. This chapter considers the measures taken by the DPC to protect bank depositors and promote financial inclusion to pronounce on whether it adequately achieves this goal.

The Global Financial Crisis (GFC) of 2007–2008[18] confirmed the critical role of explicit and privately funded deposit insurance in maintaining confidence in the financial system.[19] In the throes of the GFC, the International Association of Deposit Insurers' (IADI)[20] and the Basel Committee on Banking Supervision (BCBS) issued the "Core Principles for Effective Deposit Insurance Systems" in June 2009 (revised in November 2014).[21] A Compliance Assessment Methodology for the Core Principles was completed in December 2010.[22] The Core Principles and their compliance assessment methodology (together the Core Principles) are used by jurisdictions as a benchmark for assessing the quality of their deposit insurance systems and for identifying gaps in their deposit insurance practices and measures to address them.[23]

Global, regional and national-level policymakers are increasingly embracing financial inclusion as an important priority for promoting inclusive economic growth and social development. These policymakers recognise the strength of financial inclusion as a strong influence of economic growth.[24] In 2009, the Group of Twenty (G20) formally committed to focusing on improving access to financial services for the poor, recognising that more than two billion adults around the world do not have access to formal or semi-formal financial services, with most residing in Africa, Latin America, Asia and the Middle East.[25] The significance of financial inclusion in the economic development agenda has also been characterised by the formation of networks and organisations with a specific focus on financial inclusion matters.[26] Such organisations or networks include the Alliance for Financial Inclusion (AFI)[27] and the Global Partnership for Financial Inclusion (GPFI).[28] This development has resulted in the attempt to define best practice standards to guide the implementation of financial inclusion initiatives, such as the G20 Principles for Innovative Financial Inclusion developed in 2010.[29]

For IADI, as the international standard-setting body for deposit insurers, there is also an increasing interest in analysing the discussions around financial inclusion-related topics, as a result of the growing number of technical notes from the Financial Sector Assessment Programs (FSAP) conducted since 2000 on this matter.[30] The Core Principles define financial inclusion as the extent to which individuals and entities have access to and utilise formal financial services.[31] The Core Principles, among others, state that "deposit insurers should make efforts to stay abreast of financial inclusion initiatives and associated technological innovations occurring in their jurisdictions, particularly those affecting unsophisticated small-scale depositors".[32]

Van Roosebeke and Defina pointed out that the utilisation of financial technology ("FinTech") and the Covid-19 pandemic are among the emerging issues that are expected to significantly affect the activities of deposit insurers in the near future.[33] In recent years, e-money products have become increasingly popular and improved access to digital financial services for people previously unserved or underserved by the traditional banking sector.[34] Policy discussions concerning the extent to which deposit insurers cover these products yield considerations regarding several models, including the direct, passthrough and exclusion approaches.[35] Deposit insurer coverage leads to challenges regarding the identification and pricing of risks as well as safeguards for timely reimbursement.[36] E-money service providers operate fundamentally differently from traditional banks. As such, they are exposed to unique risks via (at times) difficult-to-characterise transmission channels thus revealing uncertainty for the deposit insurer.[37] In addition, cyber security is increasingly becoming a factor of risk to the provision and availability of digital financial products and thus to financial stability as a whole.[38] Monitoring, pricing and potentially managing operational resilience risks at member institutions may be a challenge to deposit insurers because of potential information asymmetries and technical knowledge gaps.[39] Moreover, deposit insurers themselves may be exposed to cyber security risks in their operations.

In response to the Covid-19 pandemic, the Government of Zimbabwe introduced a national lockdown that saw all business activities grind to a halt except for essential services, as part of the measures to limit the spread of the deadly virus.[40] The lockdown had an adverse impact on the performance of various sectors of the economy from which member institutions derive business for sustenance. As stated by the DPC, the full impact of the pandemic is yet to be determined.[41] On a positive note, the Covid-19 pandemic has hastened the advent of the fourth industrial revolution, also known as the digital revolution.[42] The banking sector, in response to the Covid-19 pandemic, resorted to promoting the use of digital and virtual platforms for service offerings, while simultaneously downsizing the brick-and-mortar branches.[43] According to the DPC, these actions have the potential for heightening operational and credit risk within the sector through cybercrime and depressed loan collections, which call for enhanced deposit protection.[44]

In the Zimbabwean context, financial inclusion is defined as the effective use of a wide range of quality, affordable and accessible financial services, provided in a fair and transparent manner through formal or regulated entities to all Zimbabweans.[45] One of the most pronounced trends currently observed among the AFI member countries is the development of national financial inclusion strategies.[46] Zimbabwe became a member of the AFI network in 2012.[47] To increase the pace and impact of financial inclusion reforms, the Reserve Bank of Zimbabwe (RBZ), as central bank, through a stakeholder consultative process, led the development of a five-year National Financial Inclusion Strategy (2016–2020) (NFIS), which was launched on 11 March 2016 by the Minister of Finance and Economic Development.[48] The main objectives of the NFIS is to increase the overall level of access to formal financial services within the country and increase the proportion of banked adults.[49]

The DPC is an active member of the National Financial Inclusion Forum spearheaded by the RBZ to strengthen financial inclusion in Zimbabwe. Other members of the Forum include financial sector regulatory bodies, media, banking institutions and consumer advocacy bodies.[50] The DIS in Zimbabwe promotes financial inclusion by protecting a majority of the depositors, levelling the playing field, promoting confidence in formal financial institutions, affording broad access to safe and affordable small savings accounts and complementing other financial safety net players.[51]

This chapter is organised as follows. Section 15.2 analyses the link between financial inclusion and deposit insurance. Section 15.3 provides an overview of the Core Principles that promote financial inclusion. Section 15.4 studies the Zimbabwean DIS and concentrates on the measures taken by the DPC to protect bank depositors and promote financial inclusion to pronounce on whether it adequately achieves this objective. Section 15.5 concludes and presents some recommendations.

15.2 Financial inclusion and deposit insurance

Financial exclusion plays a key role in the creation and amplification of poverty by limiting the extent to which poor and marginalised communities have access to financial services.[52] Generally, an individual is considered financially excluded when one is not able to access some or all the services offered by mainstream financial institutions in one's country of residence due to problems associated with access, conditions, prices, marketing or self-exclusion.[53] Banking institutions have often argued that it is too expensive to invest in traditional infrastructure in the form of brick-and-mortar branches, which are required to reach the under-served population segments due to high transaction costs and huge set-up costs.[54] In most cases, the physical infrastructure in the form of the road network, electricity and telephone services is often sparse and dilapidated if not dysfunctional.[55] Commercial banks have proactively leveraged alternative delivery channels such as mobile phone banking and agency banking to increase outreach efficiency while keeping transaction costs low.[56]

Financial inclusion is defined as an absence of price or non-price barriers in the use of financial services.[57] Financial inclusion means that individuals and businesses have access to useful and affordable financial products and services that meet their needs, namely, transactions, payments, savings, credit and insurance, all of which must be delivered in a responsible and sustainable way.[58] Financial inclusion efforts seek to ensure that all households and businesses, irrespective of income level, have access to and can effectively use the appropriate financial services they need to improve their lives.[59] On a larger scale, financial inclusion is linked to a country's economic and social development and plays a key role in reducing extreme poverty.[60] Some of the benefits of financial inclusion include freedom from the clutches of informal lenders or loan sharks; enhances financial deepening; promotes inclusive and equitable economic growth; boosts employment opportunities; promotes formalisation of the economy; and promotes the growth of formal sources of credit, poverty reduction and enhances financial stability.[61]

An EDIS is a key component of the financial safety net[62] for many countries, which also includes prudential regulation and supervision, lender of last resort facilities and a bank resolution framework.[63] As discussed previously, deposit insurance enhances financial stability and can promote competition in the financial sector, which can lead to a reduction in poverty.[64] Potential depositors will have greater trust in banks if they believe their savings are insured and this will lead more individuals to open bank accounts.[65] Deposit insurance can also promote confidence in financial institutions and thus potentially promote savings among the poor.[66]

Despite the noticeable connection between financial inclusion and deposit insurance, researchers have argued that the role of deposit insurance in promoting financial inclusion through financial stability and confidence-building is the most indirect.[67] According to the IADI, most explicit deposit insurance systems are not designed to have a direct effect on the poorest segments of society.[68] The IADI points out that although most deposit insurance systems are designed to protect small depositors, the poorest segments of the population are often not participants in the formal financial sector and do not fall within the group of small depositors that benefit from deposit insurance.[69]

Demaestri and others agree with this view and note that they are not aware of any country that has adopted a deposit insurance system that explicitly states poverty reduction as an objective.[70] They are of the view that deposit insurance systems can provide benefits to the very poor indirectly by contributing to the stability of the financial system and by ensuring that the cost of financial rescues is borne by the banking industry and not the taxpayers. Most deposit insurers do not have an explicit objective to promote financial inclusion.[71] Instead, the most common objectives of deposit insurers include contributing to financial stability by reducing the incentives for insured depositors (primarily small depositors) to remove their deposits from a bank unexpectedly, protecting less financially sophisticated depositors, improving competition in the financial system by levelling the playing field for smaller banks or enhancing contestability and reducing the use of public funds in financial rescues.[72] Indeed, all these objectives indirectly benefit the poorest of society, but they do not necessarily contribute directly to the furtherance of financial access.[73]

In a comment to the Demaestri paper, Isoard y Viesca also maintained that a sound deposit insurance system can contribute to poverty alleviation indirectly by fostering financial stability and the sound functioning of the payments system.[74] Isoard y Viesca is of the view that addressing financial inclusion requires that public policy encourages the existence of simple and accessible financial intermediation services to promote savings among the poor and generate their confidence in financial institutions. They suggest that deposit insurance should be extended to other financial intermediaries such as savings institutions, credit unions, mutual funds and informal microfinance institutions (MFIs), but that separate funds should be established for each type of intermediary covered.[75]

On whether deposit insurance can play a more direct role in promoting financial inclusion, the AIDI is of the view that, from a practical standpoint, deposit insurance policies and procedures as expressed in the Core Principles and individual deposit insurer mandates may directly affect financial inclusion, mainly through policies and practices governing membership, coverage, funding and public awareness.[76] For example, whether membership is compulsory or voluntary and whether it includes specialised microfinance providers along with mainstream banks; the level and scope of coverage and whether very small deposits and small depositors are offered the benefits of insurance; the type of funding systems employed and how the deposit insurance system is financed, the funding treatment of specialised microfinance institutions as compared with mainstream banks may have an impact on risk-taking in the financial sector and the evolution of the industry as well as the cost of serving the poor if the costs of deposit insurance are passed along to consumers; and lastly how the deposit insurer conducts public awareness and the extent to which the public, particularly the lower income segments, are aware of important nuances in deposit insurance protections may make a difference in the degree of confidence and trust poor populations have in the mainstream banking system.[77]

Therefore, it is submitted that, although most deposit insurers do not have an explicit objective to promote financial inclusion, specific policies in deposit insurance systems that encourage simple and accessible financial intermediation services may directly affect financial inclusion.

15.3 IADI Core Principles promoting financial inclusion

15.3.1 Background

The IADI was established in 2002 to contribute to the enhancement of deposit insurance effectiveness and safety by promoting guidance and international cooperation.[78] The IADI and the BCBS issued the Core Principles in June 2009 (revised in November 2014).[79] A compliance assessment methodology for the Core Principles was completed in December 2010.[80] The Core Principles and their compliance assessment methodology (together the Core Principles) are used by jurisdictions as a benchmark for assessing the quality of their deposit insurance systems and identifying gaps in their deposit insurance practices and measures to address them.[81] The Core Principles are also used by the International Monetary Fund (IMF) and the World Bank, in the context of the Financial Sector Assessment Program (FSAP), to assess the effectiveness of jurisdictions' DIS and practices.[82] The Core Principles are reflective of, and designed to be adaptable to, a broad range of jurisdictional circumstances, settings and structures.[83]

The Core Principles are intended as a voluntary framework supporting effective deposit insurance practices. National authorities are free to put in place supplementary measures that they deem necessary to achieve effective deposit insurance in their jurisdictions.[84] Furthermore, the Core Principles are not designed to cover all the needs and circumstances of every banking system. Instead, specific country circumstances should be more appropriately considered in the context of existing laws and powers to fulfil the public policy objectives and mandate of the deposit insurance system.[85] The Compliance Assessment part of the Core Principles is intended to help the deposit insurer benchmark their deposit insurance system against the Core Principles – to judge how well the system is meeting its public policy objectives. The assessment can also aid the deposit insurer and policymakers in making improvements to the deposit insurance system.[86]

As an association that members join voluntarily, the IADI has limited ability to directly influence the practices and public policy objectives of its members.[87] The IADI is not a rulemaking body and lacks direct authority to influence its members to alter their public policy objectives or adopt new practices or positions with respect to financial inclusion or other matters.[88] However, the IADI can facilitate dialogue among its members to discuss the various policy and operational issues that may arise from financial inclusion initiatives and innovations both within and outside of the traditional banking sector, and the implications of such developments for deposit insurers.

The AIDI Core Principles observe that, while in most jurisdictions promoting financial inclusion does not fall explicitly within the mandate of the deposit insurer, deposit insurers should make efforts to stay abreast of financial inclusion initiatives and associated technological innovations occurring in their jurisdictions, particularly those affecting unsophisticated small-scale depositors.[89] The involvement of deposit insurance in the promotion of financial inclusion, for example, the extension of coverage to deposit-like stored value products, should be undertaken with strong engagement and coordination with supervisory authorities and other financial safety-net participants.[90] Moreover, public awareness campaigns should adequately address the types of deposits and money transfer vehicles covered by deposit insurance and the types that are not covered to minimise potential confusion among small-scale depositors and financial service providers alike.[91]

As pointed out previously, deposit insurance policies and procedures as expressed in the Core Principles affect financial inclusion, primarily through policies and practices governing membership, coverage, funding and public awareness.[92] These specific Core Principles will be discussed in the following sections to determine the extent to which they promote financial inclusion.

15.3.2 Core Principle one: Public policy objectives

Core Principle one deals with public policy objectives and states that the principal public policy objectives for deposit insurance systems are to protect depositors and contribute to financial stability. These objectives should be formally specified and publicly disclosed, and the design of the deposit insurance system should reflect the system's public policy objectives.[93]

Demaestri and others observe that the most commonly stated objectives are to contribute to financial system stability, protect less financially sophisticated depositors, increase competition in a financial system and reduce the need for public funds to deal with financial sector problems.[94] They note that poverty reduction is not an explicit objective of any known deposit insurance system. They further observe that a common objective for most deposit insurance schemes is to contribute to the stability of a country's financial system by reducing the incentives for insured depositors, mainly small depositors to remove their deposits from a bank unexpectedly.[95] This facilitates stability, particularly in periods of economic instability, and helps reduce the potential for systemic crisis. This is usually done in conjunction with the roles of other safety net players. Indeed, by maintaining confidence in the financial system, crises are either avoided or reduced in severity, which benefits all participants, including the poor.

While IADI's mandate and that of most of its members is primarily focused on financial stability, it is not uncommon for the public policy objectives of individual deposit insurers to also include the protection of less financially sophisticated depositors, who are often distinguished by the small size of their deposits.[96] Demaestri and others are of the view that this objective offers the most direct mechanism for reducing poverty, as it primarily acts to improve the security of the poor's savings and enhance their overall economic security.[97] They point out that it is important to bear in mind that small depositors are not necessarily the poorest.[98] In most countries, the very poor have limited access to the banking system, or they lack the savings needed to participate in it, or they have little confidence in the formal financial sector. However, a stable financial system where deposits are explicitly protected may persuade the very poor to participate in the formal financial sector to a greater degree than without explicit protection.[99] Efforts to attract small depositors into the formal financial system can provide benefits for the poor and stimulate the financial system and economic growth. However, care must be taken to ensure that policies designed to draw the poor to the formal financial sector for credit and savings must be targeted and efficient.[100]

On the objective to increase competition in a financial system, a deposit insurance system may level the competitive playing field for smaller banks or as a minimum contribute to thc contestability of the market, leading to a higher number of smaller institutions, improving deposit rates and lowering lending costs in the competitive market for all banks.[101] All these can help smaller depositors and aid in financial sector development and improved accessibility and opportunities for the poor.[102] In the absence of deposit protection, depositors may prefer using large institutions that may be perceived to be less risky because they are protected by an implicit government guarantee and are considered "too big to fail" or they could have a long history with a high level of brand and franchise awareness among the public.[103] Deposit insurance is seen as a mechanism that reduces depositors' concerns about an institution's ability to repay deposits, which, sequentially allows new or less well-known banks to attract deposits and potentially avoid paying higher costs for funds.[104]

Lastly, on the objective to reduce the use of public funds in financial services, the notion of helping to ensure that the banking industry pays for its own problems can help reduce the need for public money to be used for financial rescues.[105] Demaestri and others observe that in countries where there is no formal deposit insurance scheme or where the guarantee is implicit, the cost of any attempt to protect deposits often falls directly on the taxpayers, with a probably excessive relative burden on the poor.[106] Deposit insurance schemes can reduce the government's financial obligation by limiting coverage, and by providing a mechanism through which surviving banks may cover all or a portion of the costs associated with resolving failures.[107] If deposit insurance is funded by surviving banks rather than by the government, the risk of the poor subsidising the lower-to-middle-income class small depositors is reduced.[108]

Accordingly, public policy objectives of individual deposit insurers that include the protection of small depositors improve the security of the poor's savings and promote financial inclusion by encouraging small depositors to participate in the banking system. However, the very poor do not always fall under small depositors and policies designed to draw the poor to the formal financial sector for credit and savings must be targeted and efficient. In addition, the objective to enhance competition in the banking system improves access to financial services and opportunities for the poor.

15.3.3 Core Principle Seven: Membership

Core Principle seven requires that membership in a deposit insurance system should be compulsory for all banks, including state-owned banks, and all banks should be subject to sound prudential regulation and supervision.[109] It is also required that the conditions, process and timeframe for attaining membership should be explicitly stated and transparent. Membership characteristics thus influence financial inclusion, specifically, whether membership is compulsory or voluntary and whether it includes specialised microfinance providers as well as mainstream banks.[110] Given the need to maintain the financial integrity of the deposit insurance system in times of financial stress and reduce confusion on the part of depositors over who is insured and who is not, compulsory membership has many benefits.[111] The Financial Stability Forum Working Group is of the view that membership should be granted only to institutions that accept deposits from the public, are financially sound and are subject to sound supervision and regulation to safeguard the solvency of the insurer.[112]

It is submitted that membership characteristics may promote financial inclusion by including finance companies, credit unions and microfinance institutions depending on country circumstances. Such institutions must be financially sound and subject to supervision and regulation to ensure that the deposit insurer will have the resources to pay insured depositors promptly.

15.3.4 Core Principle Eight: Coverage

Core Principle eight deals with coverage and requires that the level and scope of deposit coverage should be clearly defined. Specifically, coverage should be limited and credible and cover most depositors but leave a substantial amount of deposits exposed to market discipline. The coverage level refers to the percentage of depositors with deposits equal to or below the protection limit. International best practice benchmarks range from 90% to 99% of depositors by number. Some jurisdictions make use of the per capita income, while in others the cover level is stipulated by law, for example, in the EU and the United States.[113] Such coverage should be reviewed periodically (for example, at least every five years) to ensure that it meets the public policy objectives of the deposit insurance system. The residency status or nationality of depositors should have no effect on coverage.[114] The level and scope of coverage may also affect the extent to which deposit insurance is capable of contributing to the protection of depositors and stability. Full coverage (100%) for all deposits and depositors would affect the greatest protection for depositors but would present the greatest challenge for controlling moral hazard.[115] At the other end of the spectrum, very low coverage levels that do not protect the majority of depositors in the system would not be effective at curbing bank runs and protecting the savings of depositors.[116] Thus, coverage promotes financial inclusion if the coverage level protects the majority of depositors and a greater number of depositors will be reimbursed when a bank fails.

15.3.5 Core Principle Nine: Sources and uses of funds

Core Principle nine relates to sources and uses of funds. It requires that the deposit insurer should have readily available funds and all funding mechanisms necessary to ensure prompt reimbursement of depositors' claims, including assured liquidity funding arrangements. The responsibility for paying the cost of deposit insurance should be borne by banks. These funds must be provided on an *ex ante* basis[117] and initial start-up ("seed") funding from, for example, government or international donor organisation is permitted to help establish the deposit insurer. Emergency funding arrangements must be explicitly set out in legislation; a target size for the fund must be determined on the basis of clear, consistent and transparent criteria and achieved within a reasonable timeframe. The deposit insurer must further invest and manage its funds in a sound manner. Finally, it is required that the deposit insurer levies differential but transparent premiums on its members. The ratings and rankings of individual banks resulting from such differential systems are however kept confidential.[118]

Sound funding arrangements are critical to the effectiveness of a deposit insurance system in maintaining public confidence. Demaestri and others point out that a deposit insurance system entirely financed by the government can lead to taxpayers bearing the entire cost of failures. Moreover, one of the many reasons countries have adopted deposit insurance is that in the absence of industry-funded insurance, the costs of resolving bank failures fall almost entirely on taxpayers.[119] Core Principle nine states that funds must be provided on an *ex ante* basis, which ensures that all banks contribute to building and maintaining a reserve or fund and banks that subsequently fail will have contributed to paying the cost of their failure.[120]

Therefore, *ex ante* industry funding arrangements promote financial inclusion by ensuring that depositors have confidence in the banking system and such arrangements are more effective if the ratings and rankings of contributory institutions resulting from their differential contributions are kept confidential.

15.3.6 Core Principle Ten: Public awareness

Public awareness is addressed by Core Principle ten, which requires that, to protect depositors and contribute to financial stability, the public must be informed on an ongoing basis about the benefits and limitations of the deposit insurance system. The public awareness programme should be monitored on an ongoing basis and should convey information about the scope of deposit insurance (which types of financial instruments and depositors are covered, and which are not); a list of member banks; deposit insurance coverage limits; and other information such as the mandate of the deposit insurer. In the event of a bank failure, depositors must be notified of where, how and when insured depositors will be provided with access to their funds; the information they will have to provide for the purposes of obtaining payment; whether advance or interim payments will be made; and whether any depositors will lose funds as well as the procedures whereby uninsured depositors can file claims with the liquidator for their insured portion.[121] This is of particular importance for the poor, whose financial sophistication and resources may be very limited. According to the IADI, how the deposit insurer conducts public awareness and the extent to which the public, particularly the lower-income segments, are aware of important nuances in deposit insurance protections may make a difference in the level of confidence and trust poor populations have in the mainstream banking system.[122]

It is submitted that a deposit insurer's public awareness programme promotes financial inclusion by ensuring that the public is informed of safe methods of keeping their money and also ensuring that they are aware that their deposits are protected in the event of a bank failure. In addition, financial inclusion is most likely to be achieved if the deposit insurer employs creative methods of informing the public about deposit insurance depending on a country's circumstances.

15.4 Measures by the Deposit Protection Corporation of Zimbabwe to promote financial inclusion

15.4.1 Background

Historically, the regulation and supervision of banks have included the lender of last resort function of the central bank whereby the central bank intervenes by providing liquidity and rescues a bank that experiences solvency problems.[123] Regulation and supervision of banks have traditionally formed the cornerstone of most countries' regulatory safety nets. The idea of providing liquidity to troubled banks is to prevent panic among depositors and thus avoid bank runs and also to prevent perceived dangers stemming from illiquidity developing into full-scale contagious bank failures.[124] However, as free market economies developed and became sophisticated, the banking sector also changed remarkably and started to invent products and services that were more risk-prone.[125] This caused the effectiveness of the existing regulatory tools to be questionable. Substantial bank failures (in the 1930s) induced by runs on banks resulted in depositors losing their deposits, loss of confidence in the banking systems and banking instability led to governments (with the United States as the forerunner) introducing deposit insurance schemes as a measure of ameliorating the adverse effects brought about by bank runs and protecting depositors.[126]

Subsequently, many developed and developing countries have adopted deposit insurance schemes as part of their regulatory safety nets in order to safeguard the stability of the financial system. Deposit insurance is distinguished from the lender of last resort function in that a DIS is established and operates with a clear mandate to guarantee the deposits of depositors in cases of bank failure, while the lender of last resort provides temporary liquidity to troubled banks.[127] One of the core functions of the RBZ is to maintain a stable banking system through its supervisory and lender of last resort functions.[128] The RBZ promotes and delivers depositor protection through its lender of last resort function as enshrined in the RBZ Act [Chapter 22:15] of 1964. In terms of section 11(5) of the RBZ Act, the RBZ may on such terms and conditions as it may determine act as lender of last resort for banking institutions by granting to them or for their benefit, for periods of not more than three months, loans other than those mentioned in section 59 of the Banking Act and contingent commitments.

The DIS in Zimbabwe is administered by the DPC. The DPC is a statutory body previously known as the Deposit Protection Board established on 1 July 2003 in terms of the Banking Act (Chapter 24:20) as read with Banking (Deposit Protection) Regulations, Statutory Instrument 29 of 2003.[129] The Deposit Protection Board operated a "paybox" mandate in terms whereof it was responsible for depositor pay-outs when banks failed and could not exercise any functions relating to resolving failing or failed contributory institutions or curatorship.[130] The Corporation assumed the new name in terms of the DPC Act which came into effect on 16 March 2012, which also resulted in the DPC's mandate being expanded to include responsibilities such as the resolution of failing or failed banks, judicial management and liquidation of closed banks,[131] thus a "paybox plus" mandate.[132] The enhanced mandate has enabled DPC to effectively carry out its objectives in line with international best practices. The DPC is a member of the AIDI since its inception in 2003 and it is also a member of the Africa Regional Committee (ARC), one of the eight regions of IADI.[133]

The effectiveness of a deposit insurance system is influenced not only by its design features but also by the environment within which it operates.[134] According to IADI, although the operating environment is not formally assessed, it forms the foundation for the assessment of compliance with the Core Principles. Zimbabwe's operating environment in the past two years was impacted by the Covid-19 pandemic. The RBZ responded to the financial vulnerabilities resulting from the Covid-19 pandemic by issuing a circular to banking institutions that provided policy guidance on credit relief to minimise the impact of the downturn.[135] The Covid-19 pandemic also resulted in an increase in the use of digital and virtual platforms for service offerings in the banking sector. This has the potential for heightening operational and credit risk within the sector through cybercrime and depressed loan collections, which calls for enhanced deposit protection.[136]

Zimbabwe's operating environment was also significantly impacted by changes to the foreign currency regime. In 2020, the Government of Zimbabwe, through Statutory Instrument 142 of 2019, also known as the RBZ (Legal Tender) Regulations, reversed the ban on the use of multiple currencies for the convenience of business and the transacting public.[137] Civil servants together with employees from other sectors of the economy opened Nostro FCA accounts for receiving their salaries and Covid-19 allowances without worrying that the purchasing power of their deposits may be eroded by inflation.[138] In addition, the RBZ introduced the Dutch Foreign Exchange Auction Trading System on 23 June 2020, which helped in promoting the stability of the local currency against the United States dollar as well as price stability.[139] The auction system also ushered in a more efficient price discovery mechanism in the market for foreign currency.[140]

To contain illegal foreign currency dealings, with their negative effects on the economy, the RBZ introduced a number of stringent measures, which included the closure of accounts for mobile money agents and the placement of transaction limits on mobile money.[141] These measures have had a positive impact on the restriction of black market operations and an increase in the money supply that was fuelling inflation in the economy.[142]

At the end of World War II, the Greek economy and the financial system were in chaos, and hyperinflation had wiped out pre-war savings and eroded the value of the Greek drachma.[143] The RBZ can also draw some lessons on stabilising currency from the Currency Committee, a powerful ministerial committee,[144] set up in 1946 at the height of the Greek Financial Crisis to regulate the banking system by, among others, deciding on the volume and distribution of bank credit.[145] Some of the actions taken by the Currency Committee to stabilise the currency and improve growth rates included channelling bank credit to large enterprises and investment projects at low interest rates.[146] Most prices were determined freely, although the prices of "necessities" were subject to controls. In foreign trade, domestic firms enjoyed significant protection, despite the gradual phasing out of tariffs, following participation in the General Agreement on Trade and Tariffs and Greece's association agreement with the European Commission. Business taxes were low, and provisions for the protection of property rights and accelerated depreciation ensured confidence and a high rate of return on investment.[147]

15.4.2 The DPC's public policy objectives

In line with Core Principle one, the DPC aims at meeting a number of objectives that include the protection of depositors, particularly small depositors, by providing an orderly means of compensation in the event of a deposit-taking institution becoming insolvent; contributing towards the stability of Zimbabwe's financial system; enhancing public confidence in the financial system by establishing a framework for the resolution of failing or failed member institutions; protecting the Deposit Protection Fund against loss; and enhancing competition in the financial sector by creating a level playing field through guaranteeing depositor reimbursements for both big and small member institutions and promoting sound business practices in contributory institutions.[148]

The DPC's design features are largely compliant with the Core Principles. The DPC has been reimbursing depositors of failed contributory institutions over the years and is currently compensating depositors for Afrasia, Allied, Interfin and Trust Bank. In the absence of an EDIS, depositors of several failed banking institutions that went into liquidation since the DPC's inception in 2003 would not otherwise have received any form of compensation. The DPC promotes financial inclusion in Zimbabwe by reimbursing depositors of failed banks, thus ensuring that small depositors trust the banking system and know that they are protected from losing their funds in the event of a bank failure.

15.4.3 Protecting the majority of depositors

A DIS provides assurance or a guarantee to depositors that they will receive their deposits in part or in full in the event of a bank failure. According to the DPC Act, a depositor, in relation to a member institution, means a person who has made a deposit with that institution or the trustee, executor, liquidator or other lawful representatives of a depositor or a person to whom a depositor referred to above has ceded their rights in the deposit concerned.[149] A key measurement of the effectiveness of a DIS, as articulated in most deposit insurers' public policy objectives, is the percentage of depositors fully covered by the scheme, that is, those with deposits equal to or below the protection limit. As discussed earlier, acceptable benchmarks in the international arena provide for covering 90% of the deposits by number. In practice, the coverage limit, by design, takes care of the interests of the unsophisticated depositors, who are frequently incapable of knowing the true nature of the condition and performance of a banking institution due to a lack of skills and resources as well as opaqueness of the information.[150] As a matter of principle, the establishment of a DIS catering for both individual and well-to-do corporate clients, as opposed to a scheme for small depositors alone, also reduces incidences of deliberate financial exclusion. The DPC's mandate promotes financial inclusion by providing for the protection of small depositors and both big and small member institutions in insured institutions are covered by the DIS.

In line with Core Principle eight, the depositor's place of residence or nationality does not affect deposit protection.[151] Also, in the event of a bank failure, the DPC will compensate depositors part or all of their funds that were in the closed bank up to the maximum cover limit prevailing at the time of bank closure.[152] As of October 2021, the cover limit is set at ZWL$10,000 (ten thousand Zimbabwean dollars) per depositor per bank and ZWL$500 (five hundred Zimbabwean dollars) for deposit-taking microfinance institutions effective 1 January 2020.[153] The new cover level of ZWL$10,000 per depositor per banking institution protects 98.9% of depositors in full and at a cover level of ZWL500 per depositor per deposit-taking microfinance institution, 98.5% of depositors will be covered in full. The new cover levels fulfil the Corporation's public-policy objective of ensuring that at least 90% of depositors are covered in full.[154] The DPC, therefore, promotes financial inclusion by ensuring that the majority of depositors regardless of residence or nationality are protected, which encourages depositors to open bank accounts knowing that their funds will be safe if a bank fails.

Following the separation of depositor accounts into Zimbabwean dollars and foreign currency-denominated accounts (FCAs) and/or Nostro FCAs, the DPC recently announced that such deposits will also be protected for up to USD$1,000 (one thousand United States dollars) per depositor class per bank and USD$500 (five hundred United States dollars) per deposit class per deposit-taking microfinance institution from 1 January 2022.[155] The extension of deposit protection to foreign currency accounts promotes financial inclusion by ensuring that prospective depositors will keep their money in banks without fear that their deposits might be eroded by inflation.

15.4.4 Building confidence in financial institutions

Deposit protection promotes financial inclusion by fostering confidence in financial institutions and potentially leading to greater savings among the poor provided they are informed about safe places to store their money.[156] A DIS provides peace of mind and security to depositors in knowing that their deposits will be reimbursed in the event that their contributory institution becomes illiquid or insolvent. Deposit protection reduces financial uncertainty, thereby building confidence in the financial system, and enhances financial intermediation on a nationwide basis, thereby promoting financial inclusion.[157]

In line with Core Principle nine, the DPC promotes public confidence as it receives its funding from quarterly premium levies collected from contributory institutions including those under judicial management and curatorship.[158] The DPC collects premiums on an *ex ante* basis to build the funds in advance before a bank failure. The current prescribed premium rate is 0.3% of an institution's annual average eligible deposits, with premiums payable quarterly.[159] In addition to premiums from member institutions, money can also be advanced to the Fund by the RBZ, which is a prudent move given that Zimbabwe's economy is unstable and the DIS may not have sufficient funds to make the pay-outs required if a bank fails. Depositors do not pay premiums for deposit insurance cover – it is a free service to all bank depositors. Accordingly, the DPC promotes financial inclusion by ensuring that all depositors of contributory institutions have automatic deposit insurance, thus building public confidence in financial institutions.

15.4.5 Promotes competition in the financial sector

Traditionally, larger banks because of their size, track record and brand visibility have an edge over smaller banks in attracting deposits at lower interest rates. Deposit protection makes depositors of smaller banks feel safe and protected, hence neutralising the advantages that accrue to big banks.[160] In fact, small banks can compete with the big ones as well as public with private as long as every institution provides the same depositor protection. In the absence of deposit insurance, small institutions struggle to survive, as they should pay higher rates of interest to attract deposits and, hence, take on much riskier activities.[161] Potential depositors may have greater trust in banks if they believe their savings are insured and this may lead to more individuals opening bank accounts. Deposit insurance ensures that smaller institutions can participate in the banking system and encourages more people to save their money in banks.

15.4.6 Financial literacy and public awareness

For any deposit insurer to be effective, the public must be aware of the benefits and limitations of the DIS. Most deposit protection systems carry out financial literacy and public awareness campaigns among the banked and unbanked public. The purpose of the campaigns is to raise awareness on the merits and limitations of deposit protection, deposits protected, coverage limits, types of providers, products covered (or not) and safe methods of storing money, thereby promoting the use of mainstream banking. Such campaigns are conducted through a variety of media channels, including the internet, print, electronic, point of purchase, roadshows and billboards.

Section 61 of the DPC Act deals with publicity for the deposit insurance scheme. It requires every contributory institution to ensure that all its depositors are informed of the extent to which their deposits are protected under this Act and where their deposits are protected and how they may receive compensation if the institution becomes insolvent. This provision together with the fact that the DPC has a website that publishes the objectives of the DPC, the legislation, the cover limit and the reimbursement and claim procedure aligns with Core Principle ten on public awareness.

The DPC is a member of thematic committees for people living with disabilities as well as financial literacy and consumer protection.[162] In addition to the DPC's informational brochures published in the main languages, namely, Shona, Ndebele and English, the DPC also translated the brochures into Chewa and Tonga languages to widen the coverage and awareness of the DIS.[163] To increase the financial literacy of the visually impaired, brochures are also designed in braille format and distributed to centres of the blind across the country.[164] These initiatives contribute to driving the national agenda on financial inclusion and literacy.

Despite the challenges posed by Covid-19, which mainly affected public events, the DPC leverages on digital and mass media channels such as radio, television and newspapers for increased brand visibility and informational awareness. The DPC launched the Bulawayo Regional Office in February 2020.[165] The establishment of the regional office was in response to the needs of the banking public in Bulawayo and surrounding areas in Matabeleland and Midlands for ease of access to the DPC's services.[166] The publicity from the launch event in the mainstream and digital media platforms raised awareness of the DPC. To enhance customer service quality and provide convenience to the public, initiatives such as processing claim forms online, toll-free access and support help-desk solutions were implemented.[167]

The DPC's financial literacy and public awareness programmes, therefore, promote financial inclusion by ensuring that the public is encouraged to store their money safely in the financial system because it is covered by insurance in the event of a bank failure. In addition, the DPC has come up with innovative ways to reach the poor and unserved communities outside the main cities in Zimbabwe by translating their information brochures into Chewa and Tonga languages and also designing their brochures in braille format for distribution to centres of the blind across the country. The DPC also leverages on digital and mass media channels such as radio, television and newspapers for increased brand visibility and informational awareness. It is submitted that efforts made by the DPC to inform the public about deposit insurance promote financial inclusion because potential depositors in the country will store their money in their homes under pillows if they are not aware that their deposits will be safe in banks despite the economic challenges the country may be experiencing.

15.4.7 Compulsory coverage of financial intermediaries

In line with Core Principle seven, membership to the DIS is compulsory for any registered deposit-taking institutions under the Banking Act (Chapter 24:20) and Building Societies Act (Chapter 24:02),[168] POSB Act (Chapter 24:22), IDBZ Act (Chapter 24:14) and Micro-finance Act (Chapter 24:29).[169] At present, membership includes all commercial banks, merchant banks, building societies, discount houses, finance houses, deposit-taking microfinance institutions, POSB and

IDBZ.[170] The DPC currently has 27 members, that is, 21 contributory banking institutions and six deposit-taking microfinance institutions.[171] Any depositor who banks with an insured deposit-taking institution is automatically covered, notwithstanding whether the depositor is sophisticated or not. Notably, in Zimbabwe, deposit protection was extended to cover such financial intermediaries as formal microfinance institutions. Extending protection to these institutions affords broad access to safe and affordable financial services and products to the marginalised and the unbanked public, thereby promoting financial inclusion.[172] In addition, compulsory membership prevents the problem of adverse selection, a situation where financially weak or risk-prone deposit-taking financial institutions choose to join the DIS, while financially strong depository institutions opt to stay out, leaving depositors without protection.[173]

15.4.8 Providing protection to a wide range of financial products

The DIS insures financial innovations provided by members, as long as the financial innovation meets the definition of a covered deposit. Examples of deposits that are eligible for deposit protection include current and savings deposit accounts, fixed deposits, interest accrued and/or payable on all deposits, trust accounts, shares in a building society (class B and C shares) other than capital shares, deferred shares and preference shares. Extending protection to these financial products offers depositors peace of mind knowing that their money is protected and may allow the marginalised to have access to basic financial services, especially through microfinance institutions.[174]

15.5 Conclusion

Zimbabwe has had an EDIS since 2003 with the objective to protect all depositors, whether individuals or businesses, against loss of part or all of their eligible deposits in the event of failure of a contributory institution. As discussed previously, deposit insurance is distinguished from the lender of last resort function of the RBZ in that a DIS is established and operates with a clear mandate to guarantee the deposits of depositors in cases of bank failure, while the lender of last resort provides temporary liquidity to troubled banks.

Notably, though the operating environment in which a deposit insurance system operates is outside the scope of authority of the deposit insurer, it influences the deposit insurer's ability to fulfil its mandate and determines, in part, its effectiveness in protecting depositors and contributing to a jurisdiction's financial stability. In particular, the RBZ has made efforts such as the introduction of the Dutch Foreign Exchange Auction Trading System to promote stability of the local currency against the United States dollar as well as price stability. It is submitted that the RBZ should learn from the Greece Currency Committee that managed to stabilise the Greece currency during the height of the Greek Financial Crisis by *inter alia* channelling bank credit to large enterprises and investment projects at low interest rates.

As indicated earlier, financial safety nets such as the regulatory and supervisory framework, lender of last resort, bank resolution frameworks and deposit insurance are the set of arrangements to reduce the effects of the failure of one or multiple financial institutions on depositors, the financial system and the economy. Given that the financial safety nets serve different purposes, namely assistance with liquidity support and as a means of providing support to protected depositors in an insolvency situation, it is submitted that the current legal framework dealing with depositor protection should not be harmonised.

The DIS in Zimbabwe is administered by the DPC whose policies and practices positively affect financial inclusion. First, in accordance with Core Principle seven, membership to the DIS is compulsory for any registered deposit-taking institutions, which includes all commercial banks, merchant banks, building societies, discount houses, finance houses, deposit-taking microfinance institutions, POSB and IDBZ. Compulsory membership promotes financial inclusion by ensuring that any depositor who banks with an insured deposit-taking institution is automatically covered, notwithstanding whether the depositor is sophisticated or not.

Second, in line with Core Principle eight, the DPC will compensate depositors part or all of their funds that were in the closed bank up to the maximum cover limit prevailing at the time of bank closure.[175] As of October 2021, the cover limit is set at ZWL$10,000 (ten thousand Zimbabwean dollars) per depositor per bank ensuring 98.9% of depositors will be covered in full and ZWL$500 (five hundred Zimbabwean dollars) for deposit-taking microfinance institutions effective 1 January 2020, ensuring 98.5% of depositors will be covered in full.[176] This coverage limit promotes financial inclusion as it takes care of the interests of the unsophisticated depositors, who are frequently incapable of knowing the true nature of the condition and performance of a banking institution due to a lack of skills and resources as well as the opaqueness of the information.

Third, in line with Core Principle nine, the Zimbabwean EDIS promotes depositor confidence in the financial system and financial inclusion by ensuring that the fund gets its funding from quarterly premium levies collected from contributory institutions including those under judicial management and curatorship. This provides peace of mind and security to depositors in knowing that their deposits will be reimbursed in the event that their contributory institution becomes illiquid or insolvent.

Fourth, in line with Core Principle ten, the DPC runs a public awareness programme wherein it publishes informational brochures in the main languages, namely, Shona, Ndebele and English and also translates the brochures into Chewa and Tonga languages to widen the coverage and awareness of the DIS. To increase the financial literacy of the visually impaired, brochures are also designed in braille format and distributed to centres of the blind across Zimbabwe. The DPC also leverages on digital and mass media channels such as radio, television and newspapers for increased brand visibility and informational awareness. The DPC's awareness programme promotes financial inclusion by reaching out to all communities in Zimbabwe, in particular, the poor communities to ensure that they are informed about safe methods to store their money.

As pointed out previously, the Covid-19 pandemic resulted in an increase in the use of digital and virtual platforms for service offerings in the banking system. These actions have the potential for heightening operational and credit risk within the sector through cybercrime and depressed loan collections, which calls for enhanced deposit protection. The use of digital platforms includes banks and nonbank parties. Many nonbank providers are not members of the deposit insurance system, and there are legal barriers to bringing them into the system, including not being prudentially regulated and supervised (an essential criterion for deposit insurance membership). To strengthen depositor protection in Zimbabwe in cyberspace in the Covid-19 era, it is recommended that section 23 of the DPC Act dealing with the requirements for membership to the DPC should be revised in light of the current technological developments to include nonbank parties such as asset managers as deposit-taking institutions. This action will ensure that nonbanks are subject to minimum requirements for providers to operate in a safe, sound and sustainable manner. Such action should be taken without passing too many compliance costs to the consumer that could deter access in the long term.

In addition, in terms of its powers in section 41 of the DPC Act to prescribe the classes of deposits that are protected under the DPC Act, the DPC should revise the types of deposits that are eligible for deposit protection to accommodate more innovative types of deposits. Finally, the DPC should invest in IT infrastructure and its staff's technical ability to sufficiently monitor risk profiles of member institutions that may allow for early intervention and preventive measures and thus lower the probability of resolution and/or depositor reimbursement.

Notes

1 E Demaestri, M Facundo and D Walker 'Deposit Insurance and Poverty Reduction' (2006) https://www.researchgate.net/publication/239841069_DEPOSIT_INSURANCE_AND_POVERTY_REDUCTION, accessed 14 November 2021 203, 207. See also C Van Heerden 'Deposit Protection in South Africa: Recent Developments' (2020) 35(2) *Journal of International Banking Law and Regulation* 45.

2 Ibid.

3 As observed by DW Diamond, PH Dybvig 'Bank Runs, Deposit Insurance, and Liquidity' (1983) 91(3) *Journal of Political Economy* 401, during a bank run depositors withdraw their deposits from the bank concerned because they expect such banks to fail. Diamond and Dybvig, however, point out that, in fact, these sudden withdrawals can force a bank to liquidate many of its assets at a loss (so-called "fire sales") and actually cause the bank to fail. See further D Anginer, A Demirguc-Kunt 'Bank Runs and Moral Hazard: A Review of Deposit Insurance' (2018) https://elibrary.worldbank.org/doi/abs/10.1596/1813-9450-8589, accessed on 23 April 2019 1, 3.

4 Kaufman notes that what makes the perception of bank failures more important, particularly for public policy, is the fear that "the failure may spill over to other banks and possibly beyond the banking system to the financial system as a whole, domestic macroeconomy, and other countries. Similar fears are generally not perceived for the failure of other firms. The failure of a steel mill, software manufacturer or grocery store is not widely perceived to spill over to other firms in the same industry". Lang

and Stulz note that "the surviving firms frequently benefit from losing a competitor and being able to expand their market shares". Kaufman further notes that, "because banks are closely intertwined financially with each other through lending to and borrowing from each other, holding deposit balances with each other, and the payments clearing system, a failure of any one bank is believed to be more likely to spill over to other banks and to do so more quickly". See GG Kaufman 'Bank Failures, Systemic Risk and Bank Regulation' (1996) 16(1) *Cato Journal* 17, 19; See also LHP Lang, RM Stulz 'Contagion and Competitive Intra-Industry Effects of Bankruptcy Announcements: An Empirical Analysis' (1992) 32 *Journal of financial economics* 45, 47; See further BF Jackson, 'Danger Lurking in the Shadows: Why Regulators Lack the Authority to Effectively Fight Contagion in the Shadow Banking System' (2013) 127(2) *Harvard LR* 732.

5 South African Reserve Bank, 'Designing A Deposit Insurance Scheme for South Africa – A Discussion Paper' (2017) http://www.treasury.gov.za/twinpeaks/Designing%20a%20deposit%20insurance%20scheme%20for%20South%20Africa.pdf, accessed on 7 June 2021 1, 2. See also C Van Heerden 'Deposit Protection in South Africa: Recent Developments' (2020) 35(2) *Journal of International Banking Law and Regulation* 45.

6 Deposit insurance is referred to as an "explicit" system, where the cost of protecting deposits is largely borne by the financial industry and its customers with a back-up guarantee from the government to make such protection credible. This is in contrast to a system where there is an implicit expectation that the government will step in to protect all depositors or even all creditors of a depository institution. See JC Izaguirre, T Lyman, C McGuire, D Grace, 'Deposit Insurance and Digital Financial Inclusion' (2016) https://openknowledge.worldbank.org/bitstream/handle/10986/25707/110632-BRI-PUBLIC-ADD-VC-Brief-Deposit-Insurance-and-Digital-Financial-Inclusion.pdf?sequence=1, accessed on 15 October 2021 1. See also Financial Stability Board, Thematic Peer Review on Deposit Insurance Systems, Peer Review Report, 8 February 2012 https://www.fsb.org/wp-content/uploads/r_120208.pdf, accessed on 12 April 2021 9. See further C Phiri "An Assessment of the Factors Determining Public Confidence and Its Impact on the Financial Performance And Stability of Banks In Zimbabwe" (2015), *MBA Dissertation, University of Zimbabwe* 19.

7 According to the IADI, over 110 jurisdictions have an explicit deposit insurance system as part of their 'financial safety-net'. C Van Heerden 'Deposit Protection In South Africa: Recent Developments' (2020) 35(2) *Journal of International Banking Law and Regulation* 45. See also JC Izaguirre, T Lyman, C McGuire, D Grace, 'Deposit Insurance and Digital Financial Inclusion' (2016) https://openknowledge.worldbank.org/bitstream/handle/10986/25707/110632-BRI-PUBLIC-ADD-VC-Brief-Deposit-Insurance-and-Digital-Financial-Inclusion.pdf?sequence=1, accessed on 15 October 20211.

8 Deposit Protection Corporation 'Deposit Protection' https://www.dpcorp.co.zw/deposit-protection.html, accessed on 21 December 2021.

9 S Li *An Overview of Financial Inclusion, Deposit Insurance and Financial Stability* 20 ed (2018) 177.

10 N Kleftouri 'Meeting the Rationale of Deposit Protection System' (2014) 22(4) *Journal of Financial Regulation and Compliance* 300, 301. See also Deposit Protection Corporation 'Deposit Protection' https://www.dpcorp.co.zw/deposit-protection.html, accessed on 21 December 2021.

11 CGAP 'Financial Access 2009 – Measuring Access to Financial Services Around the World' 2009 https://www.cgap.org/sites/default/files/CGAP-Financial-Access-2009.pdf, accessed on 2 November 2021 1. See also A Demirguc-Kunt and L Klapper 'Financial Inclusion in Africa: An Overview' (2012) World Bank Policy Research Working Paper 6088 2 https://openknowledge.worldbank.org/bitstream/handle/10986

/9335/WPS6088.pdf?sequence=1, accessed 17 October 2021. See further Deposit Protection Corporation 'The Role of Deposit Insurance in Promoting Financial Inclusion' https://www.dpcorp.co.zw/assets/deposit-protection-and-financial-inclusion.pdf, accessed on 16 October 2021 1.

12 S Li *An Overview of Financial Inclusion, Deposit Insurance and Financial Stability* 20 ed (2018) 176.

13 Ibid.

14 Ibid.

15 In 2019, the World Bank observed that Zimbabwe has a deposit insurance scheme but noted that in substance, those arrangements are practically non-existent given that Zimbabwe is experiencing a liquidity crisis. See The World Bank, 'Financial Safety Nets and Bank Resolution Frameworks in Southern Africa: Summary of Key Issues and Challenges' (2019) https://openknowledge.worldbank.org/bitstream/handle/10986/31512/Summary-of-KeyIssues-and-Challenges.pdf?sequence=1&isAllowed=y, accessed on 20 October 2021 7. The operating environment in 2020 and 2021 was characterised by human and economic hardships, including low capacity utilisation and nationwide lockdowns attributable to the devastating effects of the ongoing global coronavirus disease, the Covid-19 pandemic. In addition to the Covid-19, Zimbabwe's operating environment was significantly impacted by changes to the foreign currency regime. In April 2020, the Government of Zimbabwe reversed the ban on the use of multiple currencies for the convenience of business and the transacting public by repealing Statutory Instrument 142 of 2019 – RBZ (Legal Tender) Regulations. In a bid to curtail illegal foreign currency dealings, with its attendant negative ramifications on the economy, RBZ introduced a raft of stringent measures, which included closure of accounts for mobile money agents and placement of transaction limits on mobile money. These measures have had a positive impact on the curtailment of black market operations and an increase in money supply that were fuelling inflation in the economy. See Depositor Protection Corporation, 'Annual Report for the Year Ended 31 December 2020' file:///Users/ashleynyaude/Desktop/dpc-2020-annual-report.pdf, accessed on 16 October 2021 10.

16 A Nyaude 'Regulatory Measures to Address Bank Failures in Zimbabwe' (2021) *LLD thesis, University of Pretoria* 89.

17 Deposit Protection Corporation 'The Role of Deposit Insurance in Promoting Financial Inclusion' (2019) https://www.dpcorp.co.zw/assets/deposit-protection-and-financial-inclusion.pdf, accessed on 16 October 2021 2.

18 Helleiner describes the 2007–2008 global financial crisis as "the most severe since the Great Depression of the 1930s". See E Helleiner 'Understanding The 2007–2008 Global Financial Crisis: Lessons For Scholars Of International Political Economy' (2011) 14 *Annual Review of Political Science* 67. See also FS Mishkin 'Over the Cliff: From the Subprime to the Global Financial Crisis' (2011) *Journal of Economic Perspectives* 49; JE Stiglitz 'Lessons From the Global Financial Crisis of 2008' (2010) *Seoul Journal of Economics* 321.

19 D Singh and J R LaBrosse, 'Developing A Framework for Effective Financial Crisis Management' (2011) *OECD Journal: Financial Market Trends* 1, 4 observe that the financial safety net traditionally included a lender of last resort (generally a central bank, prudential regulation by a bank supervisor, a government department such as a Minister of Finance or Treasury and an EDIS).

20 The International Association of Deposit Insurers (IADI) was formed in May 2002 to enhance the effectiveness of deposit insurance systems by promoting guidance and international cooperation. Members of IADI conduct research and produce guidance for the benefit of those jurisdictions seeking to establish or improve a deposit insurance system. Members also share their knowledge and expertise through participation in international conferences and other forums. IADI currently represents 86 deposit

insurers. IADI is a non-profit organisation constituted under Swiss Law and is domiciled at the Bank for International Settlements in Basel, Switzerland.

21 International Association of Deposit Insurers, 'IADI Core Principles for Effective Deposit Insurance Systems' (November 2014) https://www.iadi.org/en/assets/File/Core%20Principles/cprevised2014nov.pdf, accessed on 17 July 2021.

22 International Association of Deposit Insurers, 'Core Principles for Effective Deposit Insurance Systems – A methodology for compliance assessment' (December 2010) https:// www.iadi.org/en/events/ methodology-for-the- assessment-of-compliance-with-the-core-principles/.pdf, accessed on 2 November 2021.

23 International Association of Deposit Insurers, 'A Handbook for the Assessment of Compliance with the Core Principles for Effective Deposit Insurance Systems' (March 2016) https://www.iadi.org/en/assets/File/Core%20Principles/IADI_CP_Assessment_Handbook_FINAL_14May2016.pdf, accessed on 2 November 2021 8.

24 Reserve Bank of Zimbabwe, 'Zimbabwe National Financial Inclusion Strategy 2016–2020' (2016) https://www.rbz.co.zw/documents/BLSS/FinancialInclusion/National-Financial-Inclusion-Strategy.pdf, accessed 3 November 2021 2.

25 International Association of Deposit Insurers, 'Financial Inclusion and Deposit Insurance' (June 2013) https://www.iadi.org/en/assets/File/Papers/Approved%20Research%20-%20Discussion%20Papers/2013-06_Financial_Inclusion_and_Deposit_Insurance_publication-clean.pdf, accessed on 2 November 2021 3.

26 Reserve Bank of Zimbabwe, 'Zimbabwe National Financial Inclusion Strategy 2016–2020' (2016) https://www.rbz.co.zw/documents/BLSS/FinancialInclusion/National-Financial-Inclusion-Strategy.pdf, accessed 3 November 2021 1.

27 AFI is a policy leadership alliance owned and led by member central banks and financial regulatory institutions with the common objective of advancing financial inclusion at the country, regional and international levels. See 'Alliance for Financial Inclusion' https://www.afi-global.org/about/, accessed 2 November 2021.

28 The Global Partnership for Financial Inclusion (GPFI) is an inclusive platform for all G20 countries, interested non-G20 countries and relevant stakeholders to carry forward work on financial inclusion, including implementation of the G20 Financial Inclusion Action Plan, endorsed at the G20 Summit in Seoul in November 2010. See 'Global Partnership for Financial Inclusion' https://www.gpfi.org/about-gpfi, accessed 3 November 2021.

29 The Global Partnership for Financial Inclusion 'G20 Principles for Innovative Financial Inclusion' https://www.gpfi.org/sites/gpfi/files/documents/G20%20Principles%20for%20Innovative%20Financial%20Inclusion%20-%20AFI%20brochure.pdf, accessed 2 November 2021.

30 International Association of Deposit Insurers, 'Deposit Insurance and Financial Inclusion: Current Trends in Insuring Digital Stored – Value Products' (2020) https://www.iadi.org/en/assets/File/Papers/Approved%20Research%20-%20Discussion%20Papers/FII_for_official_publication_final_19032020.pdf, accessed 24 October 2021 5.

31 International Association of Deposit Insurers, 'IADI Core Principles for Effective Deposit Insurance Systems' (November 2014) https://www.iadi.org/en/assets/File/Core%20Principles/cprevised2014nov.pdf, accessed on 17 July 2021 9.

32 Ibid, 16.

33 B Van Roosebeke and R Defina 'Five Emerging Issues in Deposit Insurance' (2021) MPRA Paper No. 110713 https://mpra.ub.uni-muenchen.de/110713/1/MPRA_paper_110713.pdf, accessed 22 December 2021.

34 Ibid, 5. This is particularly the case in Africa. As of July 2019, 90% of Kenyans over the age of 14 were conducting transactions through M-PESA (a prominent e-money service provider Safaricom, a subsidiary of Vodafone).

35 Ibid. Deposit insurance approaches to offer coverage for e-money accounts include the direct approach that aims to address residual risks from the failure of an e-money issuer by

making each e-money account eligible for deposit insurance coverage. The passthrough approach aims to address residual risks from the failure of a deposit-taking institution holding a float account. It does so by allowing the coverage to pass through the float account (held at an institutional member of the deposit insurance system) and reach each e-money account. The exclusion approach is a conscious decision by policymakers who consider digital stored-value products to be primarily instruments of temporary value storage to make payments or transfers. Under this approach, the term "deposit" specifically excludes digital stored-value products (e.g. in Peru and the Philippines), and these products are therefore explicitly excluded from deposit insurance coverage.

36 Ibid.

37 Ibid.

38 Ibid, 6.

39 Ibid.

40 Depositor Protection Corporation, 'Annual Report for the year ended 31 December 2020' file:///Users/ashleynyaude/Desktop/dpc-2020-annual-report.pdf, accessed on 16 October 2021 20.

41 Ibid.

42 Ibid, 10.

43 Ibid, 20.

44 Ibid.

45 Reserve Bank of Zimbabwe, 'Zimbabwe National Financial Inclusion Strategy 2016 – 2020' (2016) https://www.rbz.co.zw/documents/BLSS/FinancialInclusion/National-Financial-Inclusion-Strategy.pdf, accessed 3 November 2021 2.

46 Ibid, 1. According to the RBZ, there is increasing evidence that national financial inclusion strategies are seen today as essential by many countries because they provide a clear national vision, a widely accepted strategic framework and a robust organisational structure to facilitate the development and implementation of coordinated and sound policy reforms.

47 Ibid, 1.

48 Ibid, 4.

49 Ibid, 5.

50 Depositor Protection Corporation, 'Annual Report for the year ended 31 December 2020' file:///Users/ashleynyaude/Desktop/dpc-2020-annual-report.pdf, accessed on 16 October 2021 12. .See also JT Chipika 'Financial Inclusion in Zimbabwe, From Policy to Practice: Lessons and Way Forward' https://www.rbz.co.zw/documents/publications/speeches/Dr-Chipika--Financial-Inclusion-Forum-Presentation---19-Feb-2019.pdf, accessed on 17 October 2021.

51 Deposit Protection Corporation 'The Role of Deposit Insurance in Promoting Financial Inclusion' (2019) https://www.dpcorp.co.zw/assets/deposit-protection-and-financial-inclusion.pdf, accessed on 16 October 2021 1.

52 Deposit Protection Corporation 'The Role of Deposit Insurance in Promoting Financial Inclusion' (2019) https://www.dpcorp.co.zw/assets/deposit-protection-and-financial-inclusion.pdf, accessed on 16 October 2021 1. See also Reserve Bank of Zimbabwe, 'Zimbabwe Financial Inclusion Journey 2016 – 2000' https://www.rbz.co.zw/documents/BLSS/2021/FINANCIAL-INCLUSION--JOURNEY.pdf, accessed on 15 October 2021 2. See further JF Devlin 'A Detailed Study of Financial Exclusion in the UK' (2005) 28 *Journal of Consumer Policy* 75, 76.

53 Ibid, 1. See also PS Koku 'Financial Exclusion of the Poor: A Literature Review' (2015) 33(5) *International Journal of Bank Marketing* 654, 655.

54 Ibid, 1.

55 Ibid, 1.

56 Reserve Bank of Zimbabwe, 'Zimbabwe Financial Inclusion Journey 2016 – 2000' https://www.rbz.co.zw/documents/BLSS/2021/FINANCIAL-INCLUSION-

-JOURNEY.pdf, accessed on 15 October 2021 1. See also JC Izaguirre, T Lyman, C McGuire, D Grace, 'Deposit Insurance and Digital Financial Inclusion' (2016) https://openknowledge.worldbank.org/bitstream/handle/10986/25707/110632-BRI-PUBLIC-ADD-VC-Brief-Deposit-Insurance-and-Digital-Financial-Inclusion.pdf?sequence=1, accessed on 15 October 2021 2.

57 The World Bank 'Finance for All? Policies and Pitfalls in Expanding Access' https://openknowledge.worldbank.org/bitstream/handle/10986/6905/417920PAPER0Fi18082137291301PUBLIC1.pdf?sequence=1&isAllowed=y, accessed 2 November 2021 2.

58 Reserve Bank of Zimbabwe 'Financial Inclusion' https://www.rbz.co.zw/index.php/financial-stability/financial-inclusion, accessed on 5 November 2021. See also F Kakarahwa 'The Impact of the Deposit Protection Corporation on Financial Stability in Zimbabwe Banking Sector' (2015) *Bachelor of Business Sciences Honours Dissertations, Bindura University of Science Education* 13.

59 Reserve Bank of Zimbabwe, 'Zimbabwe Financial Inclusion Journey 2016 – 2000' https://www.rbz.co.zw/documents/BLSS/2021/FINANCIAL-INCLUSION--JOURNEY.pdf, accessed on 15 October 2021 2.

60 Ibid, 2. See also A Zins and L Weill 'The Determinants of Financial Inclusion in Africa' (2016) 6 *Review of Development Finance* 46–56.

61 Ibid. See also A Demirguc-Kunt, L Klapper, D Singer 'Financial Inclusion and Inclusive Growth: A Review of Recent Empirical Evidence' (2017) World Bank Policy Research Working Paper 8040 https://openknowledge.worldbank.org/bitstream/handle/10986/26479/WPS8040.pdf?, accessed 17 October 2021 2.

62 Financial safety nets are the set of arrangements to reduce the effects of the failure of one or multiple financial institutions on depositors, the financial system, and the economy. See further The World Bank, 'Financial Safety Nets and Bank Resolution Frameworks in Southern Africa: Key Issues and Challenges' (2019) https://openknowledge.worldbank.org/bitstream/handle/10986/31511/Key-Issues-and-Challenges.pdf?sequence=1&isAllowed=y, accessed on 25 September 2021 3. See also S Schich 'Financial Crisis: Deposit Insurance and Related Financial Safety Net Aspects' (2008) https://www.oecd.org/finance/financial-markets/41894959.pdf, accessed on 22 December 2021 4.

63 International Association of Deposit Insurers, 'Financial Inclusion and Deposit Insurance' (June 2013) https://www.iadi.org/en/assets/File/Papers/Approved%20Research%20-%20Discussion%20Papers/2013-06_Financial_Inclusion_and_Deposit_Insurance_publication-clean.pdf, accessed on 2 November 2021 43.

64 Ibid. See also B Bernet, S Walter 'Design, Structure and Implementation of a Modern Deposit Insurance Scheme' (2009) https://www.econstor.eu/bitstream/10419/163489/1/suerf-study-2009-5.pdf, accessed 7 November 2021 14.

65 Ibid. See also JC Izaguirre, T Lyman, C McGuire, D Grace, 'Deposit Insurance and Digital Financial Inclusion' (2016) https://openknowledge.worldbank.org/bitstream/handle/10986/25707/110632-BRI-PUBLIC-ADD-VC-Brief-Deposit-Insurance-and-Digital-Financial-Inclusion.pdf?sequence=1, accessed on 15 October 2021 1.

66 Ibid. A Demirguc-Kunt, L Klapper, D Singer 'Financial Inclusion and Inclusive Growth: A Review of Recent Empirical Evidence' (2017) World Bank Policy Research Working Paper 8040 https://openknowledge.worldbank.org/bitstream/handle/10986/26479/WPS8040.pdf?, accessed 17 October 2021.

67 International Association of Deposit Insurers, 'Financial Inclusion and Deposit Insurance' (2013) https://www.iadi.org/en/assets/File/Papers/Approved%20Research%20-%20Discussion%20Papers/2013-06_Financial_Inclusion_and_Deposit_Insurance_publication-clean.pdf, accessed on 2 November 2021 43.

68 Ibid.

69 Ibid.

70 E Demaestri, M Facundo and D Walker 'Deposit Insurance and Poverty Reduction' (2006) https://www.researchgate.net/publication/239841069_DEPOSIT_INSURANCE_AND_POVERTY_REDUCTION, accessed 14 November 2021 203.
71 Ibid. See also International Association of Deposit Insurers, 'Financial Inclusion and Deposit Insurance' (2013) https://www.iadi.org/en/assets/File/Papers/Approved%20Research%20-%20Discussion%20Papers/2013-06_Financial_Inclusion_and_Deposit_Insurance_publication-clean.pdf, accessed on 2 November 2021 44. See further F Kakarahwa 'The Impact of the Deposit Protection Corporation on Financial Stability in Zimbabwe Banking Sector' (2015) *Bachelor of Business Sciences Honours Dissertations, Bindura University of Science Education* 15.
72 Ibid.
73 Ibid.
74 International Association of Deposit Insurers, 'Financial Inclusion and Deposit Insurance' (2013) https://www.iadi.org/en/assets/File/Papers/Approved%20Research%20-%20Discussion%20Papers/2013-06_Financial_Inclusion_and_Deposit_Insurance_publication-clean.pdf, accessed on 2 November 2021 44.
75 Ibid.
76 Ibid.
77 Ibid, 44, 45.
78 International Association of Deposit Insurers, 'A Handbook for the Assessment of Compliance with the Core Principles for Effective Deposit Insurance Systems' (March 2016) https://www.iadi.org/en/assets/File/Core%20Principles/IADI_CP_Assessment_Handbook_FINAL_14May2016.pdf, accessed on 2 November 2021 8.
79 International Association of Deposit Insurers, 'IADI Core Principles for Effective Deposit Insurance Systems' (November 2014) https://www.iadi.org/en/assets/File/Core%20Principles/cprevised2014nov.pdf, accessed on 17 July 2021 5.
80 Ibid.
81 Ibid. See also International Association of Deposit Insurers, 'A Handbook for the Assessment of Compliance with the Core Principles for Effective Deposit Insurance Systems' (March 2016) https://www.iadi.org/en/assets/File/Core%20Principles/IADI_CP_Assessment_Handbook_FINAL_14May2016.pdf, accessed on 2 November 2021 8.
82 Ibid.
83 Ibid.
84 Ibid.
85 Basel Committee on Banking Supervision, International Association of Deposit Insurers 'Core Principles for Effective Deposit Insurance Systems' (June 2009) https://www.bis.org/publ/bcbs156.pdf, accessed 23 December 2021 2.
86 International Association of Deposit Insurers, 'IADI Core Principles for Effective Deposit Insurance Systems' (November 2014) https://www.iadi.org/en/assets/File/Core%20Principles/cprevised2014nov.pdf, accessed on 17 July 2021 42.
87 International Association of Deposit Insurers, 'Financial Inclusion and Deposit Insurance' (June 2013) https://www.iadi.org/en/assets/File/Papers/Approved%20Research%20-%20Discussion%20Papers/2013-06_Financial_Inclusion_and_Deposit_Insurance_publication-clean.pdf, accessed on 2 November 2021 9.
88 Ibid.
89 International Association of Deposit Insurers, 'IADI Core Principles for Effective Deposit Insurance Systems' (November 2014) https://www.iadi.org/en/assets/File/Core%20Principles/cprevised2014nov.pdf, accessed on 17 July 2021 5.
90 Ibid, 15, 16.
91 Ibid, 17.
92 International Association of Deposit Insurers, 'Financial Inclusion and Deposit Insurance' (June 2013) https://www.iadi.org/en/assets/File/Papers/Approved%20Research%20-%20Discussion%20Papers/2013-06_Financial_Inclusion_and

_Deposit_Insurance_publication-clean.pdf, accessed on 2 November 2021 44. See also Core Principles seven, eight, nine and ten of International Association of Deposit Insurers, 'IADI Core Principles for Effective Deposit Insurance Systems' (November 2014) https://www.iadi.org/en/assets/File/Core%20Principles/cprevised2014nov.pdf, accessed on 17 July 2021.

93 International Association of Deposit Insurers, 'IADI Core Principles for Effective Deposit Insurance Systems' (November 2014) https://www.iadi.org/en/assets/File/Core%20Principles/cprevised2014nov.pdf, accessed on 17 July 2021 18.

94 E Demaestri, M Facundo and D Walker 'Deposit Insurance and Poverty Reduction' (2006) https://www.researchgate.net/publication/239841069_DEPOSIT_INSURANCE_AND_POVERTY_REDUCTION, accessed 14 November 2021 217.

95 Ibid.

96 International Association of Deposit Insurers, 'Financial Inclusion and Deposit Insurance' (June 2013) https://www.iadi.org/en/assets/File/Papers/Approved%20Research%20%20Discussion%20Papers/2013-06_Financial_Inclusion_and_Deposit_Insurance_publication-clean.pdf, accessed on 2 November 2021 9.

97 E Demaestri, M Facundo and D Walker 'Deposit Insurance and Poverty Reduction' (2006) https://www.researchgate.net/publication/239841069_DEPOSIT_INSURANCE_AND_POVERTY_REDUCTION, accessed 14 November 2021 219.

98 Ibid.

99 Ibid.

100 Ibid.

101 Ibid. See also G Garcia and C Lindgren 'Deposit Insurance: obtaining the benefits and avoiding pitfalls' (1996) file:///Users/ashleynyaude/Downloads/[IMF%20Working%20Papers]%20Deposit%20Insurance%20(1).pdf, accessed on 11 November 2021 17.

102 Ibid.

103 Ibid.

104 Ibid.

105 Ibid, 220.

106 Ibid.

107 Ibid.

108 Ibid.

109 International Association of Deposit Insurers, 'IADI Core Principles for Effective Deposit Insurance Systems' (November 2014) https://www.iadi.org/en/assets/File/Core%20Principles/cprevised2014nov.pdf, accessed on 17 July 2021 26.

110 International Association of Deposit Insurers, 'Financial Inclusion and Deposit Insurance' (June 2013) https://www.iadi.org/en/assets/File/Papers/Approved%20Research%20-%20Discussion%20Papers/2013-06_Financial_Inclusion_and_Deposit_Insurance_publication-clean.pdf, accessed on 2 November 2021 44.

111 E Demaestri, M Facundo and D Walker 'Deposit Insurance and Poverty Reduction' (2006) https://www.researchgate.net/publication/239841069_DEPOSIT_INSURANCE_AND_POVERTY_REDUCTION, accessed 14 November 2021 222.

112 Ibid.

113 Depositor Protection Corporation 'Core Principle 8 – Coverage' https://www.dpcorp.co.zw/assets/core-principle-8---coverage.pdf, accessed on 18 October 2021.

114 Ibid, 27. It is further required that the deposit insurer should not incorporate co-insurance.

115 E Demaestri, M Facundo and D Walker 'Deposit Insurance and Poverty Reduction' (2006) https://www.researchgate.net/publication/239841069_DEPOSIT_INSURANCE_AND_POVERTY_REDUCTION, accessed 14 November 2021 223.

116 Ibid.

117 Ex ante funding refers to the regular collection of premiums, with the aim of accumulating a fund to meet future obligations (e.g. reimbursing depositors) and cover the operational and related costs of the deposit insurer. See International Association

of Deposit Insurers, 'IADI Core Principles for Effective Deposit Insurance Systems' (November 2014) https://www.iadi.org/en/assets/File/Core%20Principles/cprevised-2014nov.pdf, accessed 17 July 2021 9.

118 Ibid, 29–31.

119 E Demaestri, M Facundo and D Walker 'Deposit Insurance and Poverty Reduction' (2006) https://www.researchgate.net/publication/239841069_DEPOSIT_INSURANCE_AND_POVERTY_REDUCTION, accessed 14 November 2021 224.

120 Ibid.

121 International Association of Deposit Insurers, 'IADI Core Principles for Effective Deposit Insurance Systems' (November 2014) https://www.iadi.org/en/assets/File/Core%20Principles/cprevised2014nov.pdf, accessed 17 July 2021 32, 33.

122 International Association of Deposit Insurers, 'Financial Inclusion and Deposit Insurance' (June 2013) https://www.iadi.org/en/assets/File/Papers/Approved%20Research%20-%20Discussion%20Papers/2013-06_Financial_Inclusion_and_Deposit_Insurance_publication-clean.pdf, accessed on 2 November 2021 45.

123 U Ngaujake 'Protecting Depositors and Promoting Financial Stability in South Africa: Is there a Case for the Introduction of Deposit Insurance?' (2004) *MCom Thesis, Rhodes University* 37.

124 Ibid, 56.

125 Ibid, 37.

126 Ibid.

127 Ibid, 56.

128 The RBZ's function as a lender of last resort is provided for in section 11(5) of the Reserve Bank Act [Chapter 22:15].

129 Deposit Protection Board, 'Public-Policy Objectives, Functions, Powers and Design Features for an Explicit, Limited Deposit Protection Scheme in Zimbabwe', Board Paper No 3.2/2002 (2002) https://www.dpcorp.co.zw/assets/public-policy-objectives.pdf, accessed on 1 October 2021 3. See further Deposit Protection Corporation, 'About Deposit Protection Corporation' https://www.dpcorp.co.zw/about-dpc.html, accessed on 4 August 2021.

130 Ibid, 4. See also International Association of Deposit Insurers, 'IADI Core Principles for Effective Deposit Insurance Systems' (November 2014) https://www.iadi.org/en/assets/File/Core%20Principles/cprevised2014nov.pdf, accessed 17 July 2021 10.

131 The DPC carries out its mandate as the liquidator of closed banks through the realisation of assets and payment of liquidation dividends to creditors and uninsured depositors. See Depositor Protection Corporation, 'Annual Report for the Year Ended 31 December 2020' file:///Users/ashleynyaude/Desktop/dpc-2020-annual-report.pdf, accessed on 16 October 2021 11.

132 A "pay box plus" mandate is where the deposit insurer has additional responsibilities, such as certain resolution functions (e.g. financial support). International Association of Deposit Insurers, 'IADI Core Principles for Effective Deposit Insurance Systems' (November 2014) https://www.iadi.org/en/assets/File/Core%20Principles/cprevised-2014nov.pdf, accessed 17 July 2021 10.

133 Members of IADI are entities that, under law or agreements, have a deposit insurance system and have been approved for membership in the Association. The membership benefits include the possibility to participate in the development of standards, guidance and assessment methodologies to enhance the effectiveness of deposit insurance systems; share expertise and information on deposit insurance and bank resolution issues through training, development and educational programmes; engage in technical assistance workshops and the unique Self-Assessment Technical Assistance Program (SATAP). See International Association of Deposit Insurers, 'IADI Members and Participants' https://www.iadi.org/en/about-iadi/iadi-members-and-participants/, accessed on 1 October 2021.

134 International Association of Deposit Insurers, 'IADI Core Principles for Effective Deposit Insurance Systems' (November 2014) https://www.iadi.org/en/assets/File/Core%20Principles/cprevised2014nov.pdf, accessed 17 July 2021 11.

135 Depositor Protection Corporation, 'Annual Report for the Year Ended 31 December 2020' file:///Users/ashleynyaude/Desktop/dpc-2020-annual-report.pdf, accessed on 16 October 2021 10.

136 Ibid, 20.

137 Ibid.

138 Ibid.

139 The Dutch Foreign Exchange Auction Trading System is a formal market-based foreign exchange trading system. The adoption of a Foreign Currency Auction System is expected to bring transparency and efficiency in the trading of foreign currency in the economy. See further Reserve Bank of Zimbabwe 'Introduction of a Foreign Exchange Auction Trading System' https://www.rbz.co.zw/documents/press/June/Foreign-Exchange-Auction-System---17-6-2020.pdf, accessed on 23 December 2021.

140 Depositor Protection Corporation, 'Annual Report for the Year Ended 31 December 2020' file:///Users/ashleynyaude/Desktop/dpc-2020-annual-report.pdf, accessed on 16 October 2021 20.

141 Ibid.

142 Ibid.

143 Bank of Greece 'Rescuing the Bank's Gold Reserves 1941–1945' https://www.bankofgreece.gr/en/the-bank/history/historical-review, 22 December 2021.

144 The Currency Committee comprised the Minister of National Economy as chairman, four other Ministers and the Governor of the Bank of Greece. Within the Committee, the Bank of Greece played an important role, as it was responsible for designing and recommending policy measures that were, as a rule, approved by the Committee. Bank of Greece 'Rescuing the Bank's Gold Reserves 1941–1945' https://www.bankofgreece.gr/en/the-bank/history/historical-review, 22 December 2021.

145 G Alogoskoufis 'The Two Faces of Janus: Institutions, Policy Regimes and Macroeconomic Performance in Greece' (1995) 10 *Economic Policy* 149, 153.

146 Ibid, 154.

147 Ibid.

148 S5(2) of the Depositor Protection Corporation Act (Chapter 24:29).

149 S2 of the Depositor Protection Corporation Act (Chapter 24:29).

150 Depositor Protection Corporation 'Core Principle 8 – Coverage' https://www.dpcorp.co.zw/assets/core-principle-8---coverage.pdf, accessed on 18 October 2021. See also N Kleftouri 'Meeting the Rationale of Deposit Protection System' (2014) 22(4) *Journal of Financial Regulation and Compliance* 302, 303.

151 S39 of the DPC Act.

152 S41(2) of the DPC Act.

153 Deposit Protection Corporation, 'Deposit Protection' https://www.dpcorp.co.zw/deposit-protection.html#sub-top-8, accessed on 1 October 2021. Section 42 of the DPC Act states that when calculating the amount of a protected deposit, any liability of the depositor concerned towards the insolvent institution concerned, whether the liability is present or future, shall be deducted from the amount of the deposit; and if the depositor has two or more protected deposits of the same class with the same insolvent contributory institution, the amounts standing to the credit in those deposits shall be aggregated and the deposits shall be regarded as a single deposit. Where a single deposit represents sums held by a trustee on behalf of two or more different beneficiaries, each of those sums shall be regarded as a separate deposit for the purpose of determining whether or not compensation is payable to any person under this Act. Section 43 of the DPC Act states that where a protected deposit is jointly held, the DPC shall divide the compensation payable under this section between the joint

depositors in such shares as the DPC considers appropriate in the light of the information before it, provided that, if the DPC reasonably anticipates a dispute over the share to be paid to any joint depositor, the DPC may initiate interpleader proceedings in any competent court to determine the dispute.

154 Depositor Protection Corporation, 'Deposit Protection Corporation Increases Cover Level' https://www.dpcorp.co.zw/assets/dpc-press-release-feb-2020.pdf, accessed on 21 October 2021.

155 Depositor Protection Corporation, 'Notice of Explicit Deposit Protection of Foreign Currency Denominated Accounts And/or Nostro FCA Accounts' Circular of 2021 https://www.dpcorp.co.zw/assets/public-notice-1-of-2021.pdf, accessed on 21 October 2021.

156 N Kleftouri 'Deposit Protection System's Design and Effectiveness' (2015) 16(1) *Journal of Banking Regulation*' 51, 53. See also E Giaretta and G Chesini 'Does Deposit Guarantee Scheme Increase Depositor Confidence? An Empirical Investigation' (2014) 9(4) *Journal Strategic and International Studies* 77.

157 N Kleftouri 'Meeting the Rationale of Deposit Protection System' (2014) 22(4) *Journal of Financial Regulation and Compliance* 301, 305.

158 S28 of the Depositor Protection Corporation Act [Chapter 24:29]. In terms of s2 of the Depositor Protection Corporation Act [Chapter 24:29] a contributory institution means a banking institution, building society or other organisation that is a contributory institution in terms of Part IV and whose status as such has not been suspended or revoked in terms of s27.

159 S32 of the Depositor Protection Corporation Act [Chapter 24:29] provides that any contributory institution that, without lawful excuse, fails or refuses to pay any contribution that is payable by it shall be guilty of an offence and liable to a fine not exceeding five times the amount of the contribution.

160 Ibid, 309.

161 Ibid

162 Depositor Protection Corporation, 'Annual Report for the Year Ended 31 December 2020' file:///Users/ashleynyaude/Desktop/dpc-2020-annual-report.pdf, accessed on 16 October 2021 12.

163 Ibid.

164 Ibid.

165 Depositor Protection Corporation 'Minister of Finance Officially Opens Deposit Protection Corporation's Bulawayo Regional Office' (2020) https://www.dpcorp.co.zw/assets/dpc_press_release_feb-2020_byo-launch.pdf, accessed on 19 October 2021.

166 Ibid.

167 Depositor Protection Corporation, 'Annual Report for the Year Ended 31 December 2020' file:///Users/ashleynyaude/Desktop/dpc-2020-annual-report.pdf, accessed on 16 October 2021 12.

168 S23 of the Depositor Protection Corporation Act (Chapter 24:29).

169 S25 of the Depositor Protection Corporation Act (Chapter 24:29).

170 Deposit Protection Corporation, 'Deposit Protection' https://www.dpcorp.co.zw/deposit-protection.html#sub-top-8, accessed on 1 October 2021.

171 Depositor Protection Corporation, 'Annual Report for the Year Ended 31 December 2020' file:///Users/ashleynyaude/Desktop/dpc-2020-annual-report.pdf, accessed on 16 October 2021 11.

172 JC Izaguirre, T Lyman, C McGuire, D Grace, 'Deposit Insurance and Digital Financial Inclusion' (2016) https://openknowledge.worldbank.org/bitstream/handle/10986/25707/110632-BRI-PUBLIC-ADD-VC-Brief-Deposit-Insurance-and-Digital-Financial-Inclusion.pdf?sequence=1, accessed on 15 October 2021 2. See also Depositor Protection Corporation, 'Membership' https://www.dpcorp.co.zw/assets/core-principle-7---membership.pdf, accessed on 16 October 2021.

173 Depositor Protection Corporation, 'Annual Report for the Year Ended 31 December 2020' file:///Users/ashleynyaude/Desktop/dpc-2020-annual-report.pdf, accessed on 16 October 2021 11.
174 Deposit Protection Corporation 'The Role of Deposit Insurance in Promoting Financial Inclusion' https://www.dpcorp.co.zw/assets/deposit-protection-and-financial-inclusion.pdf, accessed on 16 October 2021 1.
175 S 41(2) of the DPC Act.
176 Depositor Protection Corporation, 'Deposit Protection Corporation Increases Cover Level' https://www.dpcorp.co.zw/assets/dpc-press-release-feb-2020.pdf, accessed on 21 October 2021.

Bibliography

G Alogoskoufis 'The two faces of Janus: Institutions, policy regimes and macroeconomic performance in Greece' (1995) 10 (20) *Economic Policy* 149.

D Anginer & A Demirguc-Kunt 'Bank runs and moral hazard: A review of deposit insurance' (2018), available at https://elibrary.worldbank.org/doi/abs/10.1596/1813-9450-8589, accessed on 23 April 2019.

Banking (Deposit Protection) Regulations, Statutory Instrument 29 of 2003.

Banking Act (Chapter 24:20).

Basel Committee on Banking Supervision, International Association of Deposit Insurers 'Core principles for effective deposit insurance systems' (June 2009), available at https://www.bis.org/publ/bcbs156.pdf, accessed 23 December 2021.

B Bernet & S Walter 'Design, structure and implementation of a modern deposit insurance scheme' (2009), available at https://www.econstor.eu/bitstream/10419/163489/1/suerf-study-2009-5.pdf, accessed 7 November 2021 14.

Building Societies Act (Chapter 24:02).

J T Chipika 'Financial inclusion in Zimbabwe, from policy to practice: Lessons and way forward', available at https://www.rbz.co.zw/documents/publications/speeches/Dr-Chipika--Financial-Inclusion-Forum-Presentation---19-Feb-2019.pdf, accessed on 17 October 2021.

E Demaestri, M Facundo & D Walker 'Deposit insurance and poverty reduction' (2006), available at https://www.researchgate.net/publication/239841069_DEPOSIT_INSURANCE_AND_POVERTY_REDUCTION, accessed on 14 November 2021 203.

A Demirguc-Kunt & L Klapper *Financial Inclusion in Africa: An Overview* (World Bank Policy Research working paper 6088, 2012) 2, available at https://openknowledge.worldbank.org/bitstream/handle/10986/9335/WPS6088.pdf?sequence=1, accessed on 17 October 2021.

A Demirguc-Kunt, L Klapper & D Singer *Financial Inclusion and Inclusive Growth: A Review of Recent Empirical Evidence* (World Bank Policy research working paper 8040, 2017), available at https://openknowledge.worldbank.org/bitstream/handle/10986/26479/WPS8040.pdf?, accessed on 17 October 2021.

Deposit Protection Board *Public-Policy Objectives, Functions, Powers and Design Features for an Explicit, Limited Deposit Protection Scheme in Zimbabwe* (Board paper no. 3.2/2002, 2002), available at https://www.dpcorp.co.zw/assets/public-policy-objectives.pdf, accessed on 1 October 2021.

Deposit Protection Corporation 'About deposit protection corporation', available at https://www.dpcorp.co.zw/about-dpc.html, accessed on 4 August 2021.

Deposit Protection Corporation 'Deposit protection', available at https://www.dpcorp.co.zw/deposit-protection.html#sub-top-8, accessed on 1 October 2021.

Deposit Protection Corporation 'The role of deposit insurance in promoting financial inclusion', available at https://www.dpcorp.co.zw/assets/deposit-protection-and-financial-inclusion.pdf, accessed on 16 October 2021 1.

Depositor Protection Corporation Act (Chapter 24:29).

J F Devlin 'A detailed study of financial exclusion in the UK' (2005) 28 *Journal of Consumer Policy* 75.

D W Diamond & P H Dybvig 'Bank runs, deposit insurance, and liquidity' (1983) 91(3) *Journal of Political Economy* 401.

E Giaretta & G Chesini 'Does deposit guarantee scheme increase depositor confidence? An empirical investigation' (2014) 9(4) *Journal Strategic and International Studies* 77.

Infrastructure Development Bank of Zimbabwe Act (Chapter 24:14).

International Association of Deposit Insurers 'Core principles for effective deposit insurance systems' (November 2014), available at https://www.iadi.org/en/assets/File/Core%20Principles/cprevised2014nov.pdf, accessed on 25 September 2021.

International Association of Deposit Insurers 'Deposit insurance and financial inclusion: Current trends in insuring digital stored-value products' (March 2020), available at https://www.iadi.org/en/assets/File/Papers/Approved%20Research%20-%20Discussion%20Papers/FII_for_official_publication_final_19032020.pdf, accessed on 2 November 2021.

International Association of Deposit Insurers 'Financial inclusion and deposit insurance' (June 2013), available at https://www.iadi.org/en/assets/File/Papers/Approved%20Research%20-%20Discussion%20Papers/2013-06_Financial_Inclusion_and_Deposit_Insurance_publication-clean.pdf, accessed on 2 November 2021.

J C Izaguirre, T Lyman, C McGuire & D Grace 'Deposit insurance and digital financial inclusion' (2016), available at https://openknowledge.worldbank.org/bitstream/handle/10986/25707/110632-BRI-PUBLIC-ADD-VC-Brief-Deposit-Insurance-and-Digital-Financial-Inclusion.pdf?sequence=1, accessed on 15 October 2021 1.

B F Jackson 'Danger lurking in the shadows: Why regulators lack the authority to effectively fight contagion in the shadow banking system' (2013) 127(2) *Havard LR* 732.

F Kakarahwa 'The impact of the deposit protection corporation on financial stability in Zimbabwe banking sector' (2015) *Bachelor of Business Sciences Honours Dissertations, Bindura University of Science Education.*

G G Kaufman 'Bank failures, systemic risk and bank regulation' (1996) 16(1) *Cato Journal* 17.

N Kleftouri 'Deposit protection system's design and effectiveness' (2015) 16(1) *Journal of Banking Regulation* 51.

N Kleftouri 'Meeting the rationale of deposit protection system' (2014) 22(4) *Journal of Financial Regulation and Compliance* 301.

P S Koku 'Financial exclusion of the poor: A literature review' (2015) 33(5) *International Journal of Bank Marketing* 655.

L H P Lang & R M Stulz 'Contagion and competitive intra-industry effects of bankruptcy announcements: An empirical analysis' (1992) 32 *Journal of Financial Economics* 45.

S Li *An Overview of Financial Inclusion, Deposit Insurance and Financial Stability* 20 ed (2018) 177.

Microfinance Act (Chapter 24:30).

F S Mishkin 'Over the Cliff: From the subprime to the global financial crisis' (2011) *Journal of Economic Perspectives* 49.

U Ngaujake *Protecting Depositors and Promoting Financial Stability in South Africa: Is There a Case for the Introduction of Deposit Insurance?* (MCom thesis, Rhodes University, 2004).

A Nyaude *Regulatory Measures to Address Bank Failures in Zimbabwe* (LLD thesis, University of Pretoria, 2021).

People's Own Savings Bank Act (Chapter 24:22).

C Phiri *An Assessment of the Factors Determining Public Confidence and Its Impact on the Financial Performance and Stability of Banks in Zimbabwe* (MBA dissertation, University of Zimbabwe, 2015).

Reserve Bank of Zimbabwe (Legal Tender) Regulations Statutory Instrument 142 of 2019.

Reserve Bank of Zimbabwe Act (Chapter 22:15).

Reserve Bank of Zimbabwe 'Zimbabwe financial inclusion journey 2016–2000',available at https://www.rbz.co.zw/documents/BLSS/2021/FINANCIAL-INCLUSION--JOURNEY.pdf, accessed on 15 October 2021.

S Schich 'Financial crisis: Deposit insurance and related financial safety net aspects' (2008), available at https://www.oecd.org/finance/financial-markets/41894959.pdf, accessed on 22 December 2021.

South African Reserve Bank 'Designing a deposit insurance scheme for South Africa – A discussion paper' (2017), available at http://www.treasury.gov.za/twinpeaks/Designing%20a%20deposit%20insurance%20scheme%20for%20South%20Africa.pdf, accessed on 7 June 2021.

J E Stiglitz 'Lessons from the global financial crisis of 2008' (2010) *Seoul Journal of Economics* 321.

The World Bank 'Financial safety nets and bank resolution frameworks in Southern Africa: Key issues and challenges' (2019), available at https://openknowledge.worldbank.org/bitstream/handle/10986/31511/Key-Issues-and-Challenges.pdf?sequence=1&isAllowed=y, accessed on 25 September 2021.

The World Bank 'Financial safety nets and bank resolution frameworks in Southern Africa: Summary of key issues and challenges' (2019), available at https://openknowledge.worldbank.org/bitstream/handle/10986/31512/Summary-of-Key-Issues-and-Challenges.pdf?sequence=1&isAllowed=y, accessed on 20 October 2021.

C Van Heerden 'Deposit protection in South Africa: Recent developments' (2020) 35(2) *Journal of International Banking Law and Regulation* 45.

B Van Roosebeke & R Defina *Five Emerging Issues in Deposit Insurance* (MPRA paper no. 110713, 2021), available at https://mpra.ub.uni-muenchen.de/110713/1/MPRA_paper_110713.pdf, accessed on 22 December 2021.

A Zins & L Weill 'The determinants of financial inclusion in Africa' (2016) 6 *Review of Development Finance* 56.

Index

Note: Page numbers in *italics* indicate figures, **bold** indicate tables in the text